Love Hina

赤松 健
あか まつ けん

by Ken Akamatsu

Vol.4

ALSO AVAILABLE FROM ⊙TOKYOPOP®

MANGA

.HACK//LEGEND OF THE TWILIGHT*
@LARGE (December 2003)
ANGELIC LAYER*
BABY BIRTH*
BATTLE ROYALE*
BRAIN POWERED*
BRIGADOON*
CARDCAPTOR SAKURA
CARDCAPTOR SAKURA: MASTER OF THE CLOW*
CHOBITS*
CHRONICLES OF THE CURSED SWORD
CLAMP SCHOOL DETECTIVES*
CLOVER
CONFIDENTIAL CONFESSIONS*
CORRECTOR YUI
COWBOY BEBOP*
COWBOY BEBOP: SHOOTING STAR*
CYBORG 009*
DEMON DIARY
DIGIMON*
DRAGON HUNTER
DRAGON KNIGHTS*
DUKLYON: CLAMP SCHOOL DEFENDERS*
ERICA SAKURAZAWA*
FAKE*
FLCL*
FORBIDDEN DANCE*
GATE KEEPERS*
G GUNDAM*
GRAVITATION*
GTO*
GUNDAM WING
GUNDAM WING: BATTLEFIELD OF PACIFISTS
GUNDAM WING: ENDLESS WALTZ*
GUNDAM WING: THE LAST OUTPOST*
HAPPY MANIA*
HARLEM BEAT
I.N.V.U.
INITIAL D*
ISLAND
JING: KING OF BANDITS*
JULINE
KARE KANO*
KINDAICHI CASE FILES, THE*
KING OF HELL
KODOCHA: SANA'S STAGE*
LOVE HINA*
LUPIN III*
MAGIC KNIGHT RAYEARTH*

MAGIC KNIGHT RAYEARTH II* (COMING SOON)
MAN OF MANY FACES*
MARMALADE BOY*
MARS*
MIRACLE GIRLS
MIYUKI-CHAN IN WONDERLAND*
MONSTERS, INC.
PARADISE KISS*
PARASYTE
PEACH GIRL
PEACH GIRL: CHANGE OF HEART*
PET SHOP OF HORRORS*
PLANET LADDER*
PLANETES*
PRIEST
RAGNAROK
RAVE MASTER*
REALITY CHECK
REBIRTH
REBOUND*
RISING STARS OF MANGA
SABER MARIONETTE J*
SAILOR MOON
SAINT TAIL
SAMURAI DEEPER KYO*
SAMURAI GIRL: REAL BOUT HIGH SCHOOL*
SCRYED*
SHAOLIN SISTERS*
SHIRAHIME-SYO: SNOW GODDESS TALES* (Dec. 2003)
SHUTTERBOX
SORCERER HUNTERS
THE SKULL MAN*
THE VISION OF ESCAFLOWNE*
TOKYO MEW MEW*
UNDER THE GLASS MOON
VAMPIRE GAME*
WILD ACT*
WISH*
WORLD OF HARTZ
X-DAY*
ZODIAC P.I. *

For more information visit www.TOKYOPOP.com

*INDICATES 100% AUTHENTIC MANGA (RIGHT-TO-LEFT FORMAT)

CINE-MANGA™

CARDCAPTORS
JACKIE CHAN ADVENTURES
JIMMY NEUTRON
KIM POSSIBLE
LIZZIE MCGUIRE
POWER RANGERS: NINJA STORM
SPONGEBOB SQUAREPANTS
SPY KIDS 2

NOVELS

KARMA CLUB (April 2004)
SAILOR MOON

TOKYOPOP KIDS

STRAY SHEEP

ART BOOKS

CARDCAPTOR SAKURA*
MAGIC KNIGHT RAYEARTH*

ANIME GUIDES

COWBOY BEBOP ANIME GUIDES
GUNDAM TECHNICAL MANUALS
SAILOR MOON SCOUT GUIDES

090503

Love Hina

By
Ken Akamatsu

TOKYOPOP
Los Angeles • Tokyo • London

Translator - Nan Rymer
English Adaptation - Adam Arnold
Retouch and Lettering - Armand Tan, Julie Taylor, Luis Reyes
Graphic Designer - Anna Kernbaum

Editor - Luis Reyes
Managing Editor - Jill Freshney
Production Coordinator - Antonio DePietro
Production Manager - Jennifer Miller
Art Director - Matt Alford
Editorial Director - Jeremy Ross
VP of Production - Ron Klamert
President & C.O.O. - John Parker
Publisher & C.E.O. - Stuart Levy

Email: editor@TOKYOPOP.com
Come visit us online at www.TOKYOPOP.com

A  Manga

TOKYOPOP Inc.
5900 Wilshire Blvd. Suite 2000
Los Angeles, CA 90036

Love Hina Volume 4

©1999 Ken Akamatsu. First published in 1999 by Kodansha Ltd., Tokyo.
English publication rights arranged through Kodansha Ltd., Tokyo.

English text copyright ©2003 TOKYOPOP Inc.

ISBN: 1-59182-015-4

First TOKYOPOP printing: July 2002

10
Printed in USA

Love Hina

The Story Thus Far ...

Fifteen years ago, Keitaro Urashima made a promise to a girl (whose name he can't quite remember) that they would go to Tokyo University together. Now at the age of twenty, he's finding it more and more difficult to keep that promise, much less find that girl again.

He has already failed the entrance exam for Tokyo University three times, and is in a state of indecision about his future, the most daunting path being to spend another year stigmatized as a ronin.

He's inherited from his globetrotting grandmother the Hinata House, a quiet residential dorm where he can work as the landlord and prepare for his upcoming exams in peace... if it wasn't for that fact that Hinata House is actually a girls' dormitory with a clientele none too pleased that their new live-in landlord is a man – or as close to a man as poor Keitaro can be. The lanky loser incessantly (and accidentally) crashes their sessions in the hot springs, walks in on them changing... and pokes his nose pretty much everywhere it can get broken, if not by the hot-headed Naru, then by one of the other Hinata inmates – Kitsune, a mid-twenties alcoholic with a diesel libido; Motoko, a swordswoman who struggles with feminine issues; Shinobu, a pre-teen princess with a colossal crush on Keitaro; and Su, a foreign girl with a big appetite.

Keitaro and Naru have just returned from a trip around Japan to clear their heads after both failing the Tokyo University entrance exam. But the next move they make may not only involve academic ramifications, but romantic ones as well ...

CONTENTS

HINATA.25 When the Cherry Blossoms Bloom 7

HINATA.26 The Hinata House Runaway 27

HINATA.27 Kendo Girl's Tiny Little Problem 47

HINATA.28 In the Downpour With You 67

HINATA.29 HELP! Working Part-Time is a Killer 87

HINATA.30 Battle! Print Club Man vs. Earthenware Girl 107

HINATA.31 Missing You at Hinata House 127

HINATA.32 A Sudden Resume 147

HINATA.33 I Love You, Sempai! 167

LOVE♡HINA

LOVE♡HINA

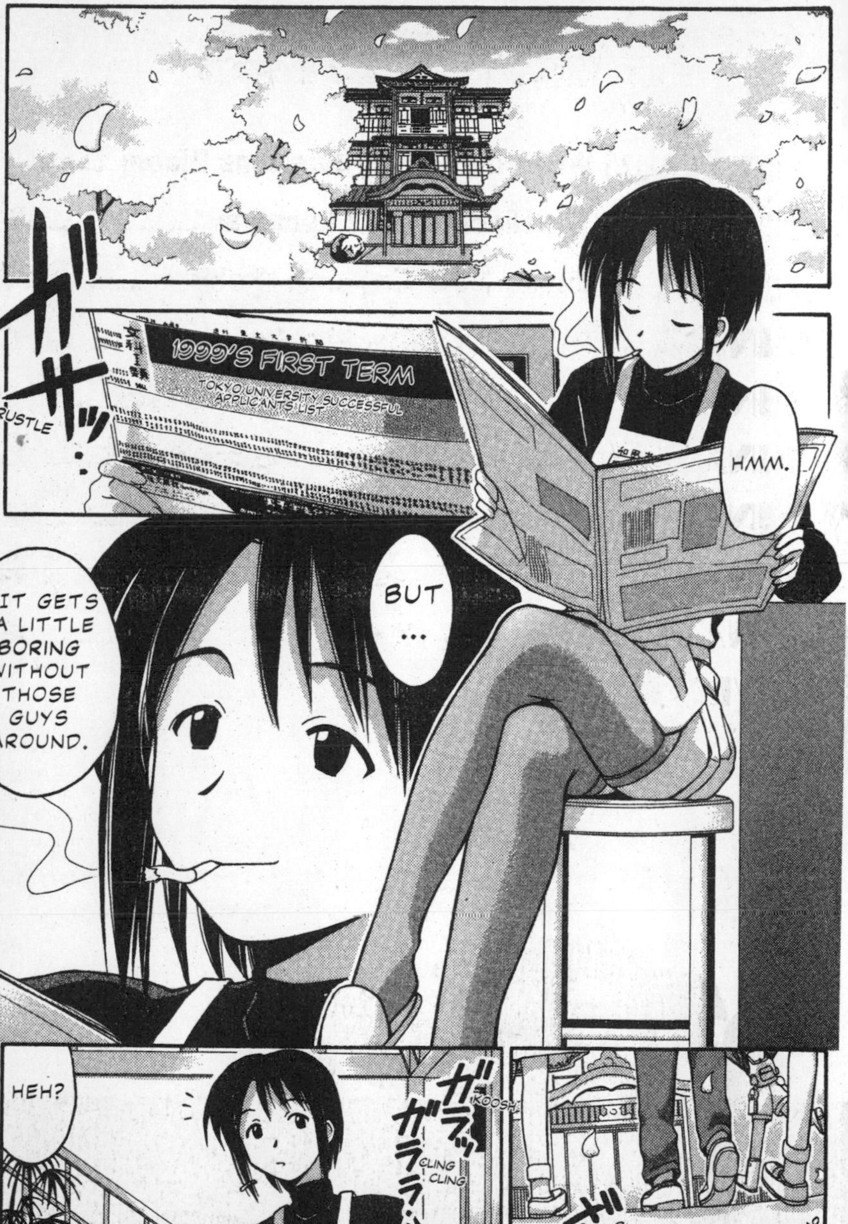
1999'S FIRST TERM
TOKYO UNIVERSITY SUCCESSFUL APPLICANTS LIST
RUSTLE
HMM.
BUT ...
...IT GETS A LITTLE BORING WITHOUT THOSE GUYS AROUND.
CLOMP
CLOMP
KOOSH
CLING CLING
HEH?

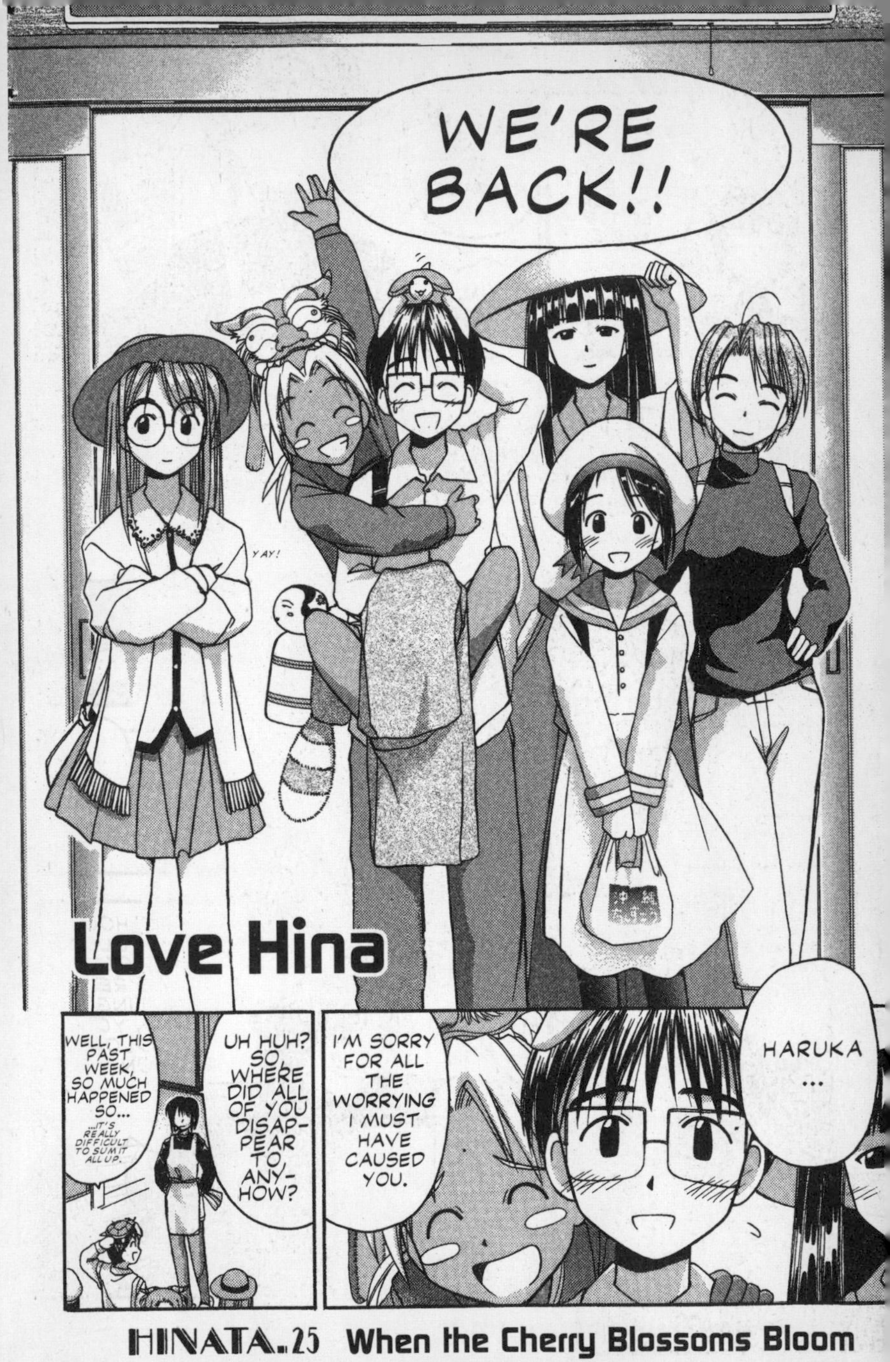
WE'RE BACK!!
YAY!
Love Hina
HARUKA ...
I'M SORRY FOR ALL THE WORRYING I MUST HAVE CAUSED YOU.
UH HUH? SO, WHERE DID ALL OF YOU DISAP-PEAR TO, ANY-HOW?
WELL, THIS PAST WEEK, SO MUCH HAPPENED SO...
...IT'S REALLY DIFFICULT TO SUM IT ALL UP.

HINATA.25 When the Cherry Blossoms Bloom

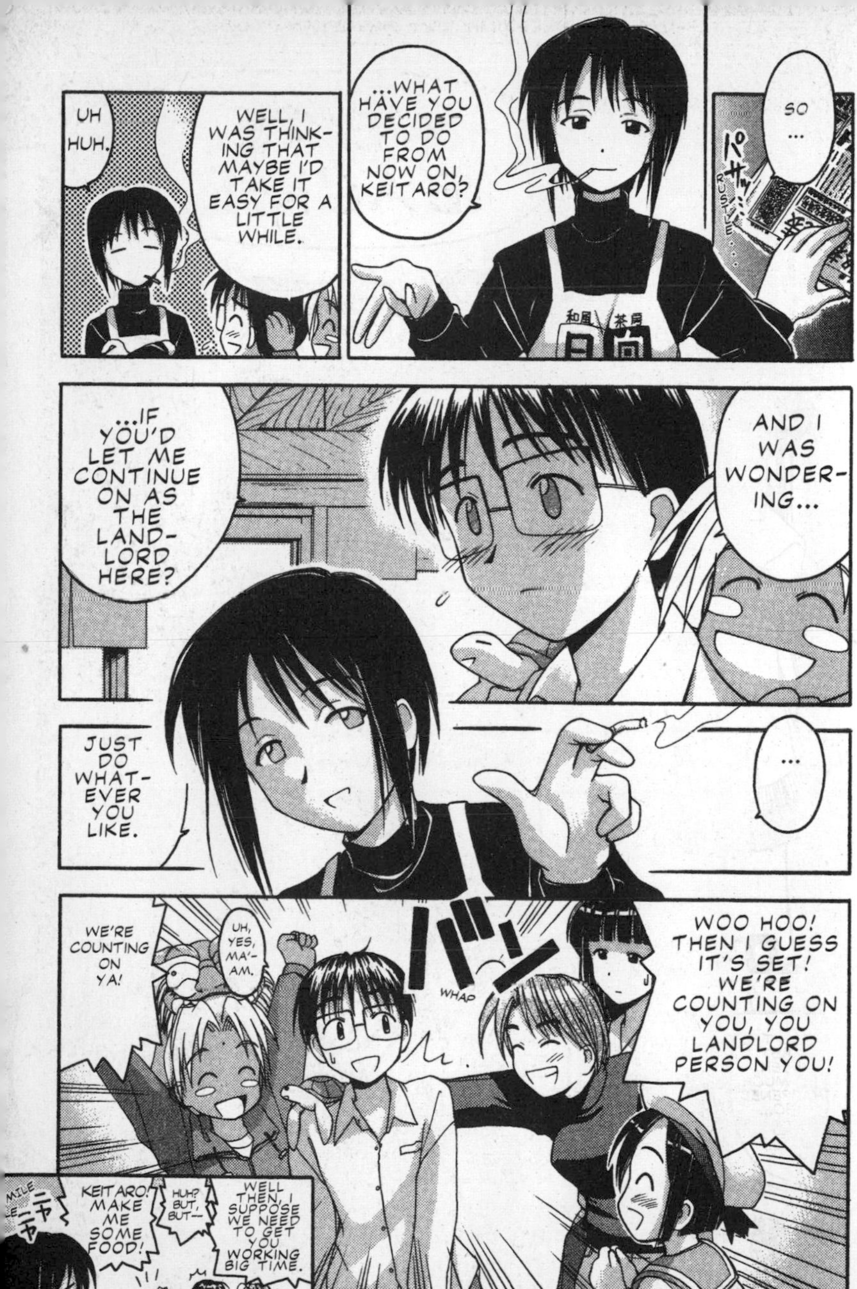
SO ...
パサッ
RUSTLE
...WHAT HAVE YOU DECIDED TO DO FROM NOW ON, KEITARO?
WELL, I WAS THINKING THAT MAYBE I'D TAKE IT EASY FOR A LITTLE WHILE.
UH HUH.
AND I WAS WONDERING...
...IF YOU'D LET ME CONTINUE ON AS THE LANDLORD HERE?
...
JUST DO WHATEVER YOU LIKE.
WOO HOO! THEN I GUESS IT'S SET! WE'RE COUNTING ON YOU, YOU LANDLORD PERSON YOU!
バン
WHAP
UH, YES, MA'AM.
WE'RE COUNTING ON YA!
ニャ
SMILE
WELL THEN, I SUPPOSE WE NEED TO GET YOU WORKING BIG TIME.
HUH? BUT, BUT—
KEITARO! MAKE ME SOME FOOD!

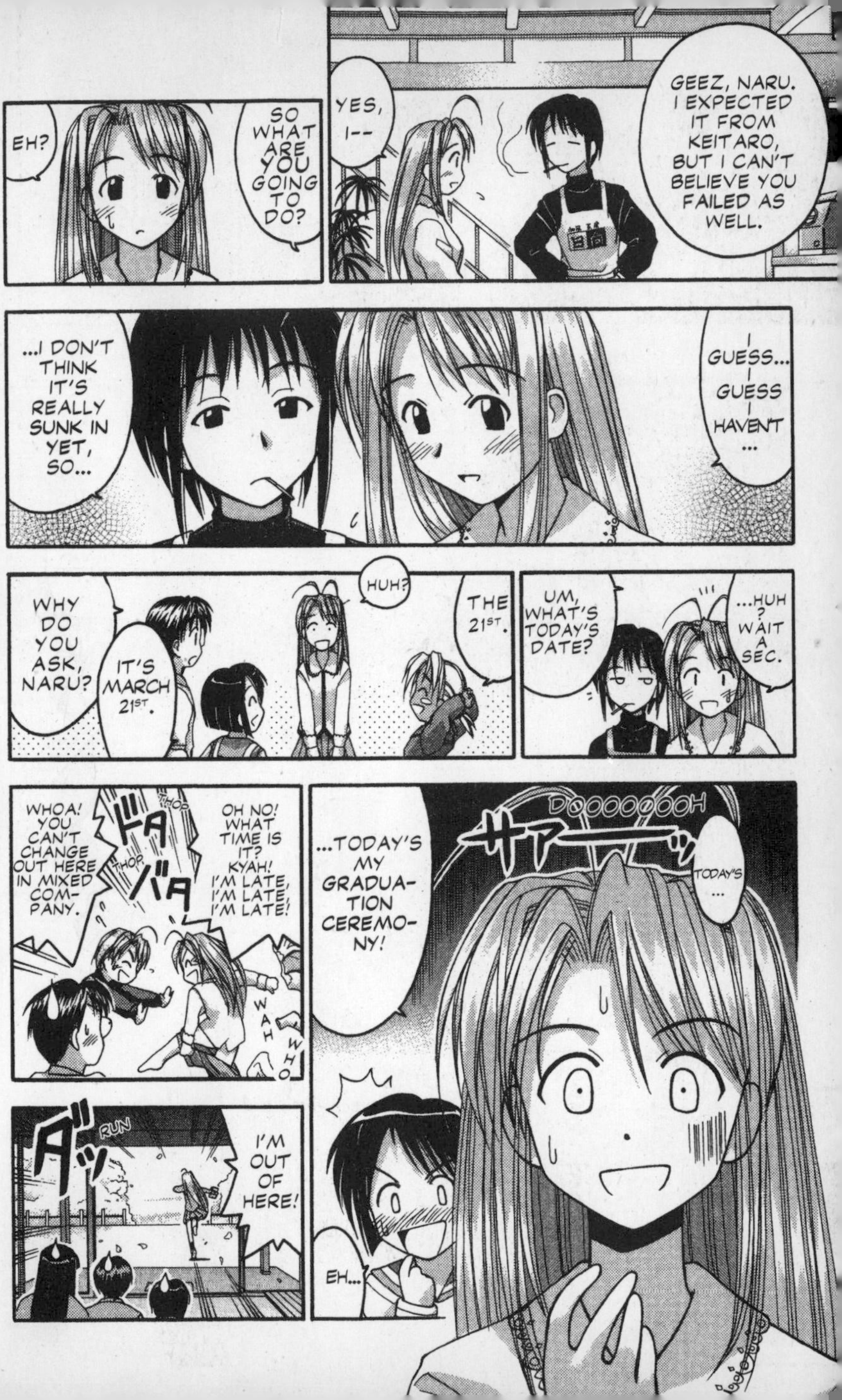
GEEZ, NARU. I EXPECTED IT FROM KEITARO, BUT I CAN'T BELIEVE YOU FAILED AS WELL.
YES, I--
SO WHAT ARE YOU GOING TO DO?
EH?
I GUESS... I GUESS I HAVEN'T ...
...I DON'T THINK IT'S REALLY SUNK IN YET, SO...
...HUH? WAIT A SEC.
UM, WHAT'S TODAY'S DATE?
THE 21ST.
HUH?
WHY DO YOU ASK, NARU?
IT'S MARCH 21ST.
DOOOOOOOOH
サァーーッ
TODAY'S ...
...TODAY'S MY GRADUATION CEREMONY!
EH...
OH NO! WHAT TIME IS IT? KYAH! I'M LATE, I'M LATE, I'M LATE!
ドタ THOP
バタ THOP
WHOA! YOU CAN'T CHANGE OUT HERE IN MIXED COMPANY.
WAH
WHO
ダッ RUN
I'M OUT OF HERE!

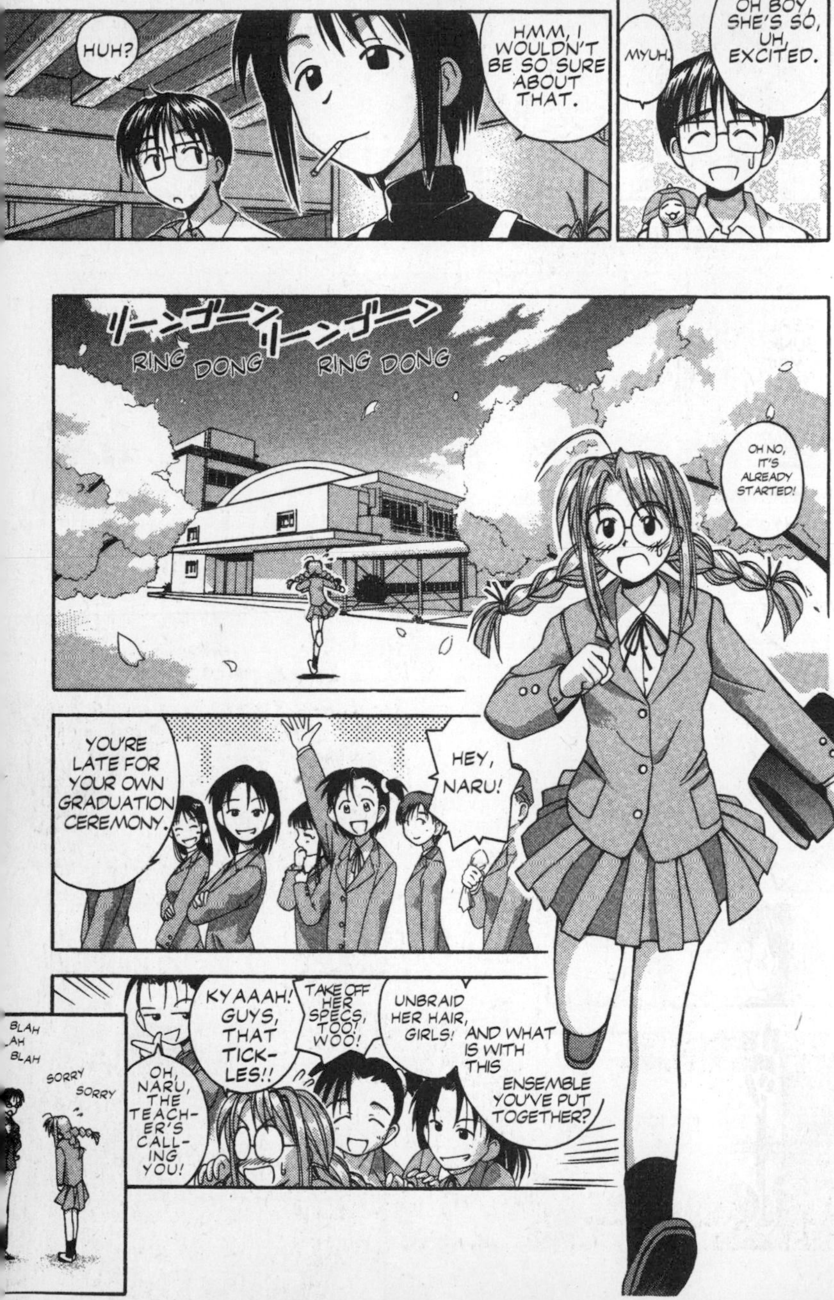
BOY OH BOY, SHE'S SO, UH, EXCITED.
MYUH.
HMM, I WOULDN'T BE SO SURE ABOUT THAT.
HUH?
リーンゴーン リーンゴーン
RING DONG RING DONG
OH NO, IT'S ALREADY STARTED!
HEY, NARU!
YOU'RE LATE FOR YOUR OWN GRADUATION CEREMONY.
UNBRAID HER HAIR, GIRLS!
AND WHAT IS WITH THIS ENSEMBLE YOU'VE PUT TOGETHER?
TAKE OFF HER SPECS, TOO! WOO!
KYAAAH! GUYS, THAT TICKLES!!
OH, NARU, THE TEACHER'S CALLING YOU!
BLAH BLAH BLAH
SORRY SORRY

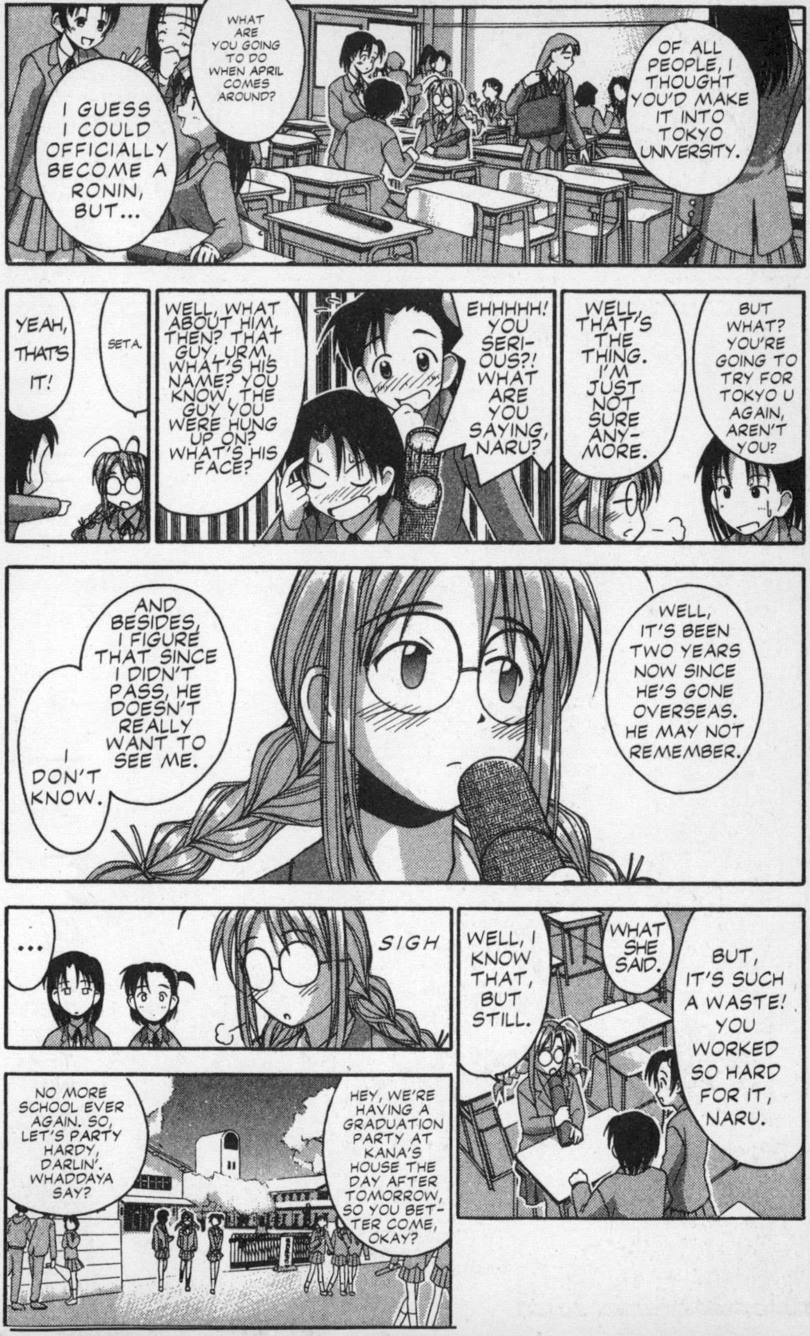
OF ALL PEOPLE, I THOUGHT YOU'D MAKE IT INTO TOKYO UNIVERSITY.
WHAT ARE YOU GOING TO DO WHEN APRIL COMES AROUND?
I GUESS I COULD OFFICIALLY BECOME A RONIN, BUT...
BUT WHAT? YOU'RE GOING TO TRY FOR TOKYO U AGAIN, AREN'T YOU?
WELL, THAT'S THE THING. I'M JUST NOT SURE ANY-MORE.
EHHHHH! YOU SERI-OUS?! WHAT ARE YOU SAYING, NARU?
WELL, WHAT ABOUT HIM, THEN? THAT GUY, URM, WHAT'S HIS NAME? YOU KNOW, THE GUY YOU WERE HUNG UP ON? WHAT'S HIS FACE?
SETA.
YEAH, THAT'S IT!
WELL, IT'S BEEN TWO YEARS NOW SINCE HE'S GONE OVERSEAS. HE MAY NOT REMEMBER.
AND BESIDES, I FIGURE THAT SINCE I DIDN'T PASS, HE DOESN'T REALLY WANT TO SEE ME.
I DON'T KNOW.
BUT, IT'S SUCH A WASTE! YOU WORKED SO HARD FOR IT, NARU.
WHAT SHE SAID.
WELL, I KNOW THAT, BUT STILL.
SIGH
...
HEY, WE'RE HAVING A GRADUATION PARTY AT KANA'S HOUSE THE DAY AFTER TOMORROW, SO YOU BET-TER COME, OKAY?
NO MORE SCHOOL EVER AGAIN. SO, LET'S PARTY HARDY, DARLIN'. WHADDAYA SAY?

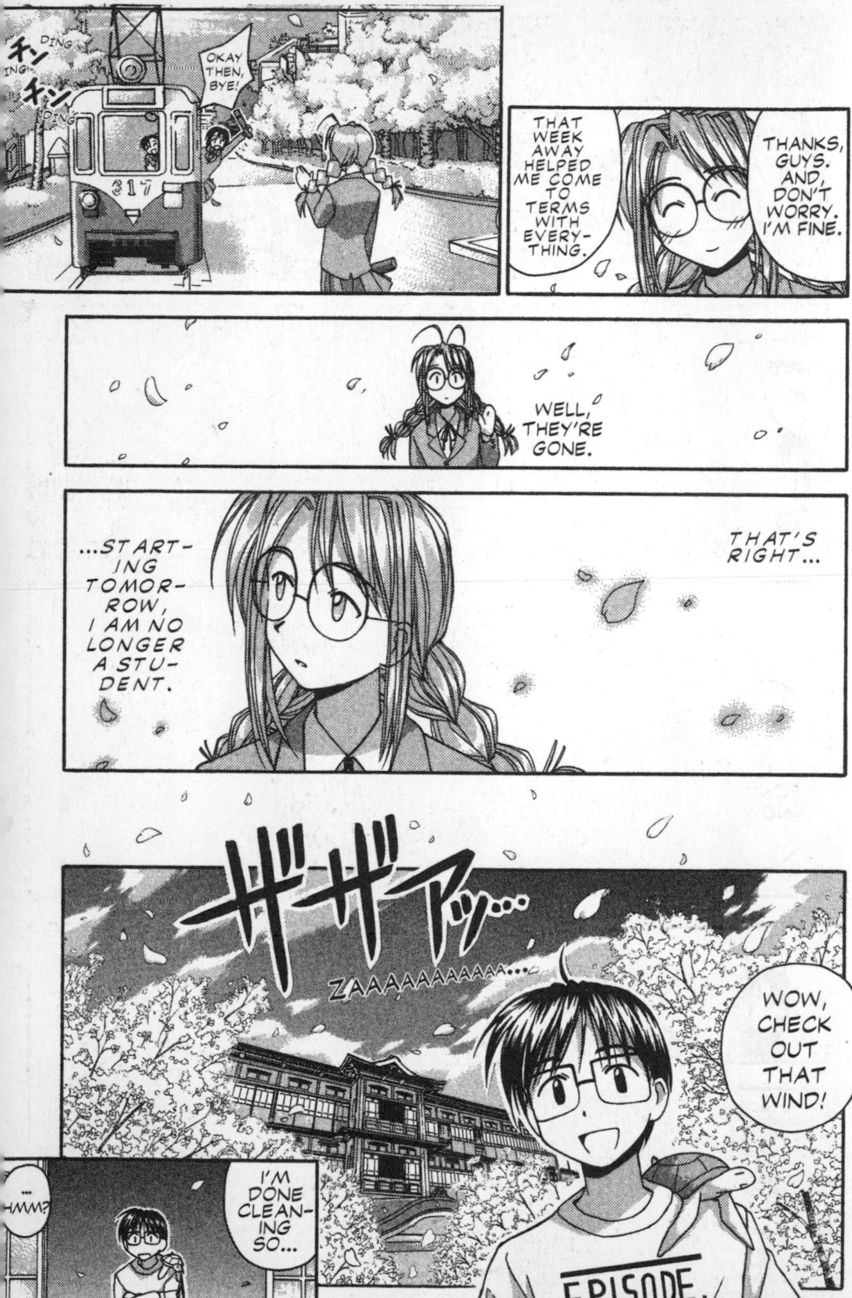
THANKS, GUYS. AND, DON'T WORRY. I'M FINE.
THAT WEEK AWAY HELPED ME COME TO TERMS WITH EVERY-THING.
OKAY THEN, BYE!
チン DING
チン DING
317
WELL, THEY'RE GONE.
THAT'S RIGHT...
...START-ING TOMOR-ROW, I AM NO LONGER A STU-DENT.
ザザアッ...
ZAAAAAAAAAA...
WOW, CHECK OUT THAT WIND!
I'M DONE CLEANING SO...
...HMM?
EPISODE.

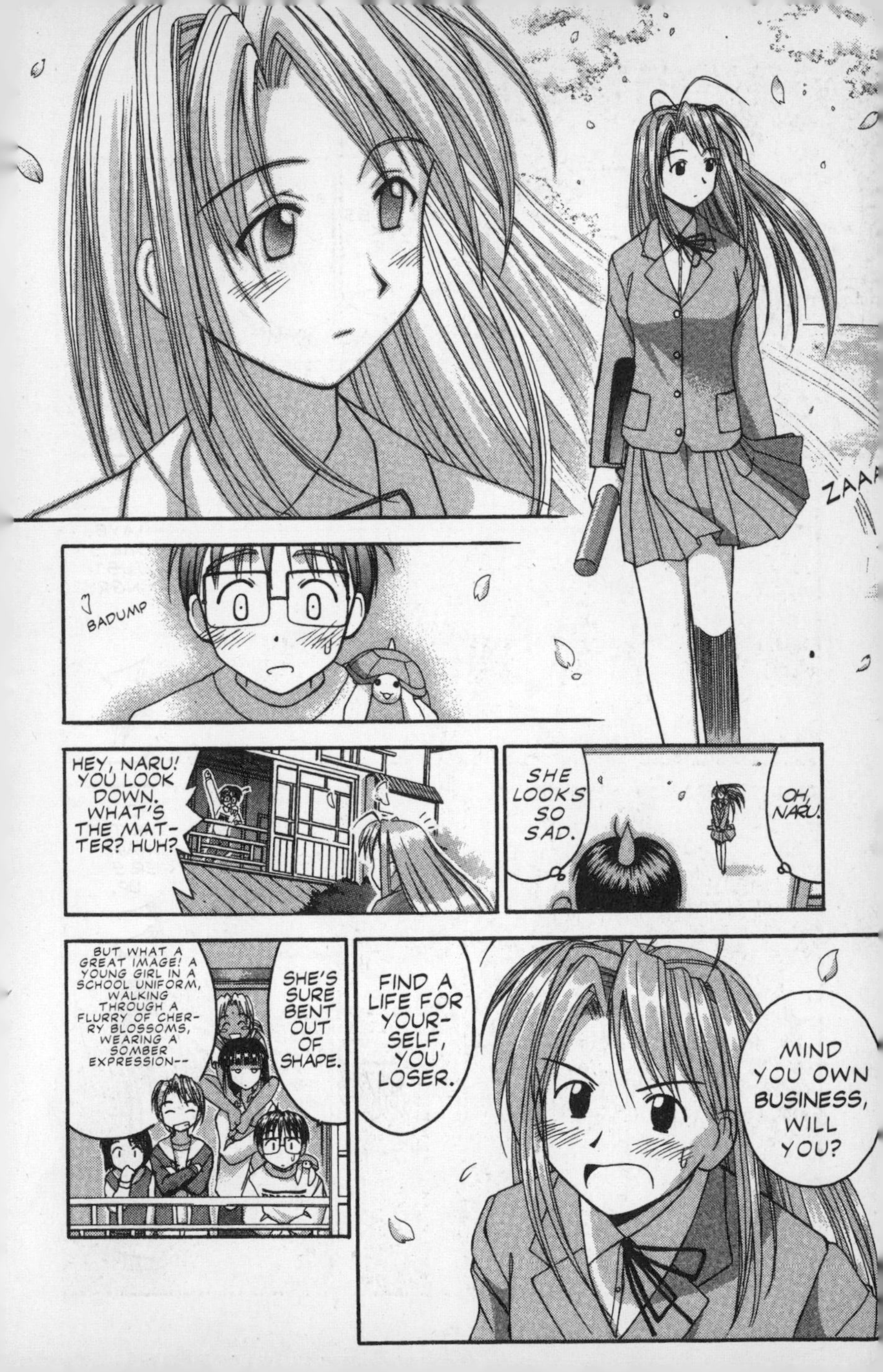
ZAA
BADUMP
OH, NARU.
SHE LOOKS SO SAD.
HEY, NARU! YOU LOOK DOWN. WHAT'S THE MATTER? HUH?
MIND YOU OWN BUSINESS, WILL YOU?
FIND A LIFE FOR YOURSELF, YOU LOSER.
SHE'S SURE BENT OUT OF SHAPE.
BUT WHAT A GREAT IMAGE! A YOUNG GIRL IN A SCHOOL UNIFORM, WALKING THROUGH A FLURRY OF CHERRY BLOSSOMS, WEARING A SOMBER EXPRESSION--

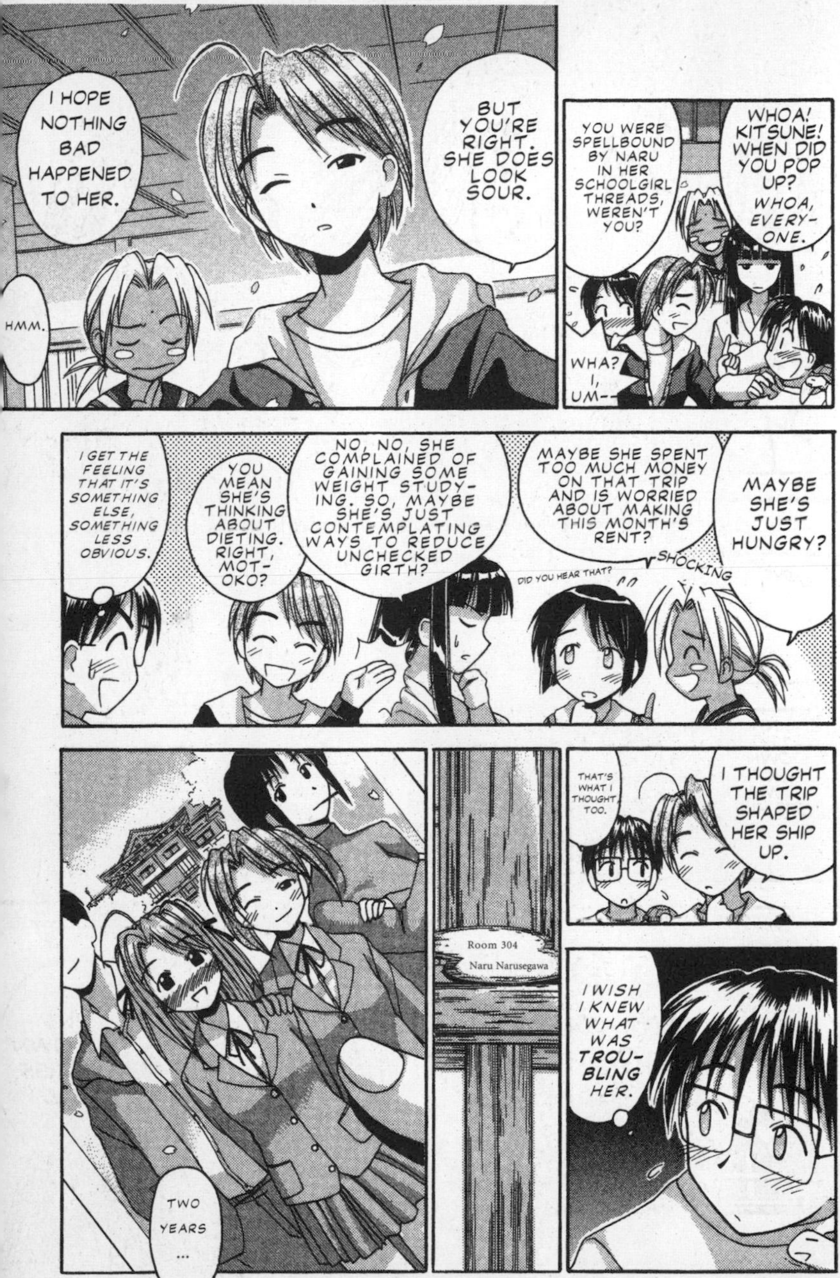
WHOA! KITSUNE! WHEN DID YOU POP UP?
WHOA, EVERYONE.
YOU WERE SPELLBOUND BY NARU IN HER SCHOOLGIRL THREADS, WEREN'T YOU?
WHA? I, UM--
BUT YOU'RE RIGHT. SHE DOES LOOK SOUR.
I HOPE NOTHING BAD HAPPENED TO HER.
HMM.
MAYBE SHE'S JUST HUNGRY?
SHOCKING
MAYBE SHE SPENT TOO MUCH MONEY ON THAT TRIP AND IS WORRIED ABOUT MAKING THIS MONTH'S RENT?
DID YOU HEAR THAT?
NO, NO, SHE COMPLAINED OF GAINING SOME WEIGHT STUDYING. SO, MAYBE SHE'S JUST CONTEMPLATING WAYS TO REDUCE UNCHECKED GIRTH?
YOU MEAN SHE'S THINKING ABOUT DIETING. RIGHT, MOTOKO?
I GET THE FEELING THAT IT'S SOMETHING ELSE, SOMETHING LESS OBVIOUS.
I THOUGHT THE TRIP SHAPED HER SHIP UP.
THAT'S WHAT I THOUGHT, TOO.
I WISH I KNEW WHAT WAS TROUBLING HER.
Room 304
Naru Narusegawa
TWO YEARS ...

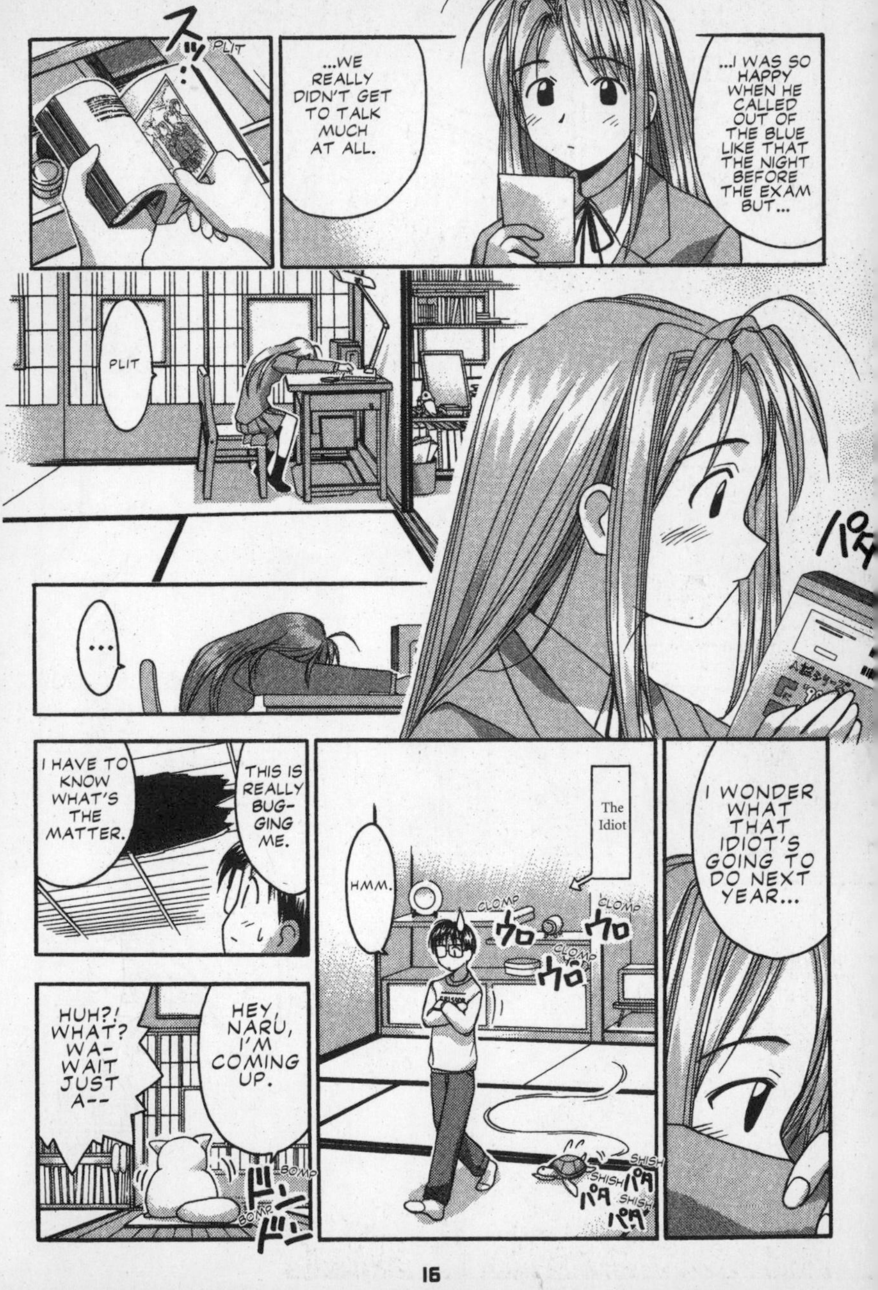
...I WAS SO HAPPY WHEN HE CALLED OUT OF THE BLUE LIKE THAT THE NIGHT BEFORE THE EXAM BUT...
...WE REALLY DIDN'T GET TO TALK MUCH AT ALL.
PLIT
PLIT
...
I WONDER WHAT THAT IDIOT'S GOING TO DO NEXT YEAR...
The Idiot
HMM.
CLOMP
CLOMP
CLOMP
SHISH
SHISH
SHISH
THIS IS REALLY BUG-GING ME.
I HAVE TO KNOW WHAT'S THE MATTER.
HEY, NARU, I'M COMING UP.
HUH?! WHAT? WA-WAIT JUST A--
BOMP
BOMP

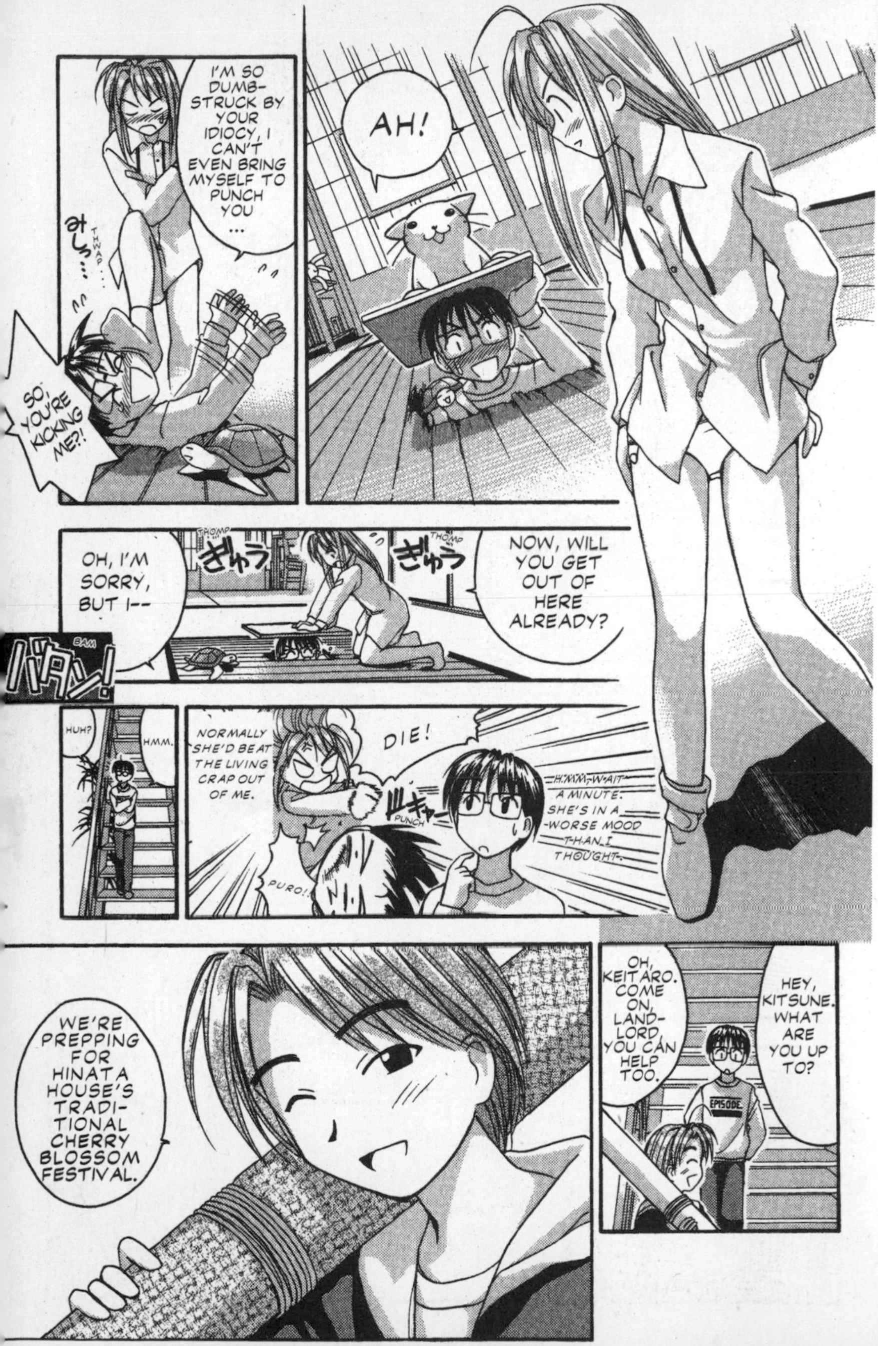
AH!
I'M SO DUMB-STRUCK BY YOUR IDIOCY, I CAN'T EVEN BRING MYSELF TO PUNCH YOU ...
みしっ
THWAP
SO, YOU'RE KICKING ME?!
NOW, WILL YOU GET OUT OF HERE ALREADY?
ぎゅう
THOMP
ぎゅう
THOMP
OH, I'M SORRY, BUT I--
バタン!
BAM
DIE!
HMM, WAIT A MINUTE. SHE'S IN A WORSE MOOD THAN I THOUGHT.
NORMALLY SHE'D BEAT THE LIVING CRAP OUT OF ME.
ギャー
PUNCH
PURO!!
HMM.
HUH?
HEY, KITSUNE. WHAT ARE YOU UP TO?
OH, KEITARO. COME ON, LAND-LORD YOU CAN HELP TOO.
EPISODE
WE'RE PREPPING FOR HINATA HOUSE'S TRADI-TIONAL CHERRY BLOSSOM FESTIVAL.

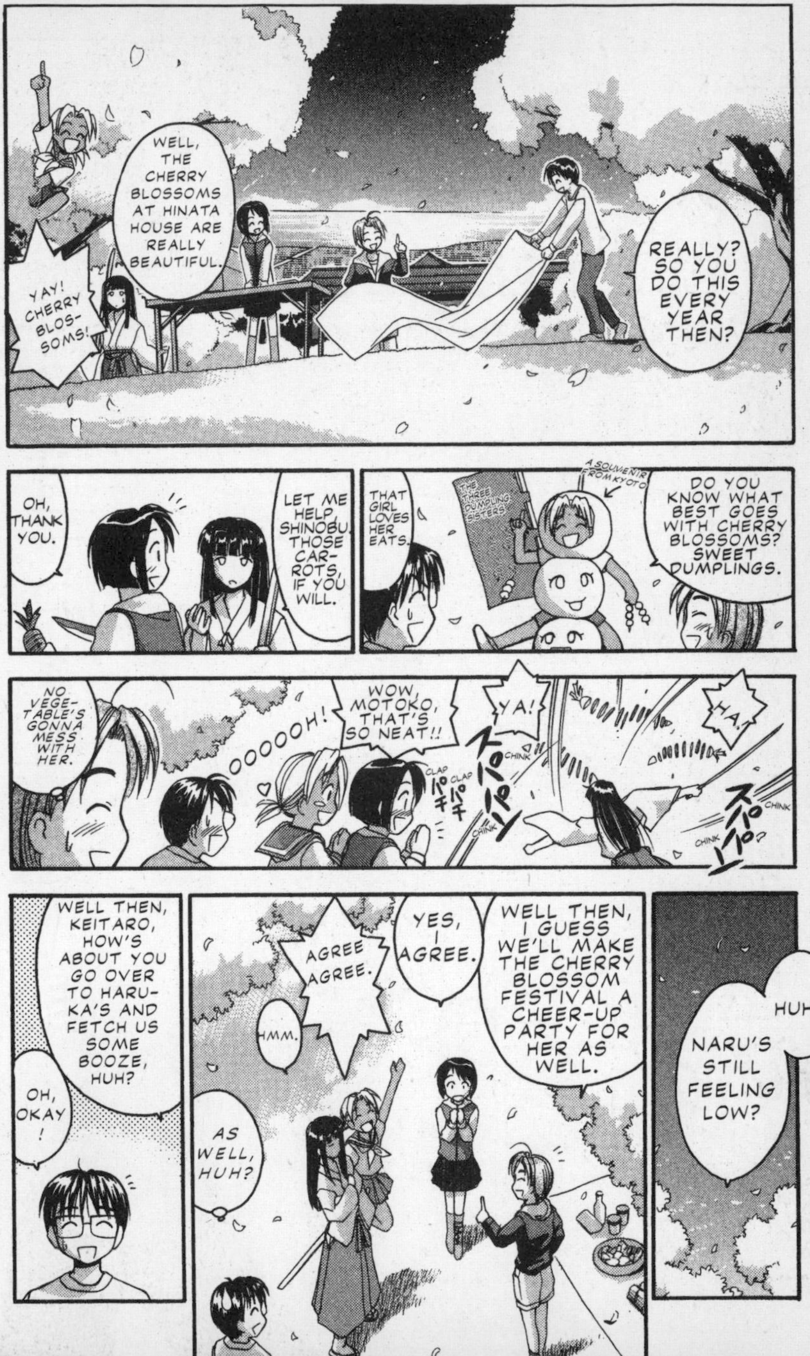
REALLY? SO YOU DO THIS EVERY YEAR THEN?
WELL, THE CHERRY BLOSSOMS AT HINATA HOUSE ARE REALLY BEAUTIFUL.
YAY! CHERRY BLOS-SOMS!
DO YOU KNOW WHAT BEST GOES WITH CHERRY BLOSSOMS? SWEET DUMPLINGS.
A SOUVENIR FROM KYOTO
THE THREE DUMPLING SISTERS
THAT GIRL LOVES HER EATS.
LET ME HELP, SHINOBU. THOSE CAR-ROTS, IF YOU WILL.
OH, THANK YOU.
HA!
CHINK
CHINK
YA!
CHINK
CHINK
WOW, MOTOKO, THAT'S SO NEAT!!
CLAP CLAP
OOOOOOH!
NO VEGE-TABLE'S GONNA MESS WITH HER.
HUH?
NARU'S STILL FEELING LOW?
WELL THEN, I GUESS WE'LL MAKE THE CHERRY BLOSSOM FESTIVAL A CHEER-UP PARTY FOR HER AS WELL.
YES, I AGREE.
AGREE AGREE.
HMM.
AS WELL, HUH?
WELL THEN, KEITARO, HOW'S ABOUT YOU GO OVER TO HARU-KA'S AND FETCH US SOME BOOZE, HUH?
OH, OKAY!

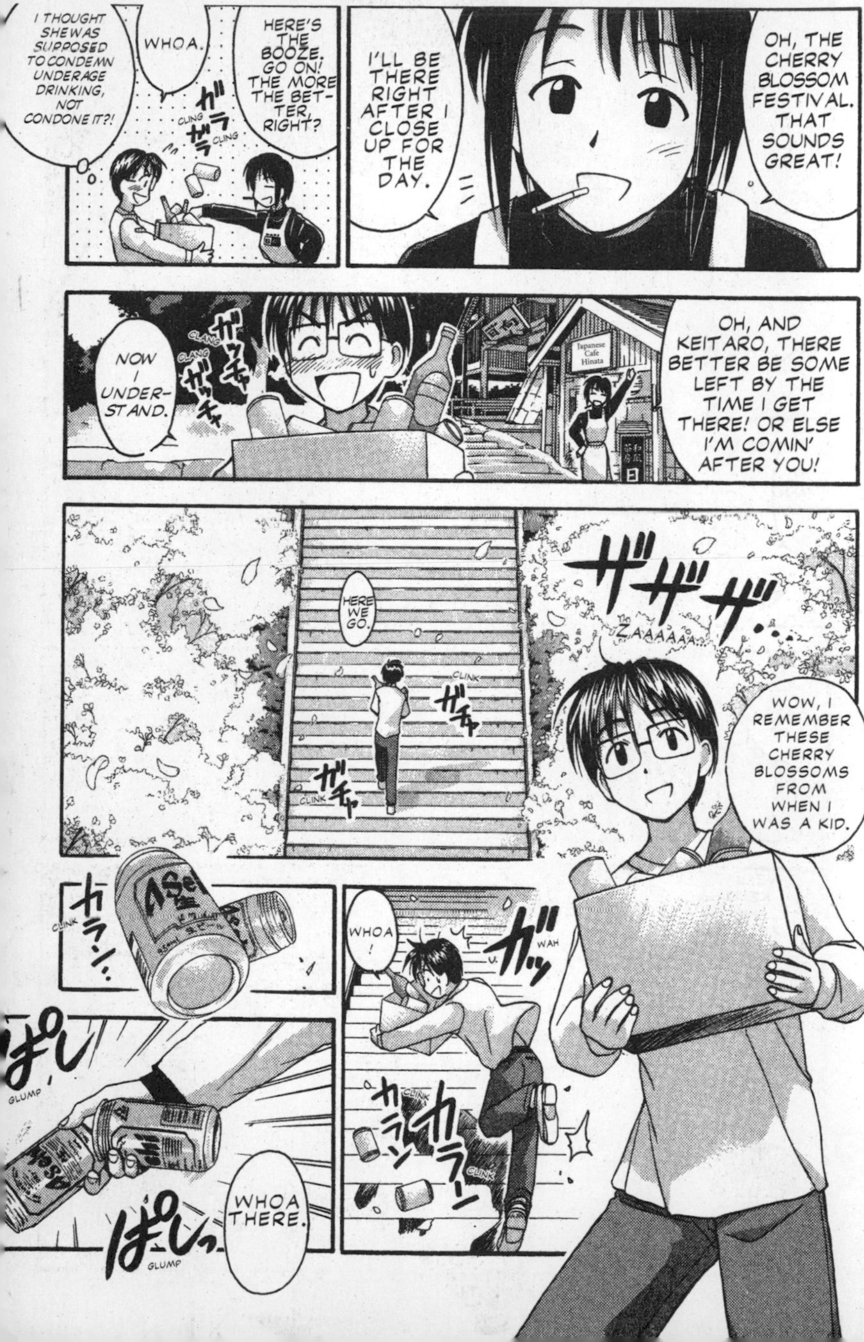
OH, THE CHERRY BLOSSOM FESTIVAL. THAT SOUNDS GREAT!
I'LL BE THERE RIGHT AFTER I CLOSE UP FOR THE DAY.
HERE'S THE BOOZE. GO ON! THE MORE THE BETTER, RIGHT?
WHOA.
ガラ CLING
ガラ CLING
I THOUGHT SHE WAS SUPPOSED TO CONDEMN UNDERAGE DRINKING, NOT CONDONE IT?!
OH, AND KEITARO, THERE BETTER BE SOME LEFT BY THE TIME I GET THERE! OR ELSE I'M COMIN' AFTER YOU!
Japanese Cafe Hinata
ガッチャ CLANG
ガッチャ CLANG
NOW I UNDERSTAND.
ザザザ
ZAAAAAA
WOW, I REMEMBER THESE CHERRY BLOSSOMS FROM WHEN I WAS A KID.
HERE WE GO.
ガチャ CLINK
ガチャ CLINK
WHOA!
ガッ WAH
カラーン CLINK
カラン CLINK
カラン CLINK
ぱしっ GLUMP
ぱしっ GLUMP
WHOA THERE.

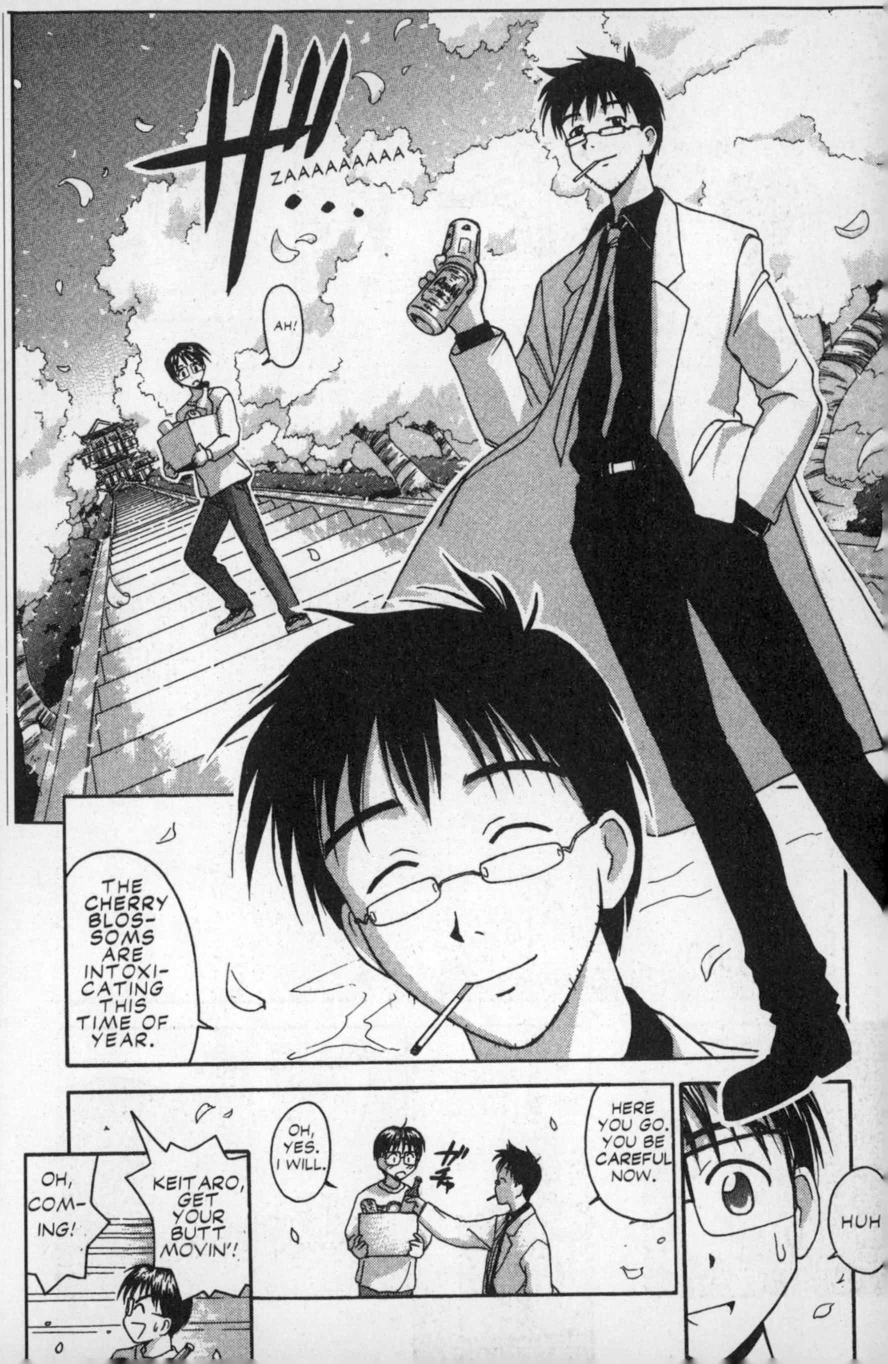
ZAAAAAAAAA
...
AH!
THE CHERRY BLOSSOMS ARE INTOXICATING THIS TIME OF YEAR.
HUH
HERE YOU GO. YOU BE CAREFUL NOW.
OH, YES. I WILL.
KEITARO, GET YOUR BUTT MOVIN'!
OH, COMING!

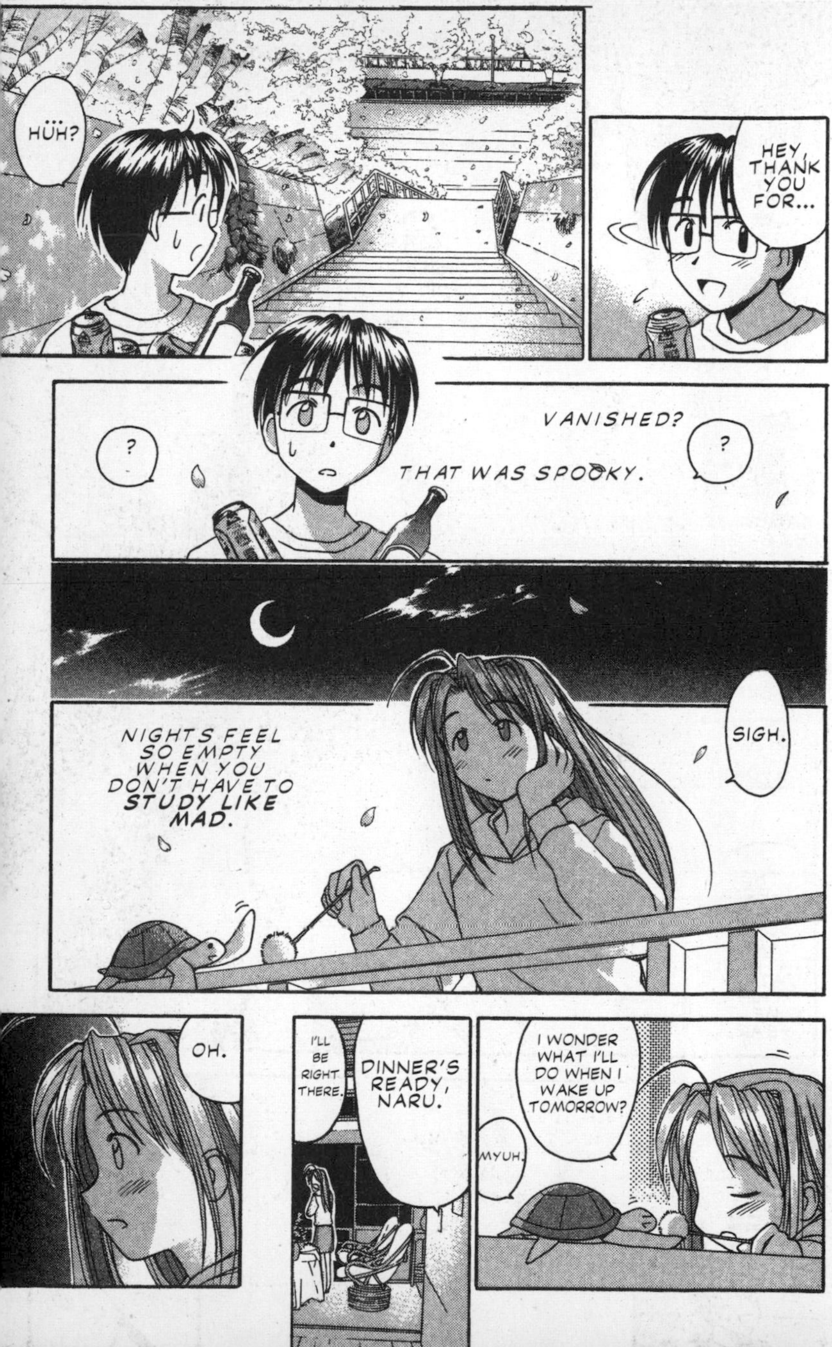
HEY, THANK YOU FOR...
...HUH?
?
VANISHED?
THAT WAS SPOOKY.
?
SIGH.
NIGHTS FEEL SO EMPTY WHEN YOU DON'T HAVE TO **STUDY LIKE MAD.**
I WONDER WHAT I'LL DO WHEN I WAKE UP TOMORROW?
MYUH.
DINNER'S READY, NARU.
I'LL BE RIGHT THERE.
OH.

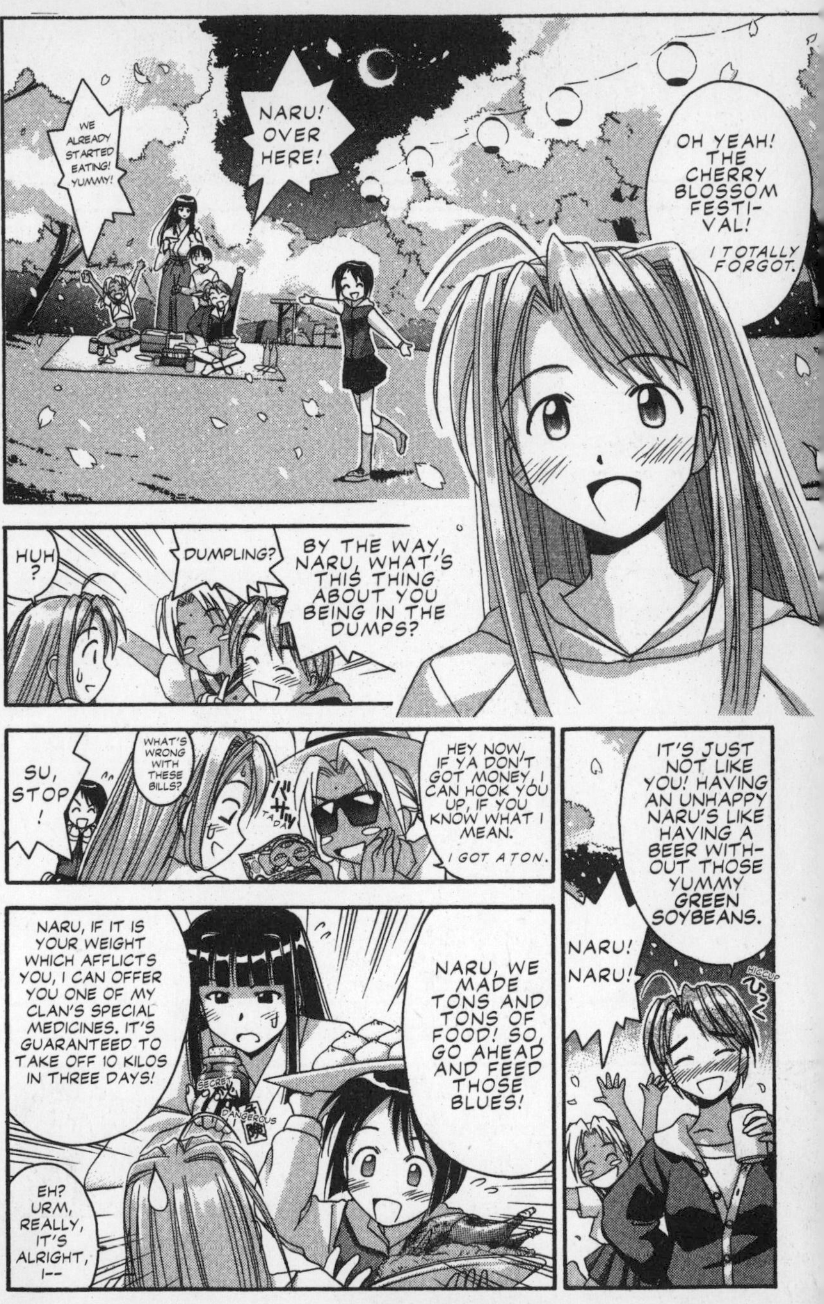
OH YEAH! THE CHERRY BLOSSOM FESTI- VAL!
I TOTALLY FORGOT.
NARU! OVER HERE!
WE ALREADY STARTED EATING! YUMMY!
BY THE WAY, NARU, WHAT'S THIS THING ABOUT YOU BEING IN THE DUMPS?
DUMPLING?
HUH?
IT'S JUST NOT LIKE YOU! HAVING AN UNHAPPY NARU'S LIKE HAVING A BEER WITH- OUT THOSE YUMMY GREEN SOYBEANS.
HICCUP
NARU! NARU!
HEY NOW, IF YA DON'T GOT MONEY, I CAN HOOK YOU UP, IF YOU KNOW WHAT I MEAN.
I GOT A TON.
TA DA
WHAT'S WRONG WITH THESE BILLS?
SU, STOP!
NARU, WE MADE TONS AND TONS OF FOOD! SO, GO AHEAD AND FEED THOSE BLUES!
NARU, IF IT IS YOUR WEIGHT WHICH AFFLICTS YOU, I CAN OFFER YOU ONE OF MY CLAN'S SPECIAL MEDICINES. IT'S GUARANTEED TO TAKE OFF 10 KILOS IN THREE DAYS!
SECRET
DANGEROUS
EH? URM, REALLY, IT'S ALRIGHT, I--

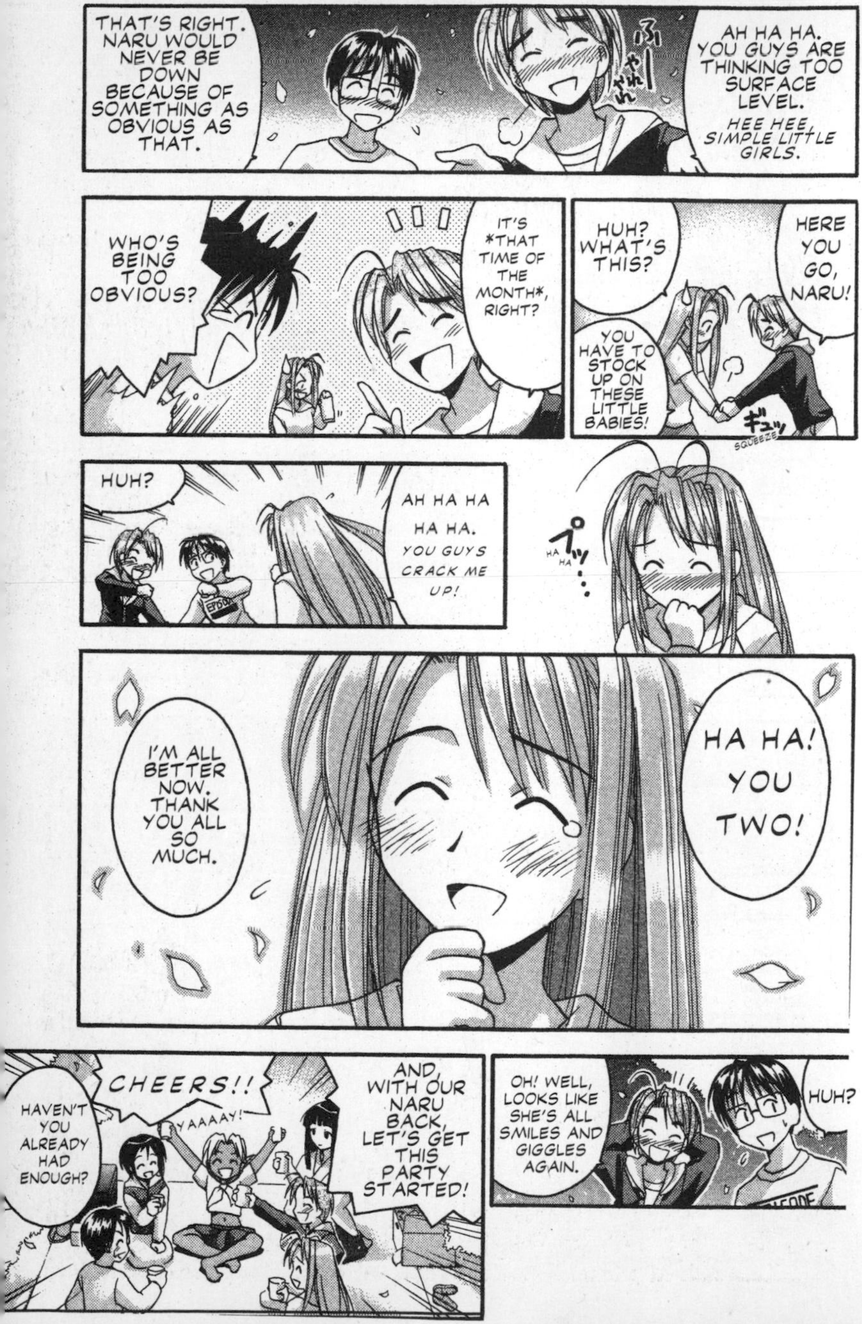
AH HA HA. YOU GUYS ARE THINKING TOO SURFACE LEVEL.
HEE HEE, SIMPLE LITTLE GIRLS.
THAT'S RIGHT. NARU WOULD NEVER BE DOWN BECAUSE OF SOMETHING AS OBVIOUS AS THAT.
HERE YOU GO, NARU!
HUH? WHAT'S THIS?
YOU HAVE TO STOCK UP ON THESE LITTLE BABIES!
SQUEEZE
IT'S *THAT TIME OF THE MONTH*, RIGHT?
WHO'S BEING TOO OBVIOUS?
HA HA
AH HA HA HA HA. YOU GUYS CRACK ME UP!
HUH?
HA HA! YOU TWO!
I'M ALL BETTER NOW. THANK YOU ALL SO MUCH.
HUH?
OH! WELL, LOOKS LIKE SHE'S ALL SMILES AND GIGGLES AGAIN.
AND, WITH OUR NARU BACK, LET'S GET THIS PARTY STARTED!
CHEERS!!
YAAAAY!
HAVEN'T YOU ALREADY HAD ENOUGH?

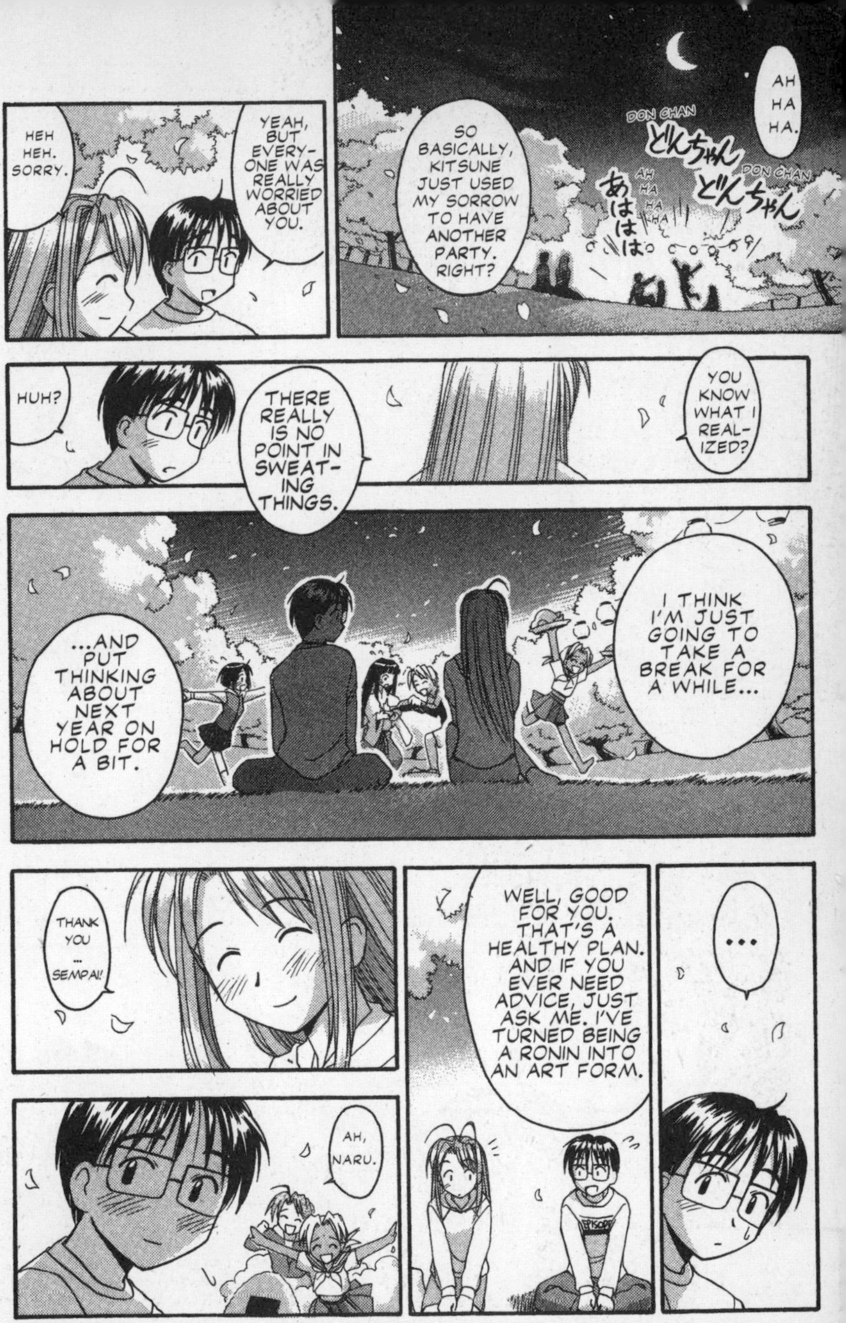
AH HA HA.
DON CHAN
どんちゃん
DON CHAN
どんちゃん
AH HA HA HA
あははは
SO BASICALLY, KITSUNE JUST USED MY SORROW TO HAVE ANOTHER PARTY. RIGHT?
YEAH, BUT EVERY-ONE WAS REALLY WORRIED ABOUT YOU.
HEH HEH. SORRY.
YOU KNOW WHAT I REAL-IZED?
THERE REALLY IS NO POINT IN SWEAT-ING THINGS.
HUH?
I THINK I'M JUST GOING TO TAKE A BREAK FOR A WHILE...
...AND PUT THINKING ABOUT NEXT YEAR ON HOLD FOR A BIT.
...
WELL, GOOD FOR YOU. THAT'S A HEALTHY PLAN. AND IF YOU EVER NEED ADVICE, JUST ASK ME. I'VE TURNED BEING A RONIN INTO AN ART FORM.
THANK YOU ... SEMPAI!
AH, NARU.

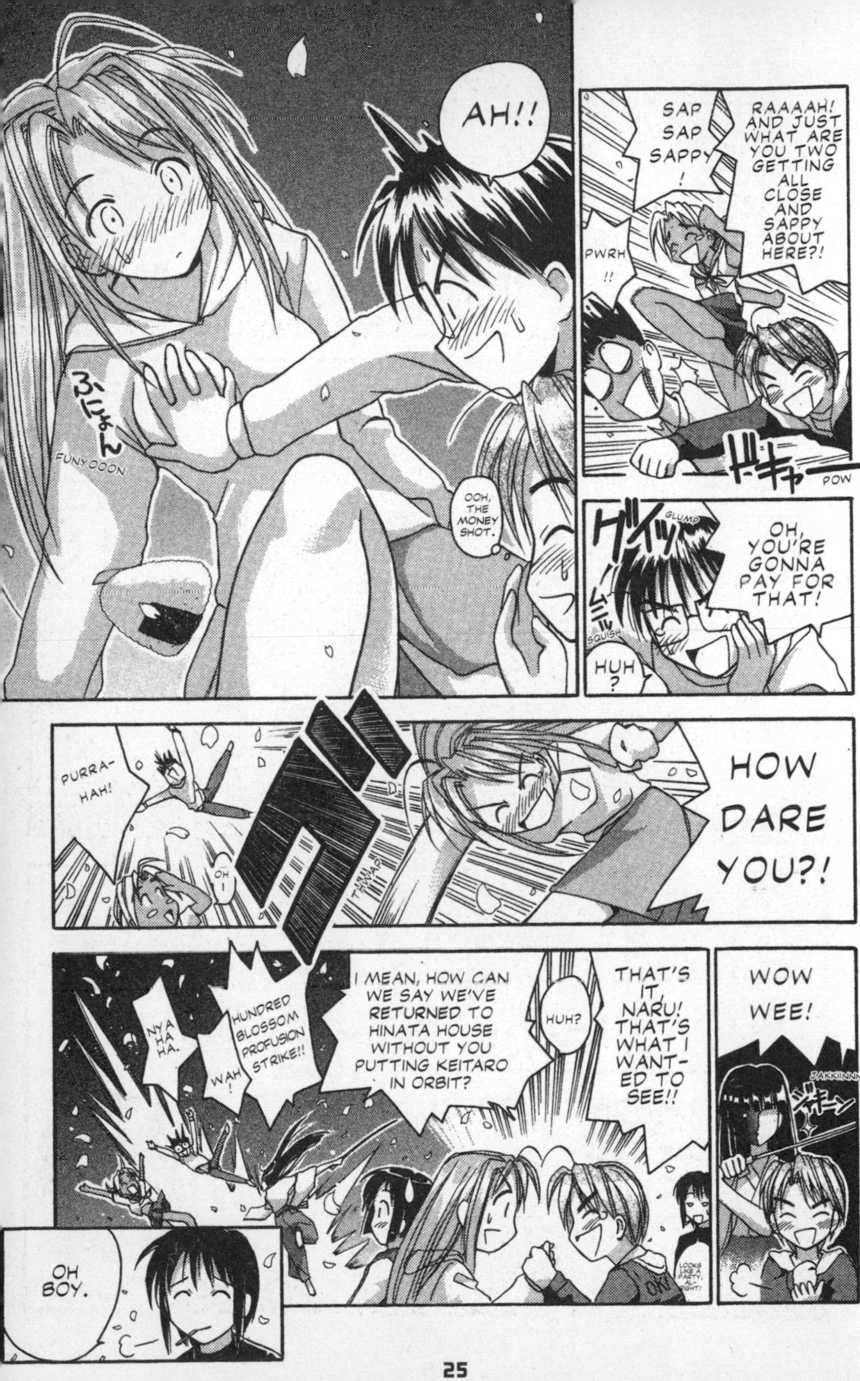
RAAAAH! AND JUST WHAT ARE YOU TWO GETTING ALL CLOSE AND SAPPY ABOUT HERE?!
SAP SAP SAPPY!
PWRH!!
POW
OH, YOU'RE GONNA PAY FOR THAT!
GLUMP
SQUISH
HUH?
AH!!
OOH, THE MONEY SHOT.
ふにょん
FUNYOOON
HOW DARE YOU?!
THWAP
OH!
PURRA-HAH!
WOW WEE!
JAKKIINNN
THAT'S IT, NARU! THAT'S WHAT I WANTED TO SEE!!
HUH?
I MEAN, HOW CAN WE SAY WE'VE RETURNED TO HINATA HOUSE WITHOUT YOU PUTTING KEITARO IN ORBIT?
HUNDRED BLOSSOM PROFUSION STRIKE!!
NYA HA HA.
WAH!
LOOKS LIKE A PARTY, ALRIGHT!
OH BOY.

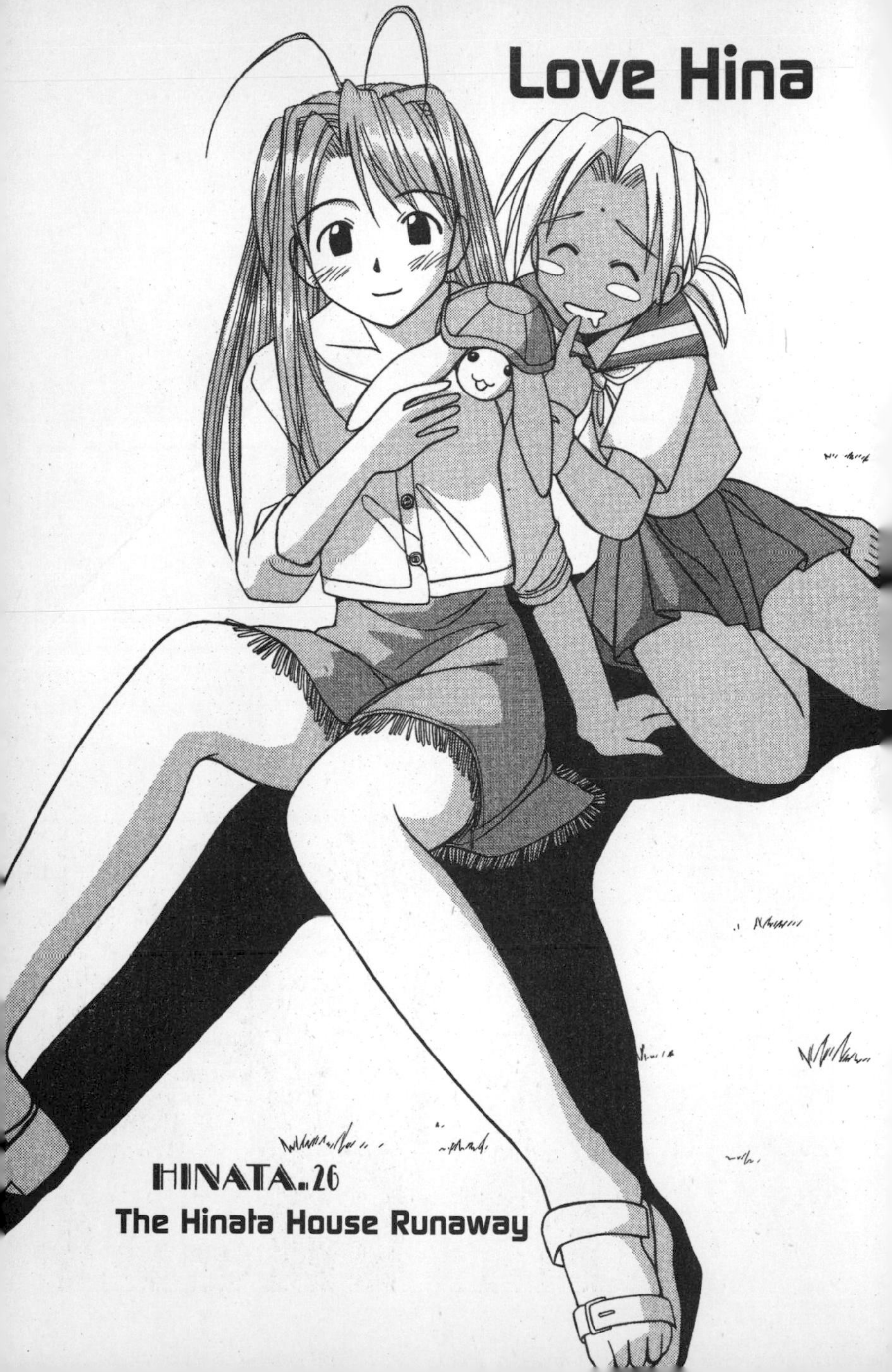
Love Hina
HINATA.26
The Hinata House Runaway

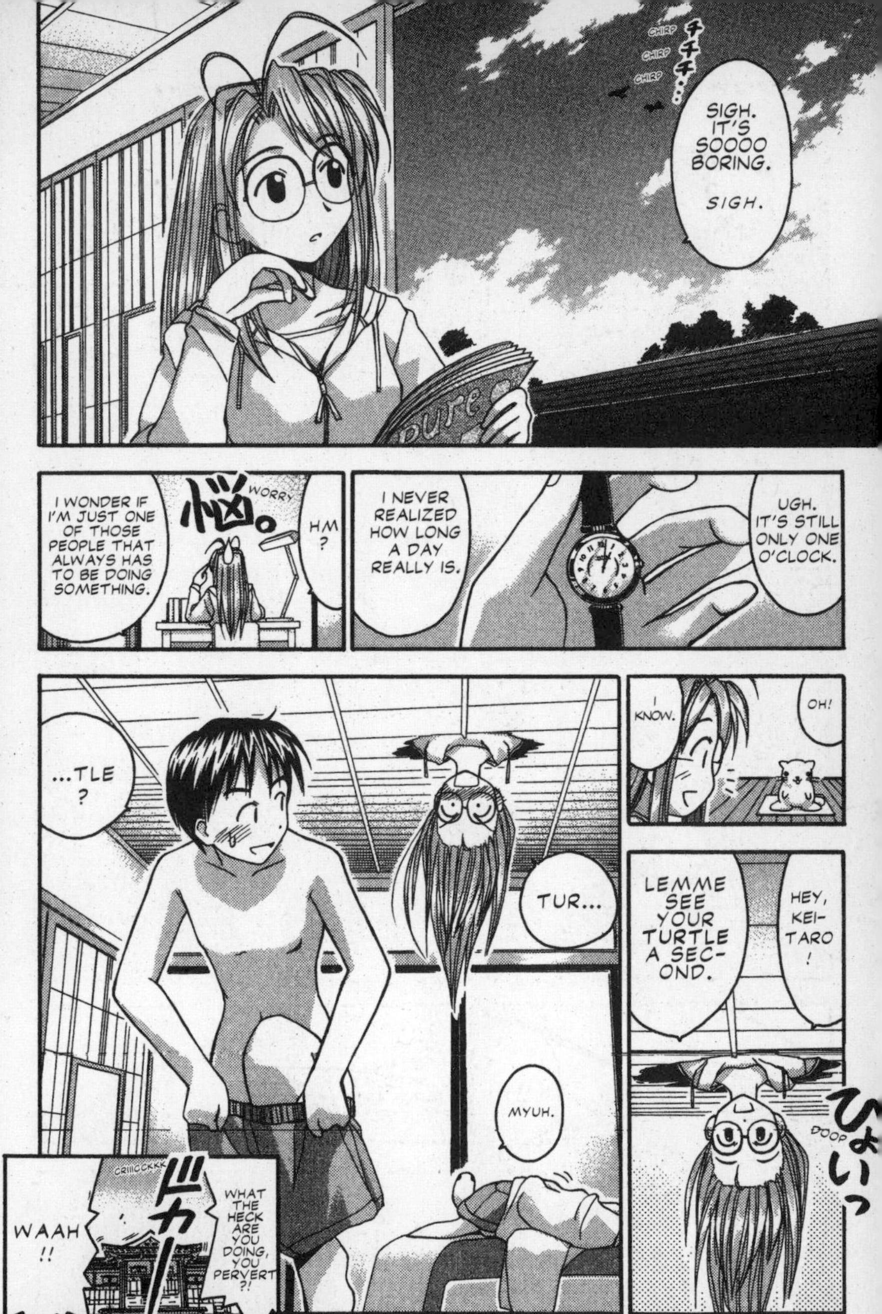
チチチ…
CHIRP
CHIRP
CHIRP
SIGH. IT'S SOOOO BORING.
SIGH.
UGH. IT'S STILL ONLY ONE O'CLOCK.
I NEVER REALIZED HOW LONG A DAY REALLY IS.
HM?
悩
WORRY
I WONDER IF I'M JUST ONE OF THOSE PEOPLE THAT ALWAYS HAS TO BE DOING SOMETHING.
OH!
I KNOW.
HEY, KEI-TARO!
LEMME SEE YOUR TURTLE A SEC-OND.
ひょいっ
DOOP
TUR...
...TLE?
MYUH.
ドカー
CRIIICKKK
WHAT THE HECK ARE YOU DOING, YOU PERVERT?!
WAAH!!

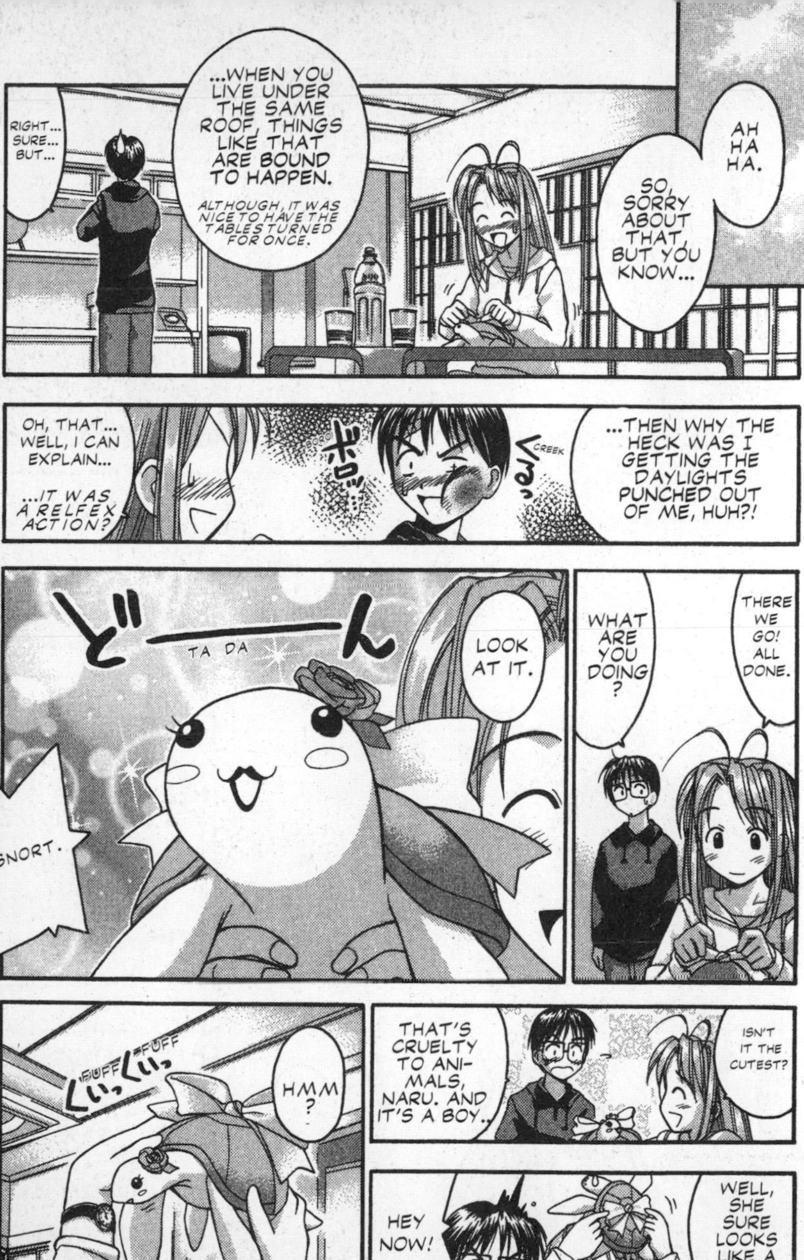
AH HA HA.
SO, SORRY ABOUT THAT, BUT YOU KNOW...
...WHEN YOU LIVE UNDER THE SAME ROOF, THINGS LIKE THAT ARE BOUND TO HAPPEN.
ALTHOUGH, IT WAS NICE TO HAVE THE TABLES TURNED FOR ONCE.
RIGHT... SURE... BUT...
...THEN WHY THE HECK WAS I GETTING THE DAYLIGHTS PUNCHED OUT OF ME, HUH?!
CREEK
BORO
OH, THAT... WELL, I CAN EXPLAIN...
...IT WAS A RELFEX ACTION?
THERE WE GO! ALL DONE.
WHAT ARE YOU DOING?
LOOK AT IT.
TA DA
SNORT.
ISN'T IT THE CUTEST?
THAT'S CRUELTY TO ANIMALS, NARU. AND IT'S A BOY..
WELL, SHE SURE LOOKS LIKE A GIRL TO ME.
HEY NOW!
HMM?
FUFF FUFF

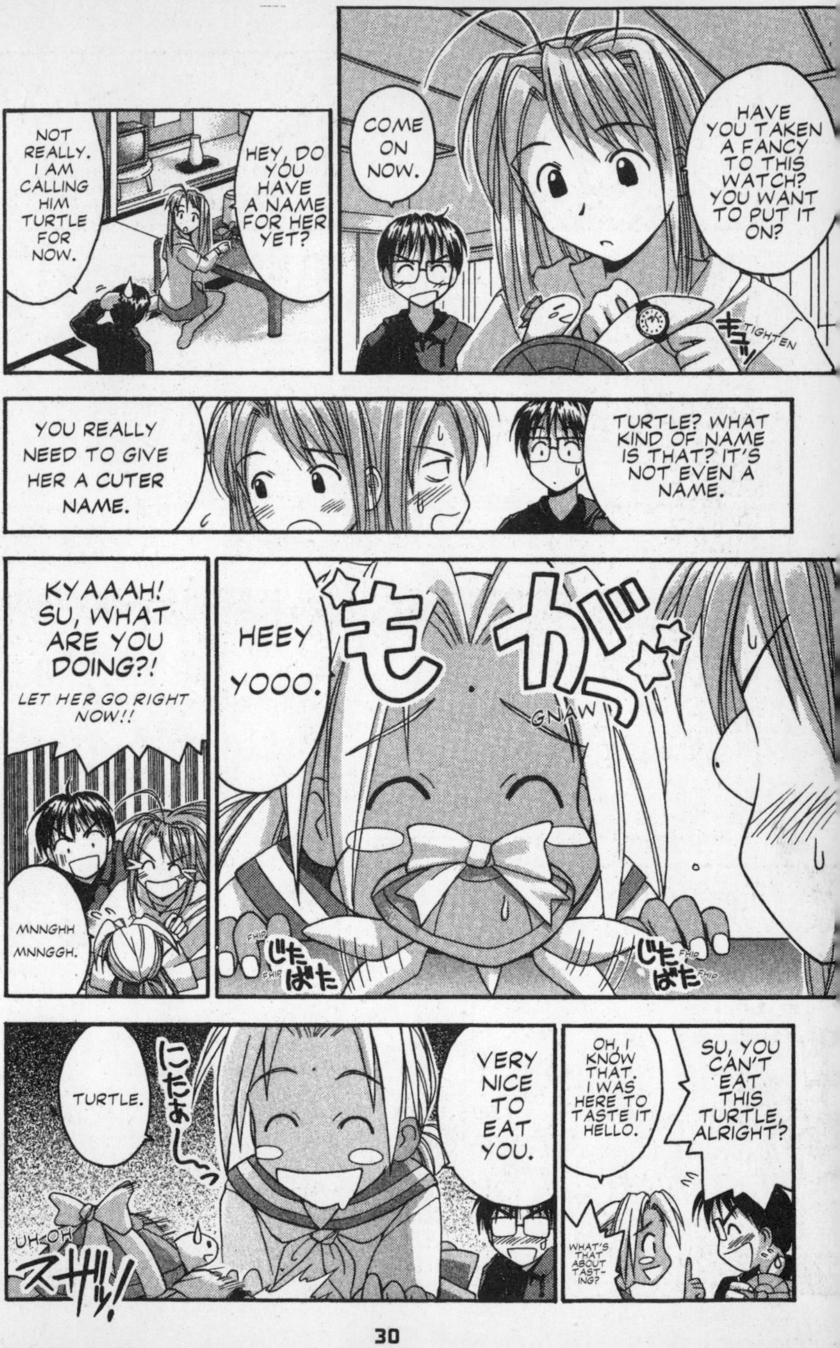
HAVE YOU TAKEN A FANCY TO THIS WATCH? YOU WANT TO PUT IT ON?
COME ON NOW.
キュッ
TIGHTEN
HEY, DO YOU HAVE A NAME FOR HER YET?
NOT REALLY. I AM CALLING HIM TURTLE FOR NOW.
TURTLE? WHAT KIND OF NAME IS THAT? IT'S NOT EVEN A NAME.
YOU REALLY NEED TO GIVE HER A CUTER NAME.
もがっ
GNAW
HEEY YOOO.
じたばた
FHIP
FHIP
じたばた
FHIP
FHIP
KYAAAH! SU, WHAT ARE YOU DOING?!
LET HER GO RIGHT NOW!!
MNNGHH MNNGGH.
SU, YOU CAN'T EAT THIS TURTLE, ALRIGHT?
OH, I KNOW THAT. I WAS HERE TO TASTE IT HELLO.
WHAT'S THAT ABOUT TASTING?
VERY NICE TO EAT YOU.
にたぁ〜っ
GRIN
TURTLE.
スザッ!
UH-OH

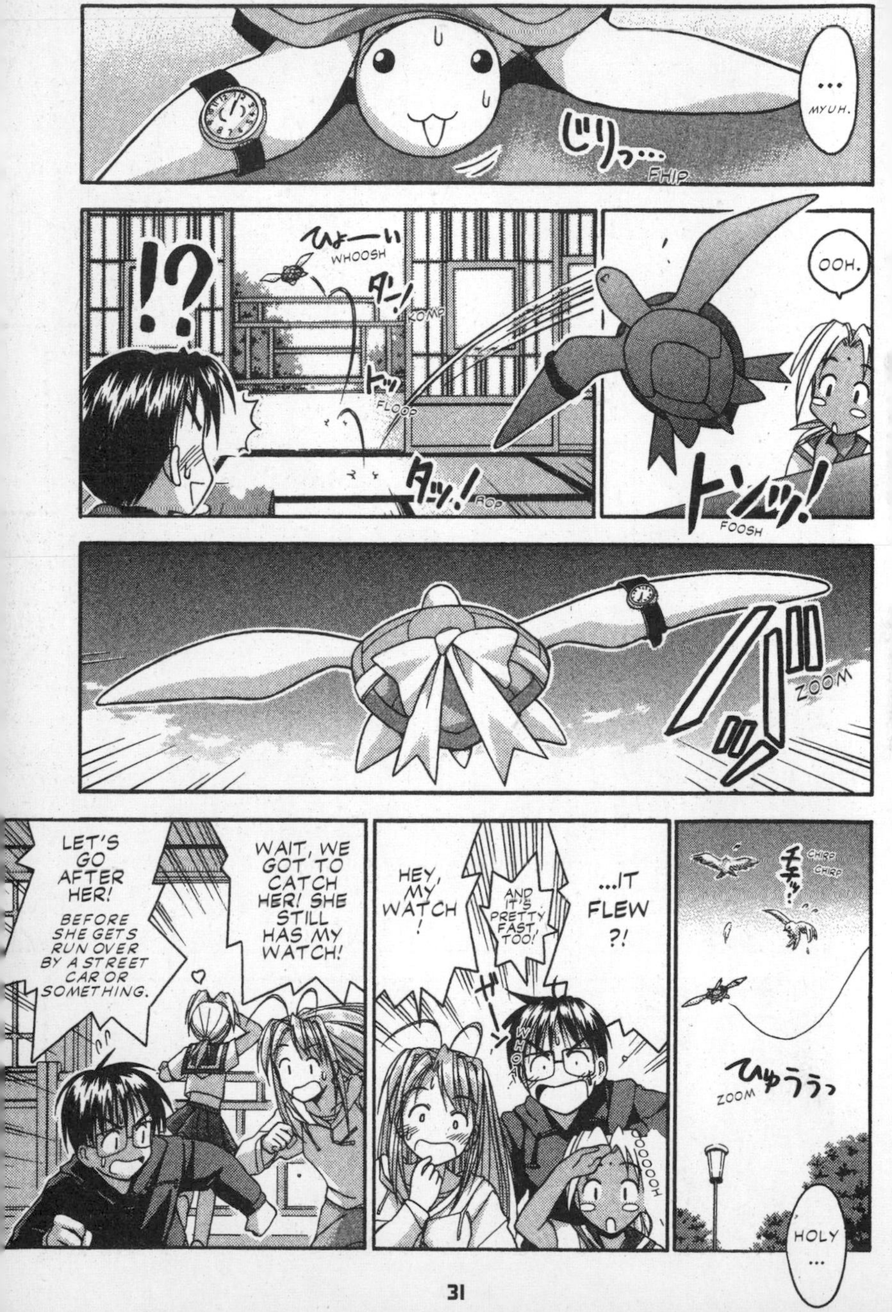

... MYUH.
FHIP
OOH.
FOOSH
!?
WHOOSH
KOMP
FLOOP
ROP
ZOOM
HOLY ...
CHIRP CHIRP
ZOOM
...IT FLEW ?!
AND IT'S PRETTY FAST TOO!
HEY, MY WATCH!
WHOA
OOOOOOH
WAIT, WE GOT TO CATCH HER! SHE STILL HAS MY WATCH!
LET'S GO AFTER HER!
BEFORE SHE GETS RUN OVER BY A STREET CAR OR SOMETHING.

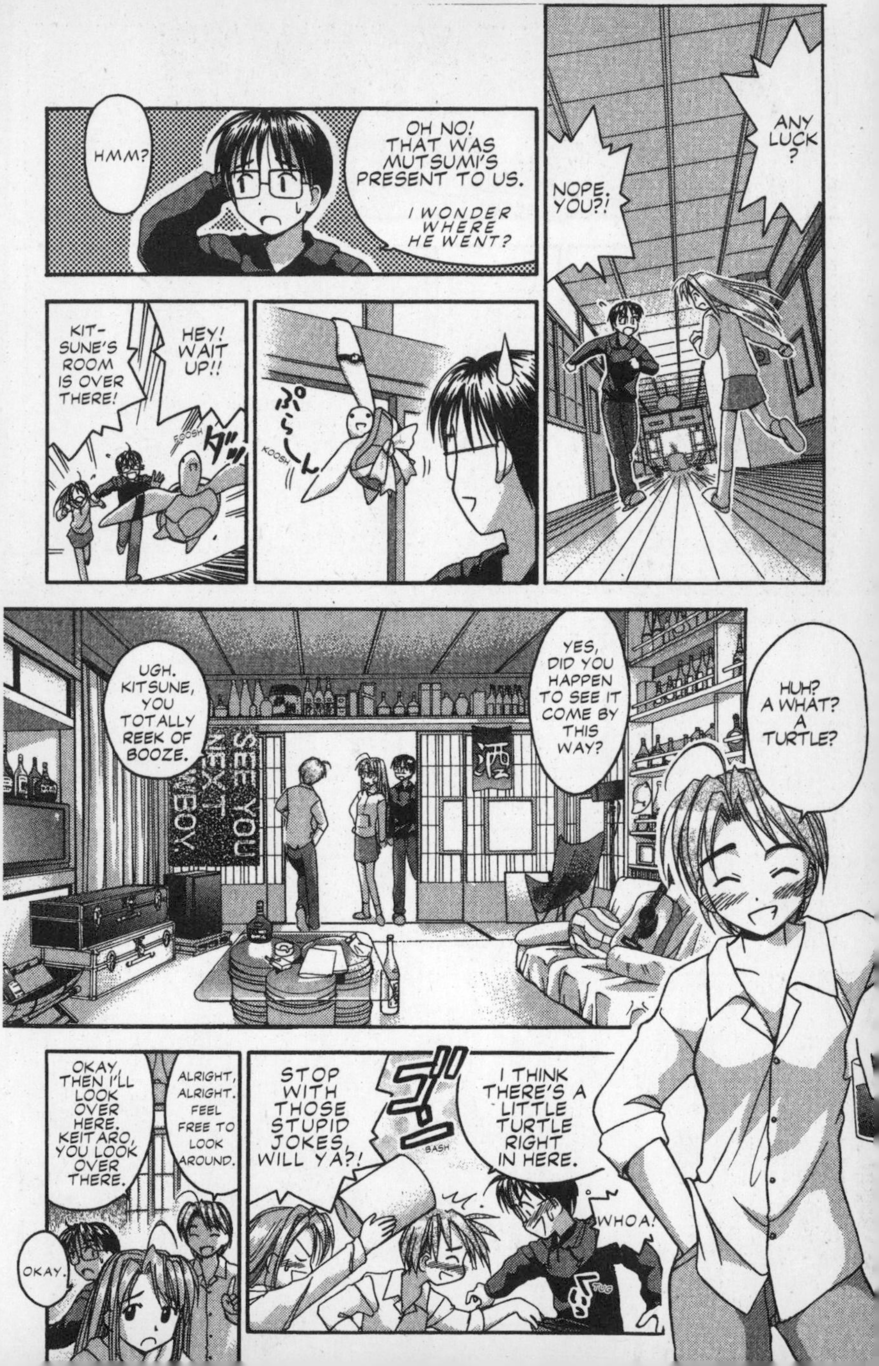
ANY LUCK?
NOPE. YOU?!
HMM?
OH NO! THAT WAS MUTSUMI'S PRESENT TO US.
I WONDER WHERE HE WENT?
KOOSH
HEY! WAIT UP!!
KIT-SUNE'S ROOM IS OVER THERE!
FOOSH
ダッ
HUH? A WHAT? A TURTLE?
YES, DID YOU HAPPEN TO SEE IT COME BY THIS WAY?
UGH. KITSUNE, YOU TOTALLY REEK OF BOOZE.
SEE YOU NEXT BOY
I THINK THERE'S A LITTLE TURTLE RIGHT IN HERE.
WHOA!
STOP WITH THOSE STUPID JOKES, WILL YA?!
BASH
TUG
ALRIGHT, ALRIGHT. FEEL FREE TO LOOK AROUND.
OKAY THEN I'LL LOOK OVER HERE. KEITARO, YOU LOOK OVER THERE.
OKAY.

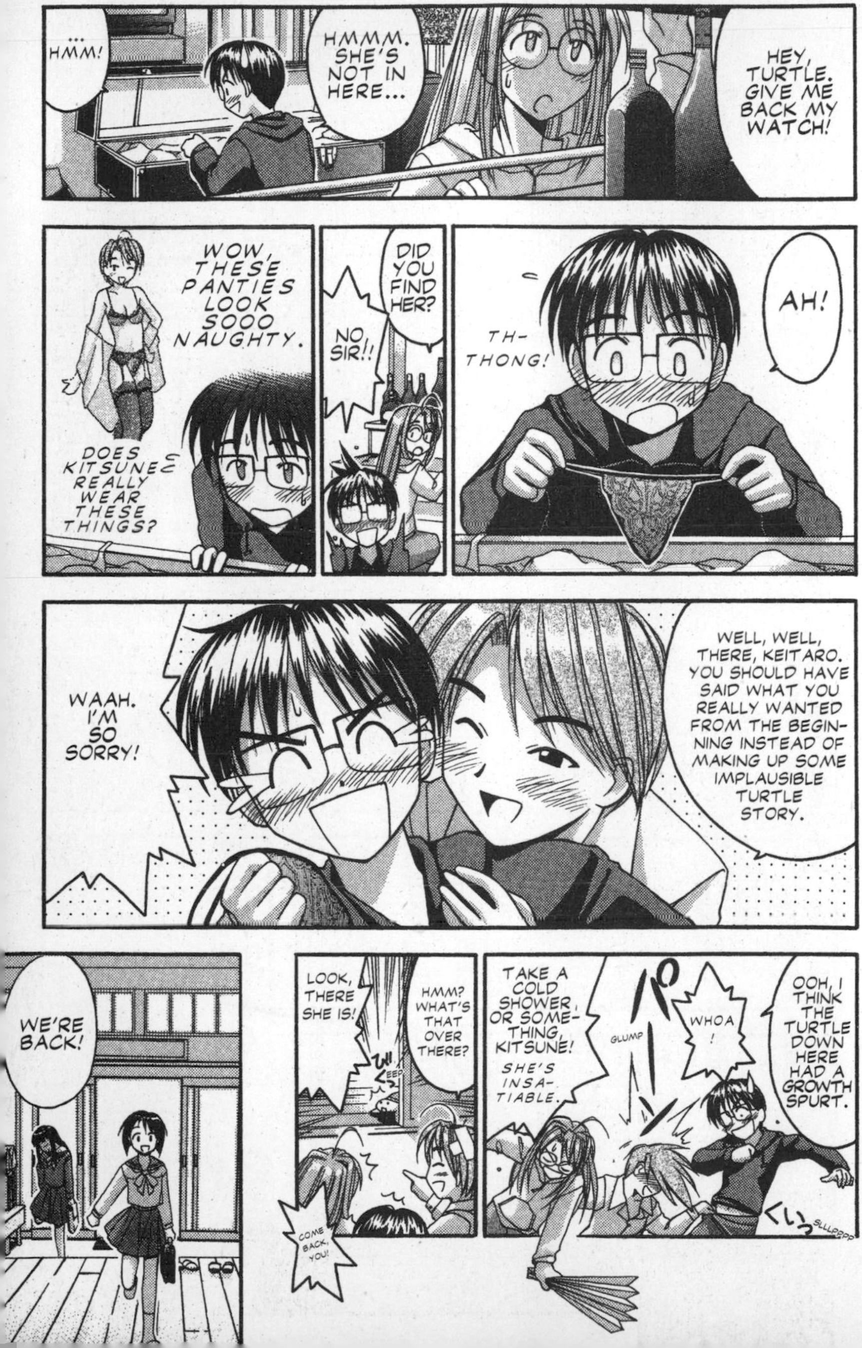

HEY, TURTLE. GIVE ME BACK MY WATCH!
HMMM. SHE'S NOT IN HERE...
... HMM!
AH!
TH- THONG!
DID YOU FIND HER?
NO SIR!!
WOW, THESE PANTIES LOOK SOOO NAUGHTY.
DOES KITSUNE REALLY WEAR THESE THINGS?
WELL, WELL, THERE, KEITARO. YOU SHOULD HAVE SAID WHAT YOU REALLY WANTED FROM THE BEGIN-NING INSTEAD OF MAKING UP SOME IMPLAUSIBLE TURTLE STORY.
WAAH. I'M SO SORRY!
OOH, I THINK THE TURTLE DOWN HERE HAD A GROWTH SPURT.
WHOA!
TAKE A COLD SHOWER OR SOME-THING, KITSUNE!
GLUMP
SHE'S INSA-TIABLE.
SLLLPPPP
HMM? WHAT'S THAT OVER THERE?
LOOK, THERE SHE IS!
EEP
COME BACK, YOU!
WE'RE BACK!

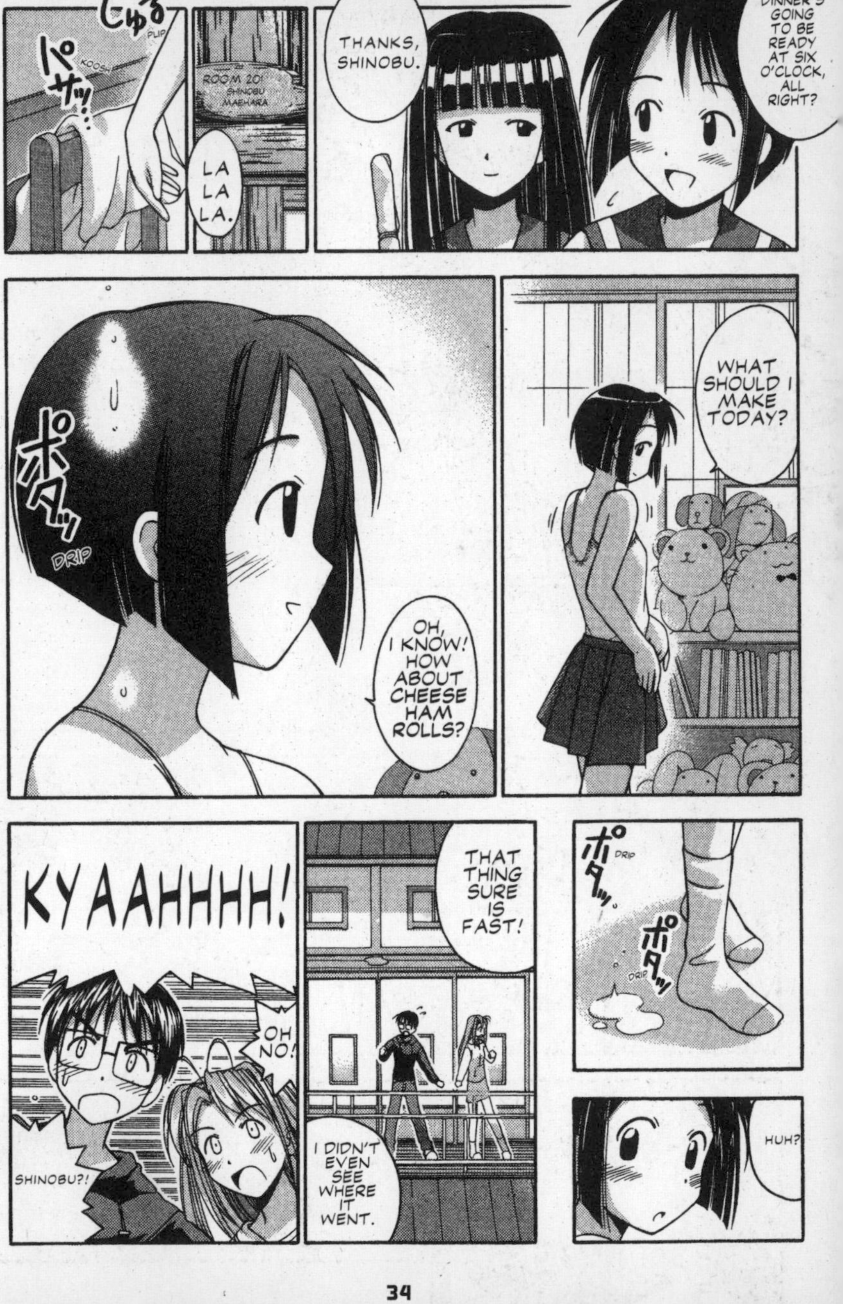
OKAY, DINNER'S GOING TO BE READY AT SIX O'CLOCK, ALL RIGHT?
THANKS, SHINOBU.
ROOM 201
SHINOBU MAEHARA
LA LA LA.
しゅる
PLIP
パサッ
KOOSH
WHAT SHOULD I MAKE TODAY?
ポタッ
DRIP
OH, I KNOW! HOW ABOUT CHEESE HAM ROLLS?
ポタッ
DRIP
ポタッ
DRIP
HUH?
THAT THING SURE IS FAST!
I DIDN'T EVEN SEE WHERE IT WENT.
KYAAHHHH!
OH NO!
SHINOBU?!

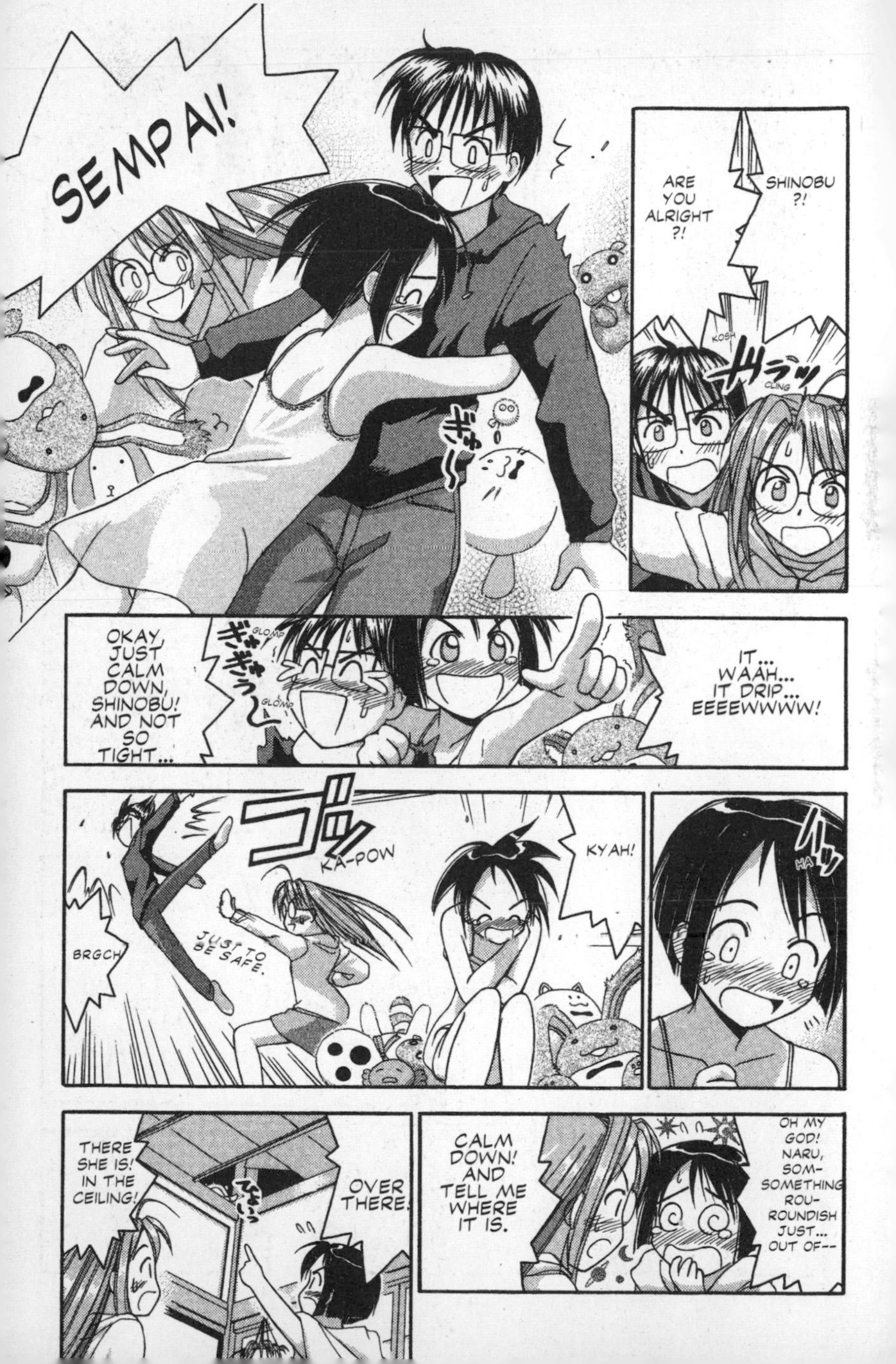
SHINOBU ?!
ARE YOU ALRIGHT ?!
ガラッ
KOSH
CLING
SEMPAI!
ぎゅ〜
IT... WAAH... IT DRIP... EEEEWWWW!
ぎゅぎゅう〜
GLOMP
GLOMP
OKAY, JUST CALM DOWN, SHINOBU! AND NOT SO TIGHT...
ハッ
HA
KYAH!
ゴッ
KA-POW
JUST TO BE SAFE.
BRGCH
OH MY GOD! NARU, SOM-SOMETHING ROU-ROUNDISH JUST... OUT OF--
CALM DOWN! AND TELL ME WHERE IT IS.
OVER THERE.
THERE SHE IS! IN THE CEILING!

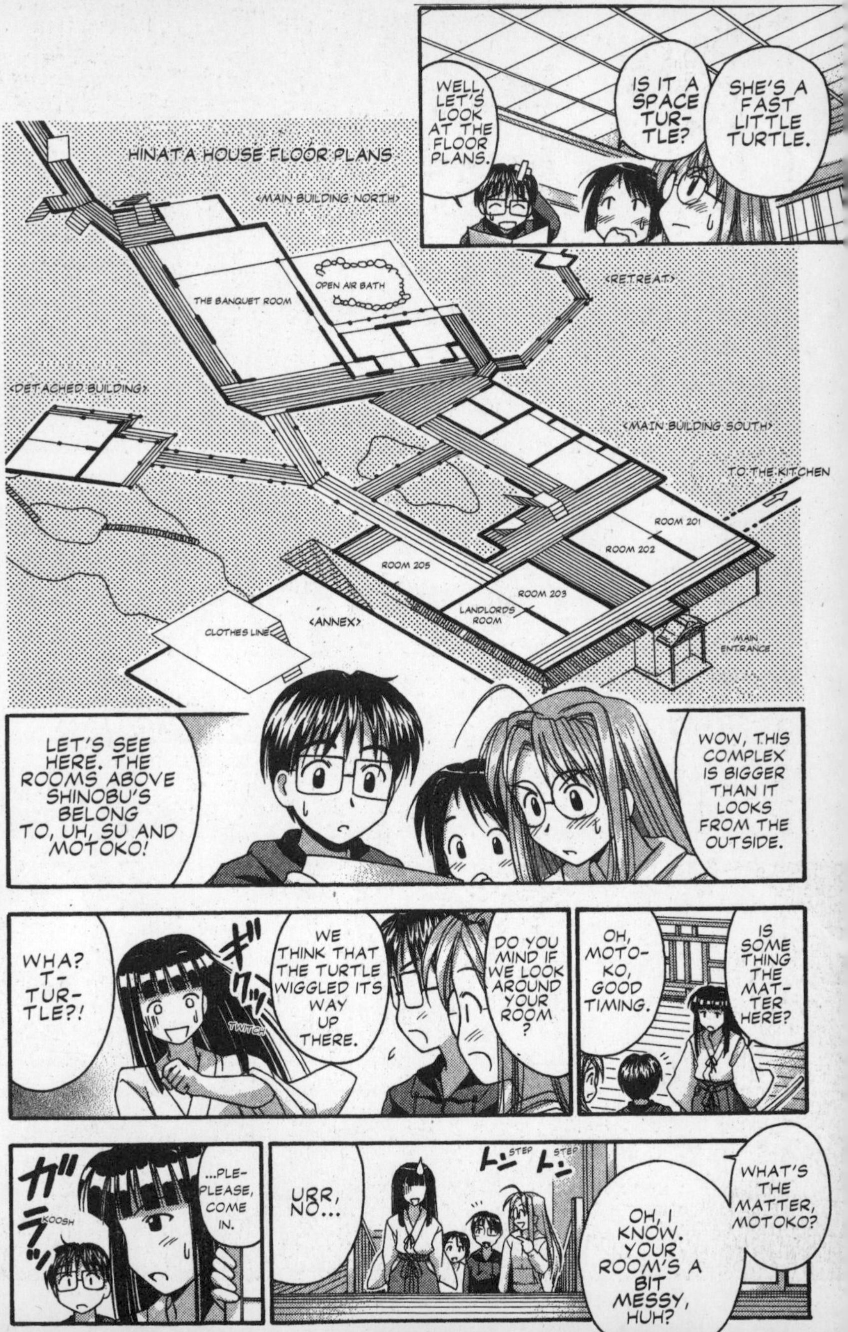
SHE'S A FAST LITTLE TURTLE.
IS IT A SPACE TUR-TLE?
WELL, LET'S LOOK AT THE FLOOR PLANS.
HINATA HOUSE FLOOR PLANS
<MAIN BUILDING NORTH>
OPEN AIR BATH
THE BANQUET ROOM
<RETREAT>
<DETACHED BUILDING>
<MAIN BUILDING SOUTH>
TO THE KITCHEN
ROOM 201
ROOM 202
ROOM 205
ROOM 203
LANDLORDS ROOM
<ANNEX>
CLOTHES LINE
MAIN ENTRANCE
WOW, THIS COMPLEX IS BIGGER THAN IT LOOKS FROM THE OUTSIDE.
LET'S SEE HERE. THE ROOMS ABOVE SHINOBU'S BELONG TO, UH, SU AND MOTOKO!
IS SOME THING THE MAT-TER HERE?
OH, MOTO-KO, GOOD TIMING.
DO YOU MIND IF WE LOOK AROUND YOUR ROOM?
WE THINK THAT THE TURTLE WIGGLED ITS WAY UP THERE.
TWITCH
WHA? T-TUR-TLE?!
WHAT'S THE MATTER, MOTOKO?
OH, I KNOW. YOUR ROOM'S A BIT MESSY, HUH?
STEP STEP
URR, NO...
...PLE-PLEASE, COME IN.
KOOSH

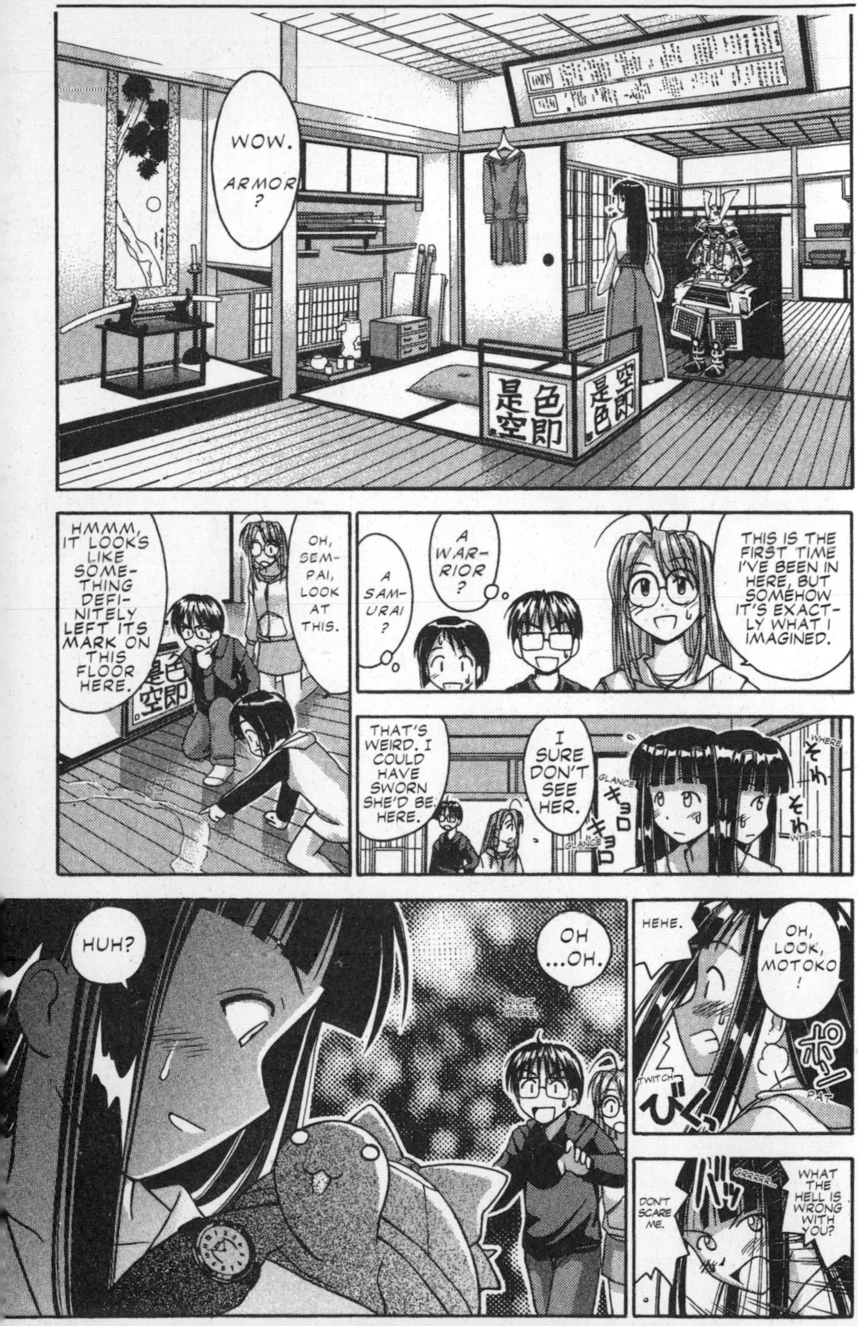
WOW.
ARMOR?
色即是空
空即是色
THIS IS THE FIRST TIME I'VE BEEN IN HERE, BUT SOMEHOW IT'S EXACTLY WHAT I IMAGINED.
A WARRIOR?
A SAMURAI?
そわそわ WHERE WHERE
キョロキョロ GLANCE GLANCE
I SURE DON'T SEE HER.
THAT'S WEIRD. I COULD HAVE SWORN SHE'D BE HERE.
OH, SEMPAI, LOOK AT THIS.
HMMM, IT LOOKS LIKE SOMETHING DEFINITELY LEFT ITS MARK ON THIS FLOOR HERE.
色即是空
OH, LOOK, MOTOKO!
HEHE.
ポン PAT
びくっ TWITCH
WHAT THE HELL IS WRONG WITH YOU?
GRRRRR...
バッ
DON'T SCARE ME.
OH ...OH.
RIGHT THERE.
HUH?

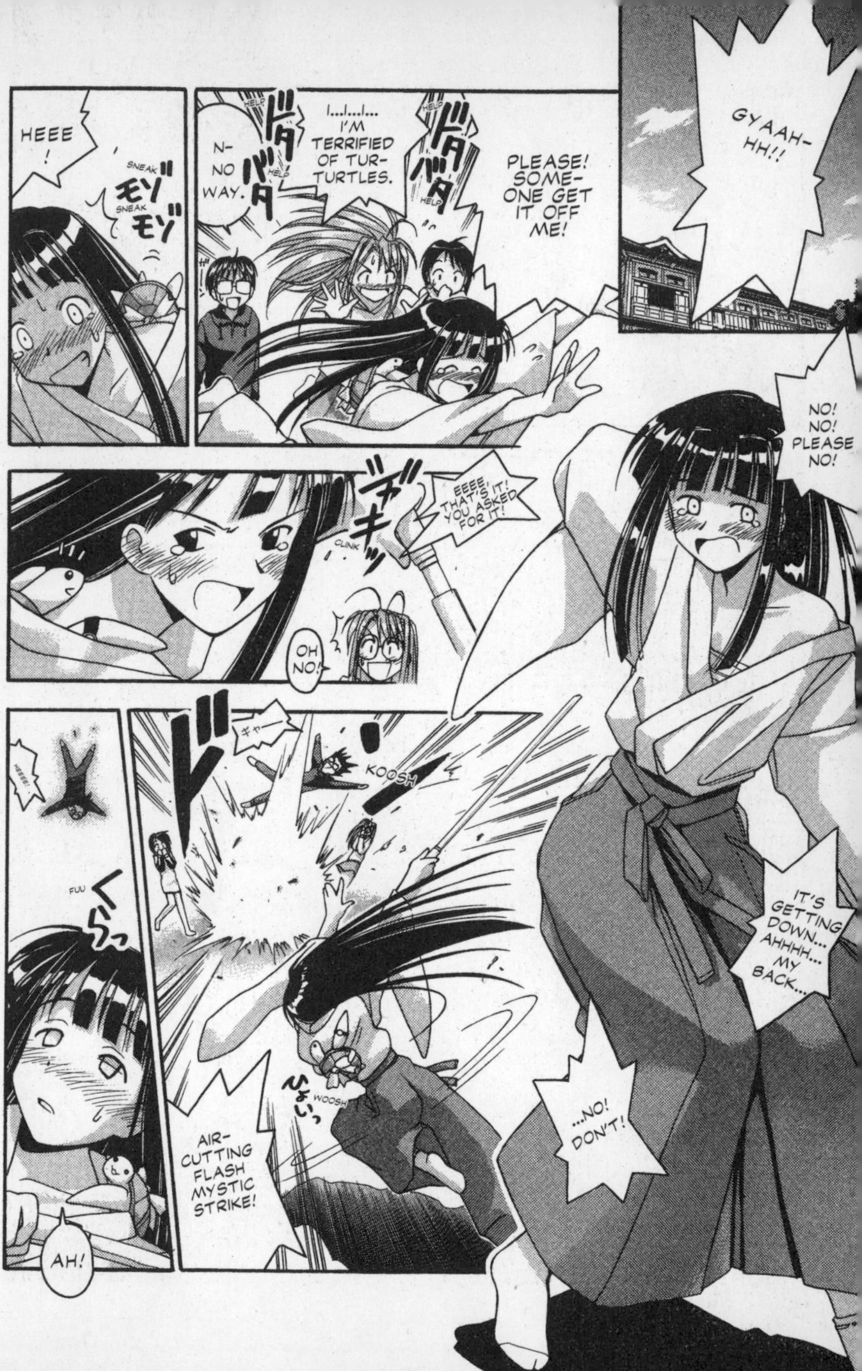
GYAAH-HH!!
HELP ドタ HELP バタ
PLEASE! SOMEONE GET IT OFF ME!
I...I...I... I'M TERRIFIED OF TUR-TURTLES.
HELP ドタ HELP バタ
N-NO WAY.
HEEE!
SNEAK モゾ SNEAK モゾ
NO! NO! PLEASE NO!
IT'S GETTING DOWN... AHHHH... MY BACK...
CLINK ガキッ
EEEE, THAT'S IT! YOU ASKED FOR IT!
OH NO!
ドッ
ギャー
KOOSH
...NO! DON'T!
WOOSH ひょいっ
AIR-CUTTING FLASH MYSTIC STRIKE!
HEEEE!
FUU くらっ
AH!

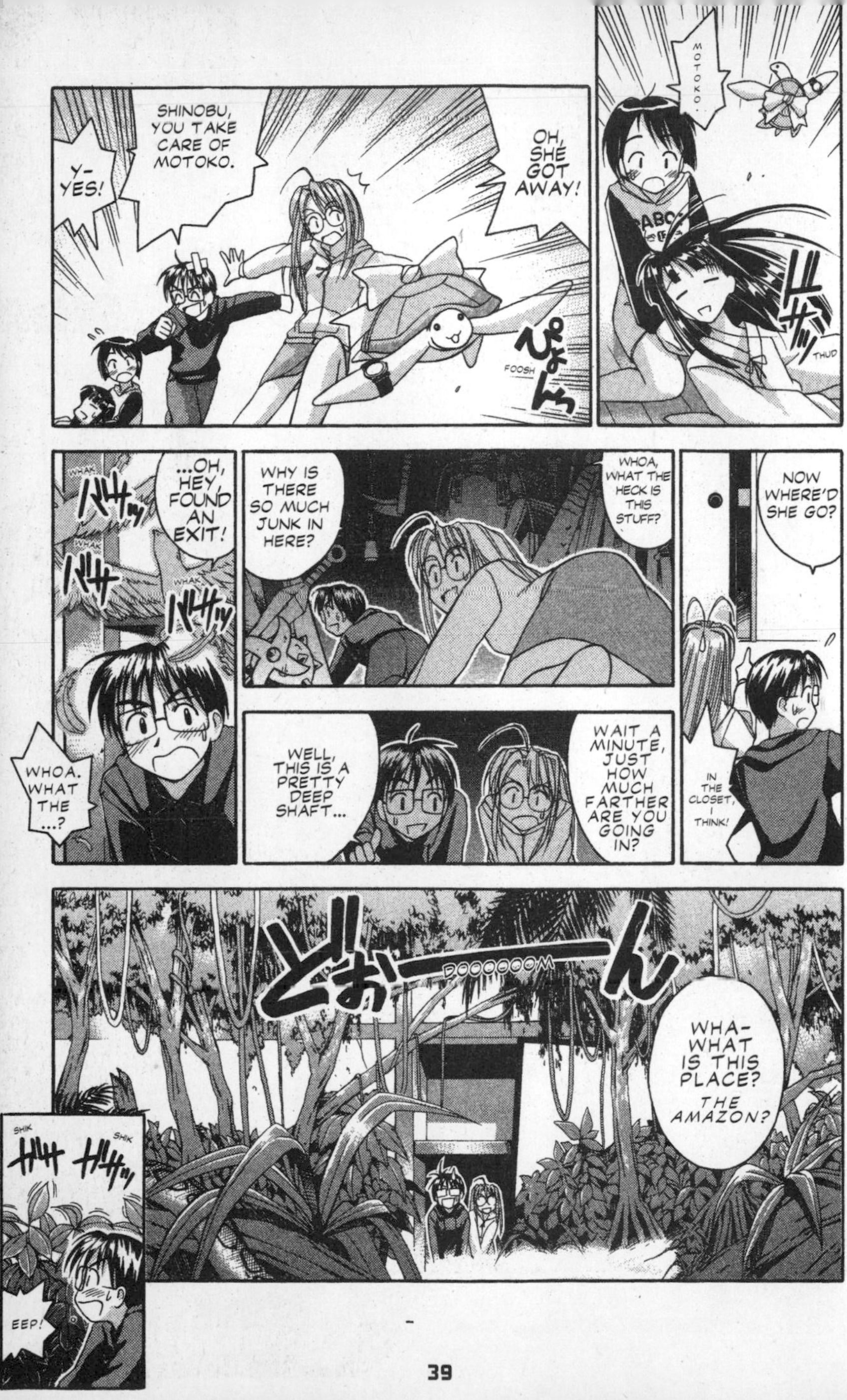
MOTOKO...
THUD
OH, SHE GOT AWAY!
SHINOBU, YOU TAKE CARE OF MOTOKO.
Y-YES!
FOOSH
NOW WHERE'D SHE GO?
IN THE CLOSET, I THINK!
WHOA, WHAT THE HECK IS THIS STUFF?
WHY IS THERE SO MUCH JUNK IN HERE?
WAIT A MINUTE, JUST HOW MUCH FARTHER ARE YOU GOING IN?
WELL, THIS IS A PRETTY DEEP SHAFT...
...OH, HEY, FOUND AN EXIT!
WHAK
WHAK
WHAK
WHOA. WHAT THE ...?
DOOOOOOM
WHA-WHAT IS THIS PLACE? THE AMAZON?
SHIK
SHIK
EEP!

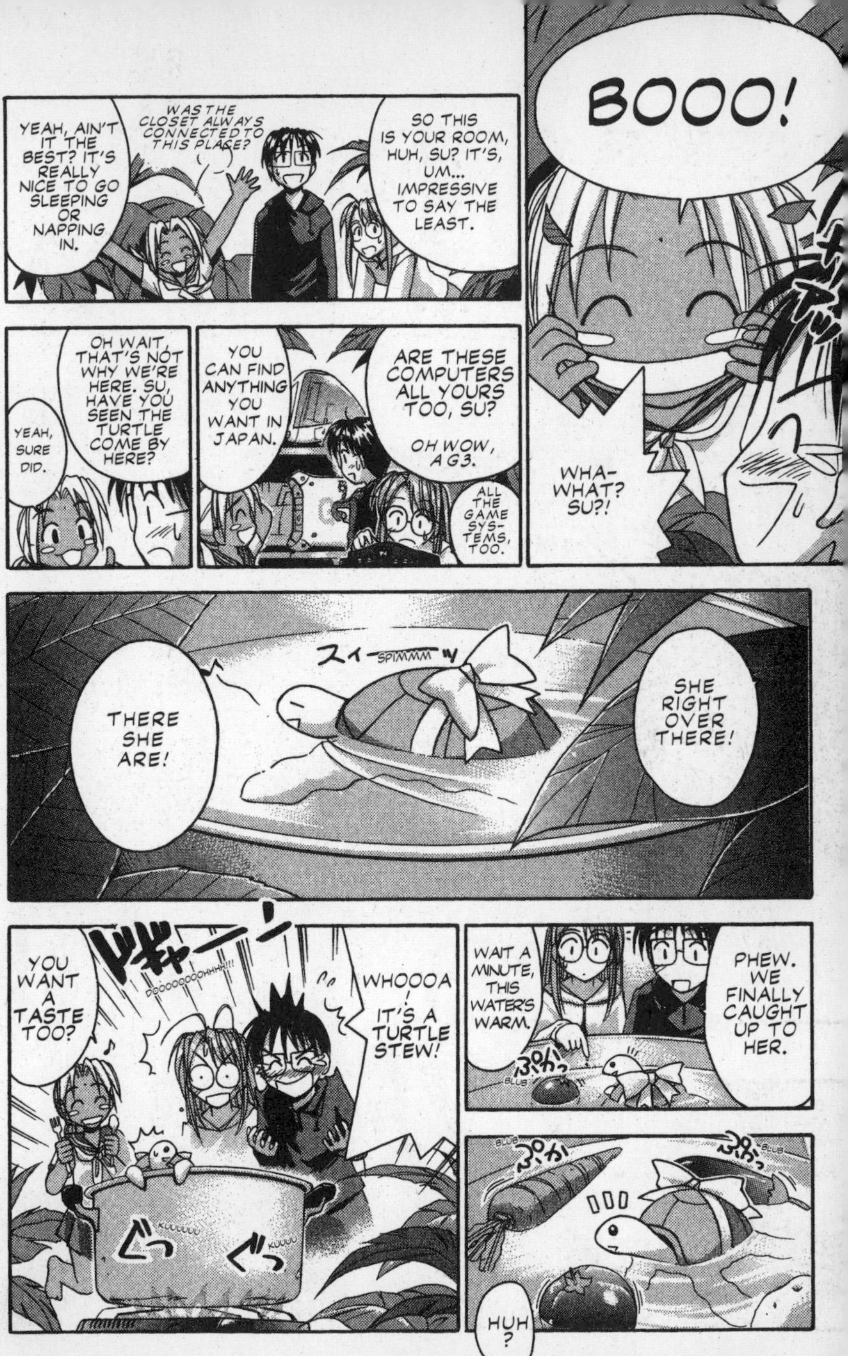

BOOO!
WHA-WHAT? SU?!
SO THIS IS YOUR ROOM, HUH, SU? IT'S, UM... IMPRESSIVE TO SAY THE LEAST.
WAS THE CLOSET ALWAYS CONNECTED TO THIS PLACE?
YEAH, AIN'T IT THE BEST? IT'S REALLY NICE TO GO SLEEPING OR NAPPING IN.
ARE THESE COMPUTERS ALL YOURS TOO, SU?
OH WOW, A G3.
YOU CAN FIND ANYTHING YOU WANT IN JAPAN.
ALL THE GAME SYSTEMS, TOO.
OH WAIT, THAT'S NOT WHY WE'RE HERE. SU, HAVE YOU SEEN THE TURTLE COME BY HERE?
YEAH, SURE DID.
SHE RIGHT OVER THERE!
SPIMMM
THERE SHE ARE!
PHEW. WE FINALLY CAUGHT UP TO HER.
WAIT A MINUTE, THIS WATER'S WARM.
BLUB
BLUB
BLUB
HUH?
WHOOOA! IT'S A TURTLE STEW!
YOU WANT A TASTE TOO?

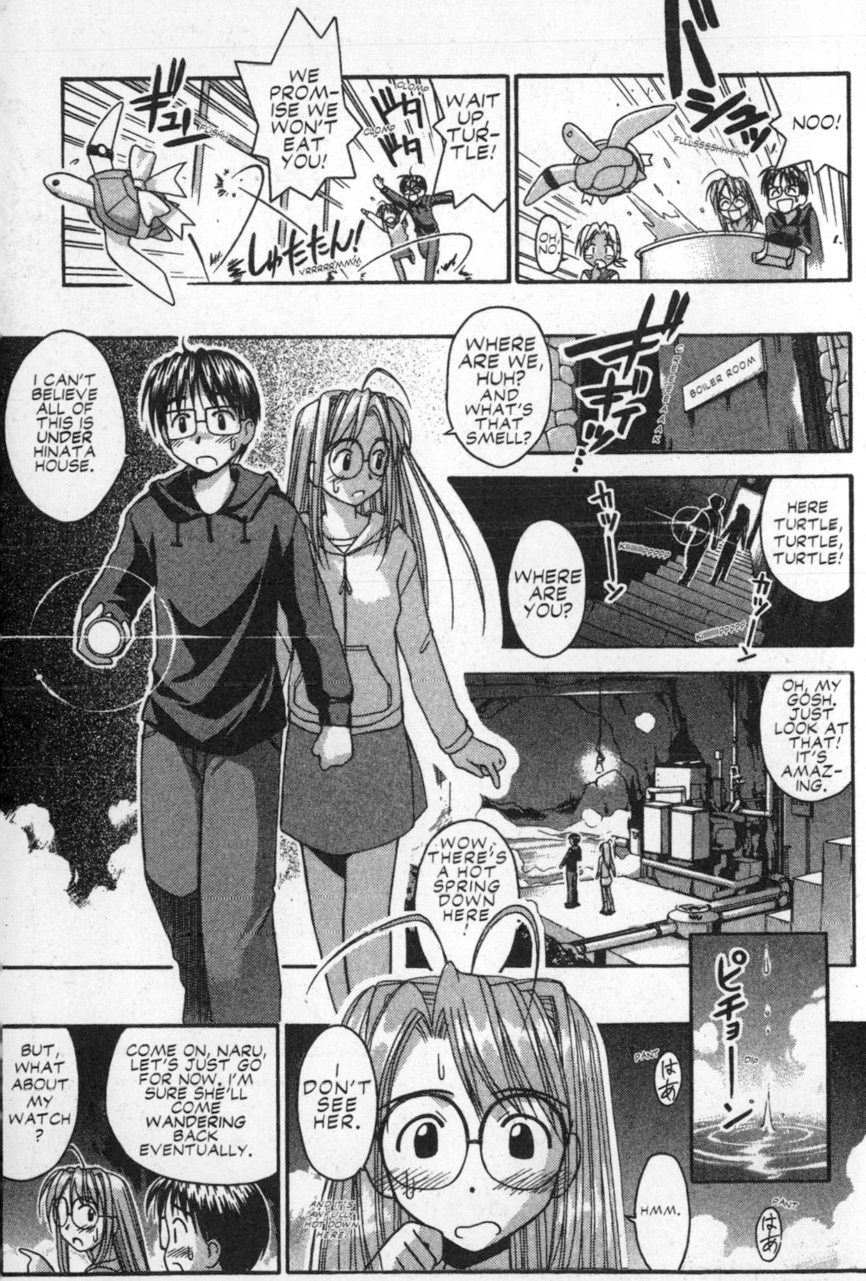
NOO!
FLLLSSSSHHHHHH
OH, NO.
WE PROMISE WE WON'T EAT YOU!
WAIT UP, TURTLE!
CLOMP
CLOMP
VRRRRRMMM
WHERE ARE WE, HUH? AND WHAT'S THAT SMELL?
BOILER ROOM
HERE TURTLE, TURTLE, TURTLE!
WHERE ARE YOU?
OH, MY GOSH. JUST LOOK AT THAT! IT'S AMAZING.
WOW, THERE'S A HOT SPRING DOWN HERE!
I CAN'T BELIEVE ALL OF THIS IS UNDER HINATA HOUSE.
IT'S SULPHER.
PANT
DIP
PANT
I DON'T SEE HER.
HMM.
AND IT'S AWFULLY HOT DOWN HERE.
COME ON, NARU, LET'S JUST GO FOR NOW. I'M SURE SHE'LL COME WANDERING BACK EVENTUALLY.
BUT, WHAT ABOUT MY WATCH?

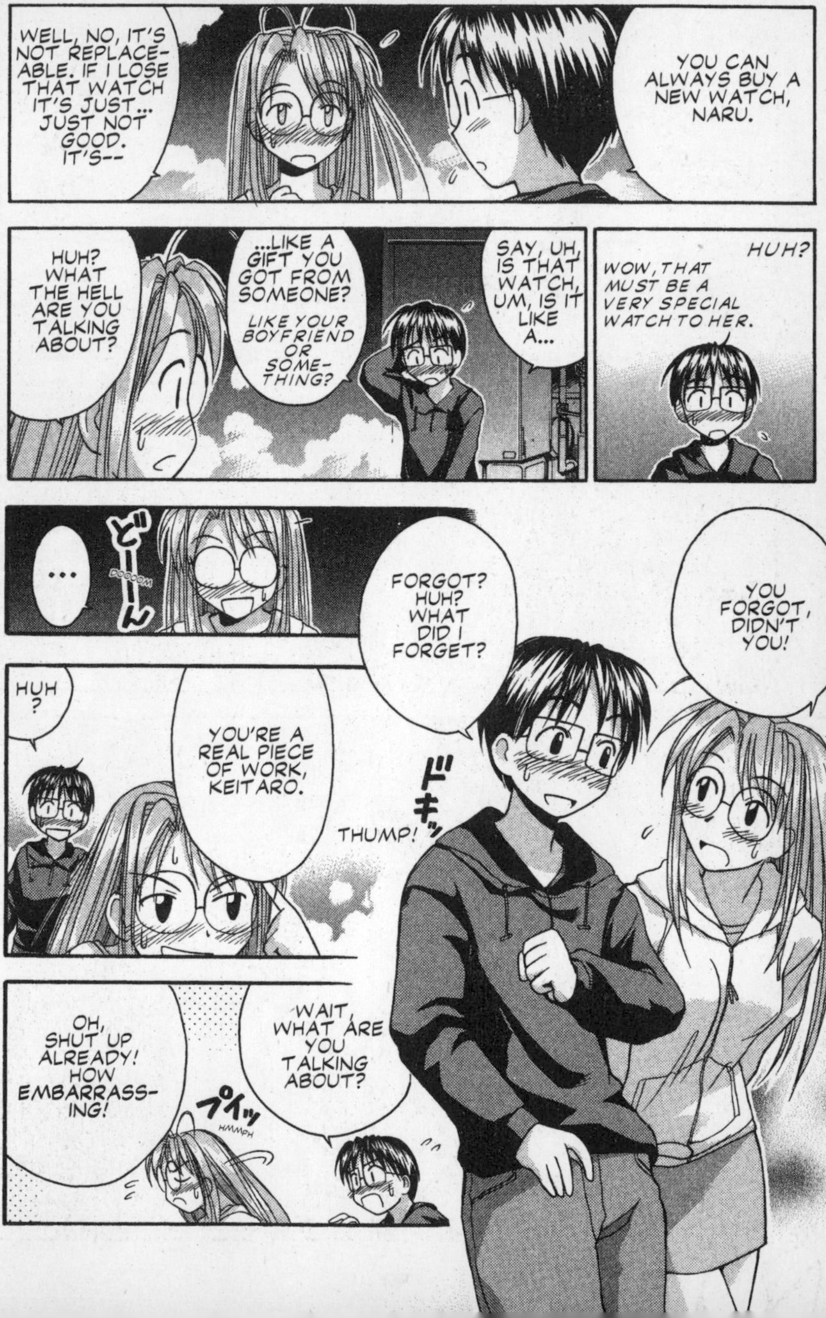
YOU CAN ALWAYS BUY A NEW WATCH, NARU.
WELL, NO, IT'S NOT REPLACEABLE. IF I LOSE THAT WATCH IT'S JUST... JUST NOT GOOD. IT'S--
HUH?
WOW, THAT MUST BE A VERY SPECIAL WATCH TO HER.
SAY, UH, IS THAT WATCH, UM, IS IT LIKE A...
...LIKE A GIFT YOU GOT FROM SOMEONE?
LIKE YOUR BOYFRIEND OR SOMETHING?
HUH? WHAT THE HELL ARE YOU TALKING ABOUT?
どーん
DOOOOM
...
YOU FORGOT, DIDN'T YOU!
FORGOT? HUH? WHAT DID I FORGET?
ドキッ
THUMP!
YOU'RE A REAL PIECE OF WORK, KEITARO.
HUH?
WAIT, WHAT ARE YOU TALKING ABOUT?
OH, SHUT UP ALREADY! HOW EMBARRASSING!
プイッ
HMMPH

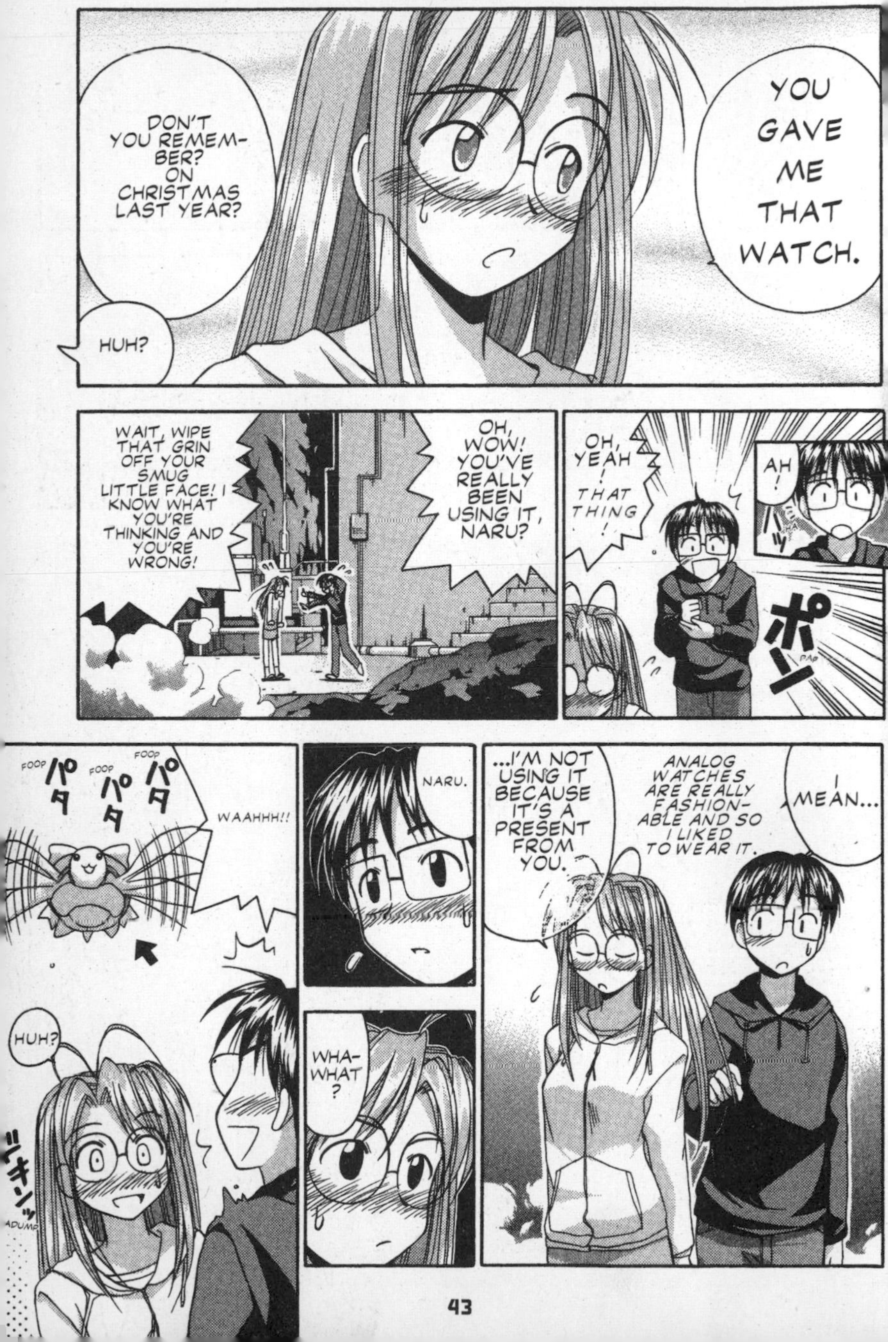
YOU GAVE ME THAT WATCH.
DON'T YOU REMEMBER? ON CHRISTMAS LAST YEAR?
HUH?
AH!
OH, YEAH! THAT THING!
PAP
OH, WOW! YOU'VE REALLY BEEN USING IT, NARU?
WAIT, WIPE THAT GRIN OFF YOUR SMUG LITTLE FACE! I KNOW WHAT YOU'RE THINKING AND YOU'RE WRONG!
I MEAN...
ANALOG WATCHES ARE REALLY FASHIONABLE AND SO I LIKED TO WEAR IT.
...I'M NOT USING IT BECAUSE IT'S A PRESENT FROM YOU.
NARU.
WHA-WHAT?
WAAHHH!!
FOOP
FOOP
FOOP
HUH?
ADUMP

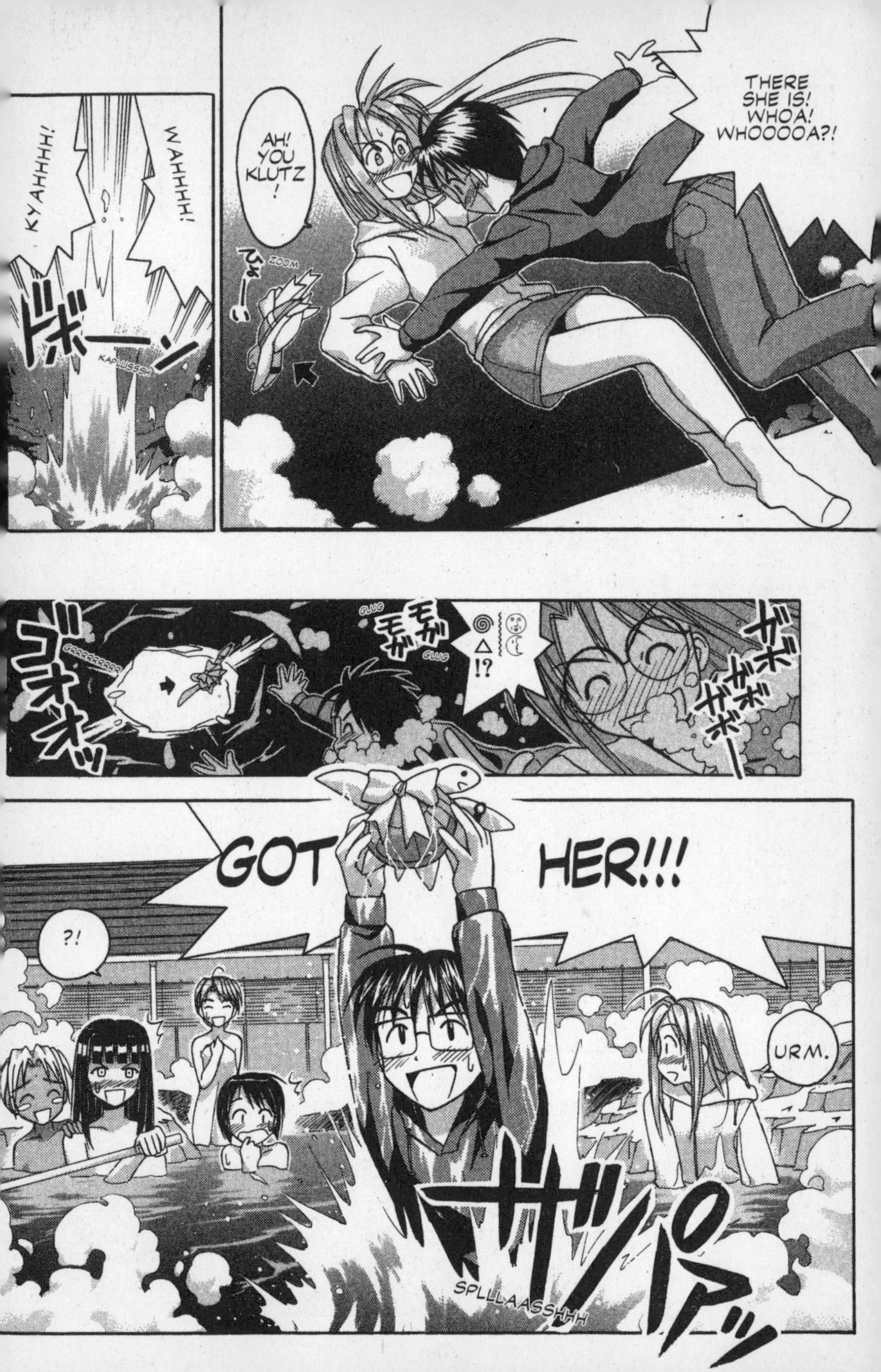
THERE SHE IS! WHOA! WHOOOOA?!
AH! YOU KLUTZ!
ひょー
ZOOM
WAHHHH!
KYAHHHH!
ドボーン
KAPLUSSSH
ガボガボガボー
◎△!?
モガモガ
GLUG
GLUG
ゴオオッ
GOT HER!!!
URM.
?!
ザパァッ
SPLLLAASSHHH

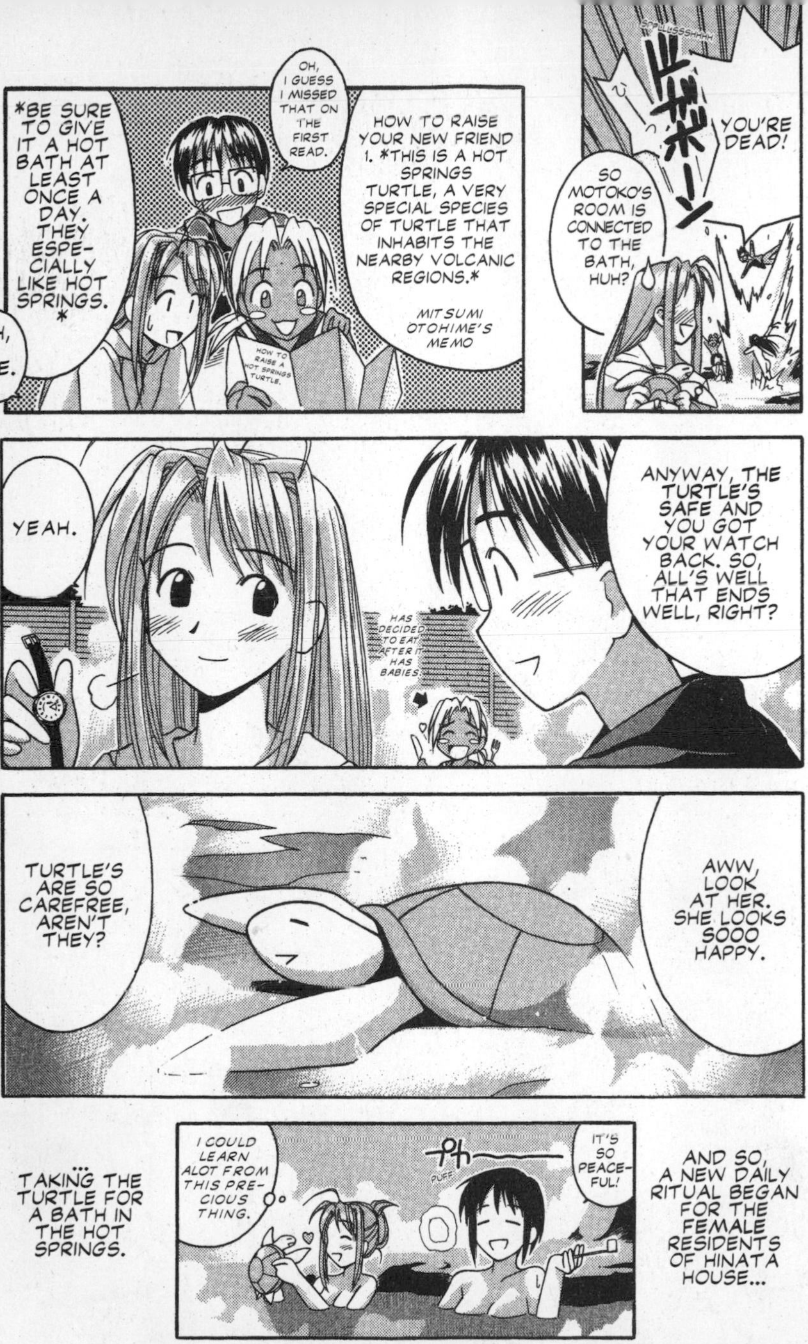

SPPLLLSSSHHHH
YOU'RE DEAD!
SO MOTOKO'S ROOM IS CONNECTED TO THE BATH, HUH?
HOW TO RAISE YOUR NEW FRIEND 1. *THIS IS A HOT SPRINGS TURTLE, A VERY SPECIAL SPECIES OF TURTLE THAT INHABITS THE NEARBY VOLCANIC REGIONS.*
MITSUMI OTOHIME'S MEMO
OH, I GUESS I MISSED THAT ON THE FIRST READ.
BE SURE TO GIVE IT A HOT BATH AT LEAST ONCE A DAY. THEY ESPECIALLY LIKE HOT SPRINGS.
HOW TO RAISE A HOT SPRINGS TURTLE.
OH, I SEE.
ANYWAY, THE TURTLE'S SAFE AND YOU GOT YOUR WATCH BACK. SO, ALL'S WELL THAT ENDS WELL, RIGHT?
HAS DECIDED TO EAT AFTER IT HAS BABIES.
YEAH.
AWW, LOOK AT HER. SHE LOOKS SOOO HAPPY.
TURTLE'S ARE SO CAREFREE, AREN'T THEY?
AND SO, A NEW DAILY RITUAL BEGAN FOR THE FEMALE RESIDENTS OF HINATA HOUSE...
IT'S SO PEACEFUL!
PUFF
I COULD LEARN ALOT FROM THIS PRECIOUS THING.
...TAKING THE TURTLE FOR A BATH IN THE HOT SPRINGS.

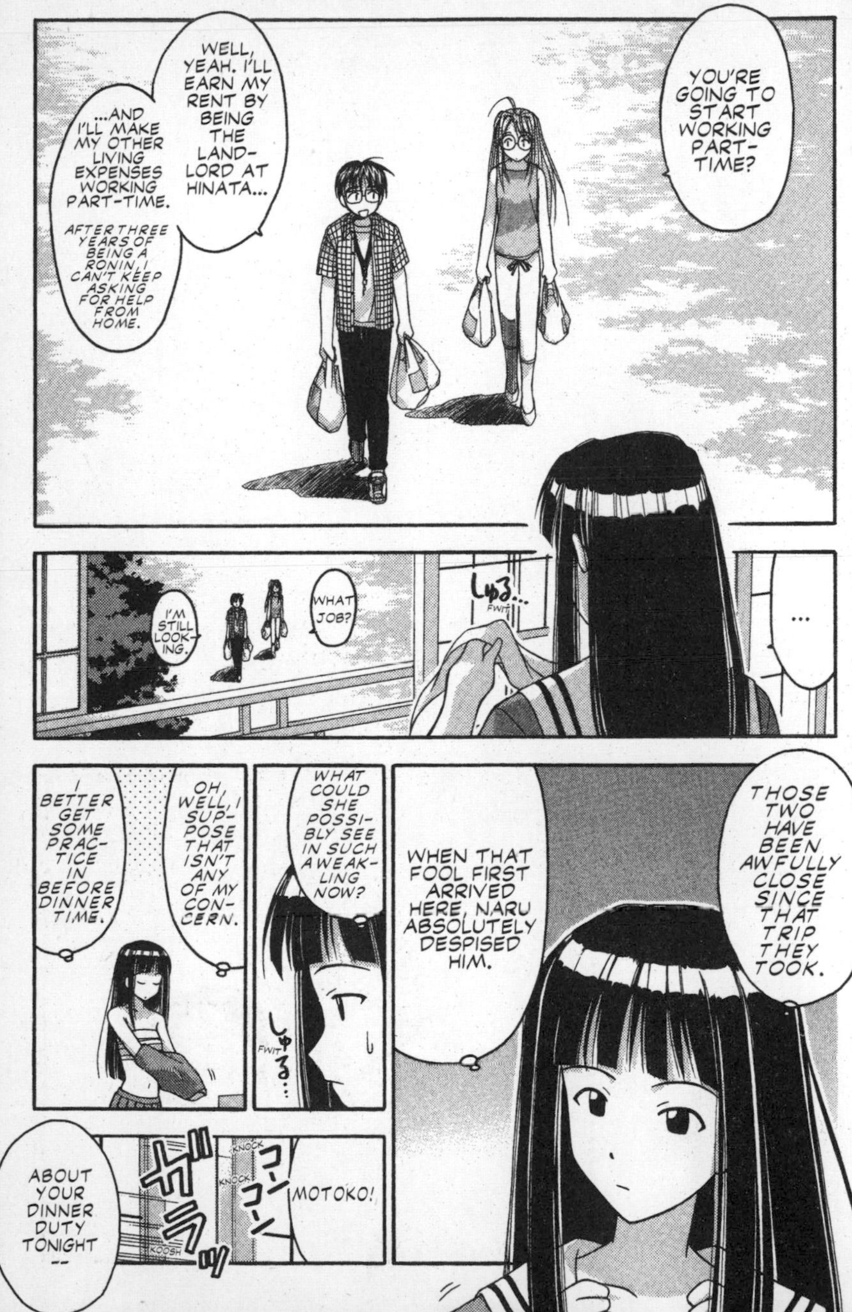
YOU'RE GOING TO START WORKING PART-TIME?
WELL, YEAH. I'LL EARN MY RENT BY BEING THE LANDLORD AT HINATA...
...AND I'LL MAKE MY OTHER LIVING EXPENSES WORKING PART-TIME.
AFTER THREE YEARS OF BEING A RONIN, I CAN'T KEEP ASKING FOR HELP FROM HOME.
...
しゅる... FWIT
WHAT JOB?
I'M STILL LOOKING.
THOSE TWO HAVE BEEN AWFULLY CLOSE SINCE THAT TRIP THEY TOOK.
WHEN THAT FOOL FIRST ARRIVED HERE, NARU ABSOLUTELY DESPISED HIM.
WHAT COULD SHE POSSIBLY SEE IN SUCH A WEAKLING NOW?
しゅる... FWIT
OH, WELL, I SUPPOSE THAT ISN'T ANY OF MY CONCERN.
I BETTER GET SOME PRACTICE IN BEFORE DINNER TIME.
MOTOKO!
コンコン KNOCK KNOCK
ガラッ KOOSH
ABOUT YOUR DINNER DUTY TONIGHT --

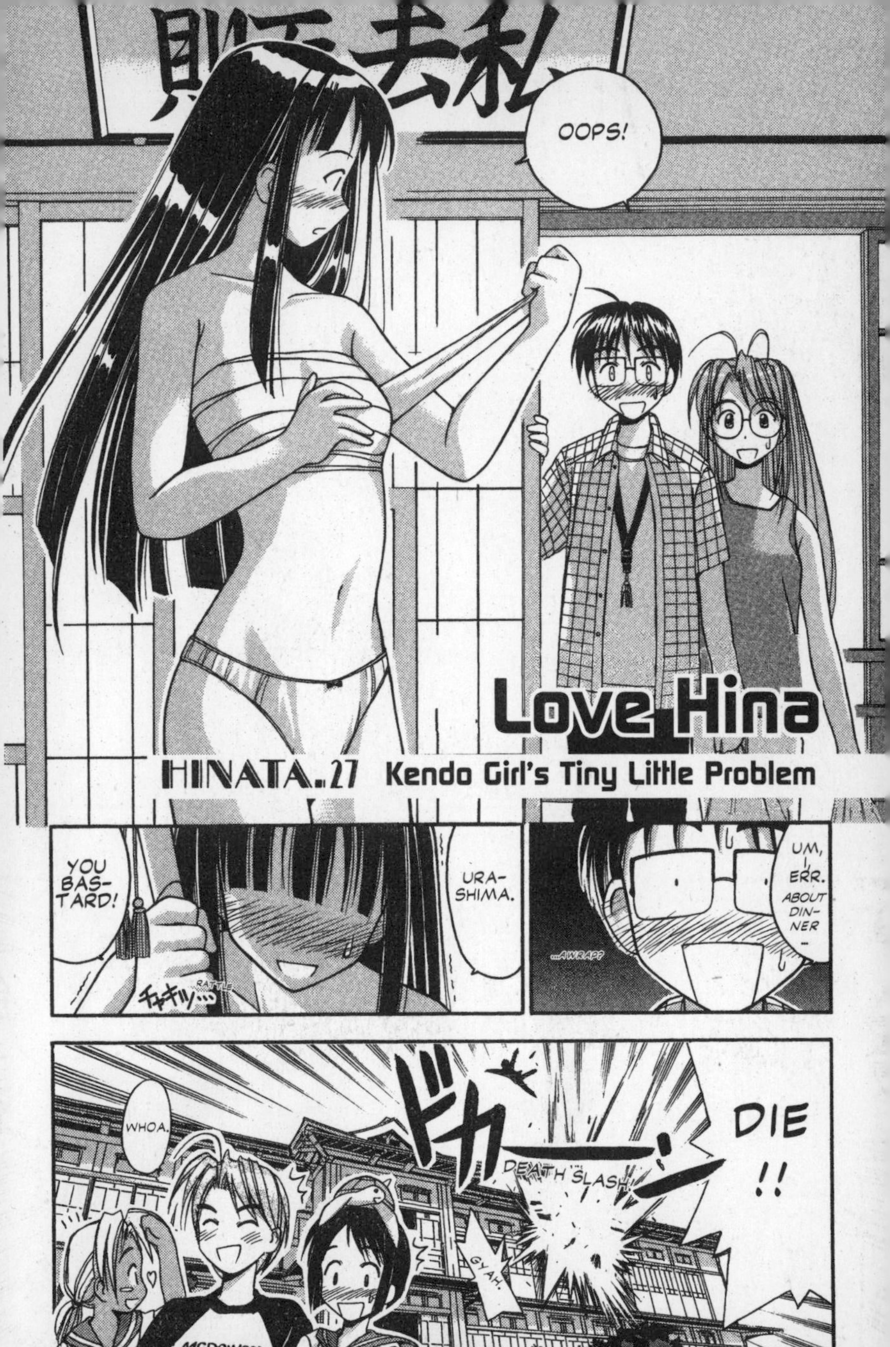
OOPS!
Love Hina
HINATA..27 Kendo Girl's Tiny Little Problem
UM, I, ERR.
ABOUT DINNER...
...AWRAP?
URA-SHIMA.
YOU BAS-TARD!
チャキリ...
RATTLE
DIE!!
ドカー
DEATH SLASH!
GYAH.
WHOA.

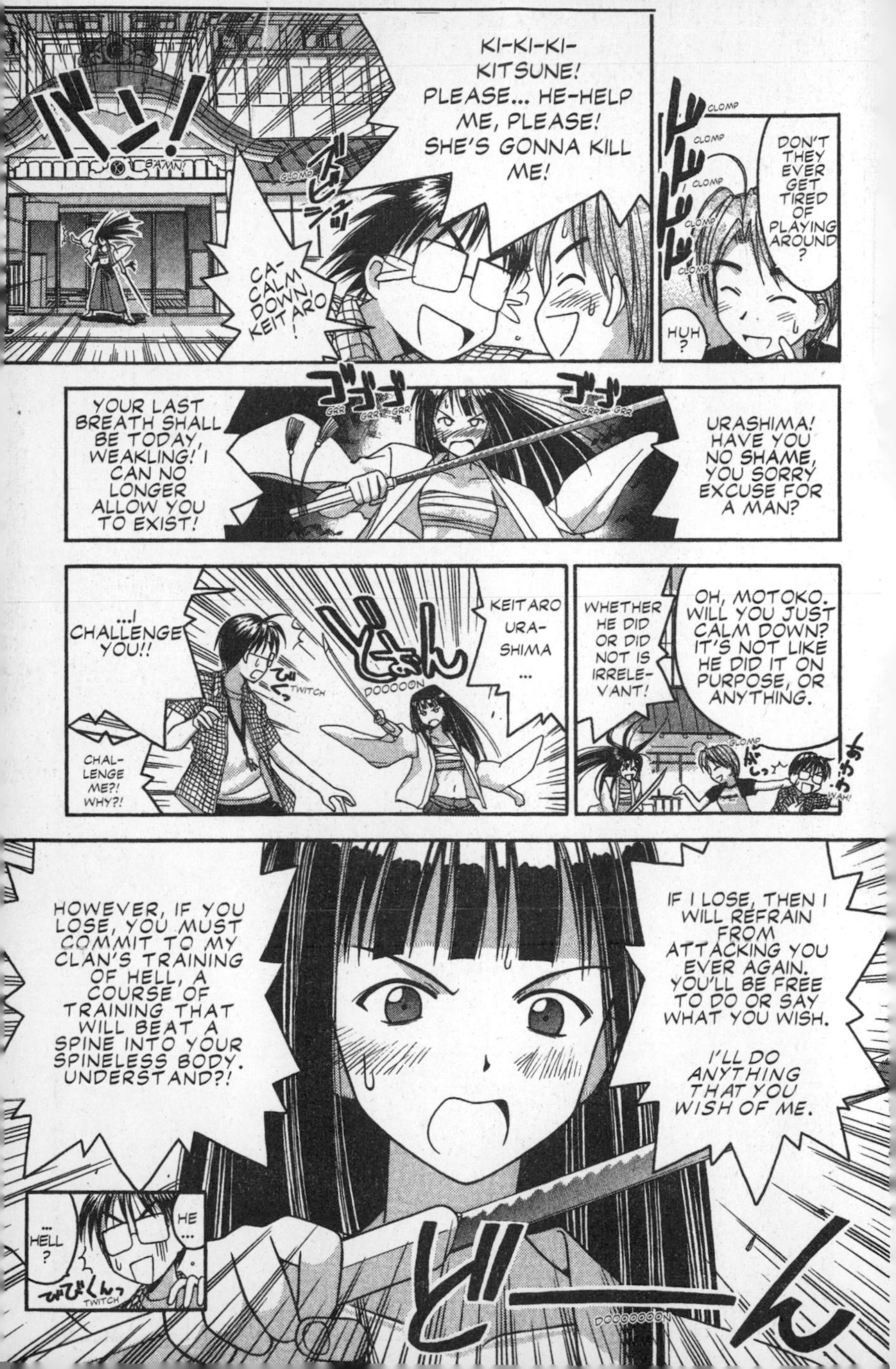
CLOMP
CLOMP
CLOMP
CLOMP
CLOMP
DON'T THEY EVER GET TIRED OF PLAYING AROUND?
HUH?
BAMN!
CLOMP
KI-KI-KI-KITSUNE! PLEASE... HE-HELP ME, PLEASE! SHE'S GONNA KILL ME!
CA-CALM DOWN, KEITARO!
URASHIMA! HAVE YOU NO SHAME, YOU SORRY EXCUSE FOR A MAN?
GRR GRR
GRR GRR GRR
YOUR LAST BREATH SHALL BE TODAY, WEAKLING! I CAN NO LONGER ALLOW YOU TO EXIST!
OH, MOTOKO. WILL YOU JUST CALM DOWN? IT'S NOT LIKE HE DID IT ON PURPOSE, OR ANYTHING.
WHETHER HE DID OR DID NOT IS IRRELEVANT!
CLOMP
WAH!
KEITARO URASHIMA...
DOOOOON
...I CHALLENGE YOU!!
TWITCH
CHALLENGE ME?! WHY?!
IF I LOSE, THEN I WILL REFRAIN FROM ATTACKING YOU EVER AGAIN. YOU'LL BE FREE TO DO OR SAY WHAT YOU WISH.
I'LL DO ANYTHING THAT YOU WISH OF ME.
HOWEVER, IF YOU LOSE, YOU MUST COMMIT TO MY CLAN'S TRAINING OF HELL, A COURSE OF TRAINING THAT WILL BEAT A SPINE INTO YOUR SPINELESS BODY. UNDERSTAND?!
HE...
...HELL?
TWITCH
DOOOOOOON

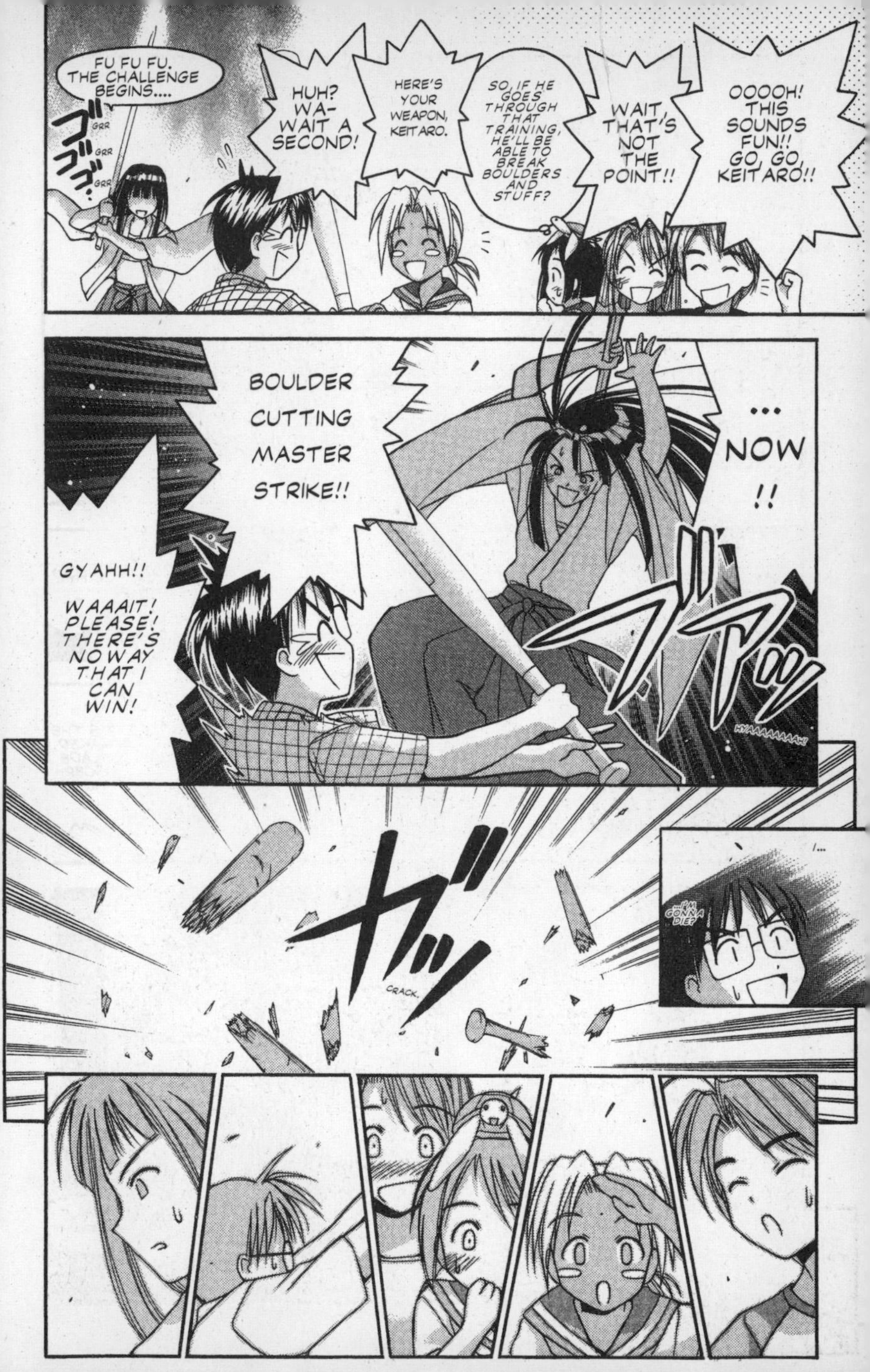
OOOOH! THIS SOUNDS FUN!! GO, GO, KEITARO!!
WAIT, THAT'S NOT THE POINT!!
SO, IF HE GOES THROUGH THAT TRAINING, HE'LL BE ABLE TO BREAK BOULDERS AND STUFF?
HERE'S YOUR WEAPON, KEITARO.
HUH? WA-WAIT A SECOND!
FU FU FU. THE CHALLENGE BEGINS....
GRR
GRR
GRR
...NOW!!
BOULDER CUTTING MASTER STRIKE!!
HYAAAAAAAAAAH!
GYAHH!!
WAAAIT! PLEASE! THERE'S NO WAY THAT I CAN WIN!
I...
I'M GONNA DIE!
CRACK.

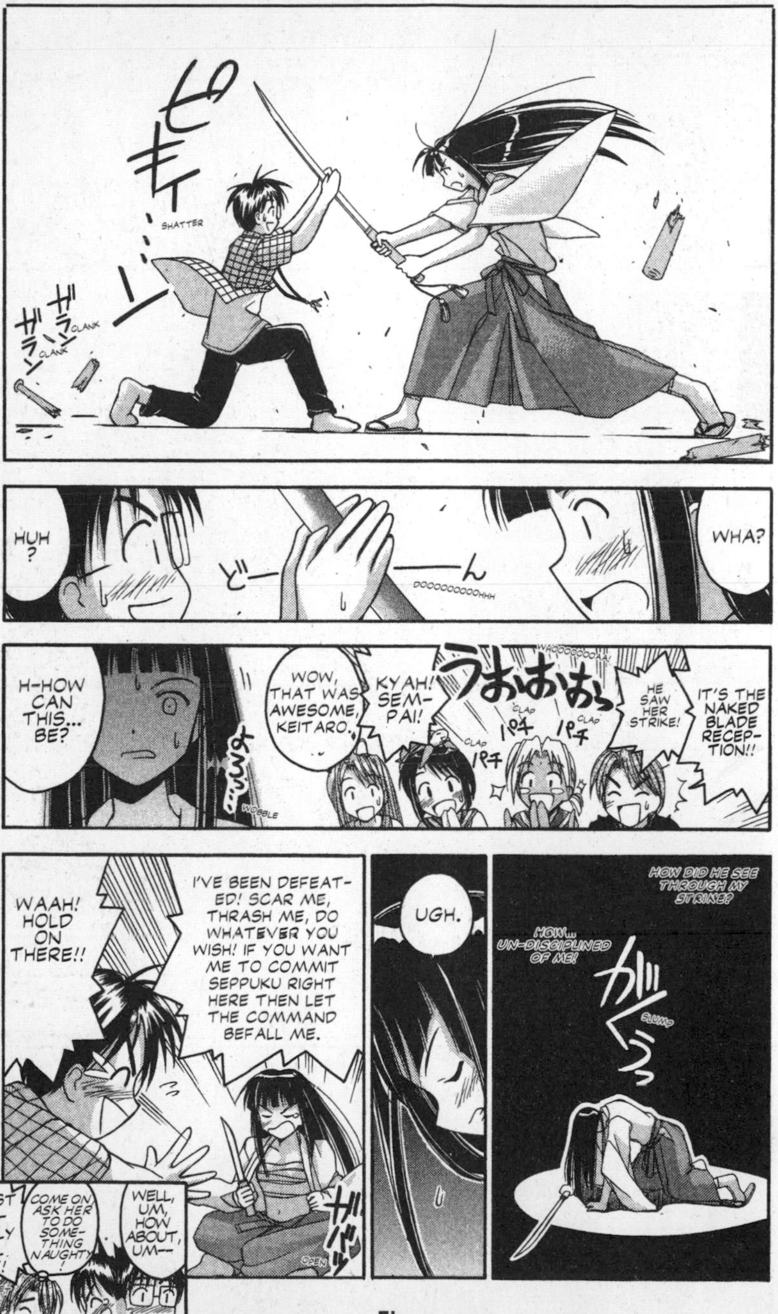

ピキイ…ン
SHATTER
ガランガラン
CLANK CLANK
WHA?
どーーーん
DOOOOOOOOOHHH
HUH?
IT'S THE NAKED BLADE RECEPTION!!
HE SAW HER STRIKE!
CLAP CLAP CLAP
WHOOOOOOOAA!
KYAH! SEMPAI!
WOW, THAT WAS AWESOME, KEITARO.
WOBBLE
H-HOW CAN THIS... BE?
HOW DID HE SEE THROUGH MY STRIKE?
HOW... UN-DISCIPLINED OF ME!
SLUMP
UGH.
I'VE BEEN DEFEATED! SCAR ME, THRASH ME, DO WHATEVER YOU WISH! IF YOU WANT ME TO COMMIT SEPPUKU RIGHT HERE THEN LET THE COMMAND BEFALL ME.
WAAH! HOLD ON THERE!!
OPEN
WELL, UM, HOW ABOUT, UM--
COME ON ASK HER TO DO SOME-THING NAUGHTY!
I MOST CER-TAINLY WILL NOT!
SPET SPET

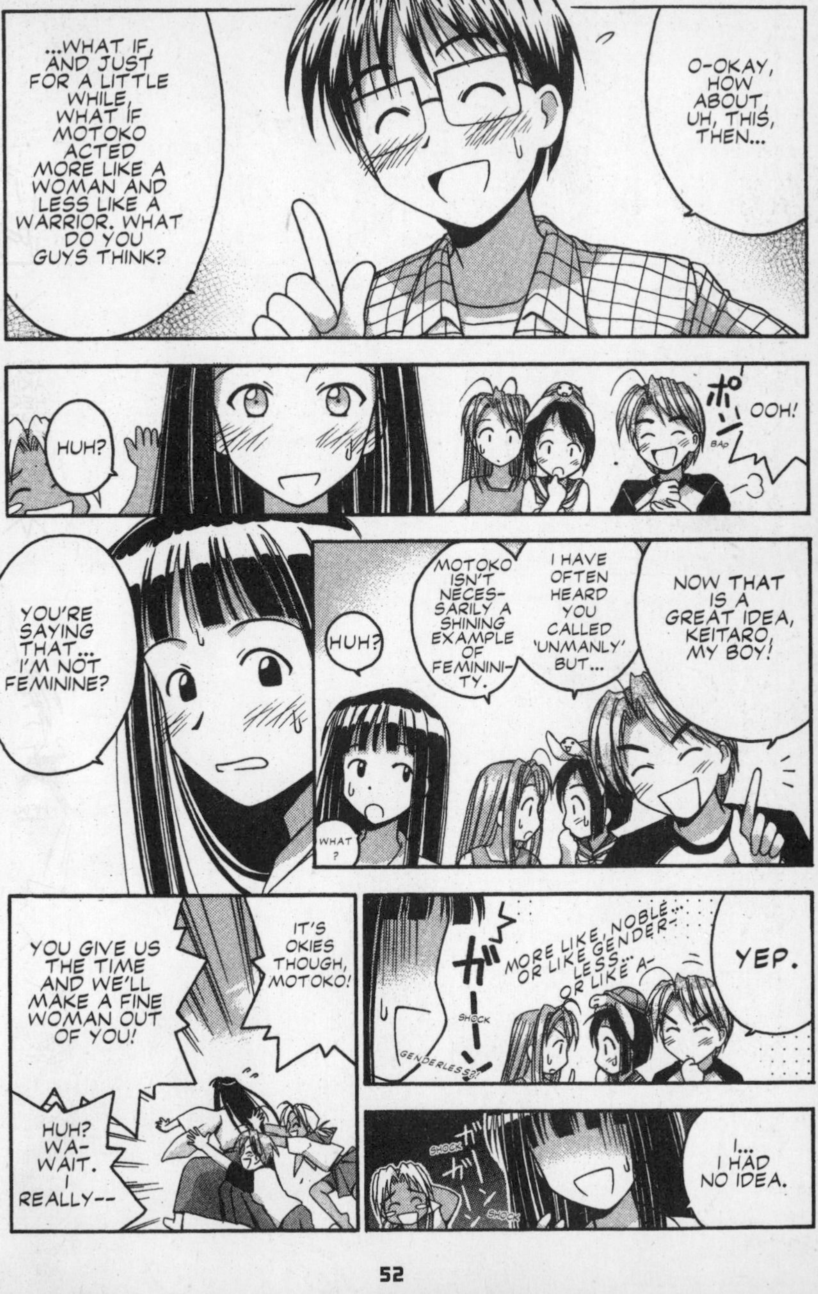
O-OKAY, HOW ABOUT, UH, THIS, THEN...
...WHAT IF, AND JUST FOR A LITTLE WHILE, WHAT IF MOTOKO ACTED MORE LIKE A WOMAN AND LESS LIKE A WARRIOR. WHAT DO YOU GUYS THINK?
OOH!
ポン
BAp
HUH?
NOW THAT IS A GREAT IDEA, KEITARO, MY BOY!
I HAVE OFTEN HEARD YOU CALLED 'UNMANLY' BUT...
MOTOKO ISN'T NECES-SARILY A SHINING EXAMPLE OF FEMININI-TY.
HUH?
WHAT?
YOU'RE SAYING THAT... I'M NOT FEMININE?
YEP.
MORE LIKE NOBLE... OR LIKE GENDER-LESS... OR LIKE A-
ガーン
SHOCK
GENDERLESS?!
I... I HAD NO IDEA.
SHOCK
SHOCK
IT'S OKIES THOUGH, MOTOKO!
YOU GIVE US THE TIME AND WE'LL MAKE A FINE WOMAN OUT OF YOU!
HUH? WA-WAIT. I REALLY--

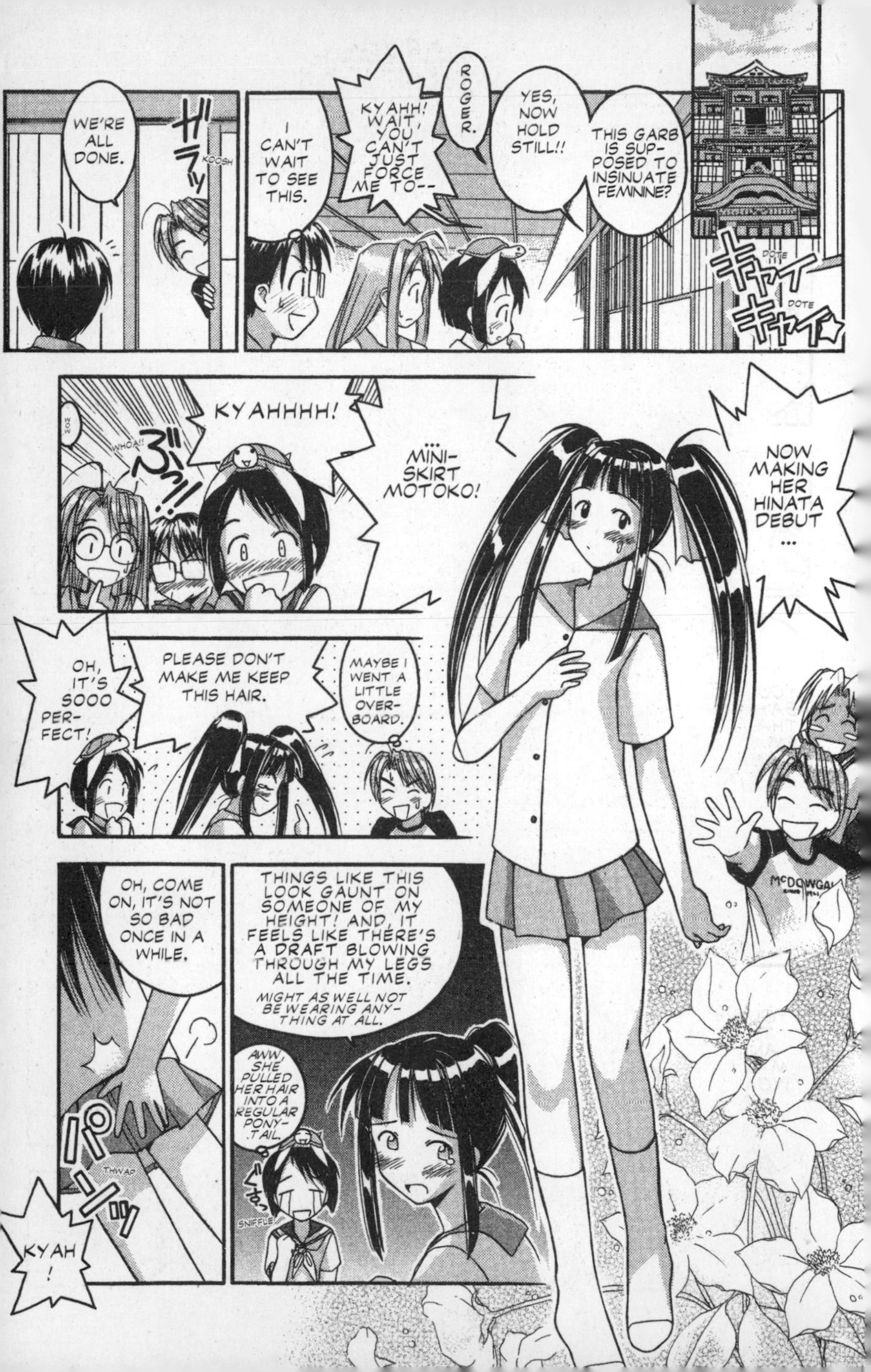
キャイ DOTE
キャイ DOTE
THIS GARB IS SUPPOSED TO INSINUATE FEMININE?
YES, NOW HOLD STILL!!
ROGER.
KYAHH! WAIT, YOU CAN'T JUST FORCE ME TO--
I CAN'T WAIT TO SEE THIS.
ガラッ KOOSH
WE'RE ALL DONE.
NOW MAKING HER HINATA DEBUT ...
...MINI-SKIRT MOTOKO!
KYAHHHH!
ぶっ WHOA!!
WOW
MAYBE I WENT A LITTLE OVERBOARD.
PLEASE DON'T MAKE ME KEEP THIS HAIR.
OH, IT'S SOOO PERFECT!
THINGS LIKE THIS LOOK GAUNT ON SOMEONE OF MY HEIGHT! AND, IT FEELS LIKE THERE'S A DRAFT BLOWING THROUGH MY LEGS ALL THE TIME.
MIGHT AS WELL NOT BE WEARING ANYTHING AT ALL.
AWW, SHE PULLED HER HAIR INTO A REGULAR PONYTAIL.
ぐすっ SNIFFLE!
OH, COME ON, IT'S NOT SO BAD ONCE IN A WHILE.
パーンッ THWAP
KYAH!

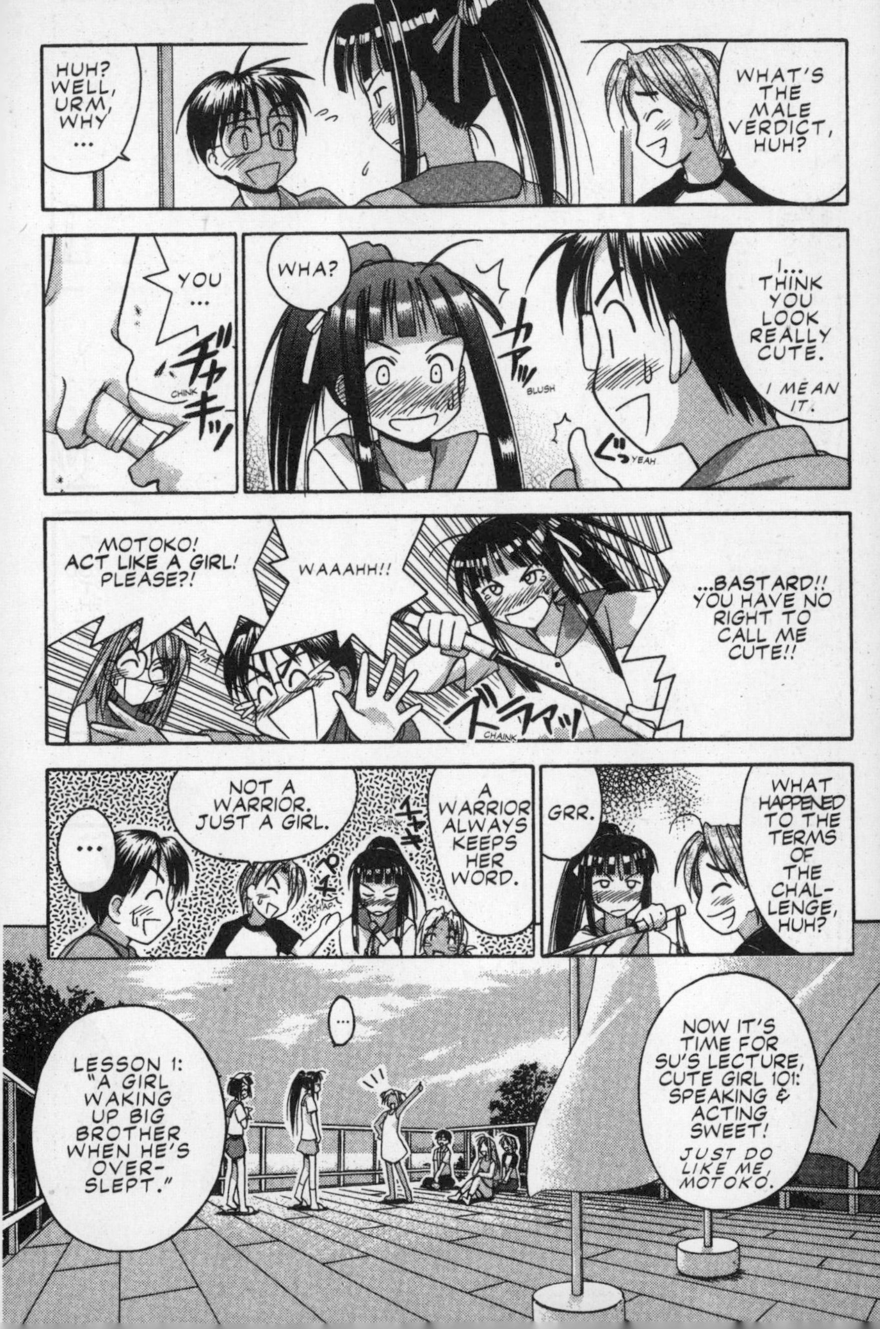
WHAT'S THE MALE VERDICT, HUH?
HUH? WELL, URM, WHY ...
I... THINK YOU LOOK REALLY CUTE.
I MEAN IT.
YEAH
BLUSH
WHA?
YOU ...
CHINK
...BASTARD!! YOU HAVE NO RIGHT TO CALL ME CUTE!!
CHAINK
WAAAHH!!
MOTOKO! ACT LIKE A GIRL! PLEASE?!
WHAT HAPPENED TO THE TERMS OF THE CHAL-LENGE, HUH?
GRR.
A WARRIOR ALWAYS KEEPS HER WORD.
CHINK
THAP
NOT A WARRIOR. JUST A GIRL.
...
NOW IT'S TIME FOR SU'S LECTURE, CUTE GIRL 101: SPEAKING & ACTING SWEET!
JUST DO LIKE ME, MOTOKO.
...
LESSON 1: "A GIRL WAKING UP BIG BROTHER WHEN HE'S OVER-SLEPT."

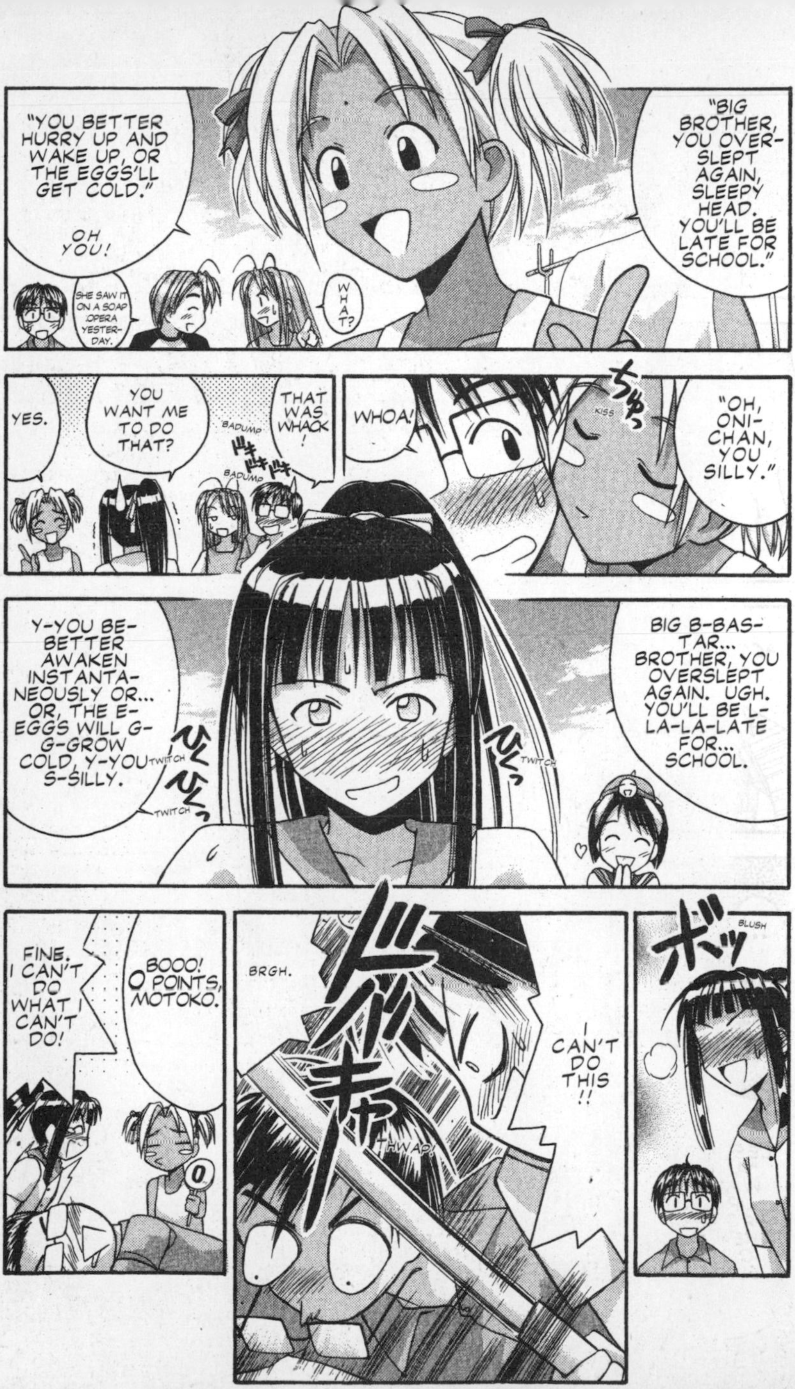
"BIG BROTHER, YOU OVER-SLEPT AGAIN, SLEEPY HEAD. YOU'LL BE LATE FOR SCHOOL."
"YOU BETTER HURRY UP AND WAKE UP, OR THE EGG'S'LL GET COLD."
OH YOU!
WHAT?
SHE SAW IT ON A SOAP OPERA YESTER-DAY.
ちゅっ
KISS
"OH, ONI-CHAN, YOU SILLY."
WHOA!
THAT WAS WHACK!
ドキドキドキ
BADUMP
BADUMP
YOU WANT ME TO DO THAT?
YES.
BIG B-BAS-TAR... BROTHER, YOU OVERSLEPT AGAIN. UGH. YOU'LL BE L-LA-LA-LATE FOR... SCHOOL.
ぴくっ
TWITCH
Y-YOU BE-BETTER AWAKEN INSTANTA-NEOUSLY OR... OR, THE E-EGG'S WILL G-G-GROW COLD, Y-YOU S-SILLY.
ぴく
TWITCH
ぴくっ
TWITCH
ボッ
BLUSH
ドバキャ
THWAP!
I CAN'T DO THIS!!
BRGH.
BOOO! 0 POINTS, MOTOKO.
FINE. I CAN'T DO WHAT I CAN'T DO!
0

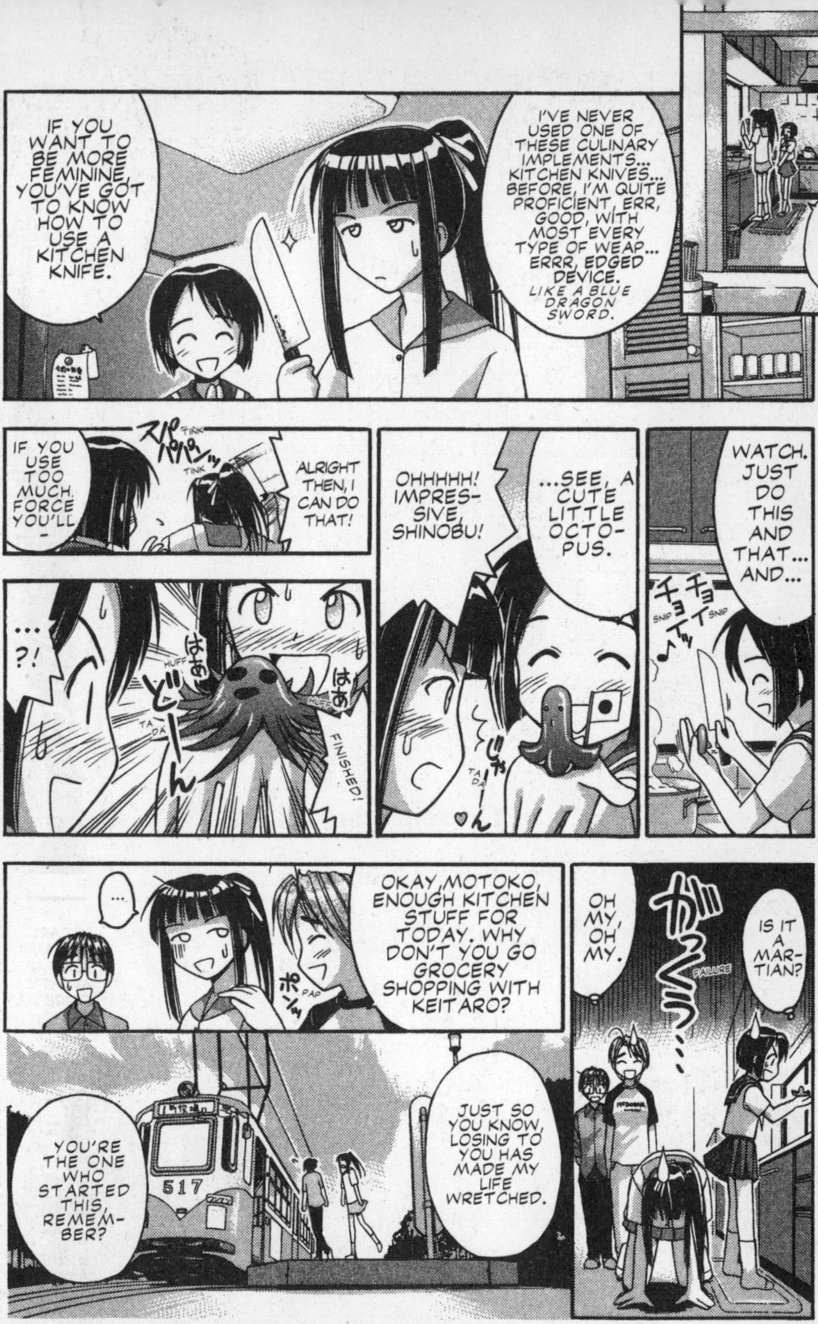
HM ...
I'VE NEVER USED ONE OF THESE CULINARY IMPLEMENTS... KITCHEN KNIVES... BEFORE, I'M QUITE PROFICIENT, ERR, GOOD, WITH MOST EVERY TYPE OF WEAP... ERRR, EDGED DEVICE.
LIKE A BLUE DRAGON SWORD.
IF YOU WANT TO BE MORE FEMININE, YOU'VE GOT TO KNOW HOW TO USE A KITCHEN KNIFE.
WATCH. JUST DO THIS AND THAT... AND...
チョイチョイッ
SNIP SNIP
♪
...SEE, A CUTE LITTLE OCTOPUS.
OHHHHH! IMPRESSIVE, SHINOBU!
じゃーん
TA DA
♡
スパパパンッ
TINK TINK
ALRIGHT THEN, I CAN DO THAT!
IF YOU USE TOO MUCH FORCE YOU'LL -
はあ
HUFF
はあ
HUFF
どーーん
TA DA
FINISHED!
... ?!
IS IT A MARTIAN?
がっくう...
FAILURE
OH MY, OH MY.
OKAY, MOTOKO, ENOUGH KITCHEN STUFF FOR TODAY. WHY DON'T YOU GO GROCERY SHOPPING WITH KEITARO?
ポンッ
PAP
...
JUST SO YOU KNOW, LOSING TO YOU HAS MADE MY LIFE WRETCHED.
YOU'RE THE ONE WHO STARTED THIS, REMEMBER?
517

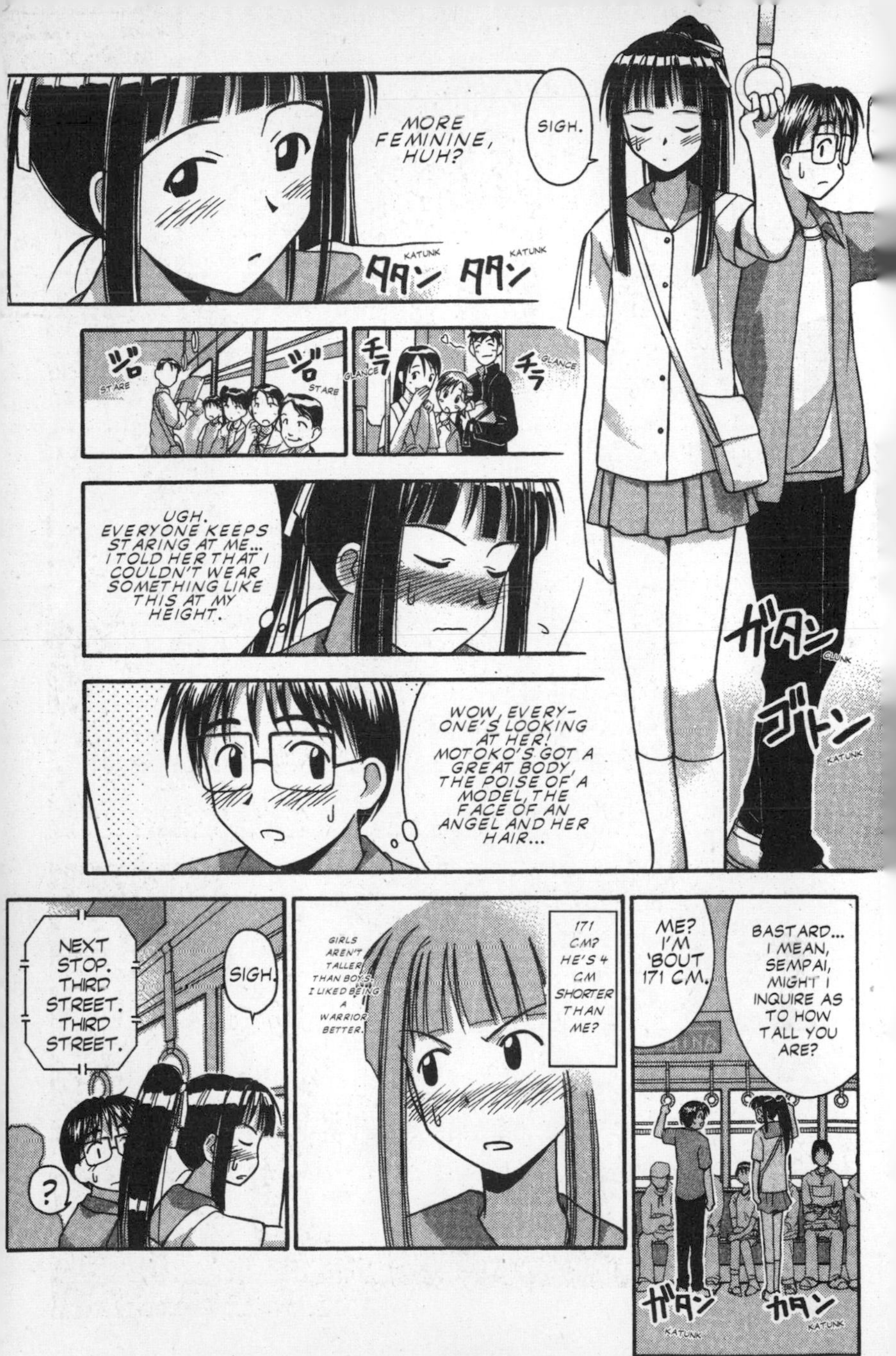
SIGH.
ガタン
CLUNK
ゴトン
KATUNK
MORE FEMININE, HUH?
タタン
KATUNK
タタン
KATUNK
チラ
GLANCE
チラ
GLANCE
ジロ
STARE
ジロ
STARE
UGH. EVERYONE KEEPS STARING AT ME... I TOLD HER THAT I COULDN'T WEAR SOMETHING LIKE THIS AT MY HEIGHT.
WOW, EVERYONE'S LOOKING AT HER! MOTOKO'S GOT A GREAT BODY, THE POISE OF A MODEL, THE FACE OF AN ANGEL AND HER HAIR...
BASTARD... I MEAN, SEMPAI, MIGHT I INQUIRE AS TO HOW TALL YOU ARE?
ME? I'M 'BOUT 171 CM.
ガタン
KATUNK
カタン
KATUNK
171 CM? HE'S 4 CM SHORTER THAN ME?
GIRLS AREN'T TALLER THAN BOYS. I LIKED BEING A WARRIOR BETTER.
SIGH.
NEXT STOP. THIRD STREET. THIRD STREET.
?

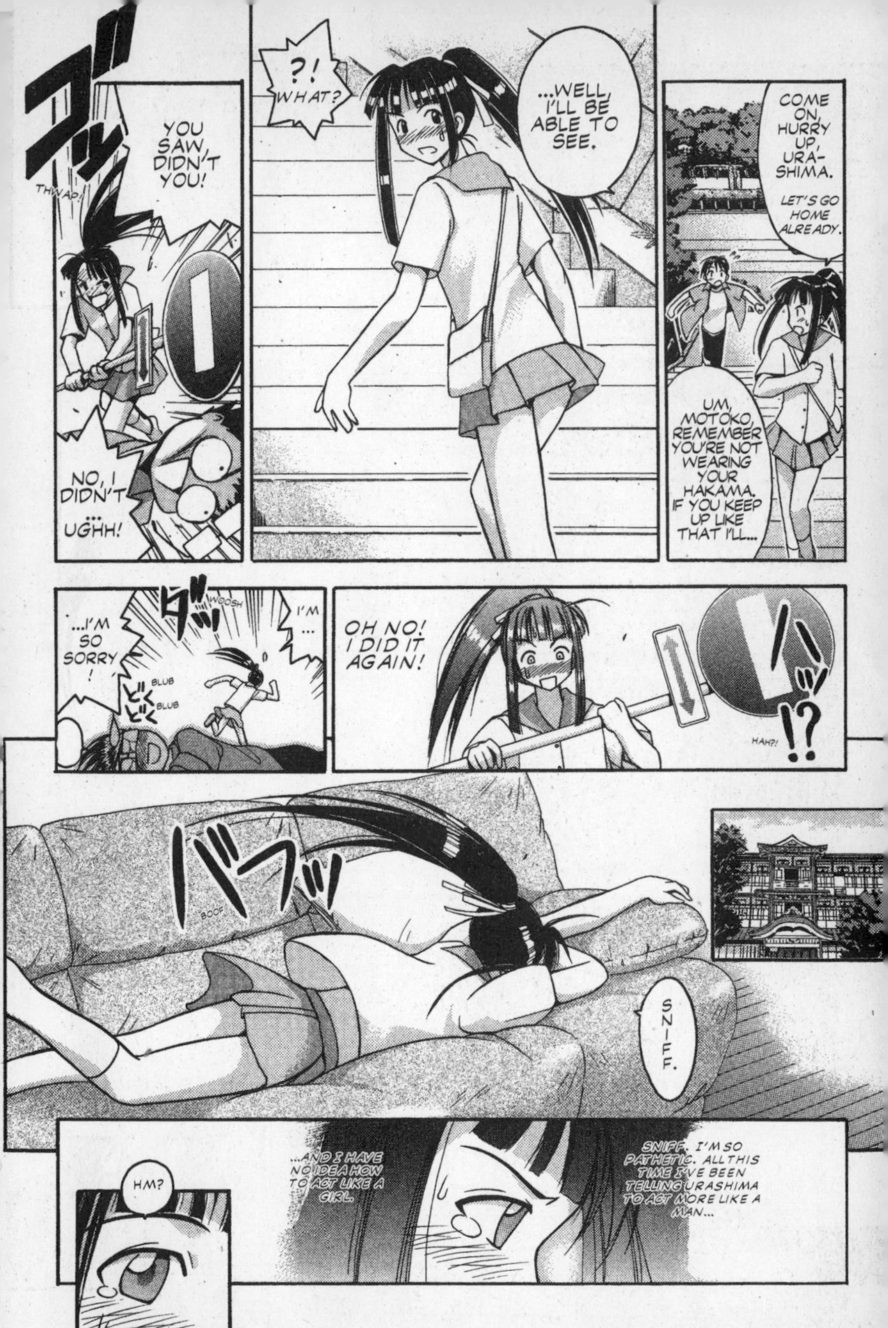
COME ON, HURRY UP, URA-SHIMA.
LET'S GO HOME ALREADY.
UM, MOTOKO, REMEMBER YOU'RE NOT WEARING YOUR HAKAMA. IF YOU KEEP UP LIKE THAT I'LL...
...WELL, I'LL BE ABLE TO SEE.
?! WHAT?
THWAP!
YOU SAW, DIDN'T YOU!
NO, I DIDN'T ... UGHH!
OH NO! I DID IT AGAIN!
HAH?!
I'M ...
WOOSH
...I'M SO SORRY!
BLUB
BLUB
BOOF
SNIFF.
SNIFF. I'M SO PATHETIC. ALL THIS TIME I'VE BEEN TELLING URASHIMA TO ACT MORE LIKE A MAN...
...AND I HAVE NO IDEA HOW TO ACT LIKE A GIRL.
HM?

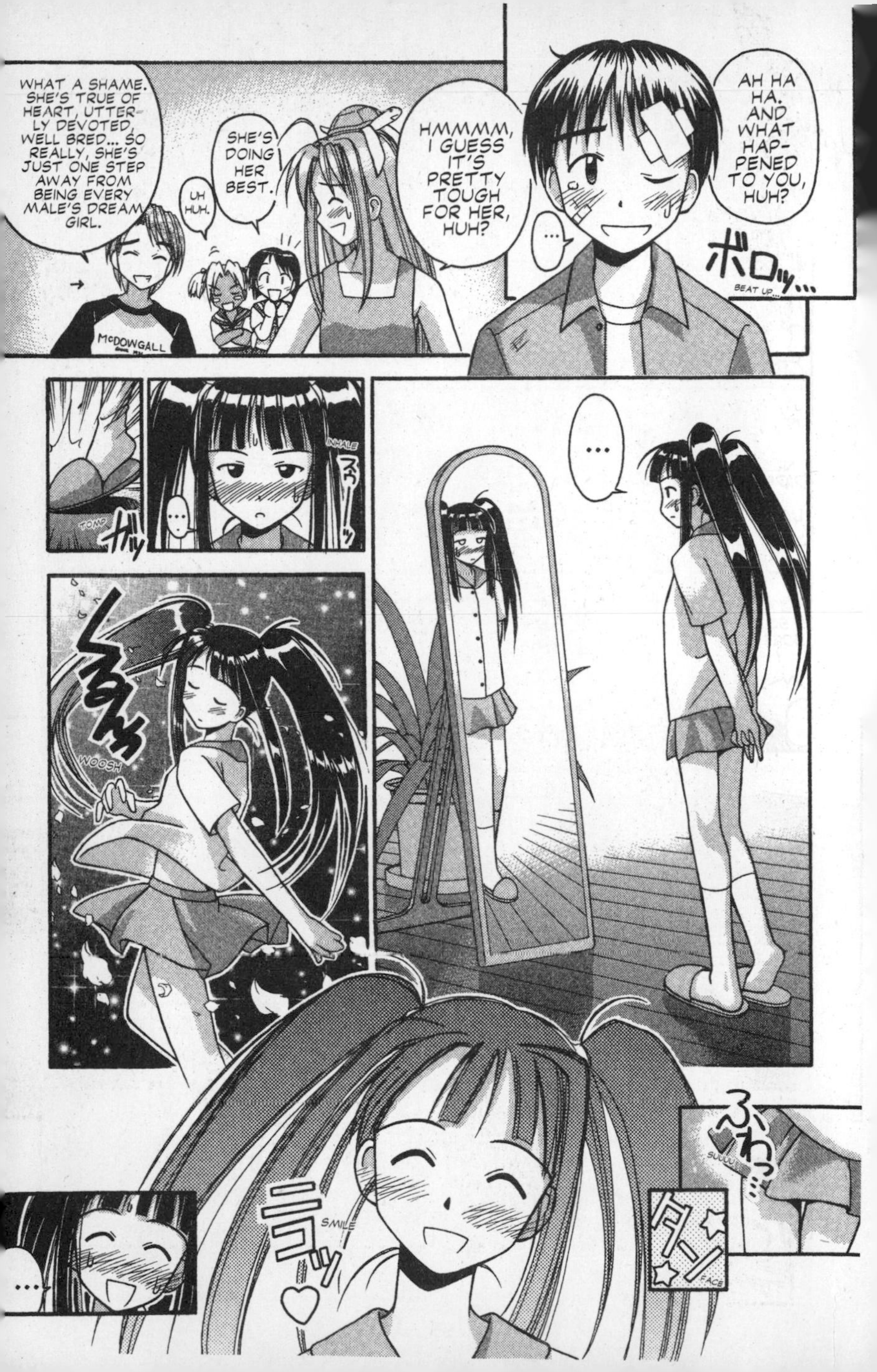
AH HA HA. AND WHAT HAP-PENED TO YOU, HUH?
ボロッ...
BEAT UP...
...
HMMMM, I GUESS IT'S PRETTY TOUGH FOR HER, HUH?
SHE'S DOING HER BEST.
UH HUH.
WHAT A SHAME. SHE'S TRUE OF HEART, UTTER-LY DEVOTED, WELL BRED... SO REALLY, SHE'S JUST ONE STEP AWAY FROM BEING EVERY MALE'S DREAM GIRL.
McDOWGALL
...
INHALE
スゥーッ
...
TOMP
ガッ
くるんっ
WOOSH
ふわっ
SUUUU
タン
FACE
ニコッ
SMILE
...

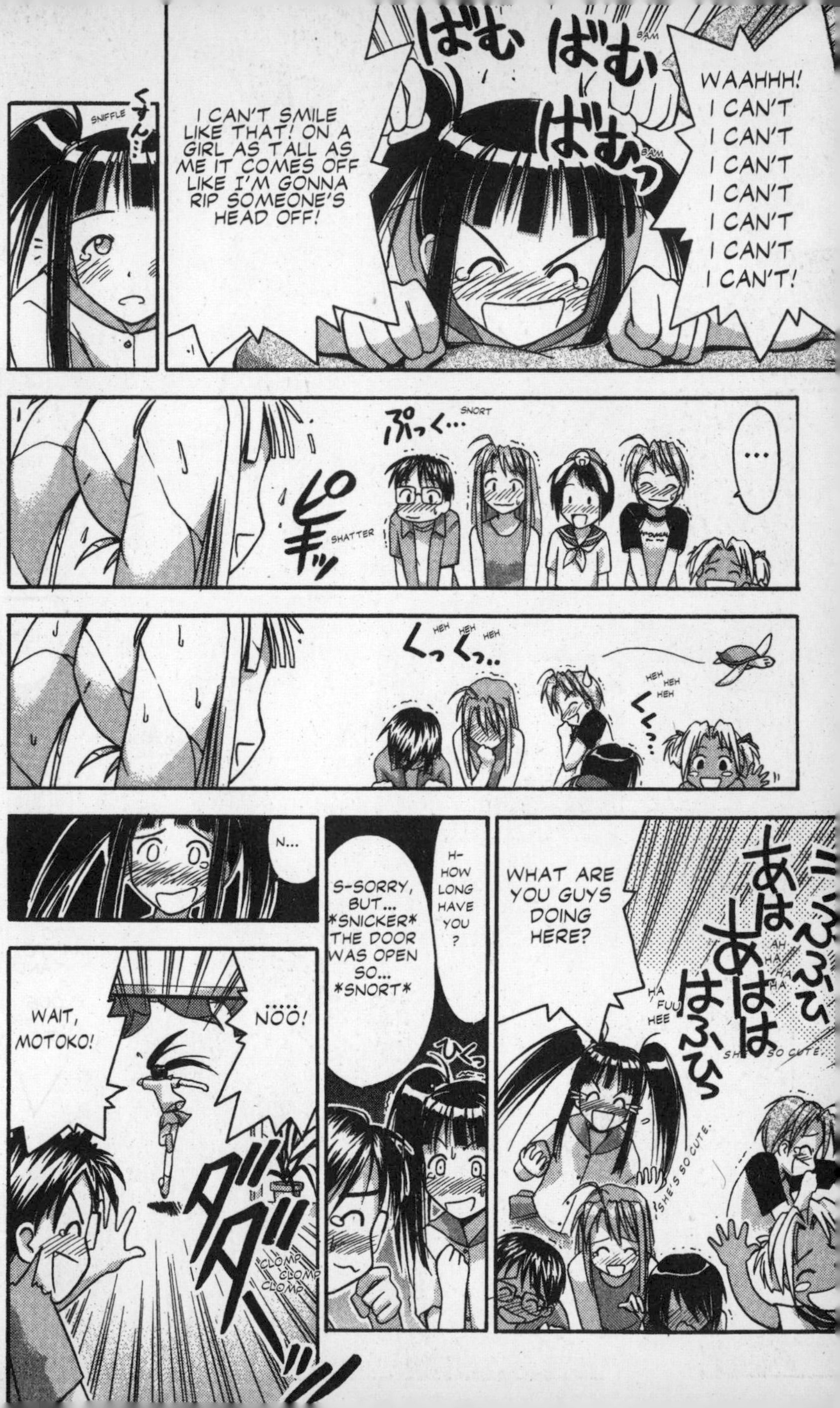
ばむ ばむ ばむっ
BAM
BAM
WAAHHH! I CAN'T I CAN'T I CAN'T I CAN'T I CAN'T I CAN'T I CAN'T!
I CAN'T SMILE LIKE THAT! ON A GIRL AS TALL AS ME IT COMES OFF LIKE I'M GONNA RIP SOMEONE'S HEAD OFF!
くすん…
SNIFFLE
...
ぷっく…
SNORT
ピキッ
SHATTER
くっくっ…
HEH HEH HEH
くくっ…
HEH HEH HEH
WHAT ARE YOU GUYS DOING HERE?
あはあは
AH HA HA HA
HA FUU HEE
SHE'S SO CUTE.
SHE'S SO CUTE.
H-HOW LONG HAVE YOU?
S-SORRY, BUT... *SNICKER* THE DOOR WAS OPEN SO... *SNORT*
N...
NÖÖ!
WAIT, MOTOKO!
CLOMP CLOMP CLOMP

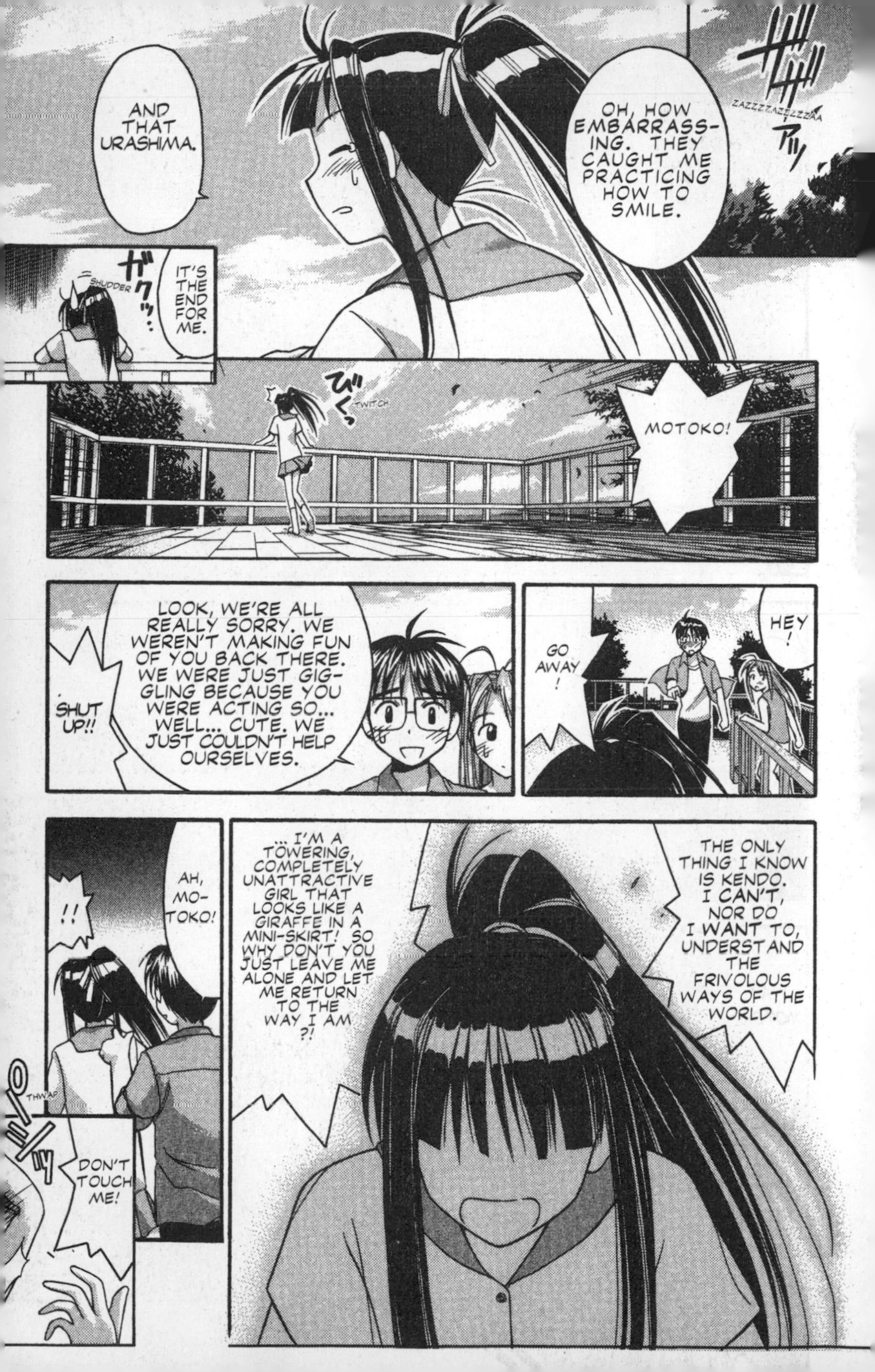
ZAZZZZAZZZZZAA
OH, HOW EMBARRASSING. THEY CAUGHT ME PRACTICING HOW TO SMILE.
AND THAT URASHIMA.
SHUDDER
IT'S THE END FOR ME.
TWITCH
MOTOKO!
HEY!
GO AWAY!
LOOK, WE'RE ALL REALLY SORRY. WE WEREN'T MAKING FUN OF YOU BACK THERE. WE WERE JUST GIGGLING BECAUSE YOU WERE ACTING SO... WELL... CUTE. WE JUST COULDN'T HELP OURSELVES.
SHUT UP!!
THE ONLY THING I KNOW IS KENDO. I CAN'T, NOR DO I WANT TO, UNDERSTAND THE FRIVOLOUS WAYS OF THE WORLD.
... I'M A TOWERING, COMPLETELY UNATTRACTIVE GIRL THAT LOOKS LIKE A GIRAFFE IN A MINI-SKIRT! SO WHY DON'T YOU JUST LEAVE ME ALONE AND LET ME RETURN TO THE WAY I AM ?!
AH, MO-TOKO!
!!
THWAP
DON'T TOUCH ME!

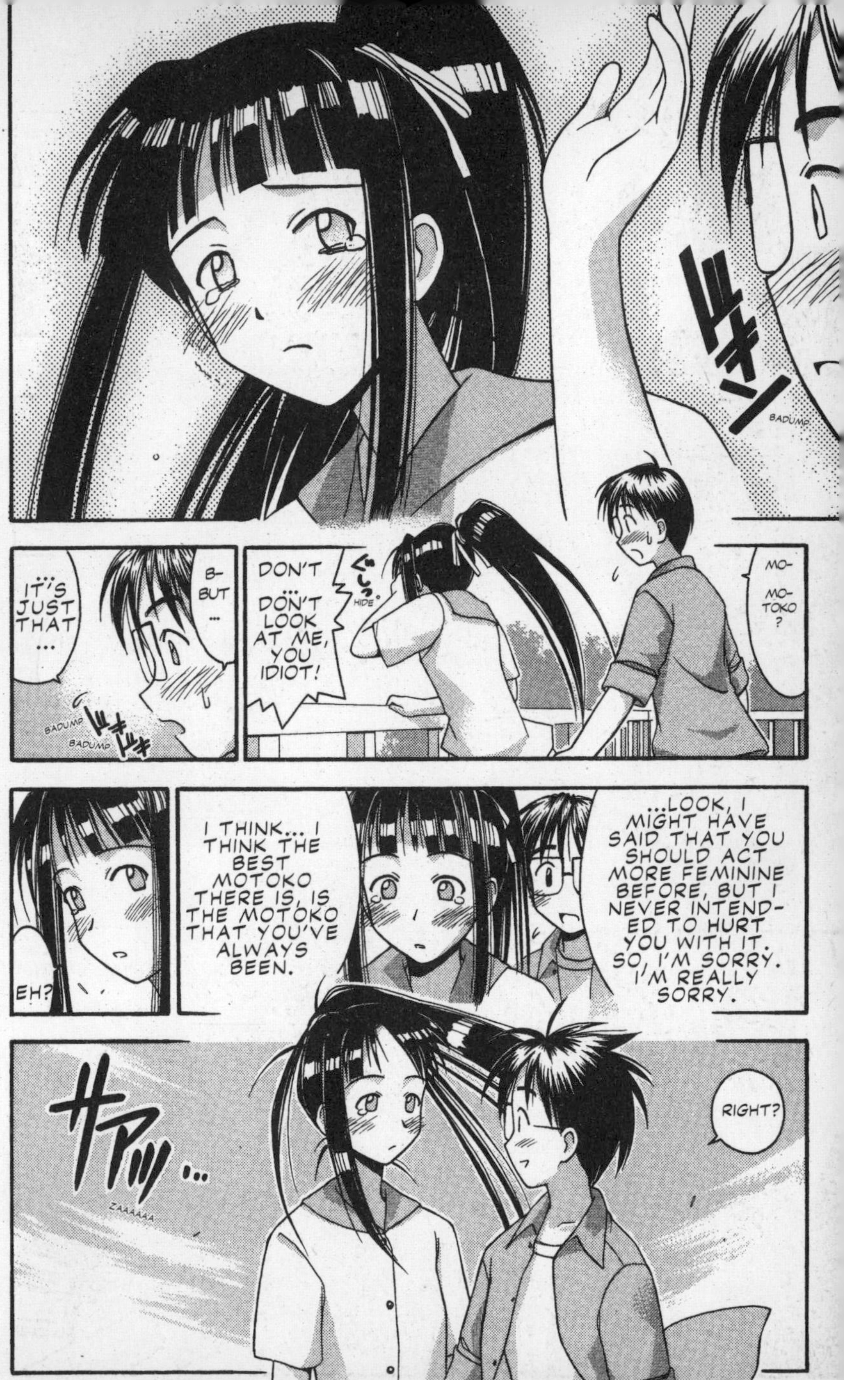
BADUMP
MO-MOTOKO?
HIDE
DON'T... DON'T LOOK AT ME, YOU IDIOT!
B-BUT...
IT'S JUST THAT...
BADUMP
BADUMP
...LOOK, I MIGHT HAVE SAID THAT YOU SHOULD ACT MORE FEMININE BEFORE, BUT I NEVER INTENDED TO HURT YOU WITH IT. SO, I'M SORRY. I'M REALLY SORRY.
I THINK... I THINK THE BEST MOTOKO THERE IS, IS THE MOTOKO THAT YOU'VE ALWAYS BEEN.
EH?
RIGHT?
ZAAAAAA

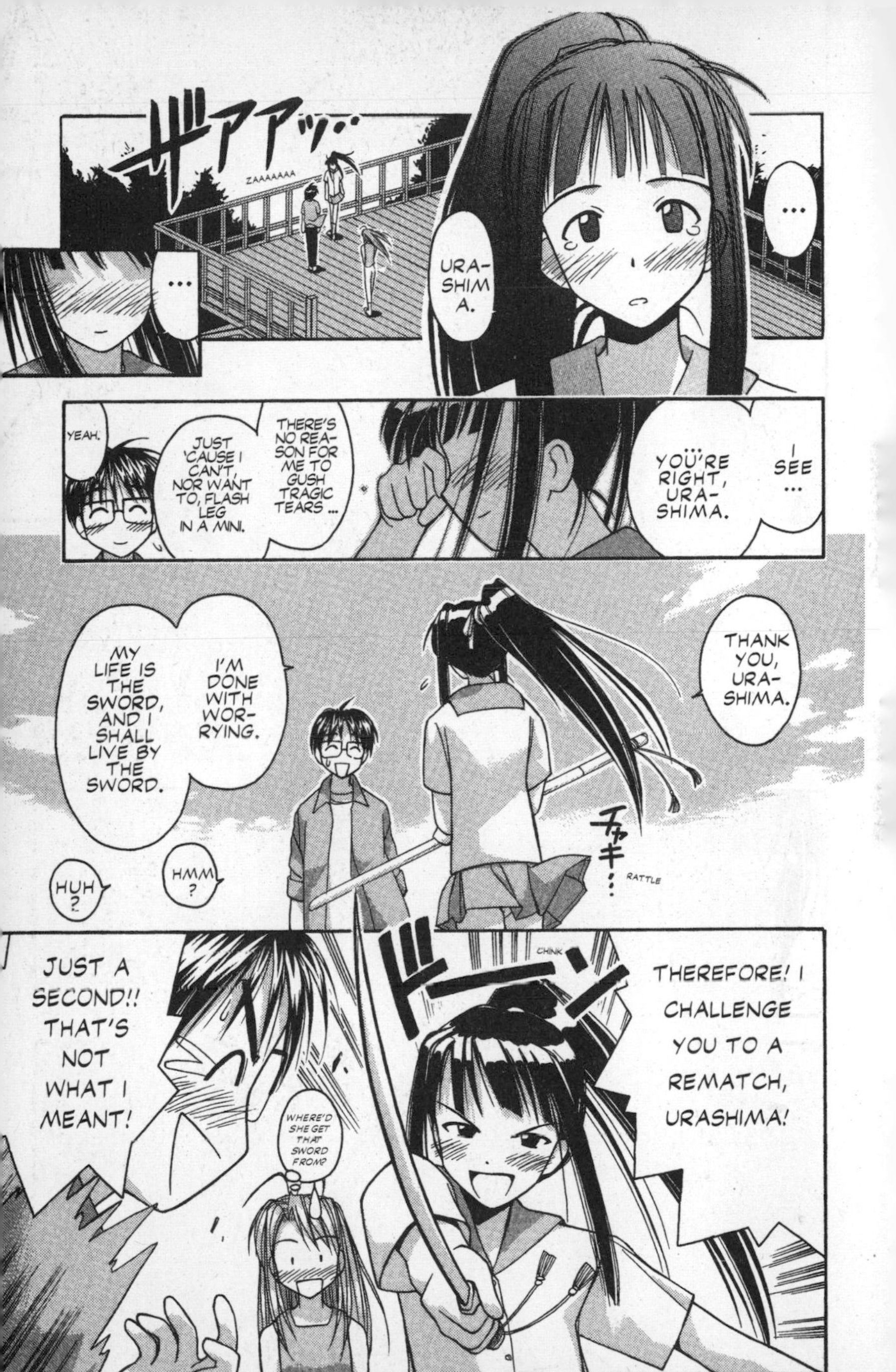
...
URA-SHIMA.
ザアアッ
ZAAAAAAA
...
I SEE ...
YOU'RE RIGHT, URA-SHIMA.
THERE'S NO REA-SON FOR ME TO GUSH TRAGIC TEARS ...
JUST 'CAUSE I CAN'T, NOR WANT TO, FLASH LEG IN A MINI.
YEAH.
THANK YOU, URA-SHIMA.
チャキ
RATTLE
I'M DONE WITH WOR-RYING.
MY LIFE IS THE SWORD, AND I SHALL LIVE BY THE SWORD.
HMM?
HUH?
THEREFORE! I CHALLENGE YOU TO A REMATCH, URASHIMA!
ドーン
CHINK
WHERE'D SHE GET THAT SWORD FROM?
JUST A SECOND!! THAT'S NOT WHAT I MEANT!

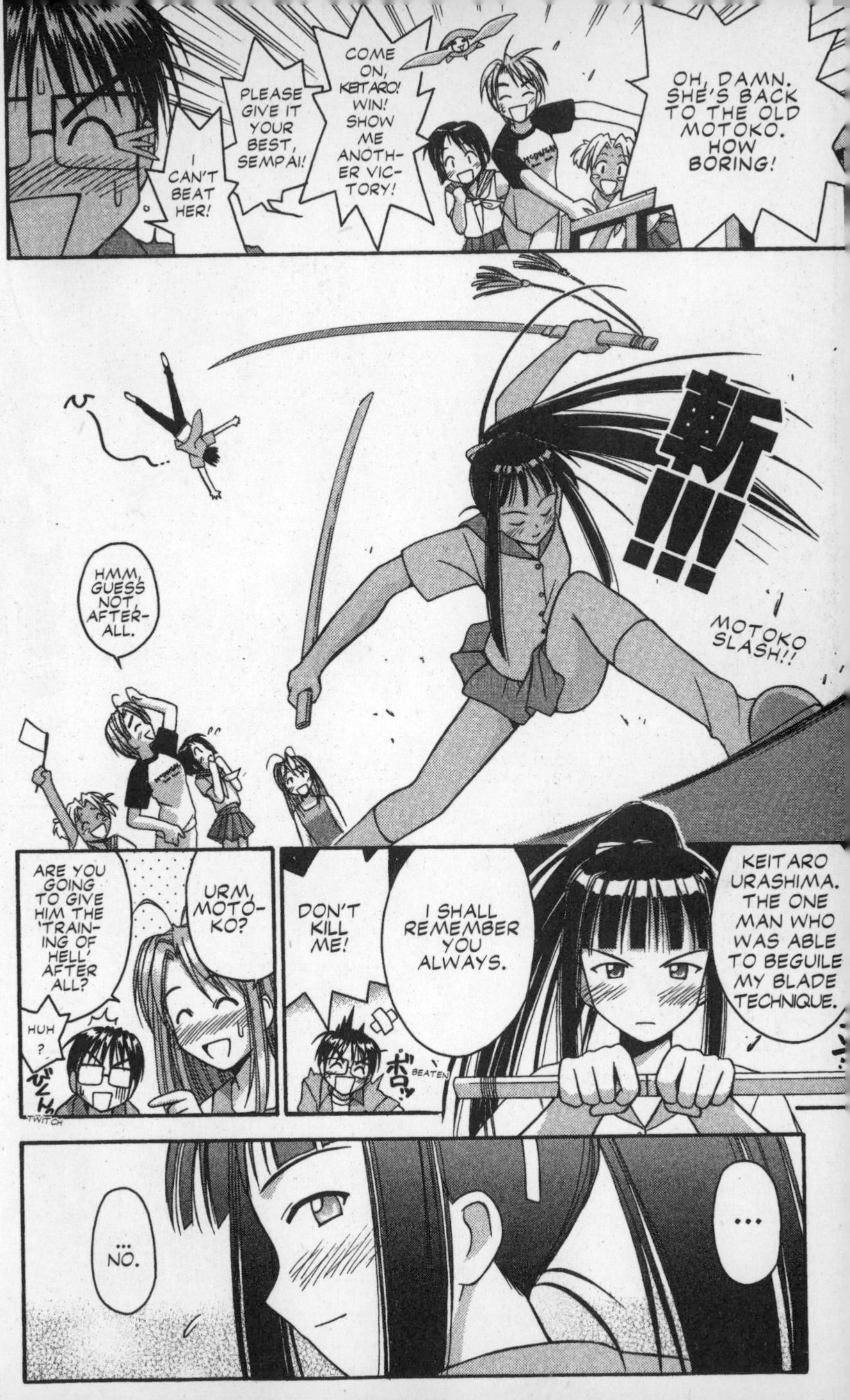
OH, DAMN. SHE'S BACK TO THE OLD MOTOKO. HOW BORING!
COME ON, KEITARO! WIN! SHOW ME ANOTHER VICTORY!
PLEASE GIVE IT YOUR BEST, SEMPAI!
I CAN'T BEAT HER!
斬!!!
MOTOKO SLASH!!
HMM, GUESS NOT, AFTER-ALL.
KEITARO URASHIMA. THE ONE MAN WHO WAS ABLE TO BEGUILE MY BLADE TECHNIQUE.
I SHALL REMEMBER YOU ALWAYS.
DON'T KILL ME!
ボロッ BEATEN
URM, MOTOKO?
ARE YOU GOING TO GIVE HIM THE 'TRAINING OF HELL' AFTER ALL?
HUH?
TWITCH
...
... NO.

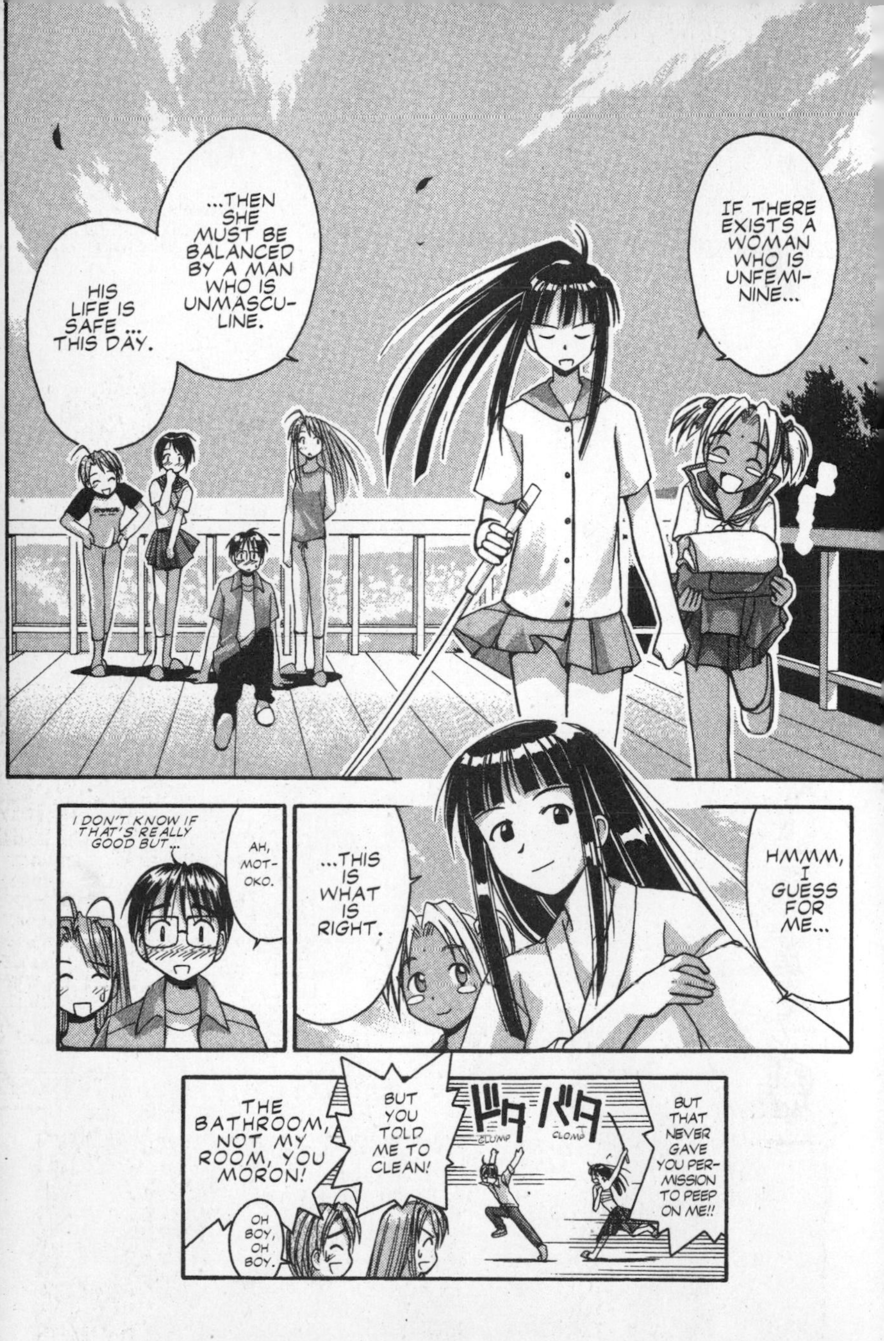
IF THERE EXISTS A WOMAN WHO IS UNFEMI-NINE...
...THEN SHE MUST BE BALANCED BY A MAN WHO IS UNMASCU-LINE.
HIS LIFE IS SAFE ... THIS DAY.
HMMM, I GUESS FOR ME...
...THIS IS WHAT IS RIGHT.
AH, MOT-OKO.
I DON'T KNOW IF THAT'S REALLY GOOD BUT...
BUT THAT NEVER GAVE YOU PER-MISSION TO PEEP ON ME!!
ドタ バタ
CLOMP CLOMP
BUT YOU TOLD ME TO CLEAN!
THE BATHROOM, NOT MY ROOM, YOU MORON!
OH BOY, OH BOY.

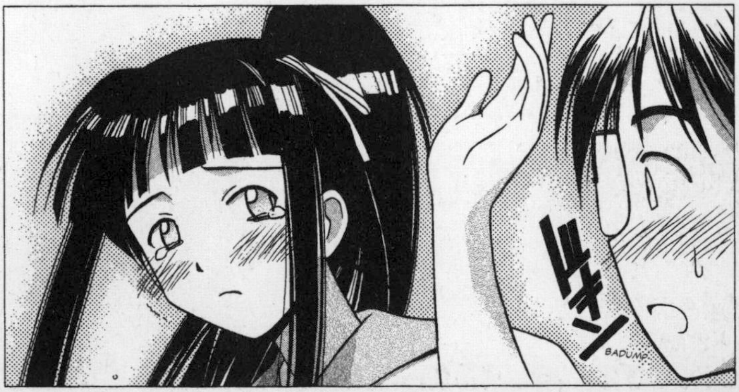
ドキン
BADUMP

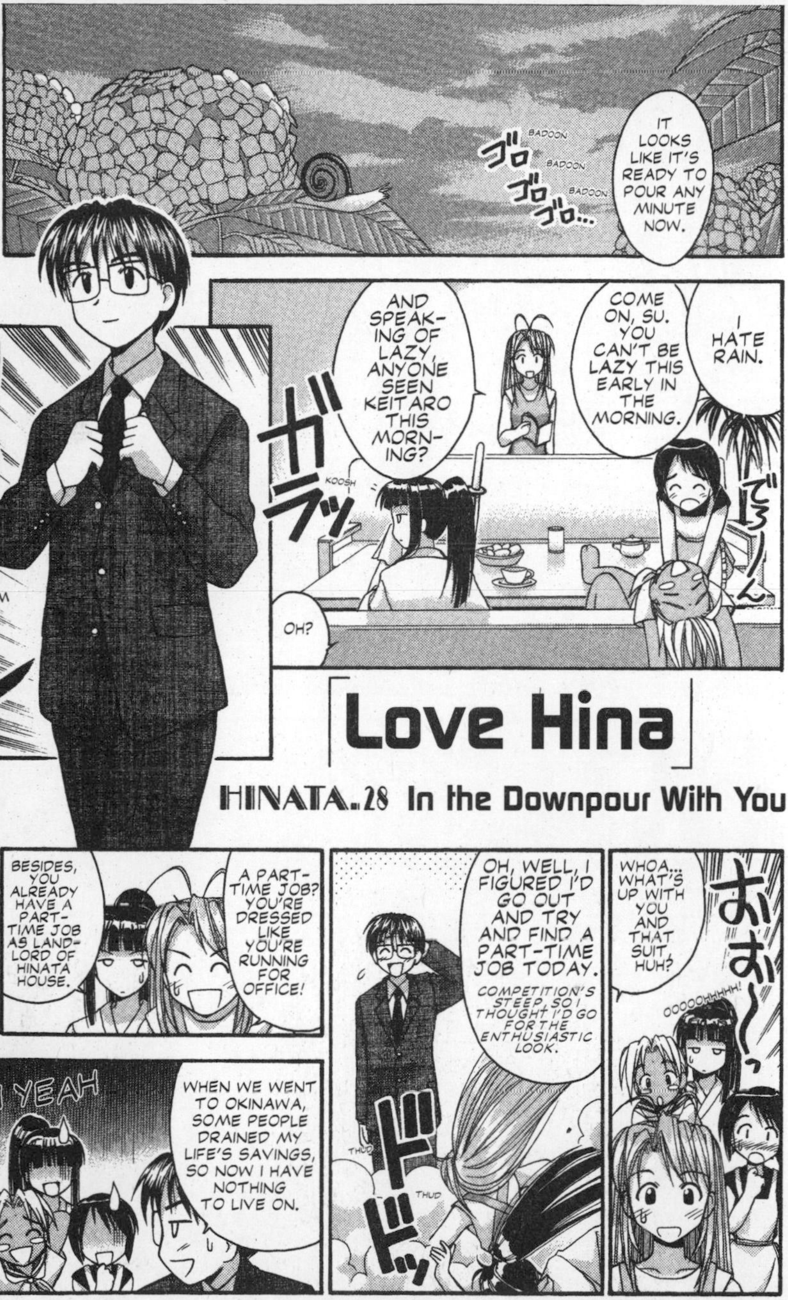
BADOON
BADOON
BADOON
IT LOOKS LIKE IT'S READY TO POUR ANY MINUTE NOW.
I HATE RAIN.
COME ON, SU. YOU CAN'T BE LAZY THIS EARLY IN THE MORNING.
AND SPEAKING OF LAZY, ANYONE SEEN KEITARO THIS MORNING?
KOOSH
OH?
BAM
WHOA... WHAT'S UP WITH YOU AND THAT SUIT, HUH?
OOOOOHHHHH!
OH, WELL, I FIGURED I'D GO OUT AND TRY AND FIND A PART-TIME JOB TODAY.
COMPETITION'S STEEP, SO I THOUGHT I'D GO FOR THE ENTHUSIASTIC LOOK.
THUD
THUD
A PART-TIME JOB? YOU'RE DRESSED LIKE YOU'RE RUNNING FOR OFFICE!
BESIDES, YOU ALREADY HAVE A PART-TIME JOB AS LANDLORD OF HINATA HOUSE.
WHEN WE WENT TO OKINAWA, SOME PEOPLE DRAINED MY LIFE'S SAVINGS, SO NOW I HAVE NOTHING TO LIVE ON.
OH YEAH
NYA HA HA.

Love Hina

HINATA.28 In the Downpour With You

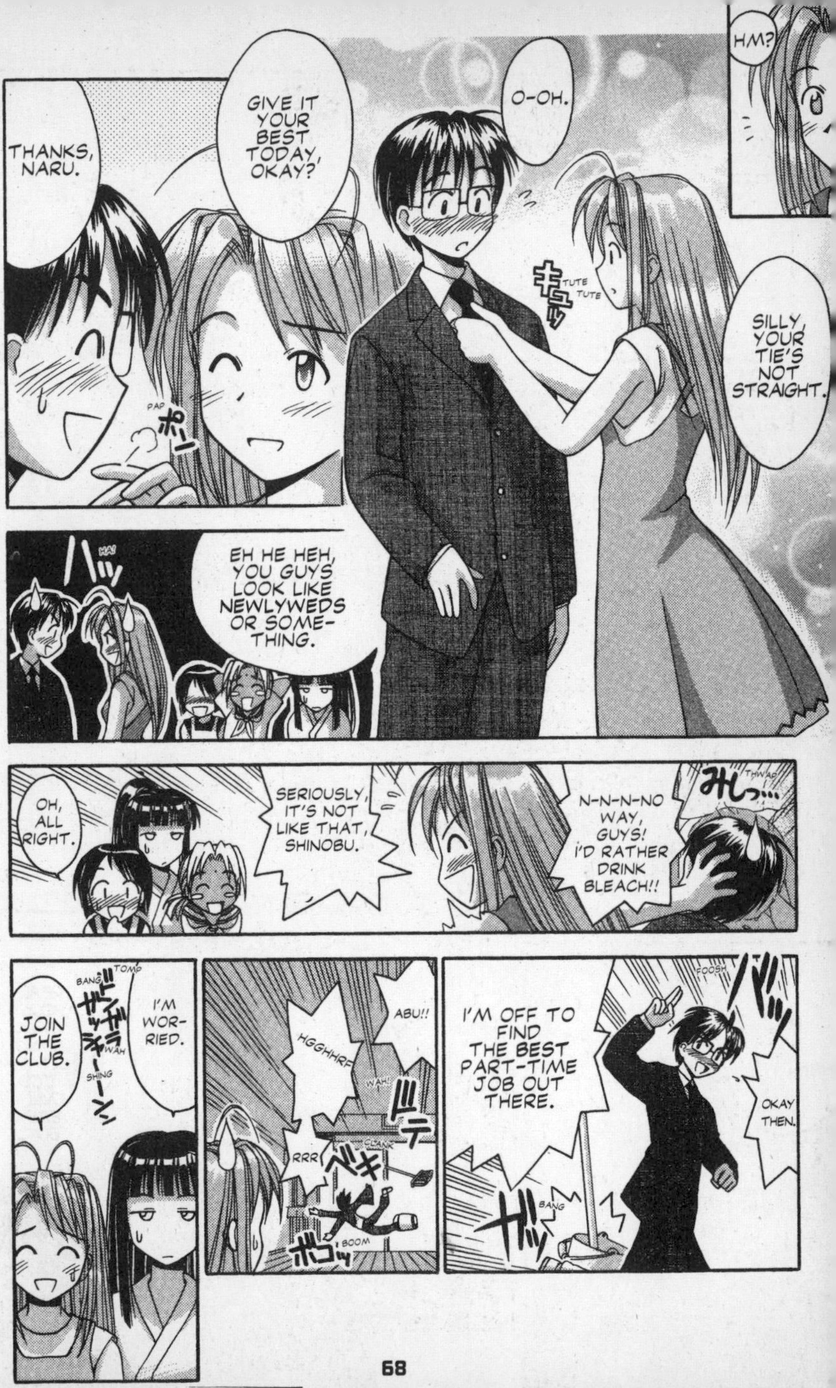
HM?
SILLY, YOUR TIE'S NOT STRAIGHT.
TUTE TUTE
O-OH.
GIVE IT YOUR BEST TODAY, OKAY?
THANKS, NARU.
PAP
HAI
EH HE HEH, YOU GUYS LOOK LIKE NEWLYWEDS OR SOME-THING.
THWAP
N-N-N-NO WAY, GUYS! I'D RATHER DRINK BLEACH!!
SERIOUSLY, IT'S NOT LIKE THAT, SHINOBU.
OH, ALL RIGHT.
FOOSH
OKAY THEN.
I'M OFF TO FIND THE BEST PART-TIME JOB OUT THERE.
BANG
ABU!!
HGGHHRF
WAH!
CLANK
RRR
BOOM
I'M WOR-RIED.
TOMP
BANG
WAH
SHING
JOIN THE CLUB.

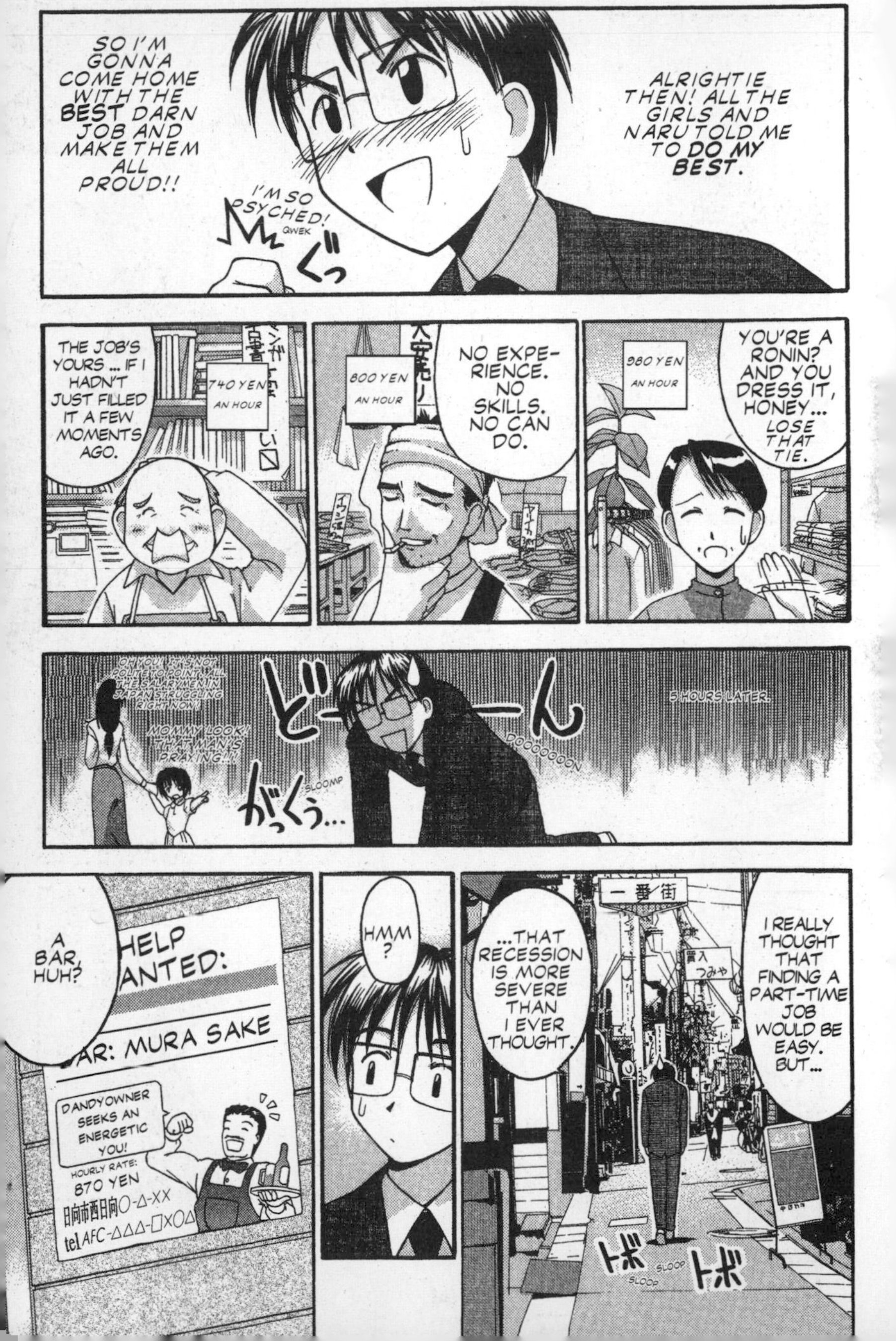
ALRIGHTIE THEN! ALL THE GIRLS AND NARU TOLD ME TO DO MY BEST.
SO I'M GONNA COME HOME WITH THE BEST DARN JOB AND MAKE THEM ALL PROUD!!
I'M SO PSYCHED!
QWEK
ぐっ
980 YEN AN HOUR
YOU'RE A RONIN? AND YOU DRESS IT, HONEY... LOSE THAT TIE.
800 YEN AN HOUR
NO EXPERIENCE. NO SKILLS. NO CAN DO.
740 YEN AN HOUR
THE JOB'S YOURS ... IF I HADN'T JUST FILLED IT A FEW MOMENTS AGO.
5 HOURS LATER.
どーーん
DOOOOOOOON
がっくぅ…
SLOOMP
MOMMY LOOK! THAT MAN'S PRAYING!!!
OH YOU! IT'S NOT POLITE TO POINT! ALL THE SALARYMEN IN JAPAN STRUGGLING RIGHT NOW!
I REALLY THOUGHT THAT FINDING A PART-TIME JOB WOULD BE EASY. BUT...
...THAT RECESSION IS MORE SEVERE THAN I EVER THOUGHT.
一番街
買入 つみや
トボ
SLOOP
トボ
SLOOP
HMM?
A BAR, HUH?
HELP
ANTED:
AR: MURA SAKE
DANDY OWNER SEEKS AN ENERGETIC YOU!
HOURLY RATE: 870 YEN
日向市西日向〇-△-XX
tel AFC-△△△-□X〇△

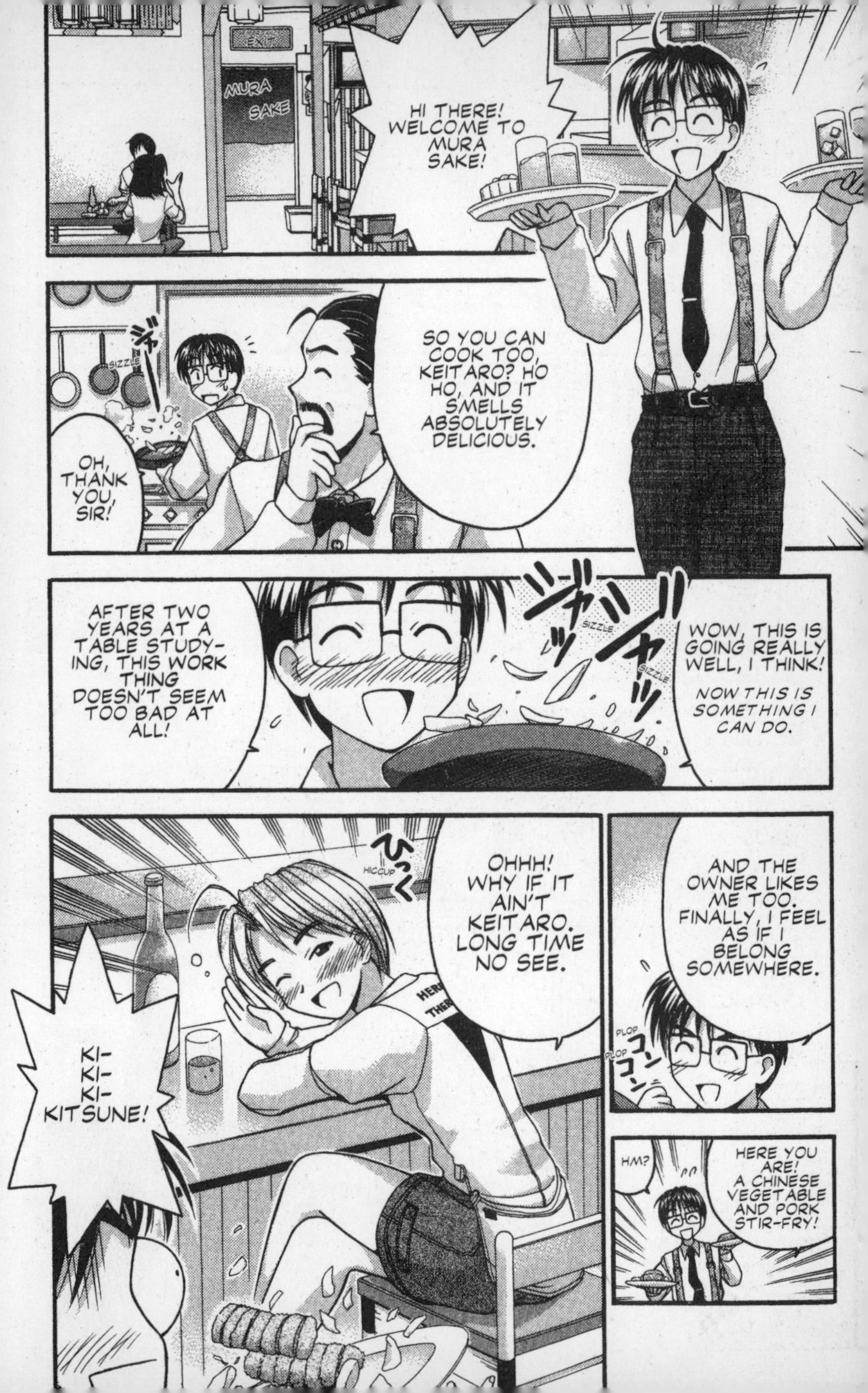
HI THERE! WELCOME TO MURA SAKE!
EXIT
MURA SAKE
SO YOU CAN COOK TOO, KEITARO? HO HO, AND IT SMELLS ABSOLUTELY DELICIOUS.
SIZZLE
OH, THANK YOU, SIR!
WOW, THIS IS GOING REALLY WELL, I THINK!
NOW THIS IS SOMETHING I CAN DO.
SIZZLE
SIZZLE
AFTER TWO YEARS AT A TABLE STUDYING, THIS WORK THING DOESN'T SEEM TOO BAD AT ALL!
AND THE OWNER LIKES ME TOO. FINALLY, I FEEL AS IF I BELONG SOMEWHERE.
PLOP
PLOP
HERE YOU ARE! A CHINESE VEGETABLE AND PORK STIR-FRY!
HM?
OHHH! WHY IF IT AIN'T KEITARO. LONG TIME NO SEE.
HICCUP
KI-KI-KI-KITSUNE!

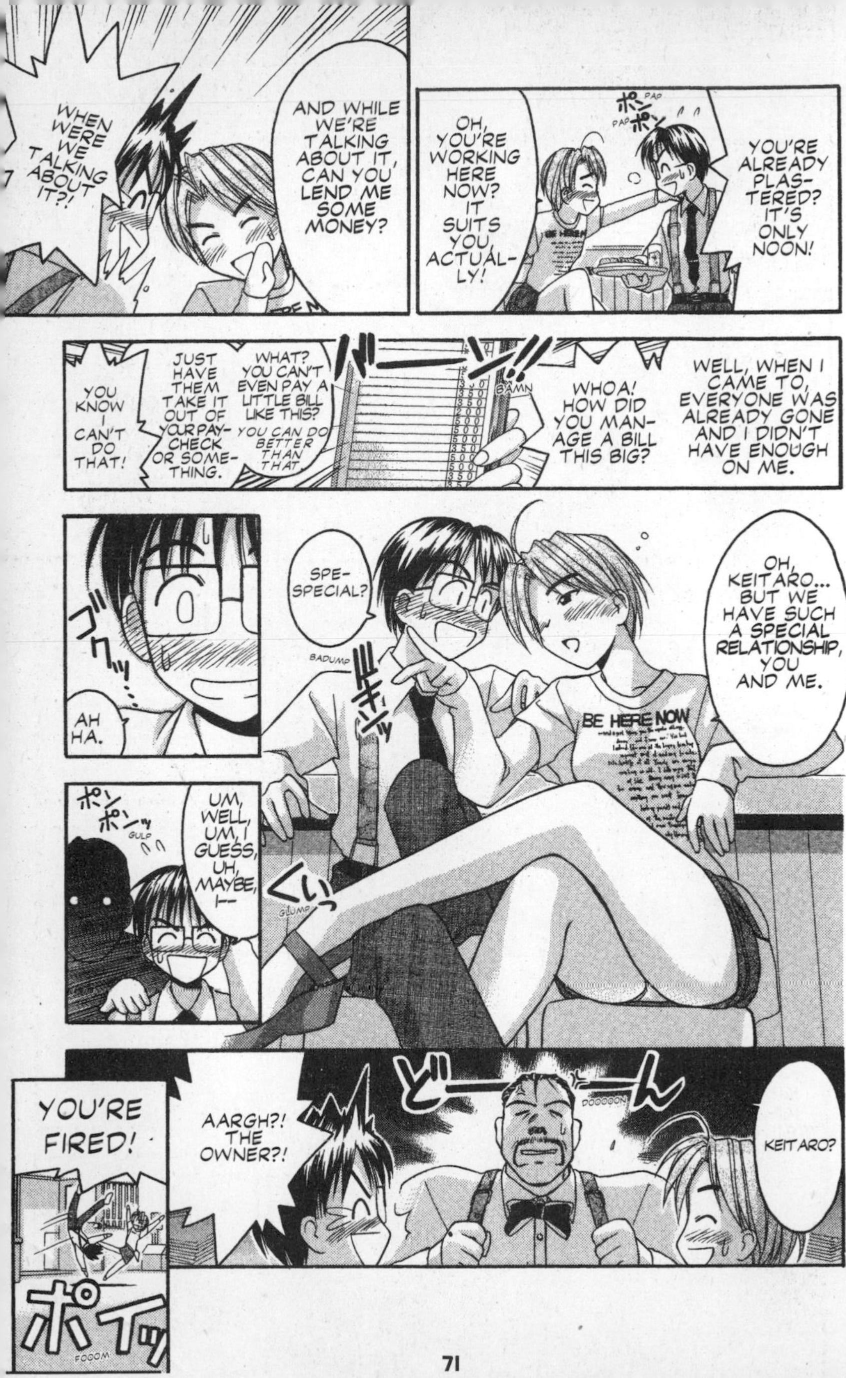
YOU'RE ALREADY PLAS-TERED? IT'S ONLY NOON!
ポン ポン
PAP PAP
OH, YOU'RE WORKING HERE NOW? IT SUITS YOU, ACTUAL-LY!
AND WHILE WE'RE TALKING ABOUT IT, CAN YOU LEND ME SOME MONEY?
WHEN WERE WE TALKING ABOUT IT?!
WELL, WHEN I CAME TO, EVERYONE WAS ALREADY GONE AND I DIDN'T HAVE ENOUGH ON ME.
WHOA! HOW DID YOU MAN-AGE A BILL THIS BIG?
バーン!!
BAMN
WHAT? YOU CAN'T EVEN PAY A LITTLE BILL LIKE THIS?
YOU CAN DO BETTER THAN THAT.
JUST HAVE THEM TAKE IT OUT OF YOUR PAY-CHECK OR SOME-THING.
YOU KNOW I CAN'T DO THAT!
OH, KEITARO... BUT WE HAVE SUCH A SPECIAL RELATIONSHIP, YOU AND ME.
SPE- SPECIAL?
BADUMP
BE HERE NOW
くいっ
GLUMP
AH HA.
UM, WELL, UM, I GUESS, UH, MAYBE, I--
GULP
KEITARO?
どーーん
DOOOOON
AARGH?! THE OWNER?!
YOU'RE FIRED!
ポイッ
FOOOM

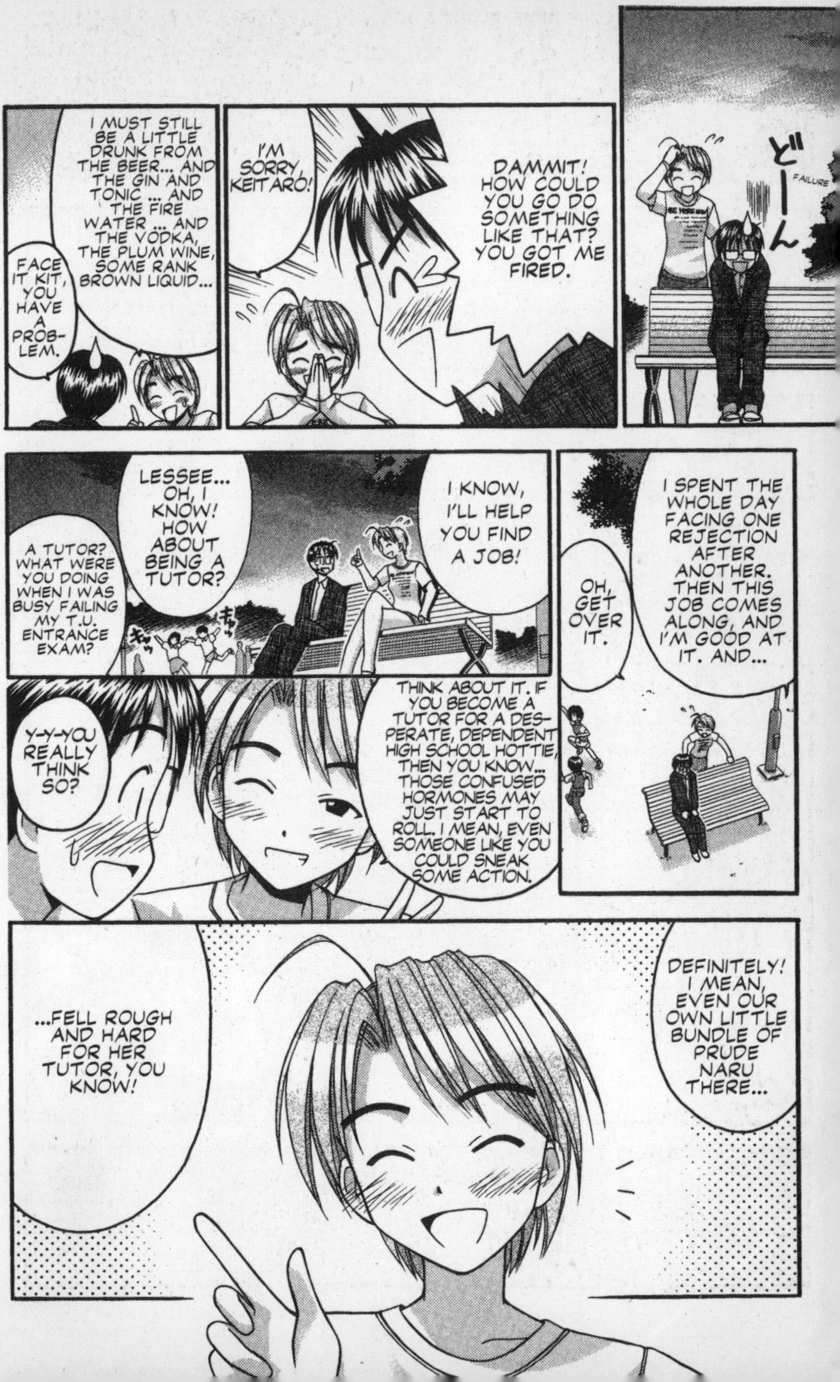
どーん
FAILURE
DAMMIT! HOW COULD YOU GO DO SOMETHING LIKE THAT? YOU GOT ME FIRED.
I'M SORRY, KEITARO!
I MUST STILL BE A LITTLE DRUNK FROM THE BEER... AND THE GIN AND TONIC ... AND THE FIRE WATER ... AND THE VODKA, THE PLUM WINE, SOME RANK BROWN LIQUID...
FACE IT KIT, YOU HAVE A PROB-LEM.
I SPENT THE WHOLE DAY FACING ONE REJECTION AFTER ANOTHER. THEN THIS JOB COMES ALONG, AND I'M GOOD AT IT. AND...
OH, GET OVER IT.
I KNOW, I'LL HELP YOU FIND A JOB!
LESSEE... OH, I KNOW! HOW ABOUT BEING A TUTOR?
A TUTOR? WHAT WERE YOU DOING WHEN I WAS BUSY FAILING MY T.U. ENTRANCE EXAM?
THINK ABOUT IT. IF YOU BECOME A TUTOR FOR A DES-PERATE, DEPENDENT HIGH SCHOOL HOTTIE, THEN YOU KNOW... THOSE CONFUSED HORMONES MAY JUST START TO ROLL. I MEAN, EVEN SOMEONE LIKE YOU COULD SNEAK SOME ACTION.
Y-Y-YOU REALLY THINK SO?
DEFINITELY! I MEAN, EVEN OUR OWN LITTLE BUNDLE OF PRUDE NARU THERE...
...FELL ROUGH AND HARD FOR HER TUTOR, YOU KNOW!

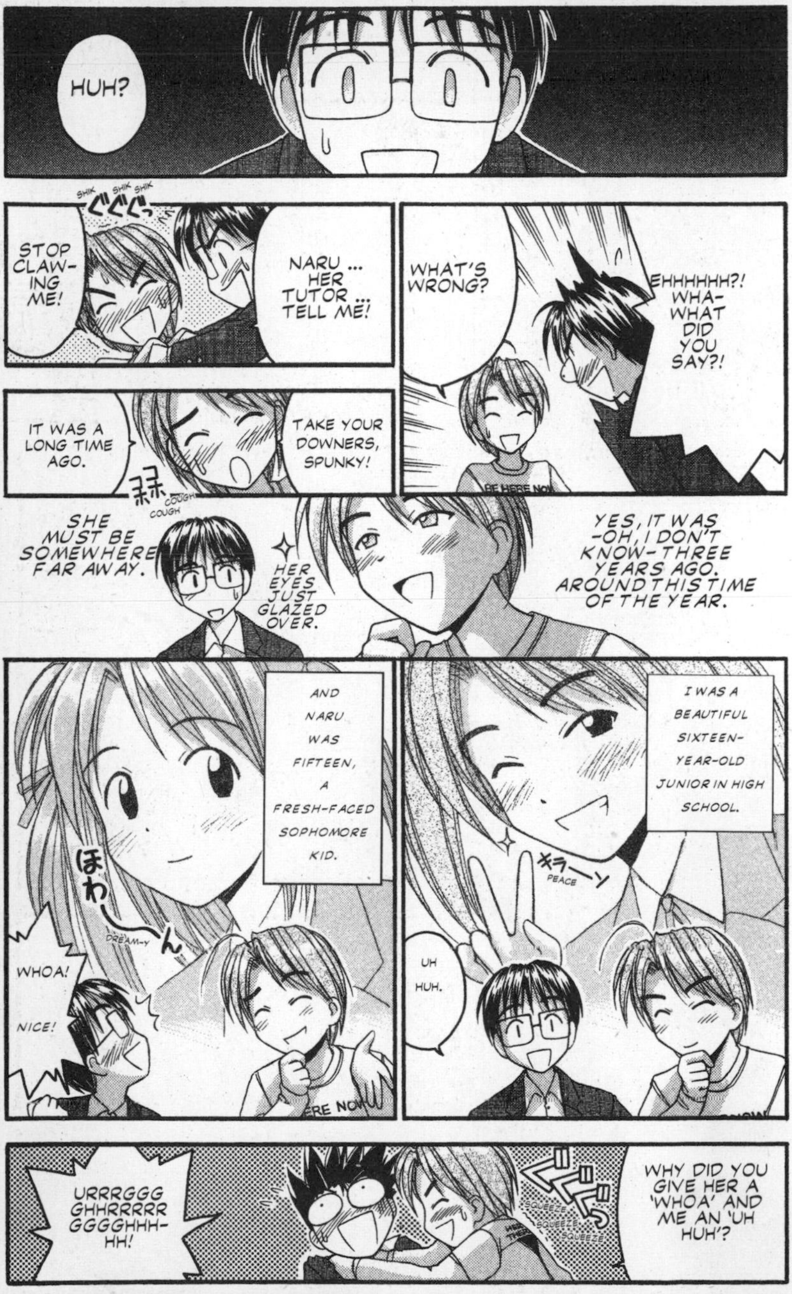
HUH?
WHAT'S WRONG?
EHHHHHH?! WHA-WHAT DID YOU SAY?!
NARU ... HER TUTOR ... TELL ME!
SHIK SHIK SHIK
ぐぐぐっ
STOP CLAWING ME!
TAKE YOUR DOWNERS, SPUNKY!
IT WAS A LONG TIME AGO.
COUGH COUGH
YES, IT WAS -OH, I DON'T KNOW- THREE YEARS AGO. AROUND THIS TIME OF THE YEAR.
HER EYES JUST GLAZED OVER.
SHE MUST BE SOMEWHERE FAR AWAY.
I WAS A BEAUTIFUL SIXTEEN-YEAR-OLD JUNIOR IN HIGH SCHOOL.
キラーン
PEACE
UH HUH.
AND NARU WAS FIFTEEN, A FRESH-FACED SOPHOMORE KID.
ほわーん
DREAM-Y
WHOA!
NICE!
WHY DID YOU GIVE HER A 'WHOA' AND ME AN 'UH HUH'?
SQUEEZE SQUEEZE SQUEEZE
URRRGGG GHHRRRRR GGGGHHH-HH!

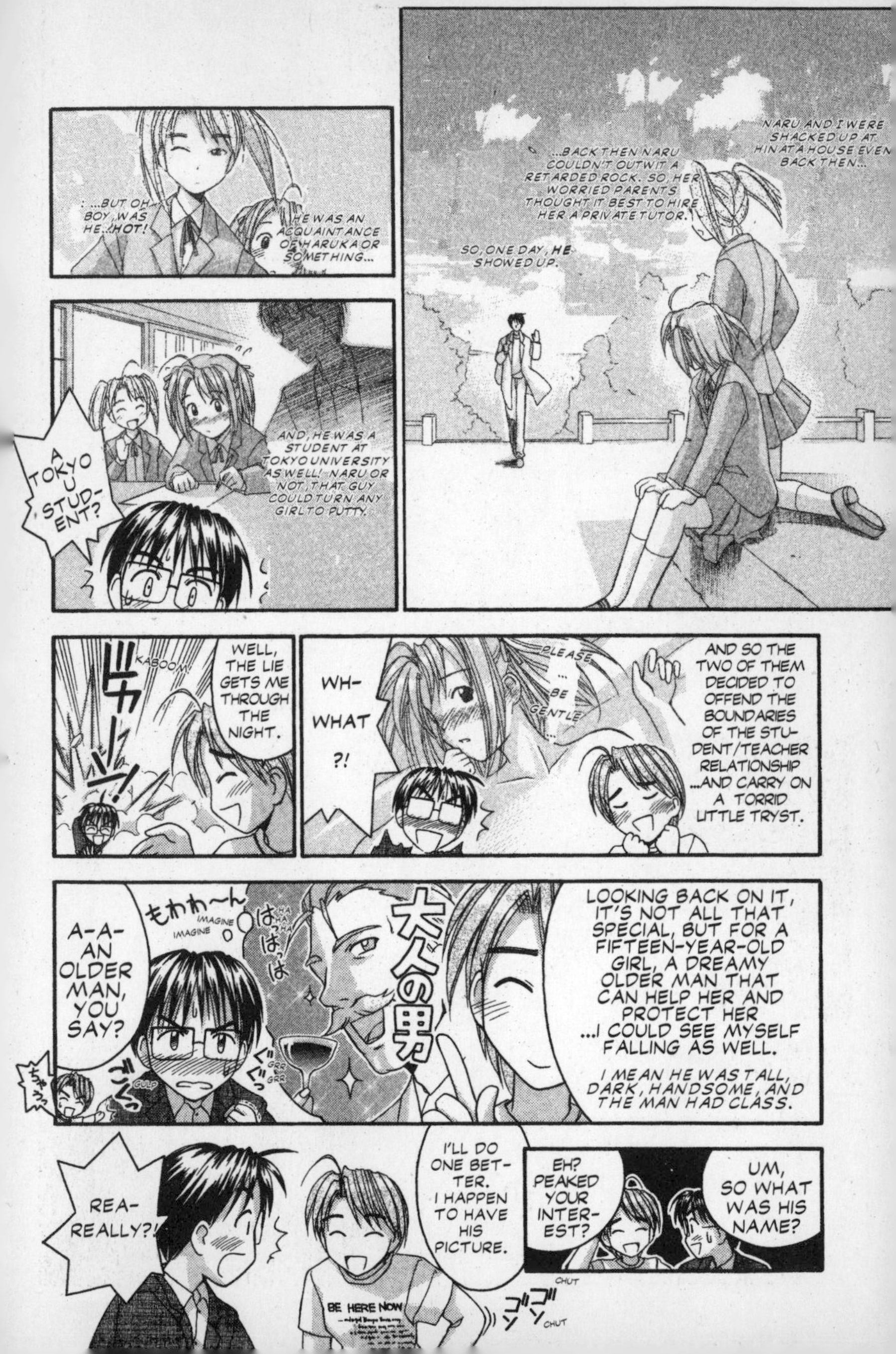

NARU AND I WERE SHACKED UP AT HINATA HOUSE EVEN BACK THEN...
...BACK THEN NARU COULDN'T OUTWIT A RETARDED ROCK. SO, HER WORRIED PARENTS THOUGHT IT BEST TO HIRE HER A PRIVATE TUTOR.
SO, ONE DAY, HE SHOWED UP.
HE WAS AN ACQUAINTANCE OF HARUKA OR SOMETHING...
...BUT OH BOY, WAS HE...HOT!
AND, HE WAS A STUDENT AT TOKYO UNIVERSITY AS WELL! NARU OR NOT, THAT GUY COULD TURN ANY GIRL TO PUTTY.
A TOKYO U STUDENT?
AND SO THE TWO OF THEM DECIDED TO OFFEND THE BOUNDARIES OF THE STUDENT/TEACHER RELATIONSHIP ...AND CARRY ON A TORRID LITTLE TRYST.
PLEASE... BE GENTLE...
WH-WHAT?!
WELL, THE LIE GETS ME THROUGH THE NIGHT.
ドカーン!
KABOOM
LOOKING BACK ON IT, IT'S NOT ALL THAT SPECIAL, BUT FOR A FIFTEEN-YEAR-OLD GIRL, A DREAMY OLDER MAN THAT CAN HELP HER AND PROTECT HER ...I COULD SEE MYSELF FALLING AS WELL.
I MEAN AN HE WAS TALL, DARK, HANDSOME, AND THE MAN HAD CLASS.
大人の男
はっはっは
HA HA HA
ぐぐっ
GRR GRR
もわわ~ん
IMAGINE IMAGINE
A-A-AN OLDER MAN, YOU SAY?
ごくっ
GULP
UM, SO WHAT WAS HIS NAME?
EH? PEAKED YOUR INTEREST?
I'LL DO ONE BETTER. I HAPPEN TO HAVE HIS PICTURE.
REA-REALLY?!
BE HERE NOW
ゴソゴソ
CHUT CHUT

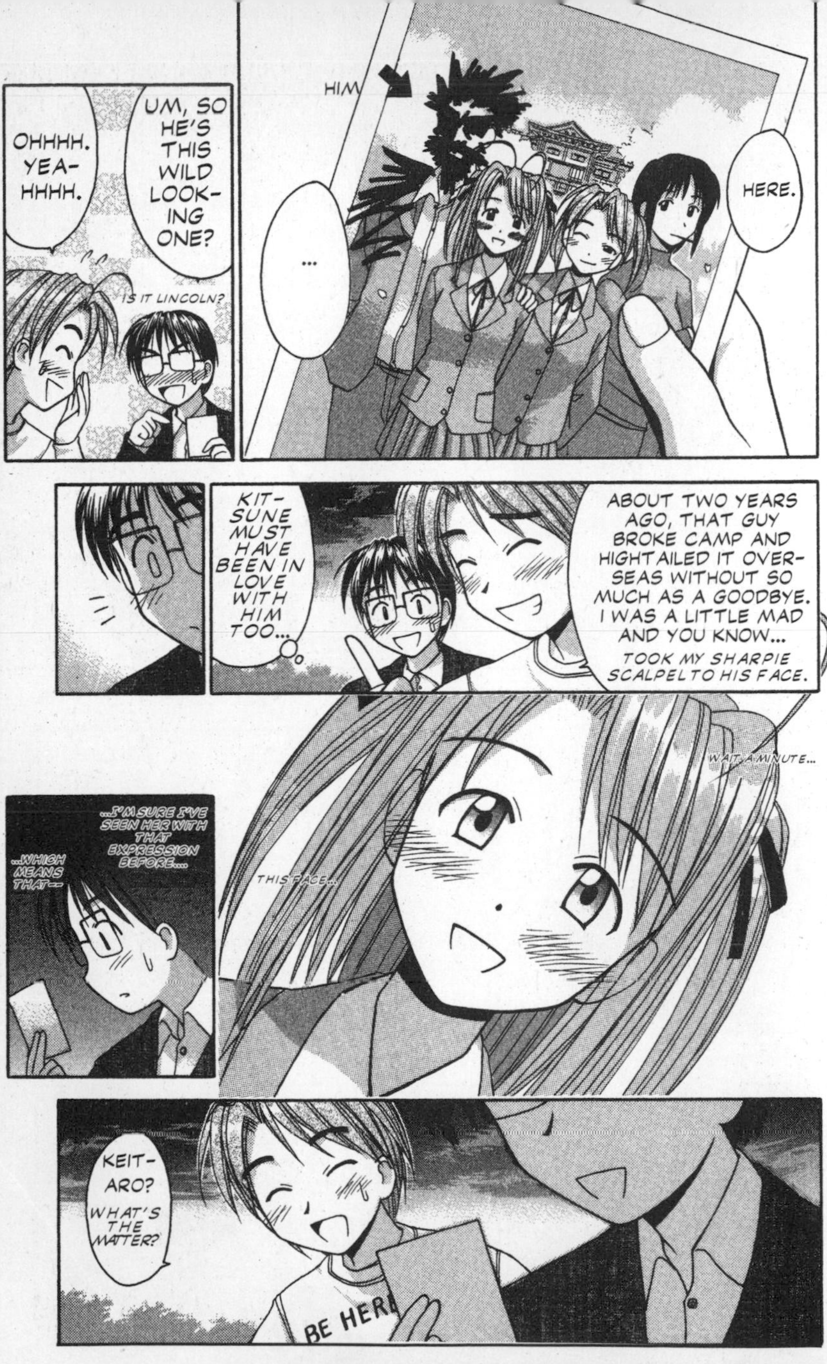
HERE.
HIM
...
UM, SO HE'S THIS WILD LOOKING-ING ONE?
OHHHH. YEA-HHHH.
IS IT LINCOLN?
ABOUT TWO YEARS AGO, THAT GUY BROKE CAMP AND HIGHTAILED IT OVER-SEAS WITHOUT SO MUCH AS A GOODBYE. I WAS A LITTLE MAD AND YOU KNOW...
TOOK MY SHARPIE SCALPEL TO HIS FACE.
KIT-SUNE MUST HAVE BEEN IN LOVE WITH HIM TOO...
WAIT A MINUTE...
THIS FACE...
...I'M SURE I'VE SEEN HER WITH THAT EXPRESSION BEFORE...
...WHICH MEANS THAT--
KEIT-ARO?
WHAT'S THE MATTER?
BE HERE

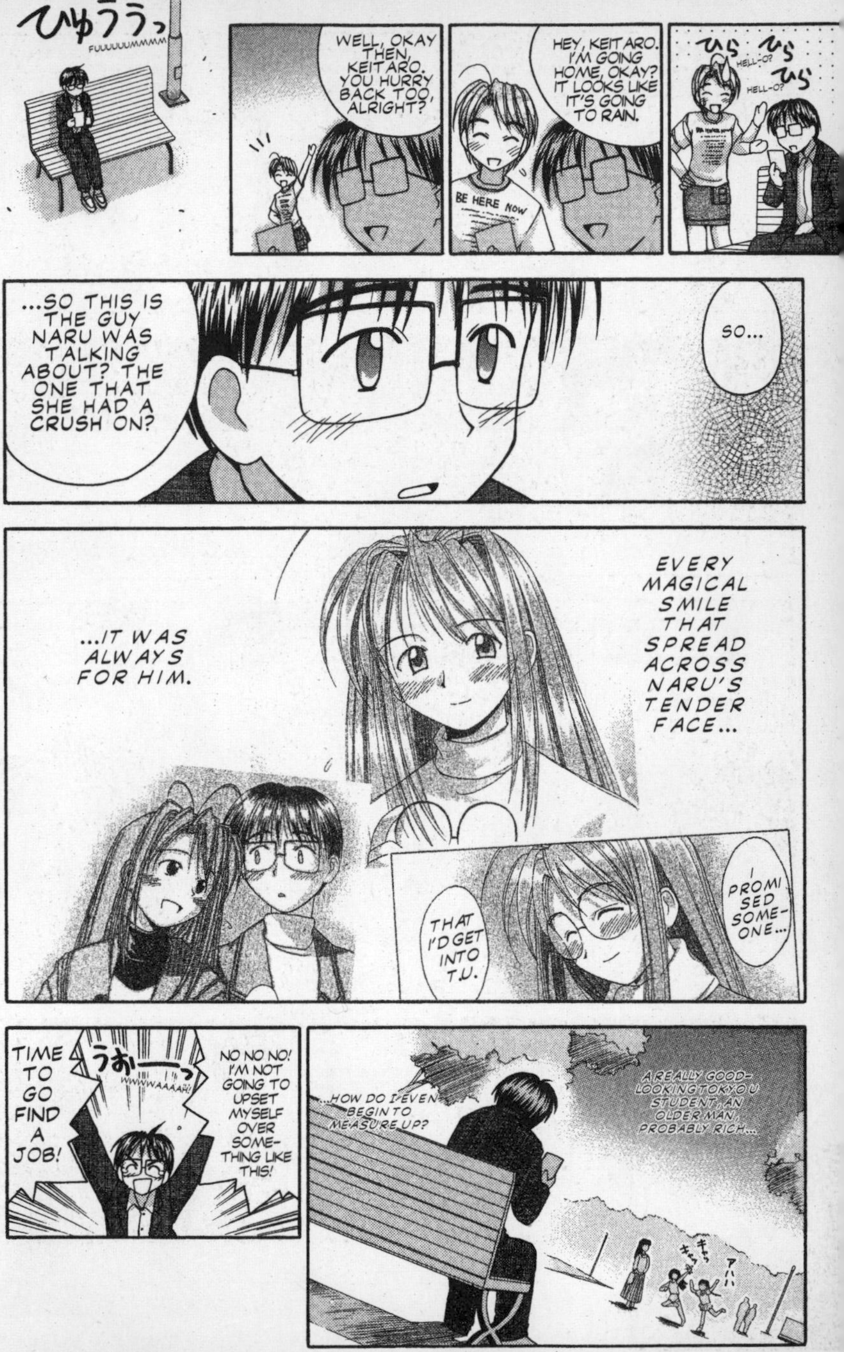

ひら ひら ひら
HELL-O?
HELL-O?
HEY, KEITARO. I'M GOING HOME, OKAY? IT LOOKS LIKE IT'S GOING TO RAIN.
BE HERE NOW
WELL, OKAY THEN, KEITARO. YOU HURRY BACK TOO, ALRIGHT?
ひゅううっ
FUUUUUUMMMM
SO...
...SO THIS IS THE GUY NARU WAS TALKING ABOUT? THE ONE THAT SHE HAD A CRUSH ON?
EVERY MAGICAL SMILE THAT SPREAD ACROSS NARU'S TENDER FACE...
...IT WAS ALWAYS FOR HIM.
I PROMISED SOMEONE...
THAT I'D GET INTO T.U.
A REALLY GOOD-LOOKING TOKYO U STUDENT, AN OLDER MAN, PROBABLY RICH...
...HOW DO I EVEN BEGIN TO MEASURE UP?
アハハ
NO NO NO! I'M NOT GOING TO UPSET MYSELF OVER SOMETHING LIKE THIS!
うおーっ
WWWWAAAAH!
TIME TO GO FIND A JOB!

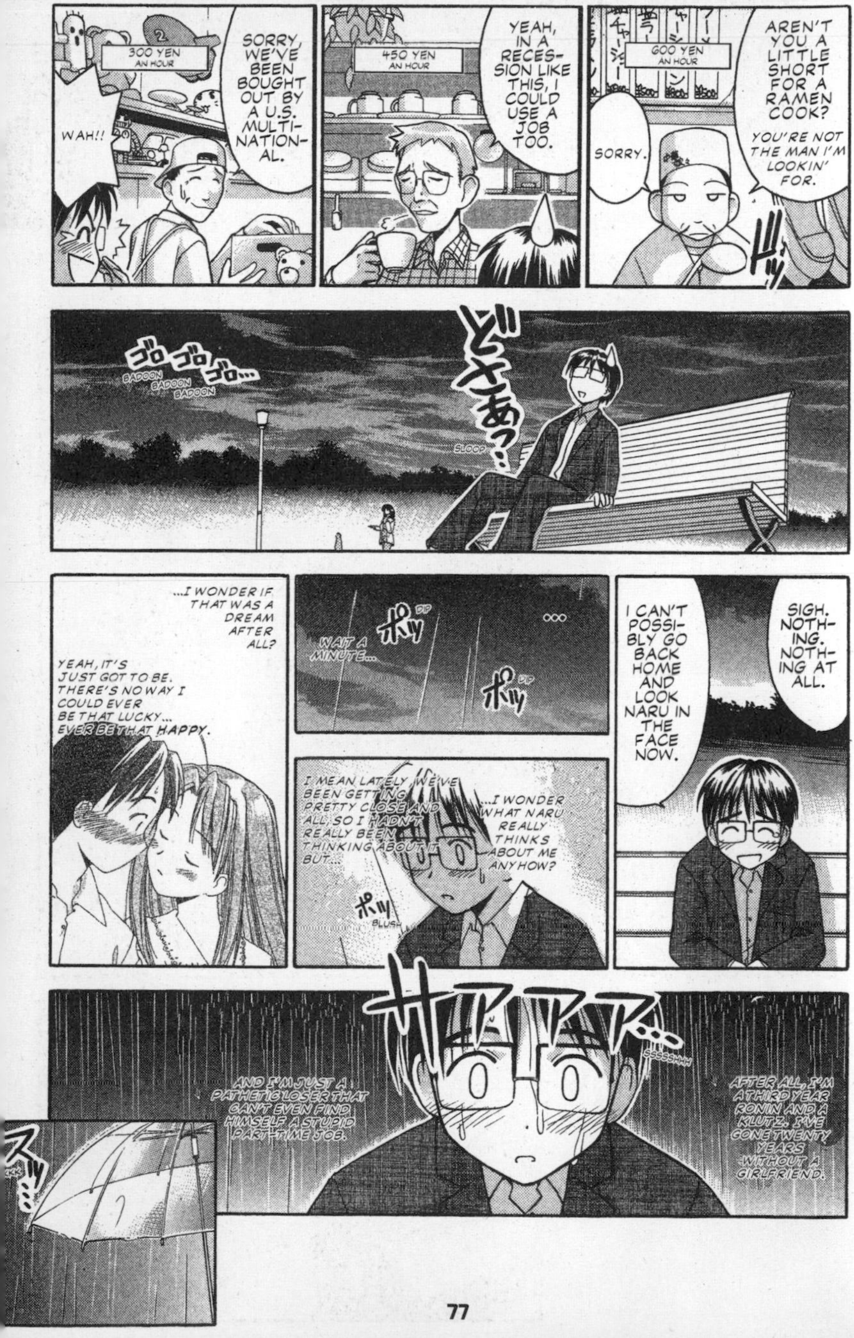
600 YEN AN HOUR
AREN'T YOU A LITTLE SHORT FOR A RAMEN COOK?
YOU'RE NOT THE MAN I'M LOOKIN' FOR.
SORRY.
450 YEN AN HOUR
YEAH, IN A RECESSION LIKE THIS, I COULD USE A JOB TOO.
300 YEN AN HOUR
SORRY, WE'VE BEEN BOUGHT OUT BY A U.S. MULTINATIONAL.
WAH!!
どさあっ
SLOOP
ゴロゴロゴロ…
BADOON BADOON BADOON
SIGH. NOTHING. NOTHING AT ALL.
I CAN'T POSSIBLY GO BACK HOME AND LOOK NARU IN THE FACE NOW.
…
WAIT A MINUTE...
ポツ
DIP
ポツ
DIP
...I WONDER WHAT NARU REALLY THINKS ABOUT ME ANYHOW?
I MEAN LATELY, WE'VE BEEN GETTING PRETTY CLOSE AND ALL, SO I HADN'T REALLY BEEN THINKING ABOUT IT BUT...
ポッ
BLUSH
...I WONDER IF THAT WAS A DREAM AFTER ALL?
YEAH, IT'S JUST GOT TO BE. THERE'S NO WAY I COULD EVER BE THAT LUCKY... EVER BE THAT HAPPY.
ザァァァ…
SSSSSHHH
AFTER ALL, I'M A THIRD YEAR RONIN AND A KLUTZ. I'VE GONE TWENTY YEARS WITHOUT A GIRLFRIEND.
AND I'M JUST A PATHETIC LOSER THAT CAN'T EVEN FIND HIMSELF A STUPID PART-TIME JOB.
スッ…

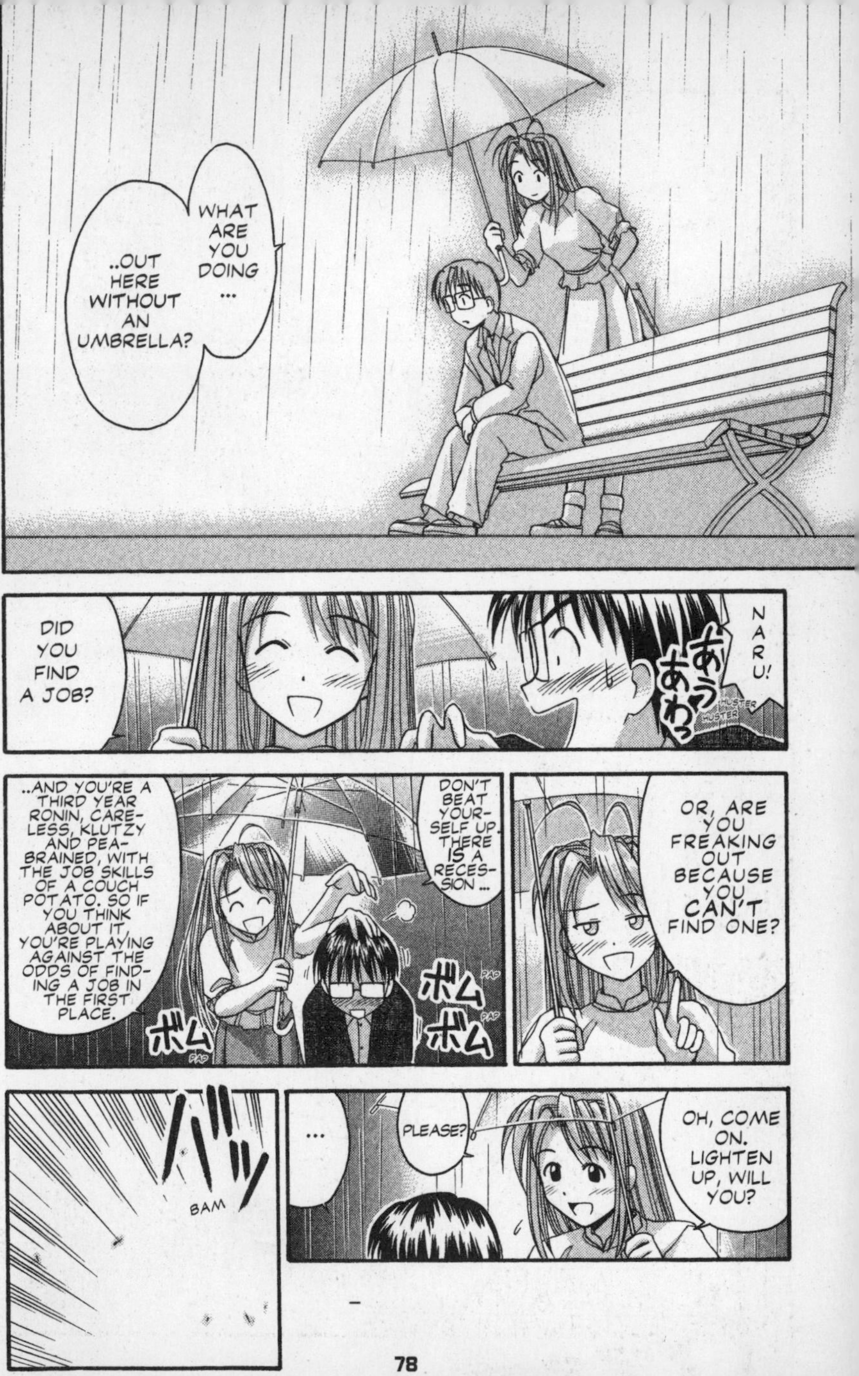
WHAT ARE YOU DOING ...
..OUT HERE WITHOUT AN UMBRELLA?
NARU!
あうあわっ
HUSTER HUSTER
DID YOU FIND A JOB?
OR, ARE YOU FREAKING OUT BECAUSE YOU CAN'T FIND ONE?
DON'T BEAT YOURSELF UP. THERE IS A RECESSION ...
..AND YOU'RE A THIRD YEAR RONIN, CARELESS, KLUTZY AND PEA-BRAINED, WITH THE JOB SKILLS OF A COUCH POTATO. SO IF YOU THINK ABOUT IT, YOU'RE PLAYING AGAINST THE ODDS OF FINDING A JOB IN THE FIRST PLACE.
ボム PAP
ボム PAP
ボム PAP
OH, COME ON. LIGHTEN UP, WILL YOU?
PLEASE?
...
バッ
BAM

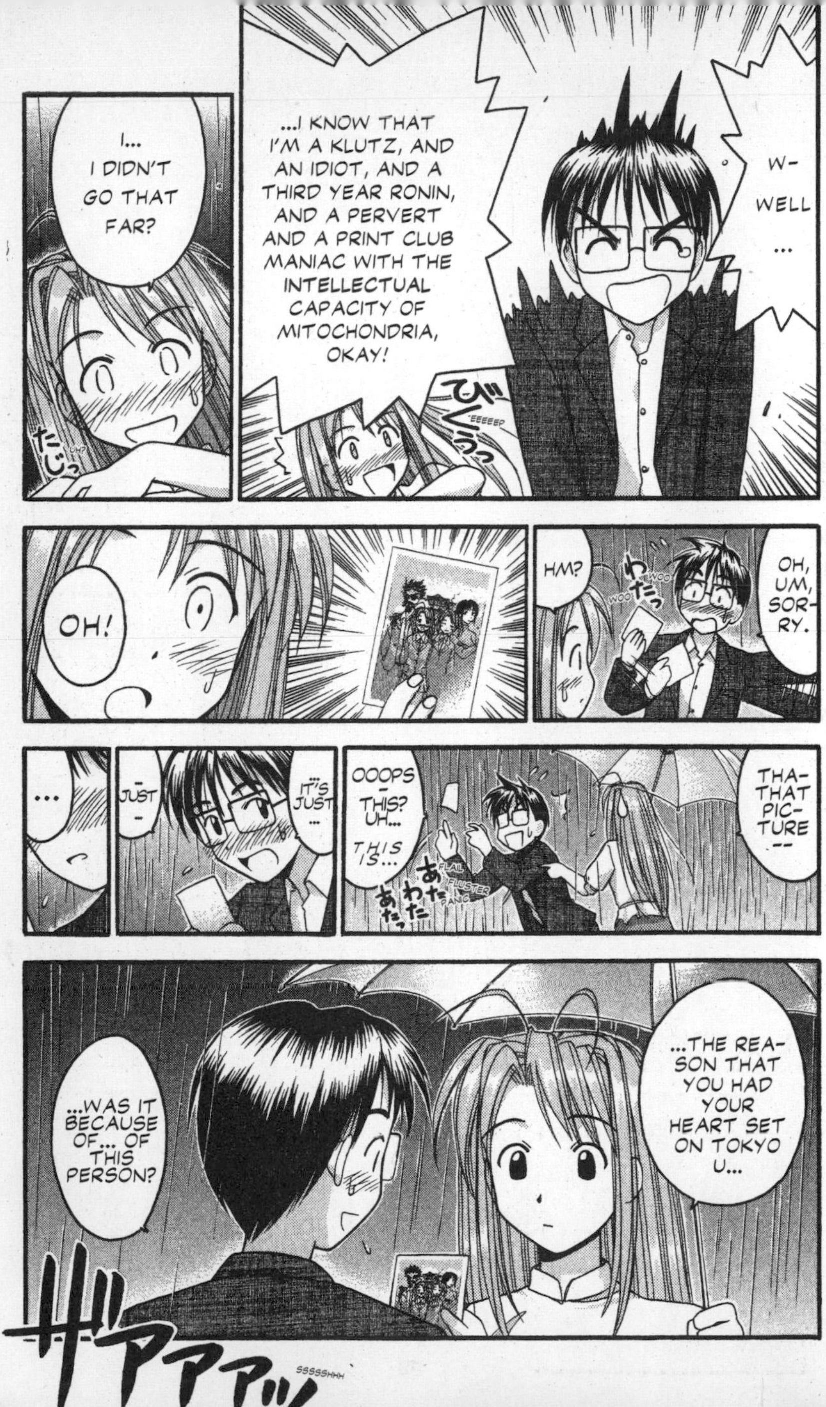
W- WELL ...
...I KNOW THAT I'M A KLUTZ, AND AN IDIOT, AND A THIRD YEAR RONIN, AND A PERVERT AND A PRINT CLUB MANIAC WITH THE INTELLECTUAL CAPACITY OF MITOCHONDRIA, OKAY!
びくうっ
EEEEEP
I... I DIDN'T GO THAT FAR?
たじっ
UH?
OH, UM, SORRY.
HM?
わたっ
WOO WOO
OH!
THA-THAT PICTURE --
OOOPS - THIS? UH...
THIS IS...
あたわた あたわたっ
FLAIL FLUSTER PANIC
...IT'S JUST ...
- JUST -
...
...THE REASON THAT YOU HAD YOUR HEART SET ON TOKYO U...
...WAS IT BECAUSE OF... OF THIS PERSON?
ザアアアッ
SSSSSHHH

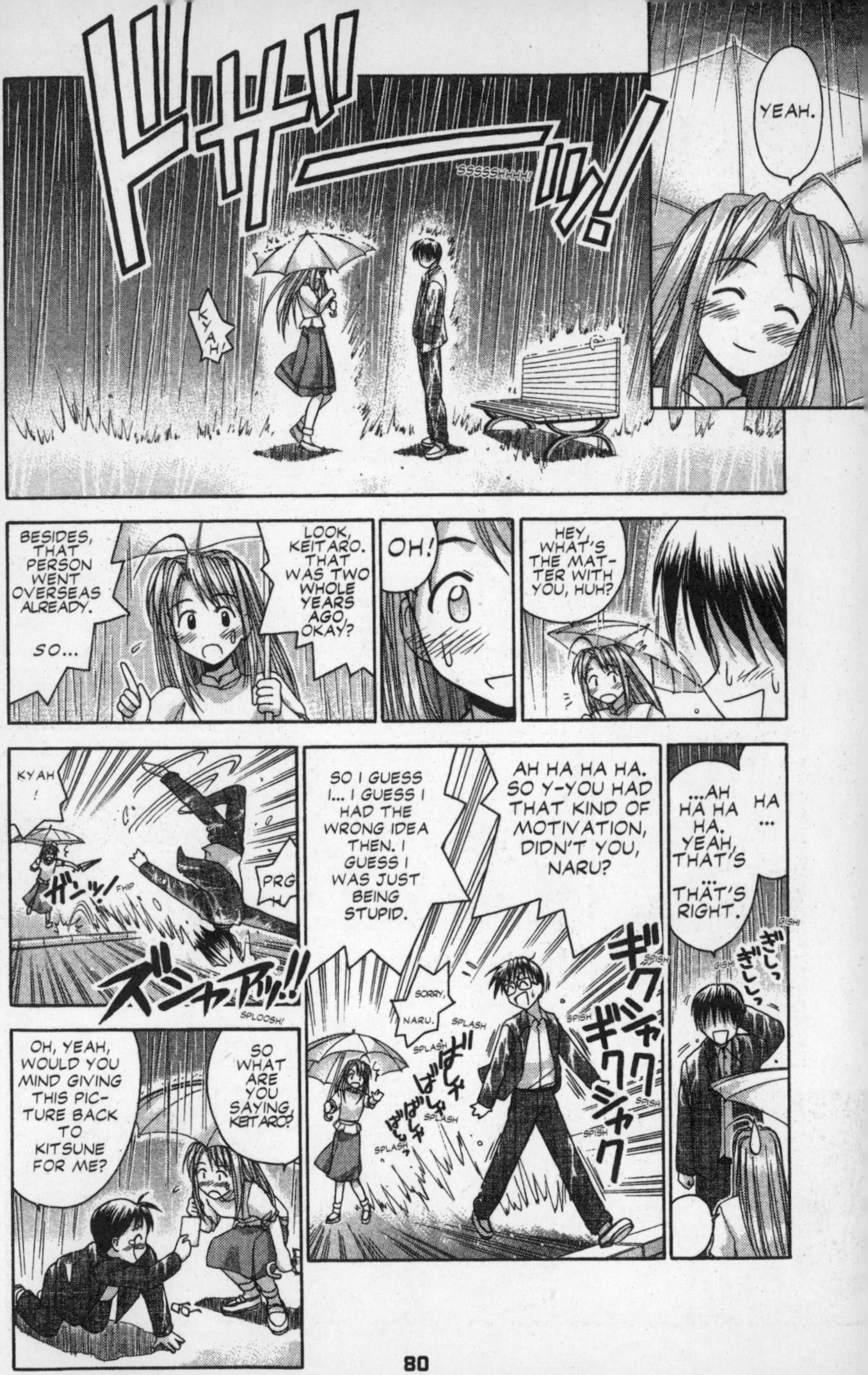
YEAH.
SSSSSHHHH!
KYAH!
HEY, WHAT'S THE MAT-TER WITH YOU, HUH?
OH!
LOOK, KEITARO. THAT WAS TWO WHOLE YEARS AGO, OKAY?
BESIDES, THAT PERSON WENT OVERSEAS ALREADY.
SO...
HA ...
...AH HA HA HA. YEAH, THAT'S ... THAT'S RIGHT.
GISHI
GISHI
AH HA HA HA. SO Y-YOU HAD THAT KIND OF MOTIVATION, DIDN'T YOU, NARU?
SO I GUESS I... I GUESS I HAD THE WRONG IDEA THEN. I GUESS I WAS JUST BEING STUPID.
SPISH
SPISH
SORRY, NARU.
SPLASH
SPLASH
SPISH
SPISH
SPLASH
SPLASH
KYAH!
PRG HU
FHIP
SPLOOSH!
SO WHAT ARE YOU SAYING, KEITARO?
OH, YEAH, WOULD YOU MIND GIVING THIS PIC-TURE BACK TO KITSUNE FOR ME?

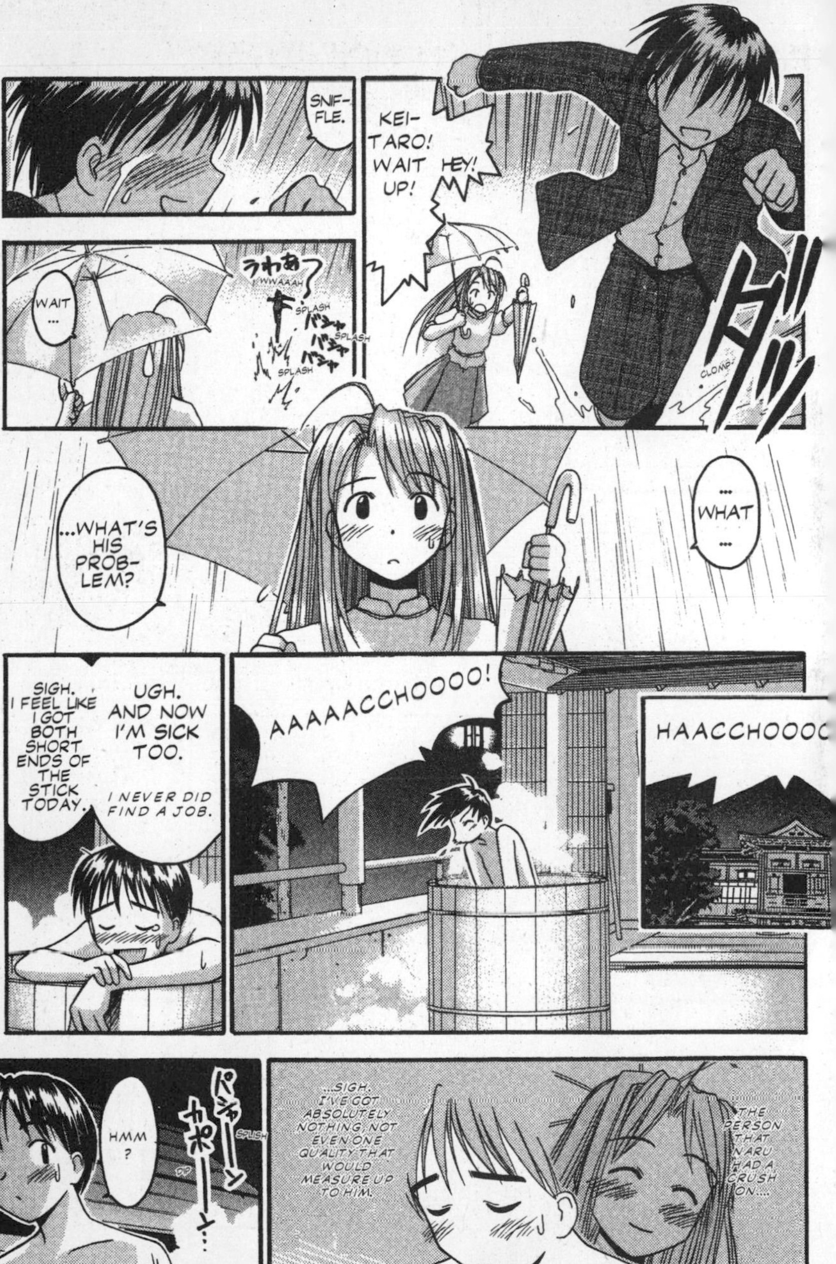
KEI-TARO! WAIT UP!
HEY!
ダッ
CLOMP
SNIF-FLE.
うわあっ
WWAAAH
バシャ
SPLASH
バシャ
SPLASH
バシャ
SPLASH
WAIT...
...WHAT...
...WHAT'S HIS PROB-LEM?
HAACCHOOOO
AAAAACCHOOOO!
UGH. AND NOW I'M SICK TOO.
I NEVER DID FIND A JOB.
SIGH. I FEEL LIKE I GOT BOTH SHORT ENDS OF THE STICK TODAY.
THE PERSON THAT NARU HAD A CRUSH ON....
...SIGH. I'VE GOT ABSOLUTELY NOTHING, NOT EVEN ONE QUALITY THAT WOULD MEASURE UP TO HIM.
パシャーン
SPLISH
カポーン...
DIP
HMM?

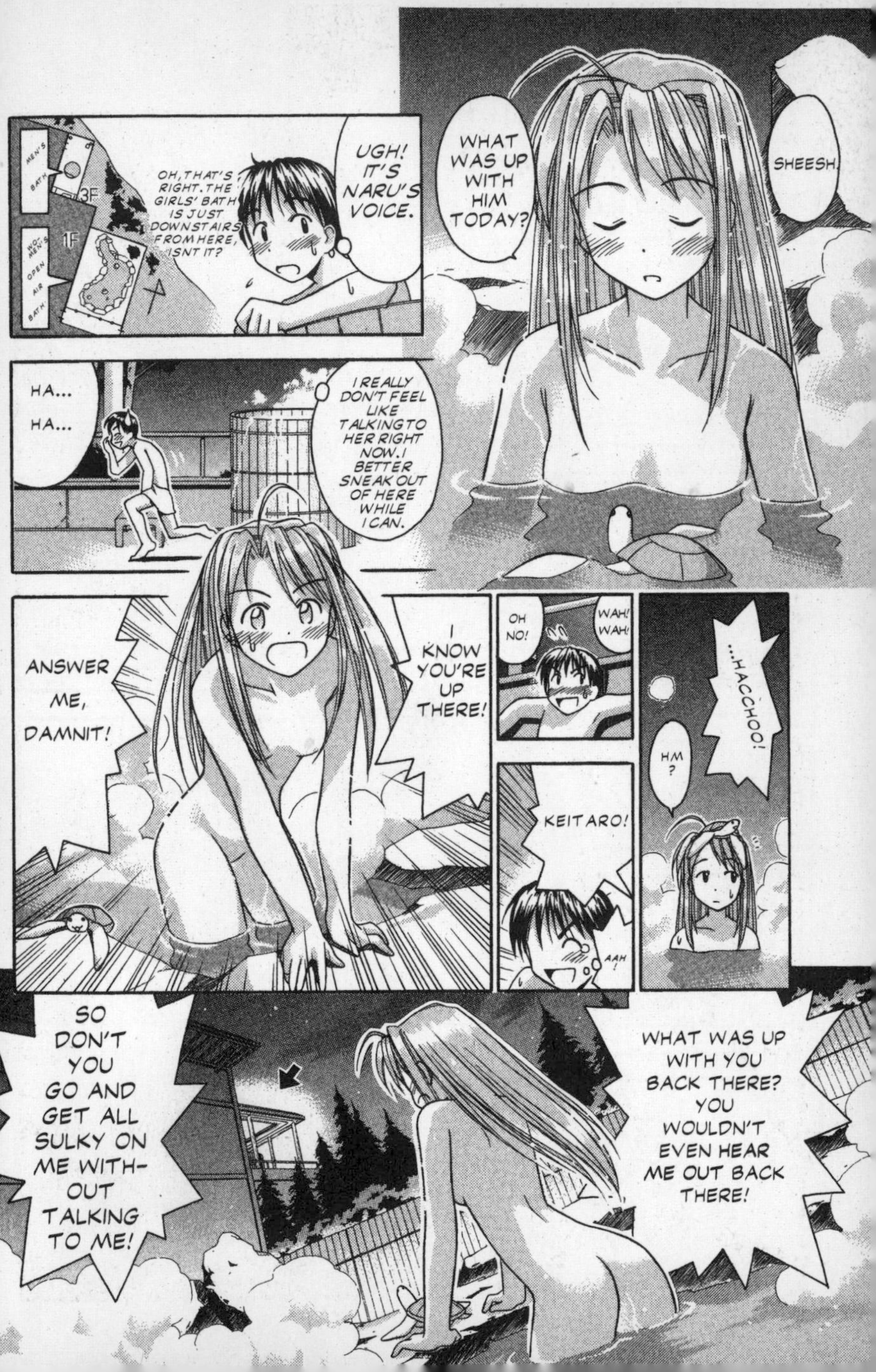
SHEESH.
WHAT WAS UP WITH HIM TODAY?
UGH! IT'S NARU'S VOICE.
OH, THAT'S RIGHT. THE GIRLS' BATH IS JUST DOWNSTAIRS FROM HERE, ISNT IT?
MEN'S BATH
3F
WOMEN'S OPEN AIR BATH
1F
I REALLY DON'T FEEL LIKE TALKING TO HER RIGHT NOW. I BETTER SNEAK OUT OF HERE WHILE I CAN.
HA... HA...
...HACCHOO!
HM?
WAH! WAH!
OH NO!
KEITARO!
AAH!
I KNOW YOU'RE UP THERE!
ANSWER ME, DAMNIT!
WHAT WAS UP WITH YOU BACK THERE? YOU WOULDN'T EVEN HEAR ME OUT BACK THERE!
SO DON'T YOU GO AND GET ALL SULKY ON ME WITH-OUT TALKING TO ME!

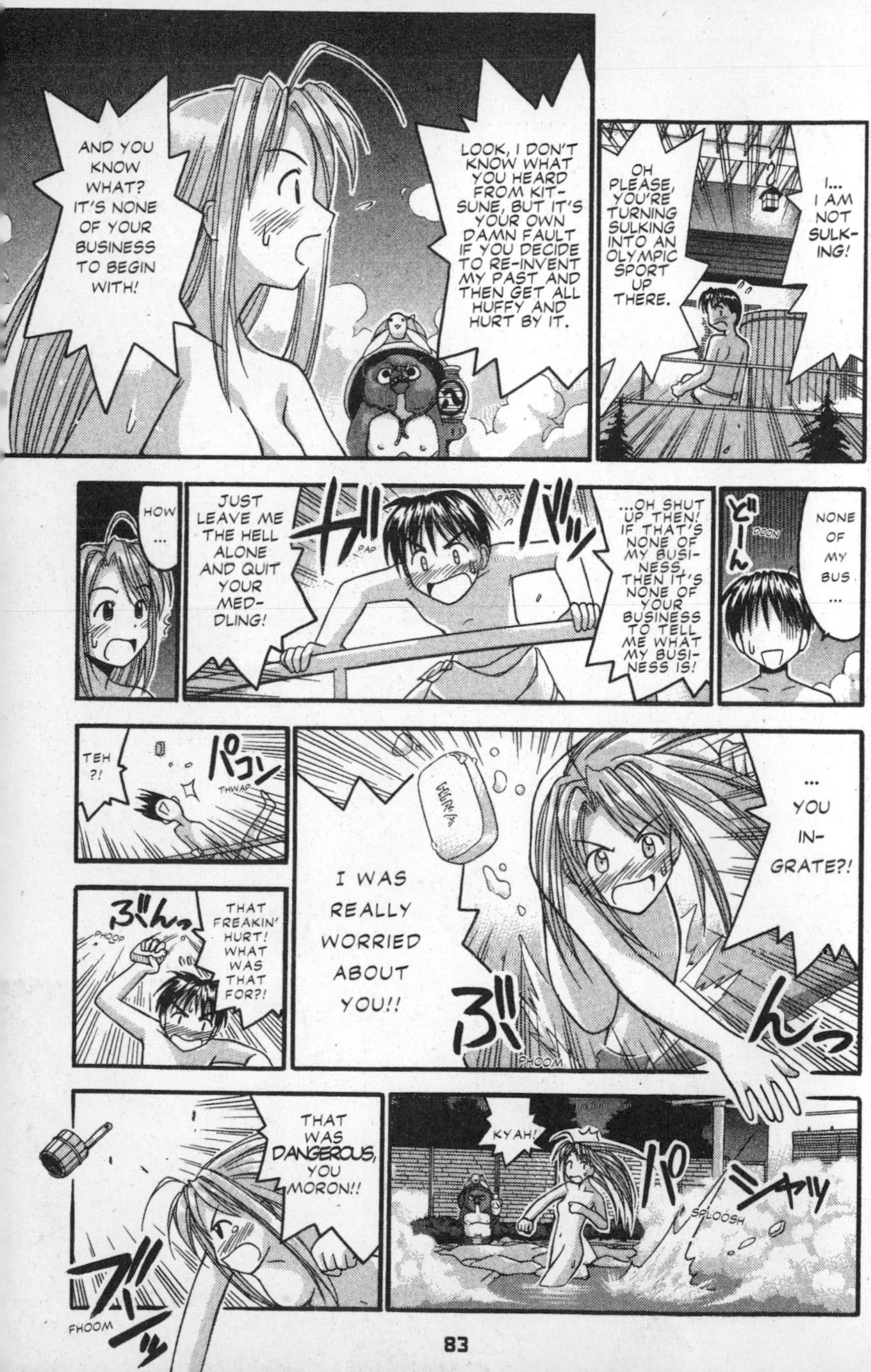
I... I AM NOT SULKING!
OH PLEASE, YOU'RE TURNING SULKING INTO AN OLYMPIC SPORT UP THERE.
LOOK, I DON'T KNOW WHAT YOU HEARD FROM KIT-SUNE, BUT IT'S YOUR OWN DAMN FAULT IF YOU DECIDE TO RE-INVENT MY PAST AND THEN GET ALL HUFFY AND HURT BY IT.
AND YOU KNOW WHAT? IT'S NONE OF YOUR BUSINESS TO BEGIN WITH!
NONE OF MY BUS...
DOON
...OH SHUT UP THEN! IF THAT'S NONE OF MY BUSI-NESS, THEN IT'S NONE OF YOUR BUSINESS TO TELL ME WHAT MY BUSI-NESS IS!
PAP
JUST LEAVE ME THE HELL ALONE AND QUIT YOUR MED-DLING!
PAP
HOW ...
... YOU IN-GRATE?!
I WAS REALLY WORRIED ABOUT YOU!!
PHOOM
TEH ?!
THWAP
THAT FREAKIN' HURT! WHAT WAS THAT FOR?!
PHOOP
KYAH!
SPLOOSH
THAT WAS DANGEROUS, YOU MORON!!
FHOOM

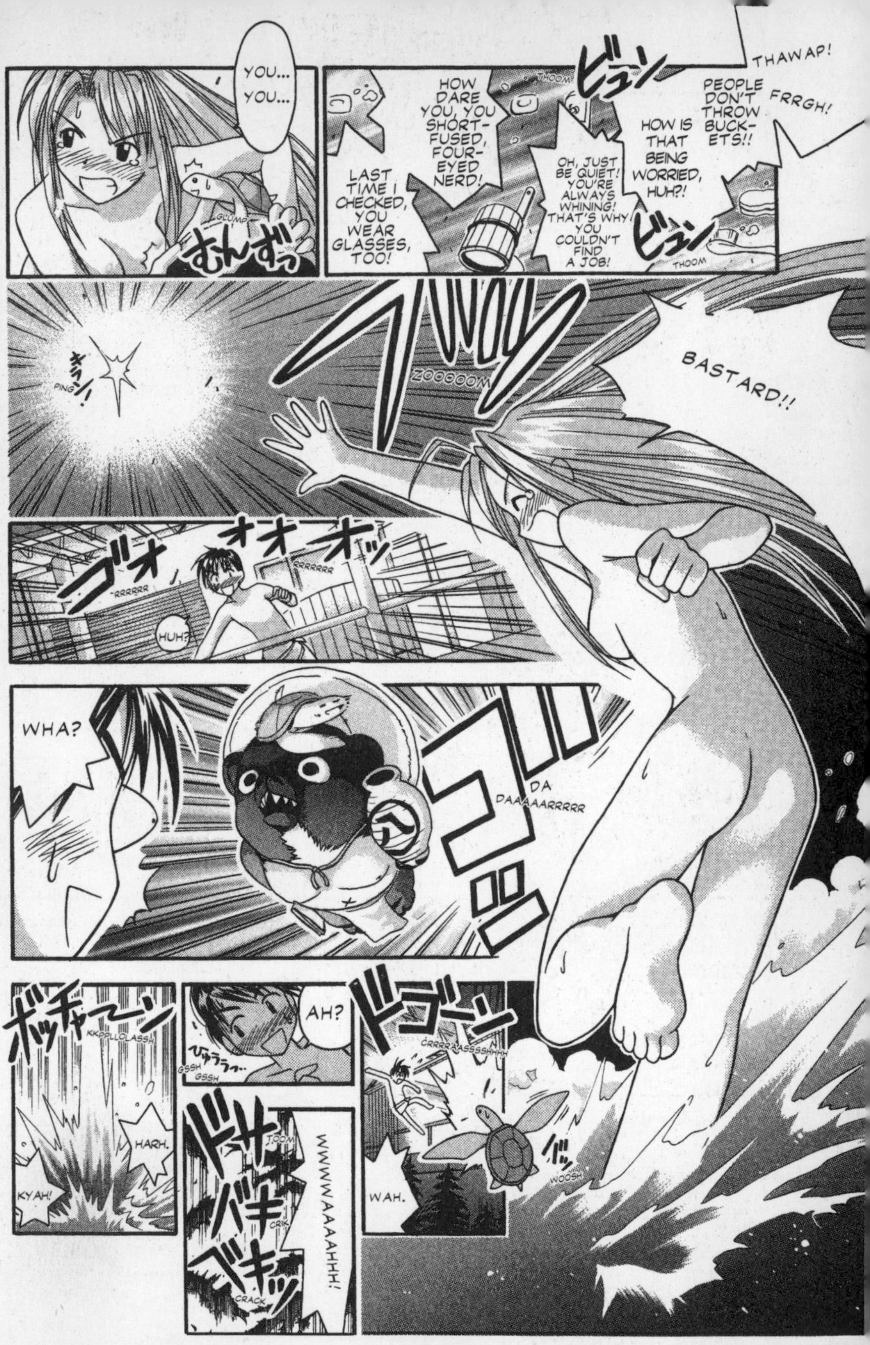
THAWAP!
PEOPLE DON'T THROW BUCK-ETS!!
FRRGH!
ビュン
THOOM
HOW IS THAT BEING WORRIED, HUH?!
ビュン
THOOM
OH, JUST BE QUIET! YOU'RE ALWAYS WHINING! THAT'S WHY YOU COULDN'T FIND A JOB!
HOW DARE YOU, YOU SHORT-FUSED, FOUR-EYED NERD!
LAST TIME I CHECKED, YOU WEAR GLASSES, TOO!
YOU... YOU...
GLUMP
むんずっ
BASTARD!!
ZOOOOOOM
キラン!
PING
ゴオオオッ
RRRRRRR
RRRRRR
HUH?
DA DAAAAARRRRR
WHA?
ドゴーン
CRRRRAASSSSHHHH
WAH.
WOOSH
AH?
GSSH GSSH
ボッチャーン
KKPPLLOLASSH
WWWWAAAAHHH!
TOOM
CRIK
CRACK
HARH.
KYAH!

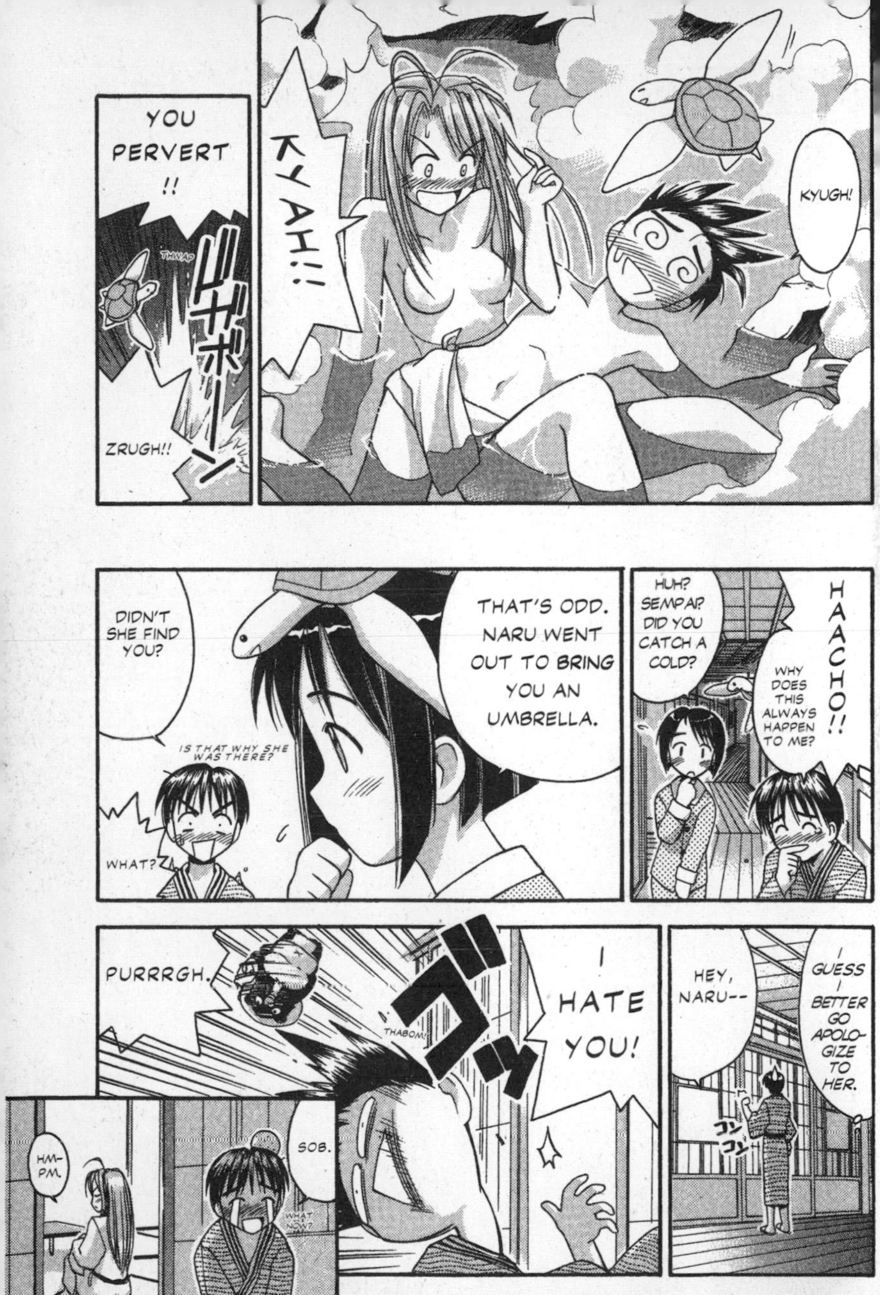
KYUGH!
KYAH!!!
YOU PERVERT !!
THWAP
ZRUGH!!
HAACHO!!
HUH? SEMPAI? DID YOU CATCH A COLD?
WHY DOES THIS ALWAYS HAPPEN TO ME?
THAT'S ODD. NARU WENT OUT TO BRING YOU AN UMBRELLA.
DIDN'T SHE FIND YOU?
IS THAT WHY SHE WAS THERE?
WHAT?
I GUESS I BETTER GO APOLOGIZE TO HER.
HEY, NARU--
I HATE YOU!
THABOM!
PURRRGH.
SOB.
WHAT NOW?
HM-PM.

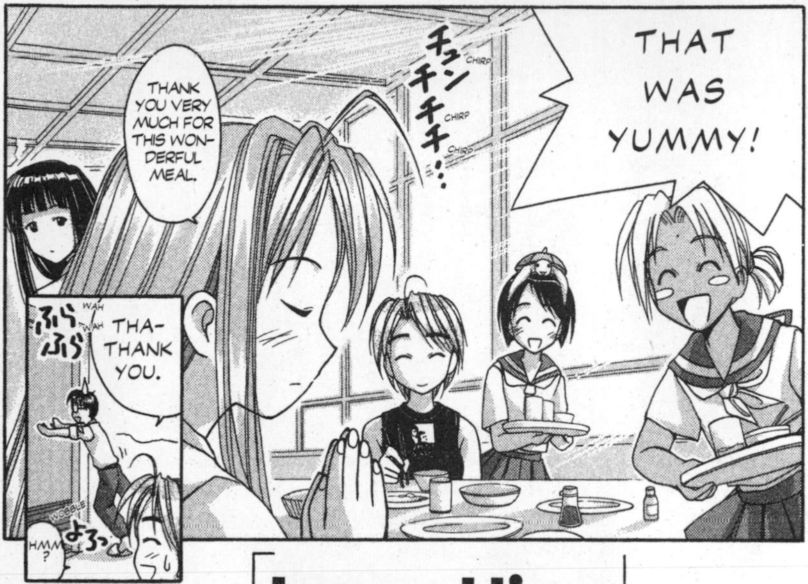
THAT WAS YUMMY!
CHIRP
CHIRP
CHIRP
THANK YOU VERY MUCH FOR THIS WONDERFUL MEAL.
WAH
WAH
THA-THANK YOU.
WOBBLE
HMM?

Love Hina

HINATA.29 HELP! Working Part-Time is a Killer

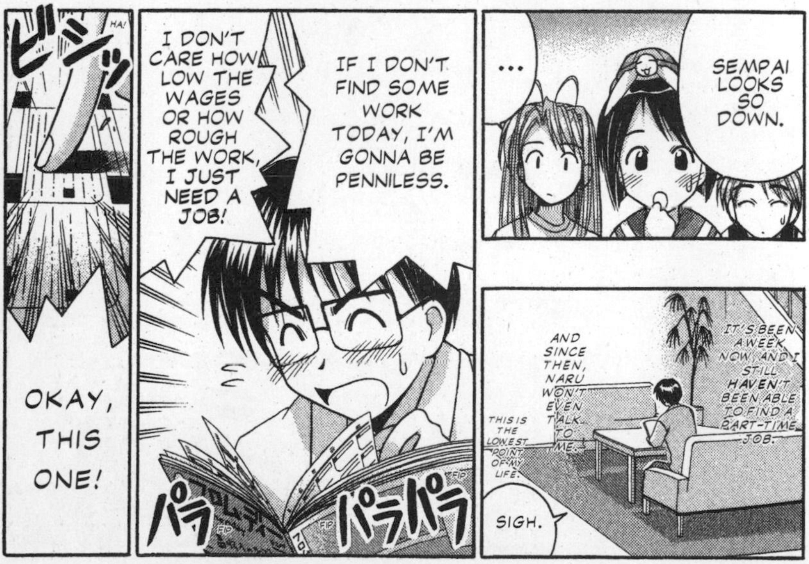
SEMPAI LOOKS SO DOWN.
...
IT'S BEEN A WEEK NOW, AND I STILL HAVEN'T BEEN ABLE TO FIND A PART-TIME JOB.
AND SINCE THEN, NARU WON'T EVEN TALK TO ME.
THIS IS THE LOWEST POINT OF MY LIFE.
SIGH.
IF I DON'T FIND SOME WORK TODAY, I'M GONNA BE PENNILESS.
I DON'T CARE HOW LOW THE WAGES OR HOW ROUGH THE WORK, I JUST NEED A JOB!
FLIP
FLIP
FLIP
HA!
OKAY, THIS ONE!

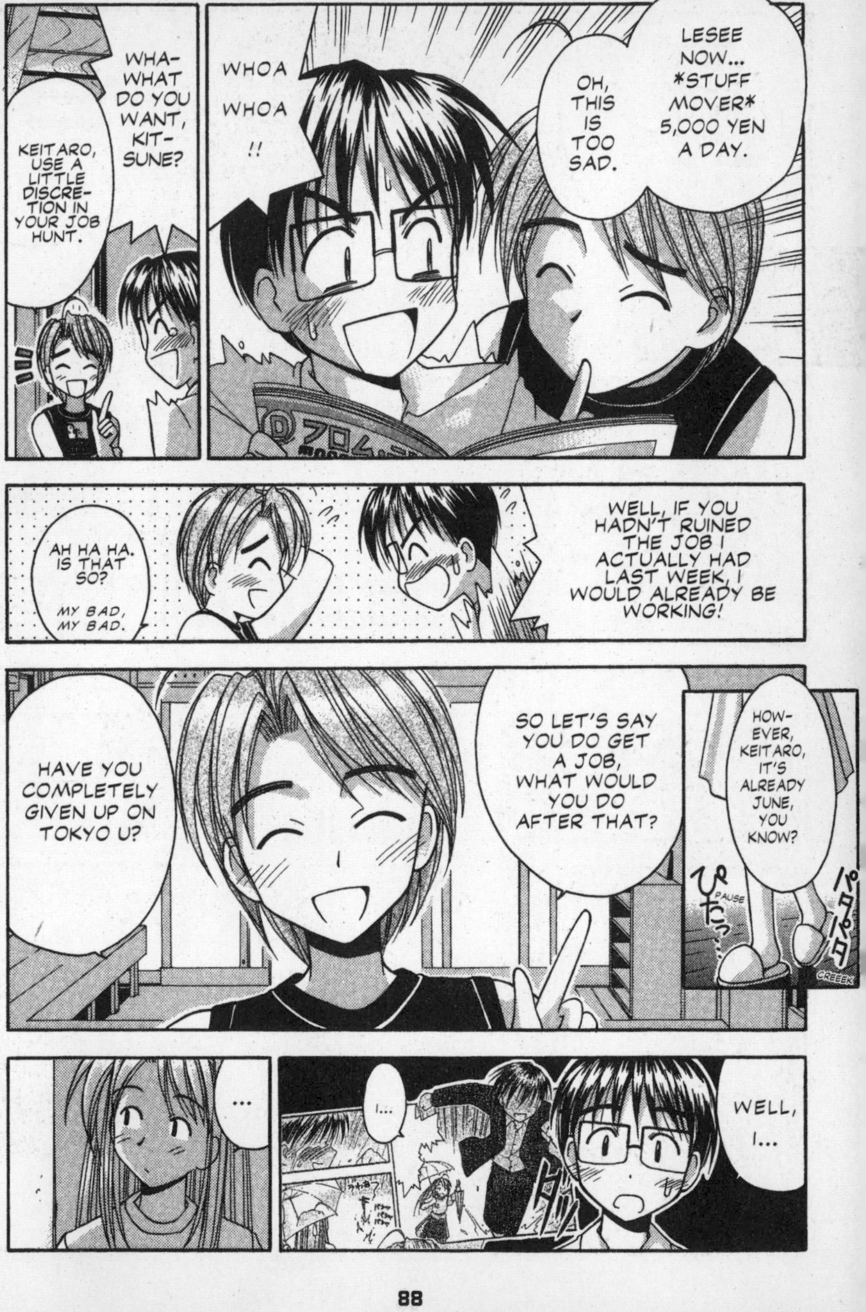
LESEE NOW... *STUFF MOVER* 5,000 YEN A DAY.
OH, THIS IS TOO SAD.
WHOA WHOA !!
WHA-WHAT DO YOU WANT, KIT-SUNE?
KEITARO, USE A LITTLE DISCRETION IN YOUR JOB HUNT.
WELL, IF YOU HADN'T RUINED THE JOB I ACTUALLY HAD LAST WEEK, I WOULD ALREADY BE WORKING!
AH HA HA. IS THAT SO?
MY BAD, MY BAD.
HOW-EVER, KEITARO, IT'S ALREADY JUNE, YOU KNOW?
PAUSE
CREEEK
SO LET'S SAY YOU DO GET A JOB, WHAT WOULD YOU DO AFTER THAT?
HAVE YOU COMPLETELY GIVEN UP ON TOKYO U?
WELL, I...
I...
...

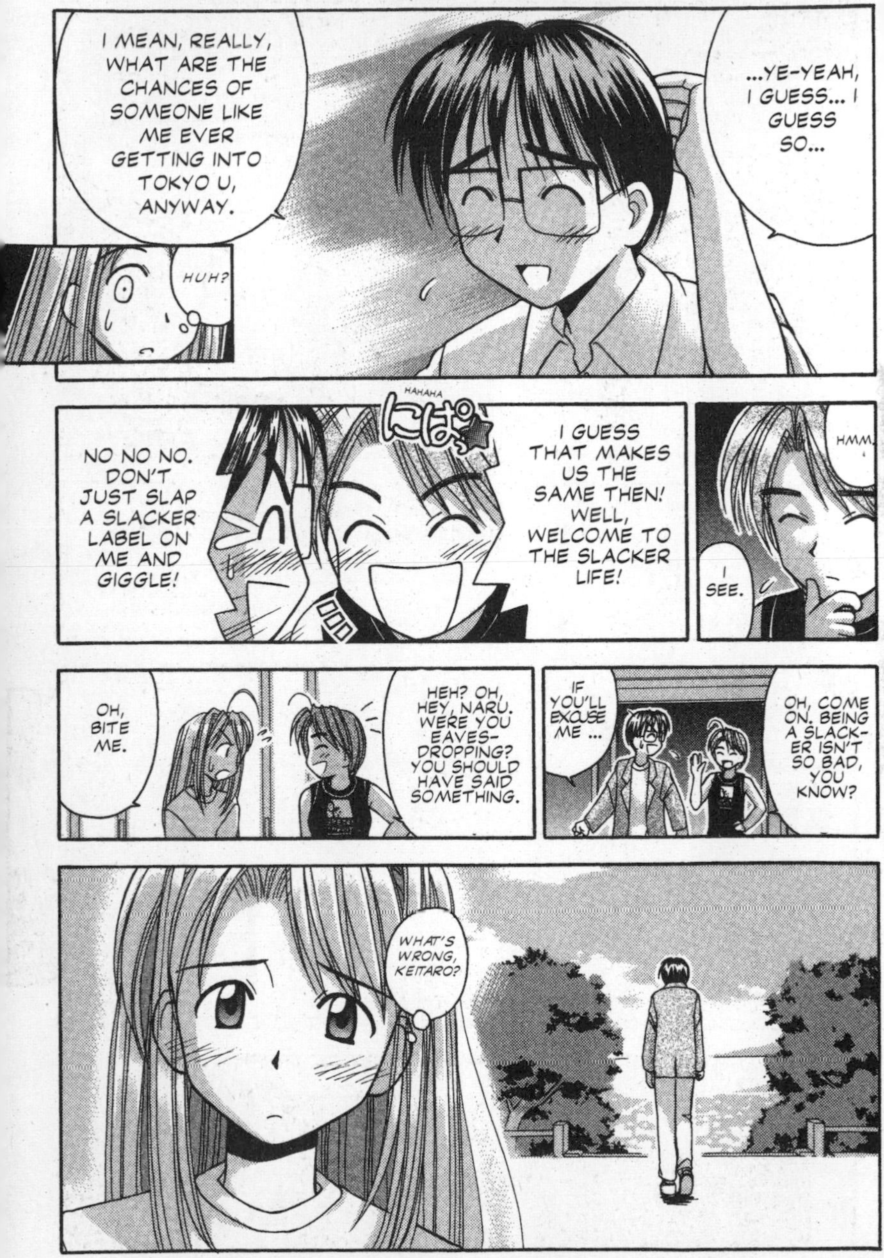
...YE-YEAH, I GUESS... I GUESS SO...
I MEAN, REALLY, WHAT ARE THE CHANCES OF SOMEONE LIKE ME EVER GETTING INTO TOKYO U, ANYWAY.
HUH?
HMM.
I SEE.
HAHAHA
にぱっ
I GUESS THAT MAKES US THE SAME THEN! WELL, WELCOME TO THE SLACKER LIFE!
NO NO NO. DON'T JUST SLAP A SLACKER LABEL ON ME AND GIGGLE!
OH, COME ON. BEING A SLACKER ISN'T SO BAD, YOU KNOW?
IF YOU'LL EXCUSE ME ...
HEH? OH, HEY, NARU. WERE YOU EAVES-DROPPING? YOU SHOULD HAVE SAID SOMETHING.
OH, BITE ME.
WHAT'S WRONG, KEITARO?

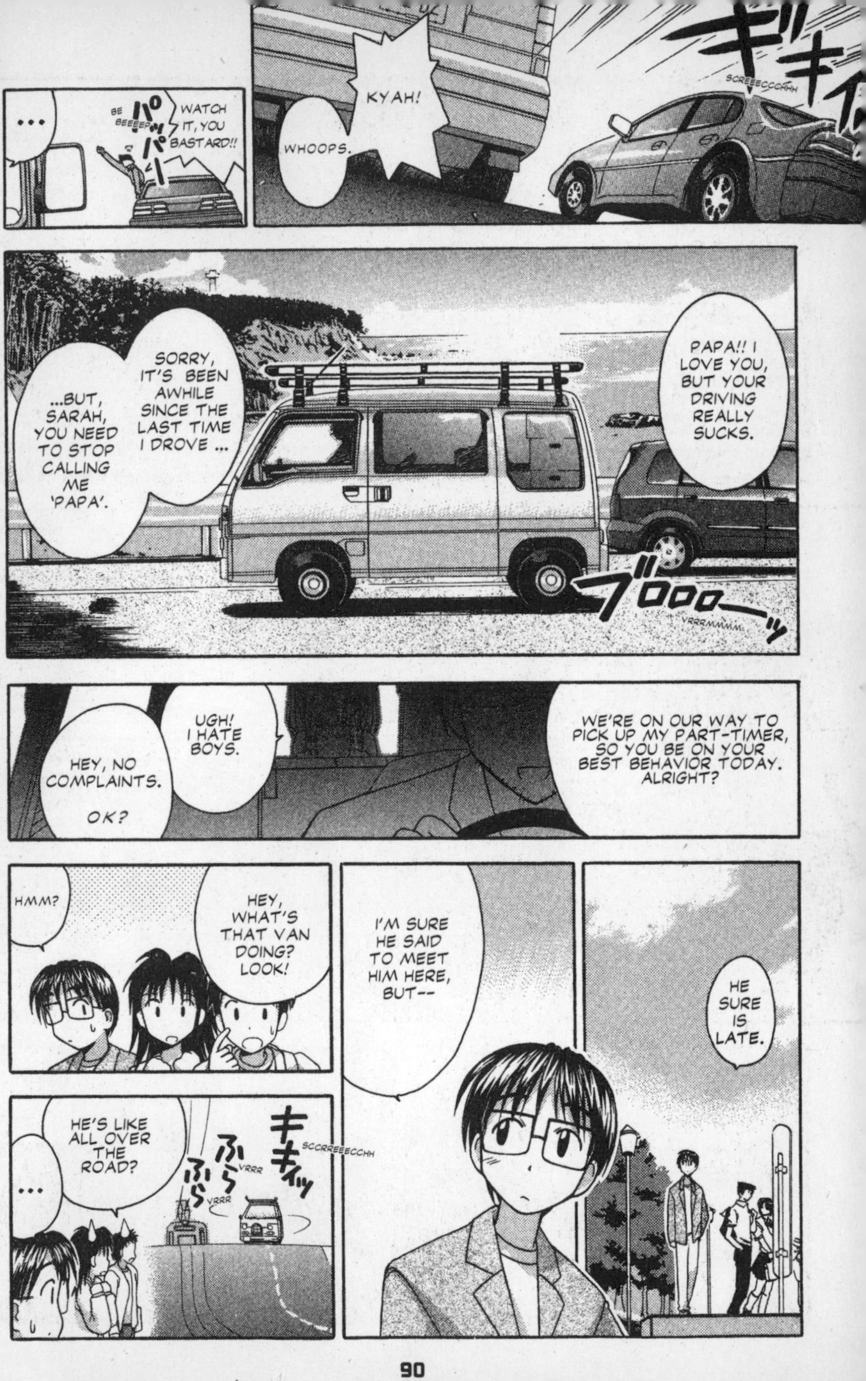
SCREEECCCHHH
KYAH!
WHOOPS.
BE BEEEEP
WATCH IT, YOU BASTARD!!
...
PAPA!! I LOVE YOU, BUT YOUR DRIVING REALLY SUCKS.
SORRY, IT'S BEEN AWHILE SINCE THE LAST TIME I DROVE ...
...BUT, SARAH, YOU NEED TO STOP CALLING ME 'PAPA'.
VRRRMMMM
WE'RE ON OUR WAY TO PICK UP MY PART-TIMER, SO YOU BE ON YOUR BEST BEHAVIOR TODAY. ALRIGHT?
UGH! I HATE BOYS.
HEY, NO COMPLAINTS. OK?
HE SURE IS LATE.
I'M SURE HE SAID TO MEET HIM HERE, BUT--
HEY, WHAT'S THAT VAN DOING? LOOK!
HMM?
SCCRREEECCHH
VRRR
VRRR
HE'S LIKE ALL OVER THE ROAD?
...

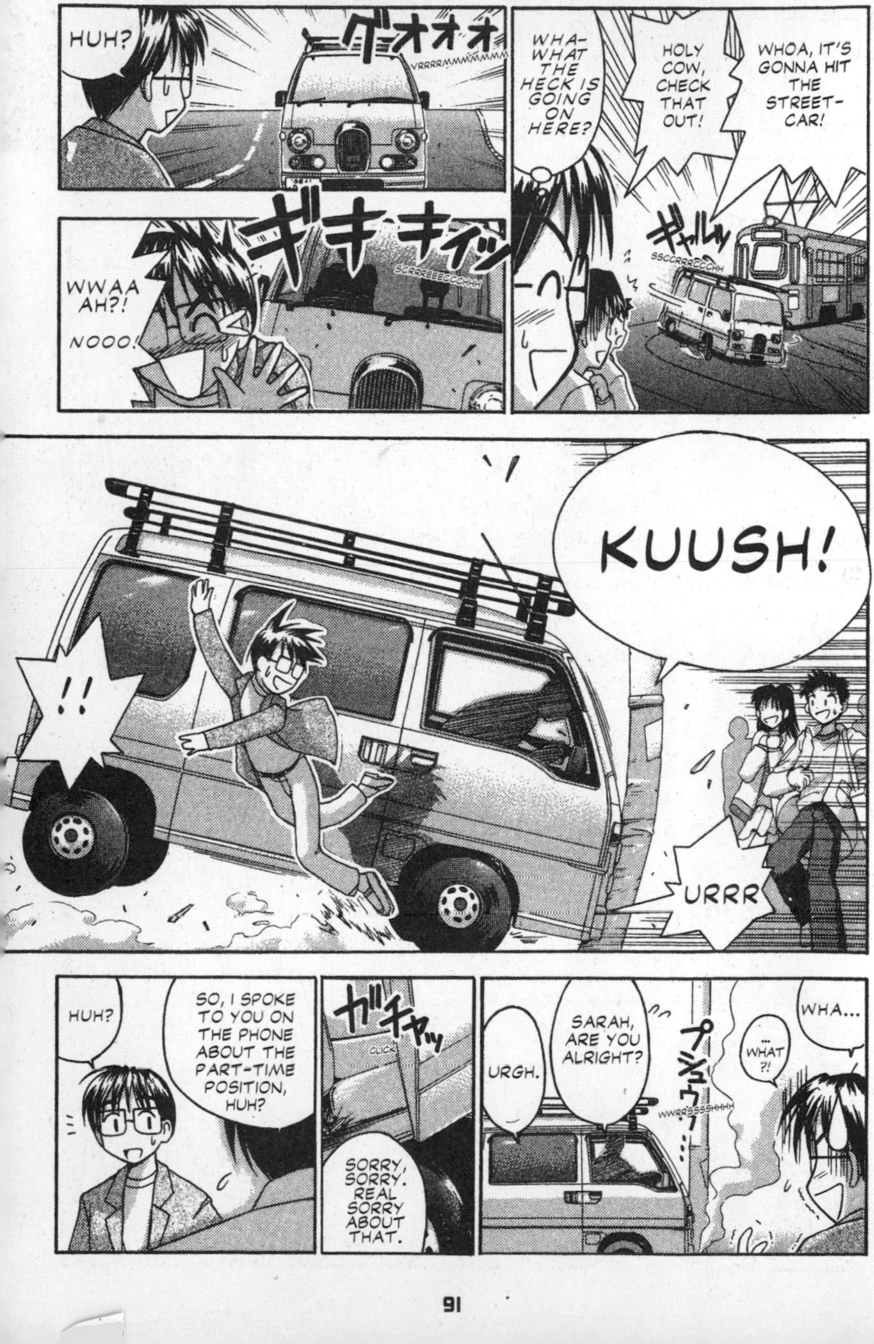
WHOA, IT'S GONNA HIT THE STREET-CAR!
HOLY COW, CHECK THAT OUT!
WHA-WHAT THE HECK IS GOING ON HERE?
SSCCRRRCCCHH
VRRRRMMMMMMM
HUH?
SCRRREEECCCHHH
WWAA AH?!
NOOO!
KUUSH!
URRR
!!
WHA...
...WHAT?!
SARAH, ARE YOU ALRIGHT?
URGH.
WWRRSSSSHHHH
CLICK
SORRY, SORRY. REAL SORRY ABOUT THAT.
SO, I SPOKE TO YOU ON THE PHONE ABOUT THE PART-TIME POSITION, HUH?
HUH?

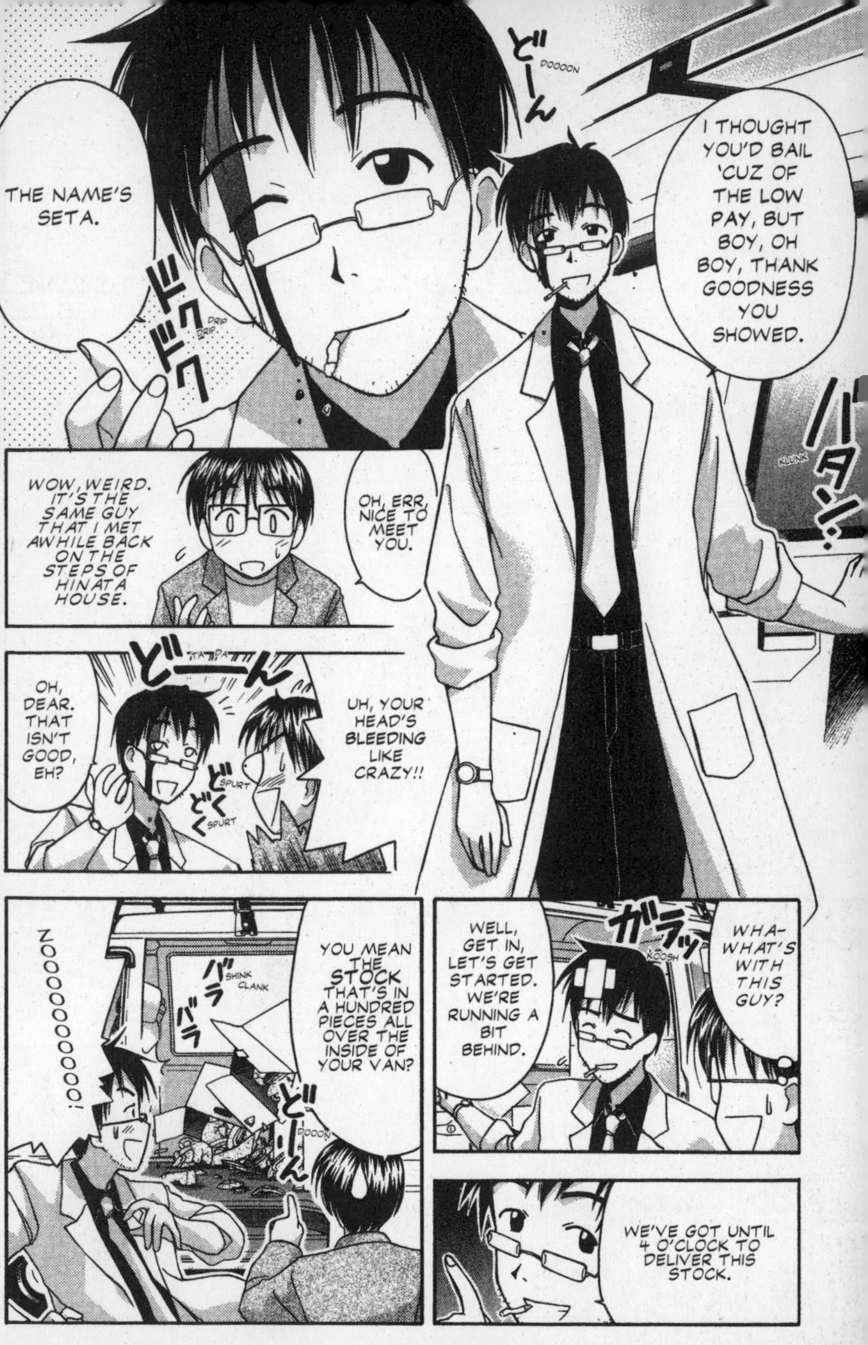
DOOOON
I THOUGHT YOU'D BAIL 'CUZ OF THE LOW PAY, BUT BOY, OH BOY, THANK GOODNESS YOU SHOWED.
KLUNK
THE NAME'S SETA.
DRIP DRIP
OH, ERR, NICE TO MEET YOU.
WOW, WEIRD. IT'S THE SAME GUY THAT I MET AWHILE BACK ON THE STEPS OF HINATA HOUSE.
TA PA
UH, YOUR HEAD'S BLEEDING LIKE CRAZY!!
OH, DEAR. THAT ISN'T GOOD, EH?
SPURT SPURT
WHA-WHAT'S WITH THIS GUY?
KOOSH
WELL, GET IN, LET'S GET STARTED. WE'RE RUNNING A BIT BEHIND.
WE'VE GOT UNTIL 4 O'CLOCK TO DELIVER THIS STOCK.
YOU MEAN THE STOCK THAT'S IN A HUNDRED PIECES ALL OVER THE INSIDE OF YOUR VAN?
SHINK CLANK
DOOON
ZOOOOOOOOOO!

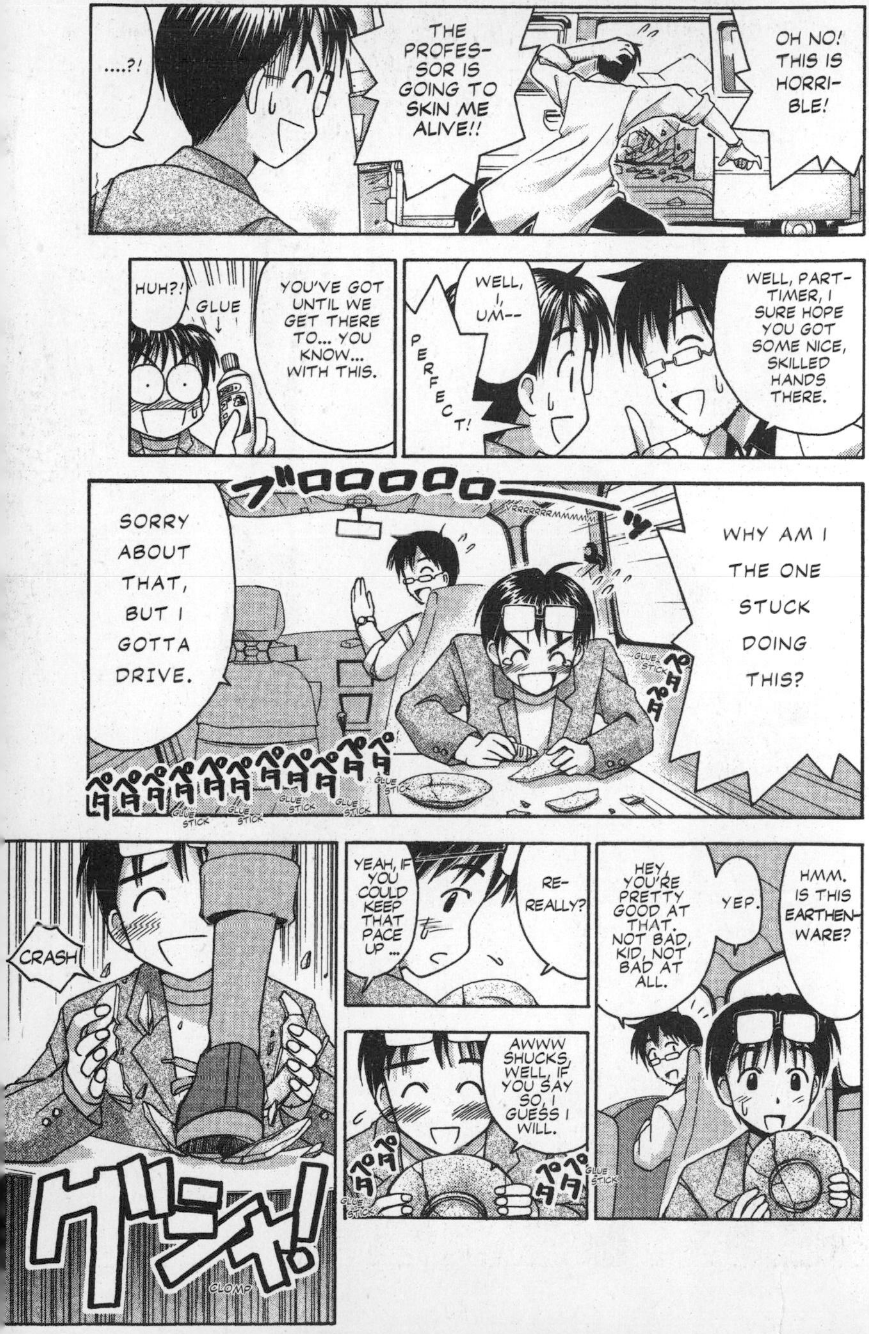
OH NO! THIS IS HORRIBLE!
THE PROFESSOR IS GOING TO SKIN ME ALIVE!!
....?!
WELL, PART-TIMER, I SURE HOPE YOU GOT SOME NICE, SKILLED HANDS THERE.
WELL, I, UM--
PERFECT!
YOU'VE GOT UNTIL WE GET THERE TO... YOU KNOW... WITH THIS.
GLUE
HUH?!
ブロロロロロ
VRRRRRRMMMMM
WHY AM I THE ONE STUCK DOING THIS?
ペタペタ
GLUE STICK
SORRY ABOUT THAT, BUT I GOTTA DRIVE.
ペタペタペタペタペタペタペタペタペタ
GLUE STICK
HMM. IS THIS EARTHENWARE?
YEP.
HEY, YOU'RE PRETTY GOOD AT THAT. NOT BAD, KID, NOT BAD AT ALL.
RE-REALLY?
YEAH, IF YOU COULD KEEP THAT PACE UP ...
AWWW SHUCKS, WELL, IF YOU SAY SO, I GUESS I WILL.
ペタペタ
GLUE STICK
CRASH
グシャ!
CLOMP

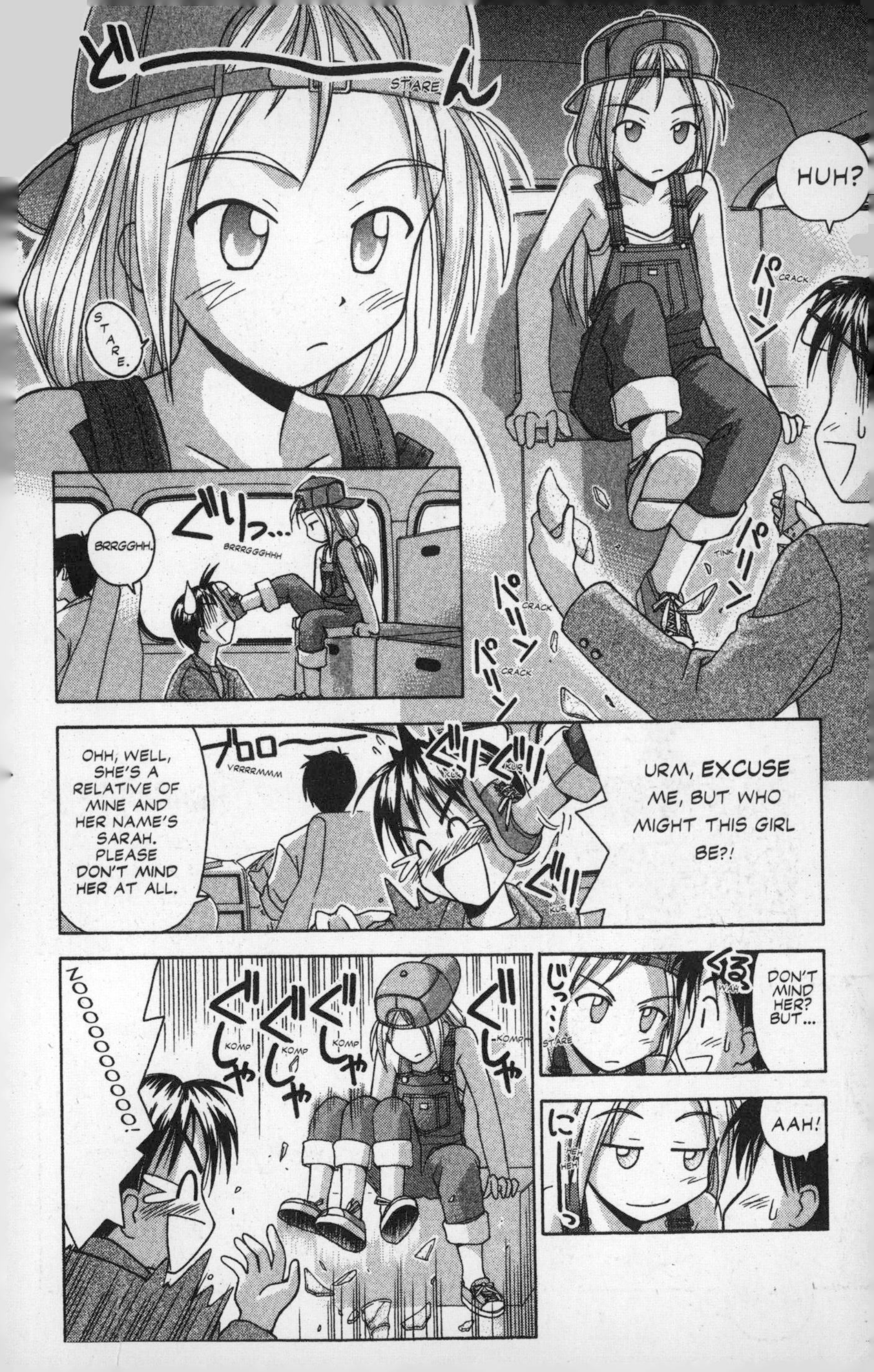
HUH?
CRACK
TINK
CRACK
CRACK
STARE
STARE.
BRRGGHH.
BRRRGGGHHH
URM, EXCUSE ME, BUT WHO MIGHT THIS GIRL BE?!
KUR
KUR
KUR
VRRRRMMM
OHH, WELL, SHE'S A RELATIVE OF MINE AND HER NAME'S SARAH. PLEASE DON'T MIND HER AT ALL.
DON'T MIND HER? BUT...
WAH
STARE
AAH!
HEH HEH
KOMP
KOMP
KOMP
KOMP
NOOOOOOOOO!

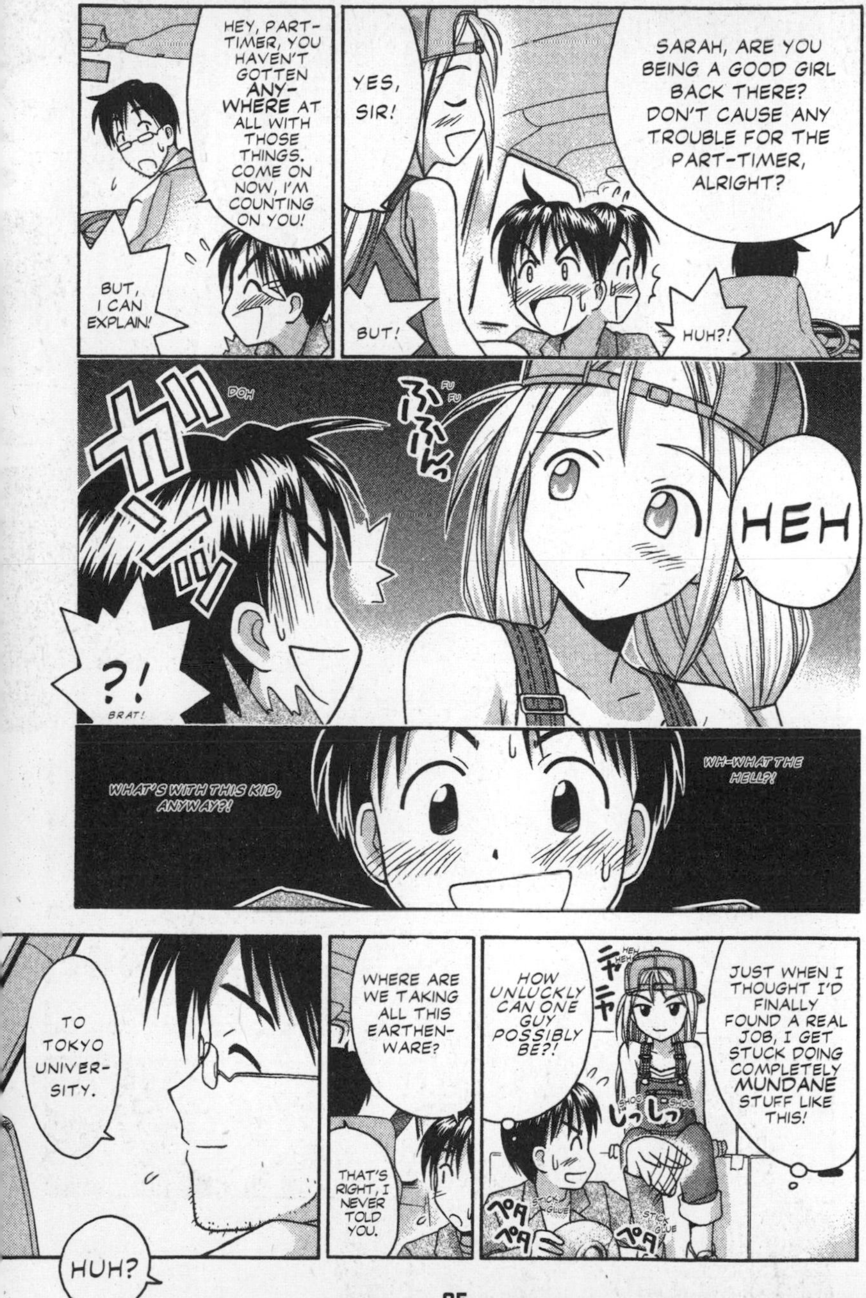
SARAH, ARE YOU BEING A GOOD GIRL BACK THERE? DON'T CAUSE ANY TROUBLE FOR THE PART-TIMER, ALRIGHT?
YES, SIR!
HUH?!
BUT!
HEY, PART-TIMER, YOU HAVEN'T GOTTEN ANY-WHERE AT ALL WITH THOSE THINGS. COME ON NOW, I'M COUNTING ON YOU!
BUT, I CAN EXPLAIN!
HEH
ふふん
FU FU
DOH
ガーン
?!
BRAT!
WH-WHAT THE HELL?!
WHAT'S WITH THIS KID, ANYWAY?!
JUST WHEN I THOUGHT I'D FINALLY FOUND A REAL JOB, I GET STUCK DOING COMPLETELY MUNDANE STUFF LIKE THIS!
ニヤニヤ
HEH HEH
HOW UNLUCKLY CAN ONE GUY POSSIBLY BE?!
しっしっ
SHOO SHOO
ペタペタ
STICK GLUE
ペタペタ
STICK GLUE
WHERE ARE WE TAKING ALL THIS EARTHEN-WARE?
THAT'S RIGHT, I NEVER TOLD YOU.
TO TOKYO UNIVER-SITY.
HUH?

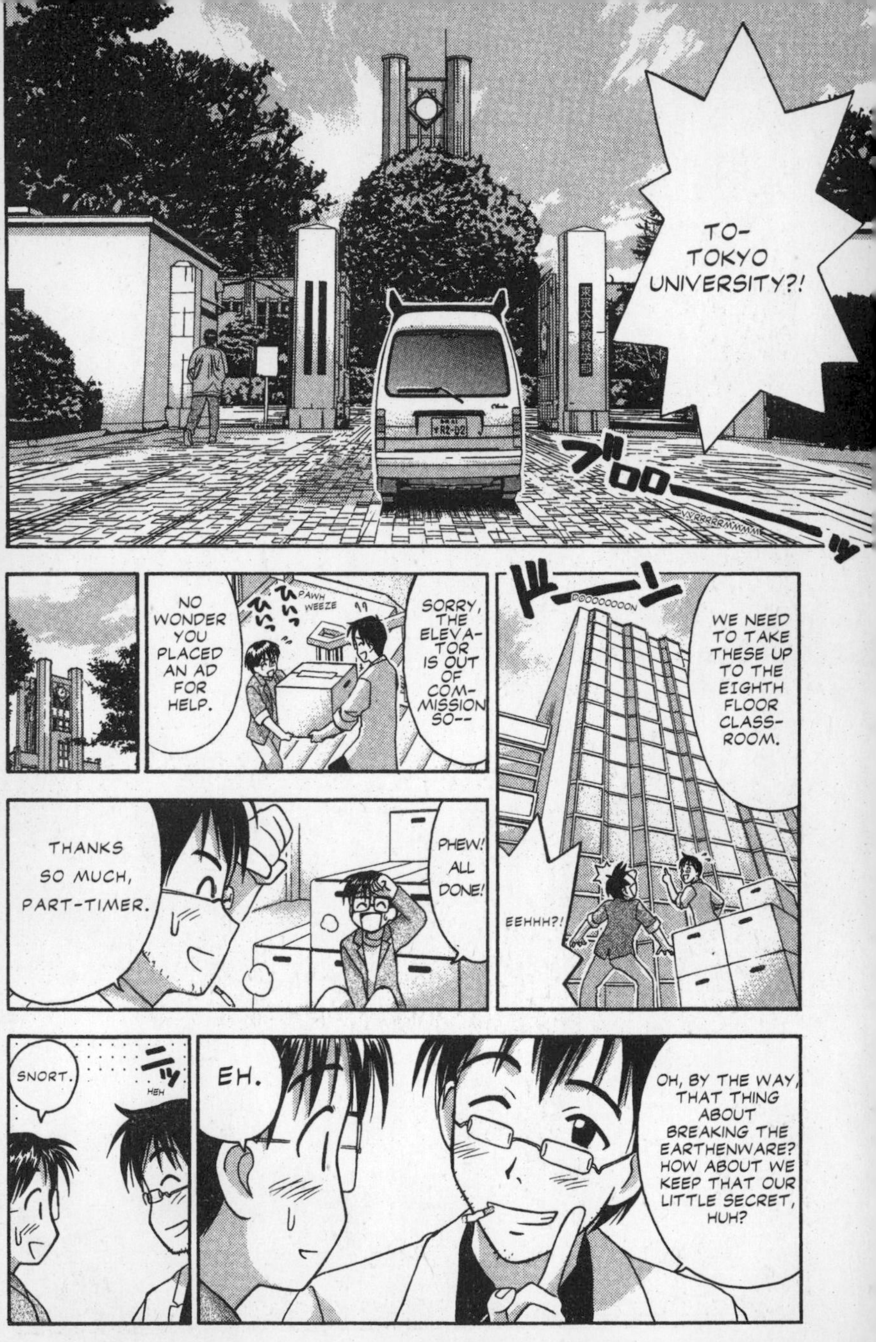
TO-TOKYO UNIVERSITY?!
ブロロー
VVRRRRRMMMM
ドーン
DOOOOOOOOON
WE NEED TO TAKE THESE UP TO THE EIGHTH FLOOR CLASSROOM.
EEHHH?!
SORRY, THE ELEVATOR IS OUT OF COMMISSION SO--
PAWH WEEZE
NO WONDER YOU PLACED AN AD FOR HELP.
PHEW! ALL DONE!
THANKS SO MUCH, PART-TIMER.
OH, BY THE WAY, THAT THING ABOUT BREAKING THE EARTHENWARE? HOW ABOUT WE KEEP THAT OUR LITTLE SECRET, HUH?
EH.
ニッ
HEH
SNORT.

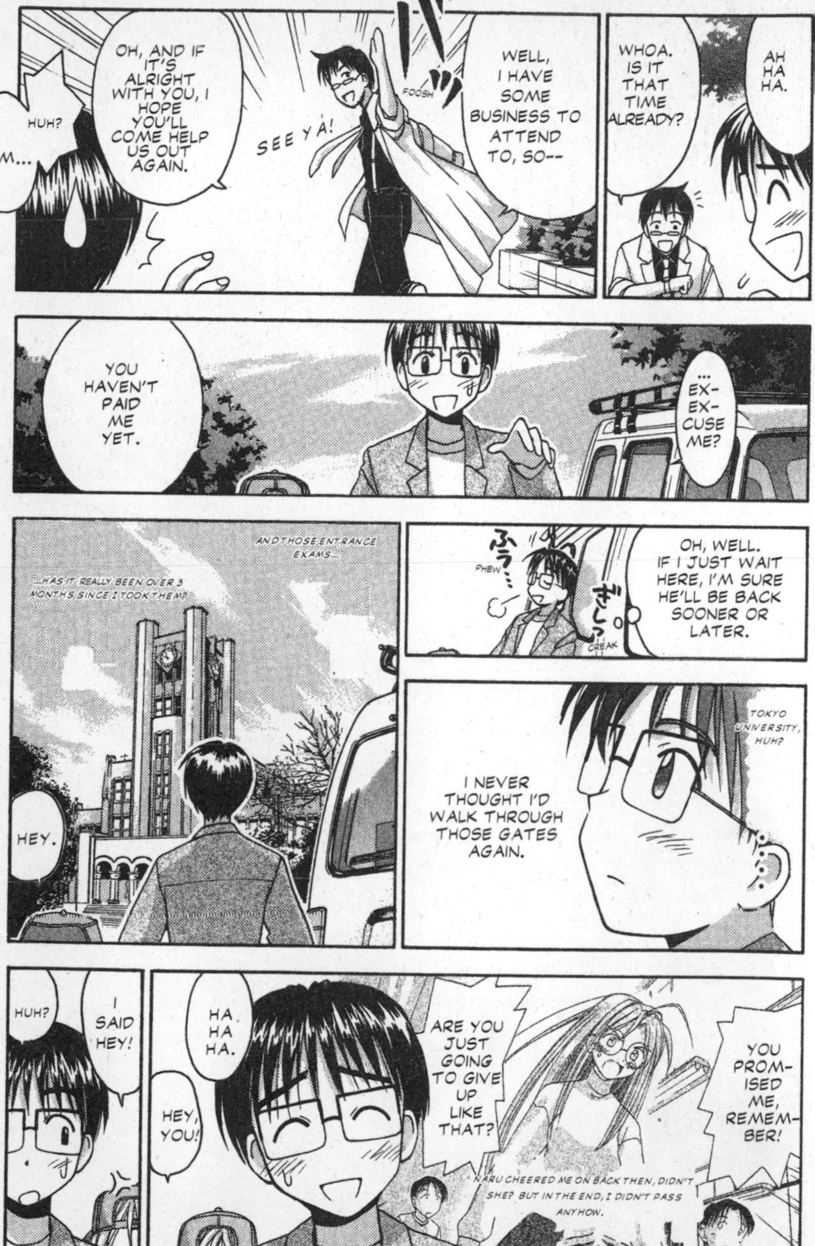
AH HA HA.
WHOA. IS IT THAT TIME ALREADY?
WELL, I HAVE SOME BUSINESS TO ATTEND TO, SO--
FOOSH
SEE YA!
OH, AND IF IT'S ALRIGHT WITH YOU, I HOPE YOU'LL COME HELP US OUT AGAIN.
HUH?
URM...
...EX-EX-CUSE ME?
YOU HAVEN'T PAID ME YET.
OH, WELL. IF I JUST WAIT HERE, I'M SURE HE'LL BE BACK SOONER OR LATER.
ぎしっ
CREAK
ふう
PHEW
TOKYO UNIVERSITY, HUH?
I NEVER THOUGHT I'D WALK THROUGH THOSE GATES AGAIN.
AND THOSE ENTRANCE EXAMS...
...HAS IT REALLY BEEN OVER 3 MONTHS SINCE I TOOK THEM?
HEY.
YOU PROMISED ME, REMEMBER!
ARE YOU JUST GOING TO GIVE UP LIKE THAT?
HA HA HA.
HEY, YOU!
NARU CHEERED ME ON BACK THEN, DIDN'T SHE? BUT IN THE END, I DIDN'T PASS ANYHOW.
I SAID HEY!
HUH?

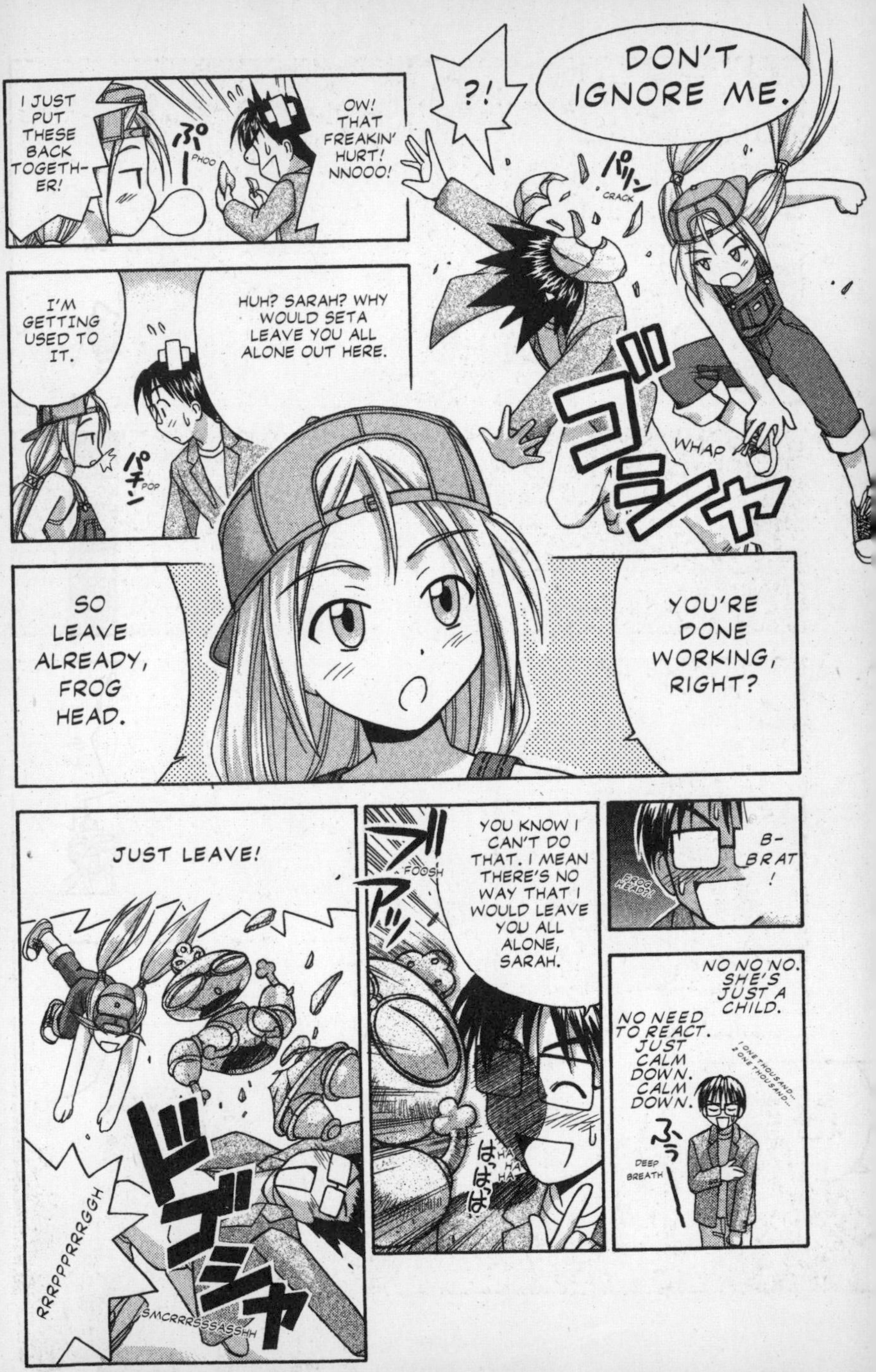
DON'T IGNORE ME.
?!
パリン CRACK
ゴシャ
WHAP
OW! THAT FREAKIN' HURT! NNOOO!
ぷー PHOO
I JUST PUT THESE BACK TOGETH-ER!
HUH? SARAH? WHY WOULD SETA LEAVE YOU ALL ALONE OUT HERE.
I'M GETTING USED TO IT.
パチン POP
YOU'RE DONE WORKING, RIGHT?
SO LEAVE ALREADY, FROG HEAD.
B-BRAT!
FROG HEAD!?
NO NO NO. SHE'S JUST A CHILD.
NO NEED TO REACT. JUST CALM DOWN. CALM DOWN.
1 ONE THOUSAND... 2 ONE THOUSAND...
ふぅ DEEP BREATH
YOU KNOW I CAN'T DO THAT. I MEAN THERE'S NO WAY THAT I WOULD LEAVE YOU ALL ALONE, SARAH.
ブアッ FOOSH
はっはっは HA HA HA
JUST LEAVE!
ドゴシャ SMCRRRSSSASSHH
RRRPPPRRRGGH

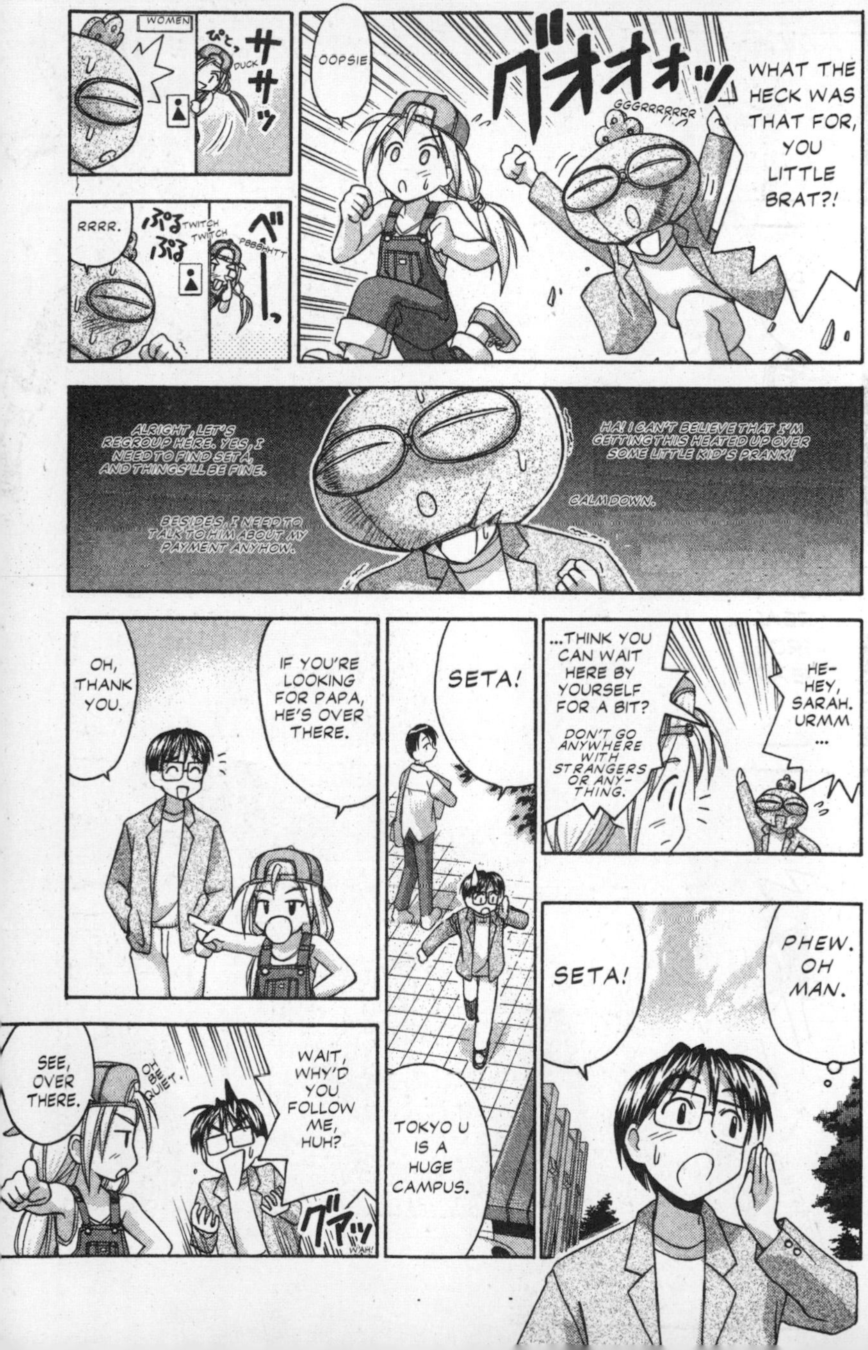
WHAT THE HECK WAS THAT FOR, YOU LITTLE BRAT?!
グオオオッ
GGGRRRRRRR
OOPSIE
WOMEN
ササッ
ぴとっ
DUCK
べーっ
PBBBHHTT
ぷるぷる
TWITCH TWITCH
RRRR.
HA! I CAN'T BELIEVE THAT I'M GETTING THIS HEATED UP OVER SOME LITTLE KID'S PRANK!
CALM DOWN.
ALRIGHT, LET'S REGROUP HERE. YES, I NEED TO FIND SETA, AND THINGS'LL BE FINE.
BESIDES, I NEED TO TALK TO HIM ABOUT MY PAYMENT ANYHOW.
HE- HEY, SARAH. URMM ...
...THINK YOU CAN WAIT HERE BY YOURSELF FOR A BIT?
DON'T GO ANYWHERE WITH STRANGERS OR ANYTHING.
PHEW. OH MAN.
SETA!
SETA!
TOKYO U IS A HUGE CAMPUS.
IF YOU'RE LOOKING FOR PAPA, HE'S OVER THERE.
OH, THANK YOU.
WAIT, WHY'D YOU FOLLOW ME, HUH?
OH BE QUIET.
SEE, OVER THERE.
グアッ
WAH!

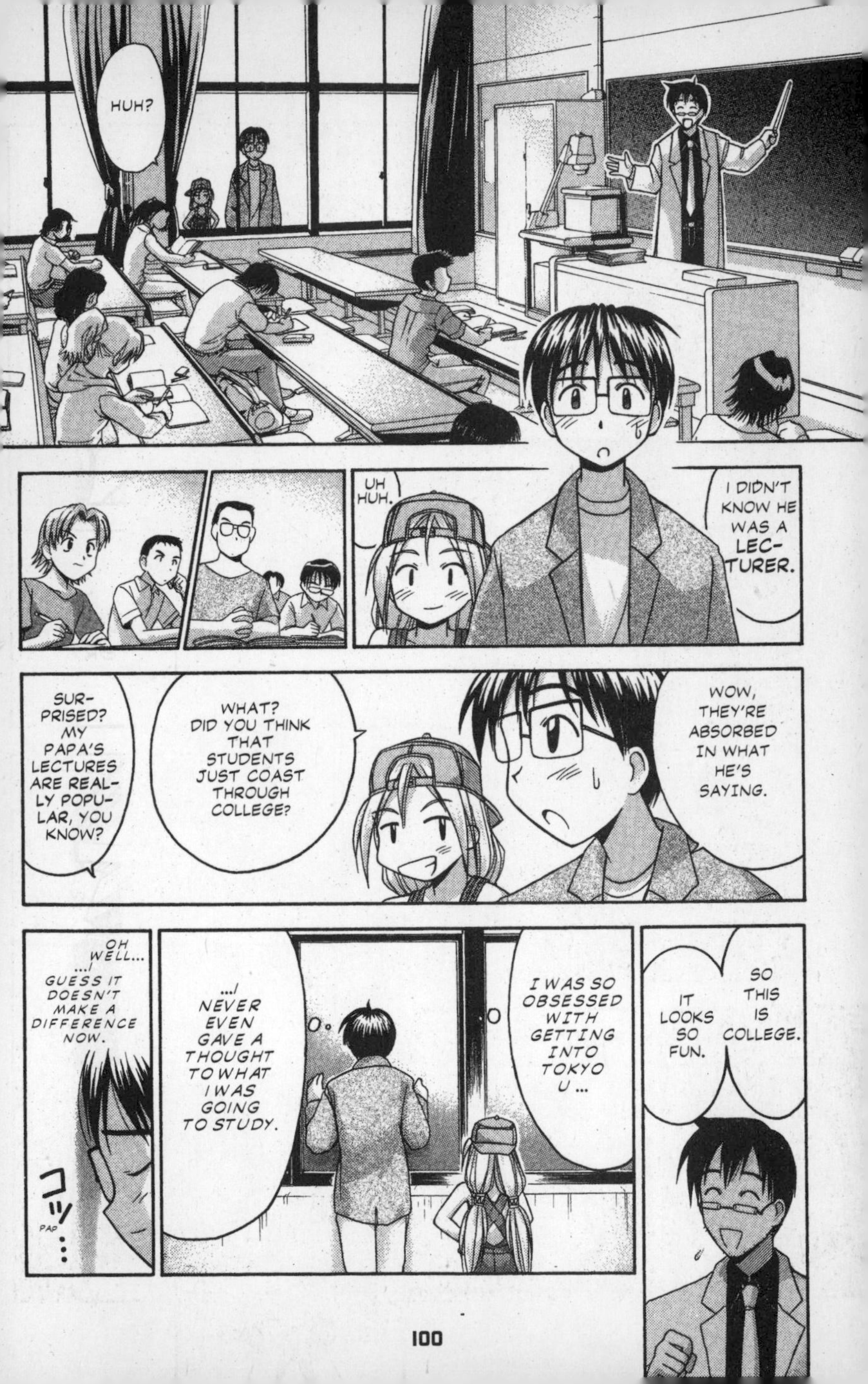
HUH?
I DIDN'T KNOW HE WAS A LEC-TURER.
UH HUH.
WOW, THEY'RE ABSORBED IN WHAT HE'S SAYING.
WHAT? DID YOU THINK THAT STUDENTS JUST COAST THROUGH COLLEGE?
SUR-PRISED? MY PAPA'S LECTURES ARE REAL-LY POPU-LAR, YOU KNOW?
SO THIS IS COLLEGE.
IT LOOKS SO FUN.
I WAS SO OBSESSED WITH GETTING INTO TOKYO U...
...I NEVER EVEN GAVE A THOUGHT TO WHAT I WAS GOING TO STUDY.
OH WELL...!
...GUESS IT DOESN'T MAKE A DIFFERENCE NOW.
コッ
PAP

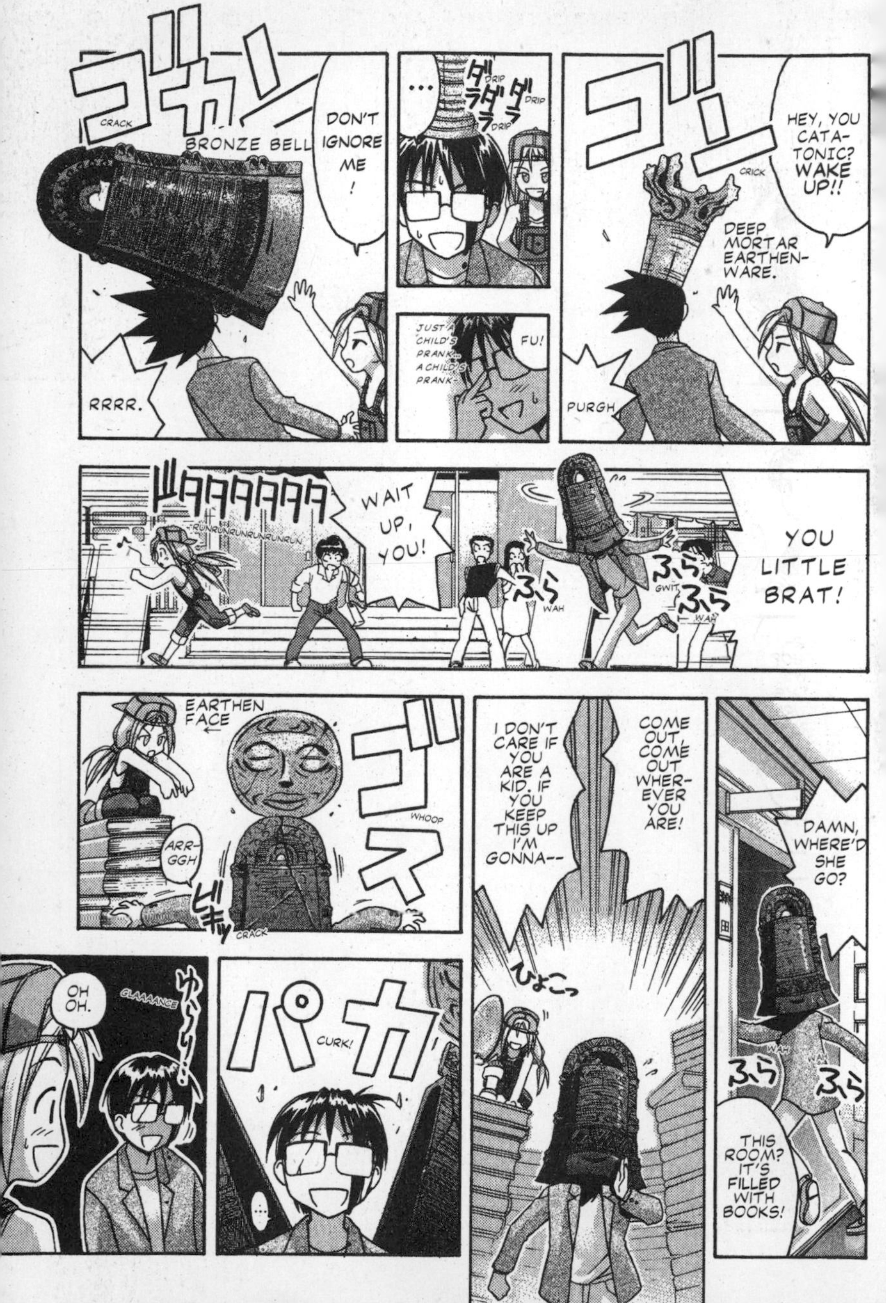
HEY, YOU CATA-TONIC? WAKE UP!!
CRICK
DEEP MORTAR EARTHEN-WARE.
PURGH
...
DRIP
DRIP
DRIP
FU!
JUST A CHILD'S PRANK... A CHILD'S PRANK--
DON'T IGNORE ME!
CRACK
BRONZE BELL
RRRR.
YOU LITTLE BRAT!
WAH
GWIT
WAH
WAIT UP, YOU!
RUNRUNRUNRUNRUNRUN
DAMN, WHERE'D SHE GO?
WAH
WAH
THIS ROOM? IT'S FILLED WITH BOOKS!
COME OUT, COME OUT WHER-EVER YOU ARE!
I DON'T CARE IF YOU ARE A KID. IF YOU KEEP THIS UP I'M GONNA--
WHOOP
EARTHEN FACE
ARR-GGH
CRACK
CURK!
...
GLAAAANCE
OH OH.

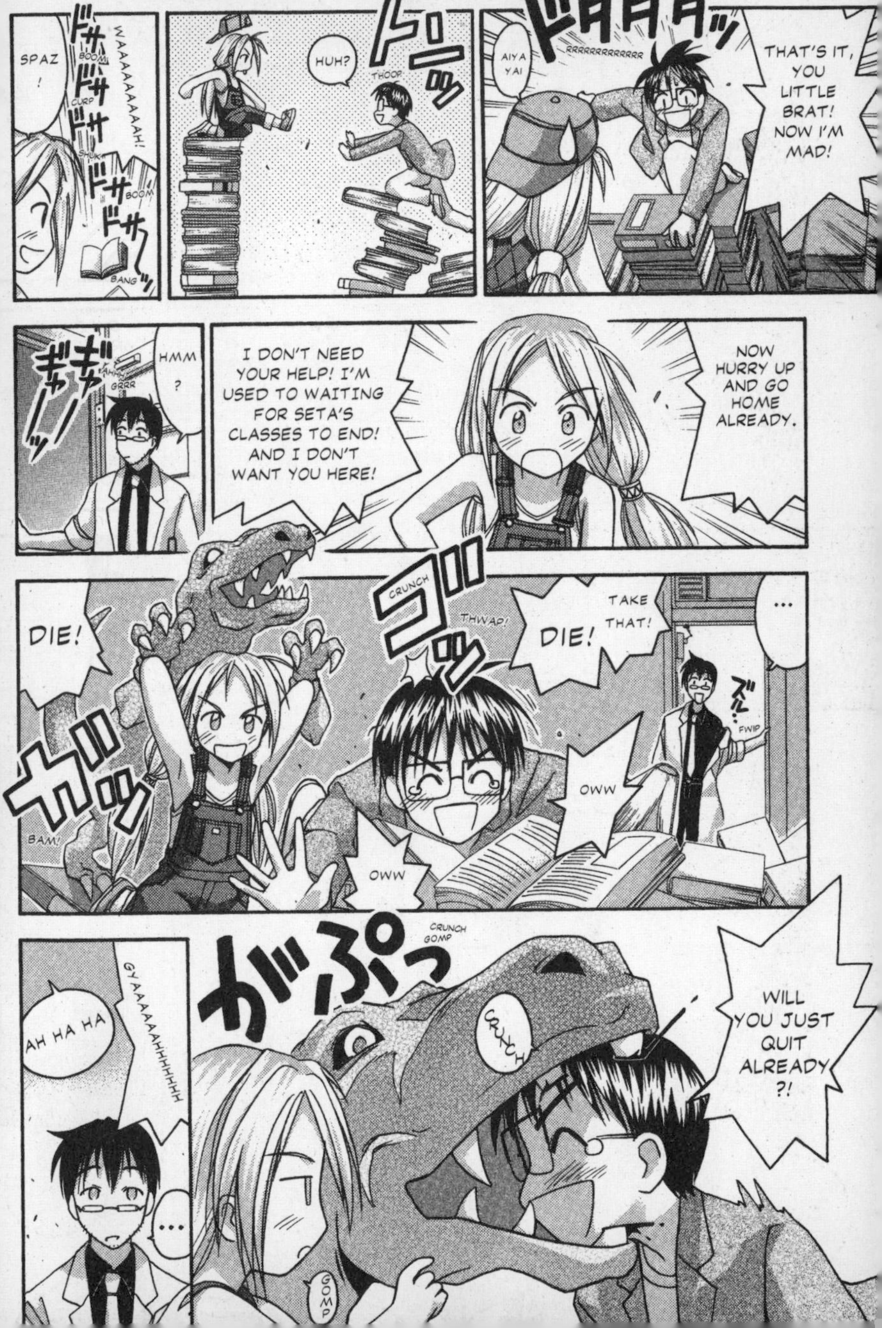
ドタタタッ
RRRRRRRRRRRRR
THAT'S IT, YOU LITTLE BRAT! NOW I'M MAD!
AIYA YAI
トーンッ
THOOP
HUH?
WAAAAAAAAAAAH!
ドサ
BOOM
ドサ
CURP
ドサ
SHUK
ドサ
BOOM
ドサッ
BANG
SPAZ!
NOW HURRY UP AND GO HOME ALREADY.
I DON'T NEED YOUR HELP! I'M USED TO WAITING FOR SETA'S CLASSES TO END! AND I DON'T WANT YOU HERE!
HMM ?
AHHH
GRRR
...
FWIP
TAKE THAT!
DIE!
ゴッ
CRUNCH
THWAP!
OWW
DIE!
BAM!
OWW
WILL YOU JUST QUIT ALREADY?!
がぷっ
CRUNCH
GOMP
CRUNCH
GOMP
GYAAAAAAAHHHHHH
AH HA HA
...

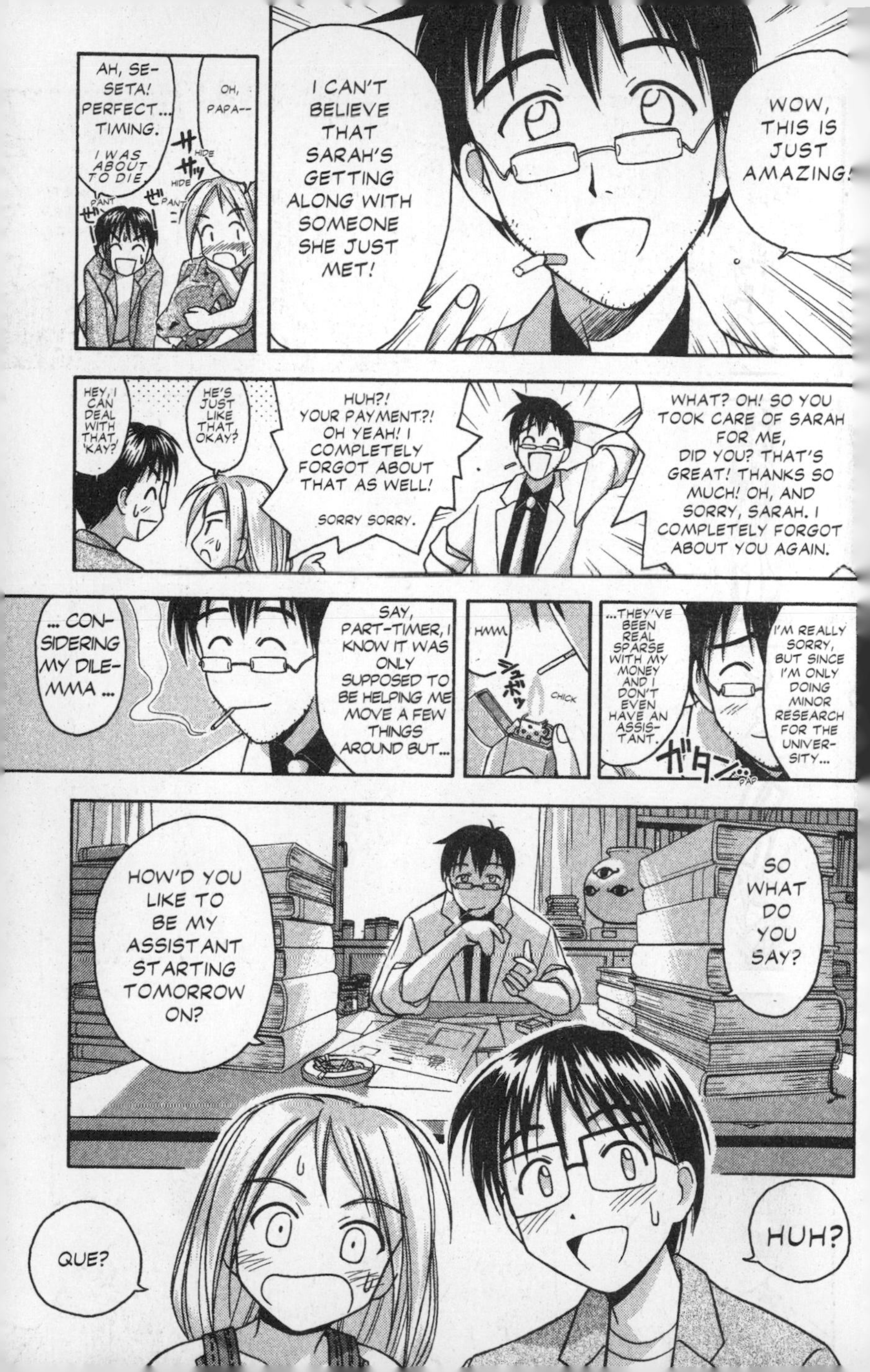
WOW, THIS IS JUST AMAZING!
I CAN'T BELIEVE THAT SARAH'S GETTING ALONG WITH SOMEONE SHE JUST MET!
OH, PAPA--
AH, SE-SETA! PERFECT... TIMING.
I WAS ABOUT TO DIE.
HIDE
HIDE
PANT
PANT
WHAT? OH! SO YOU TOOK CARE OF SARAH FOR ME, DID YOU? THAT'S GREAT! THANKS SO MUCH! OH, AND SORRY, SARAH. I COMPLETELY FORGOT ABOUT YOU AGAIN.
HUH?! YOUR PAYMENT?! OH YEAH! I COMPLETELY FORGOT ABOUT THAT AS WELL!
SORRY SORRY.
HE'S JUST LIKE THAT, OKAY?
HEY, I CAN DEAL WITH THAT, 'KAY?
I'M REALLY SORRY, BUT SINCE I'M ONLY DOING MINOR RESEARCH FOR THE UNIVERSITY...
...THEY'VE BEEN REAL SPARSE WITH MY MONEY AND I DON'T EVEN HAVE AN ASSISTANT.
PAP
HMM.
CHICK
SAY, PART-TIMER, I KNOW IT WAS ONLY SUPPOSED TO BE HELPING ME MOVE A FEW THINGS AROUND BUT...
... CONSIDERING MY DILEMMA ...
SO WHAT DO YOU SAY?
HOW'D YOU LIKE TO BE MY ASSISTANT STARTING TOMORROW ON?
HUH?
QUE?

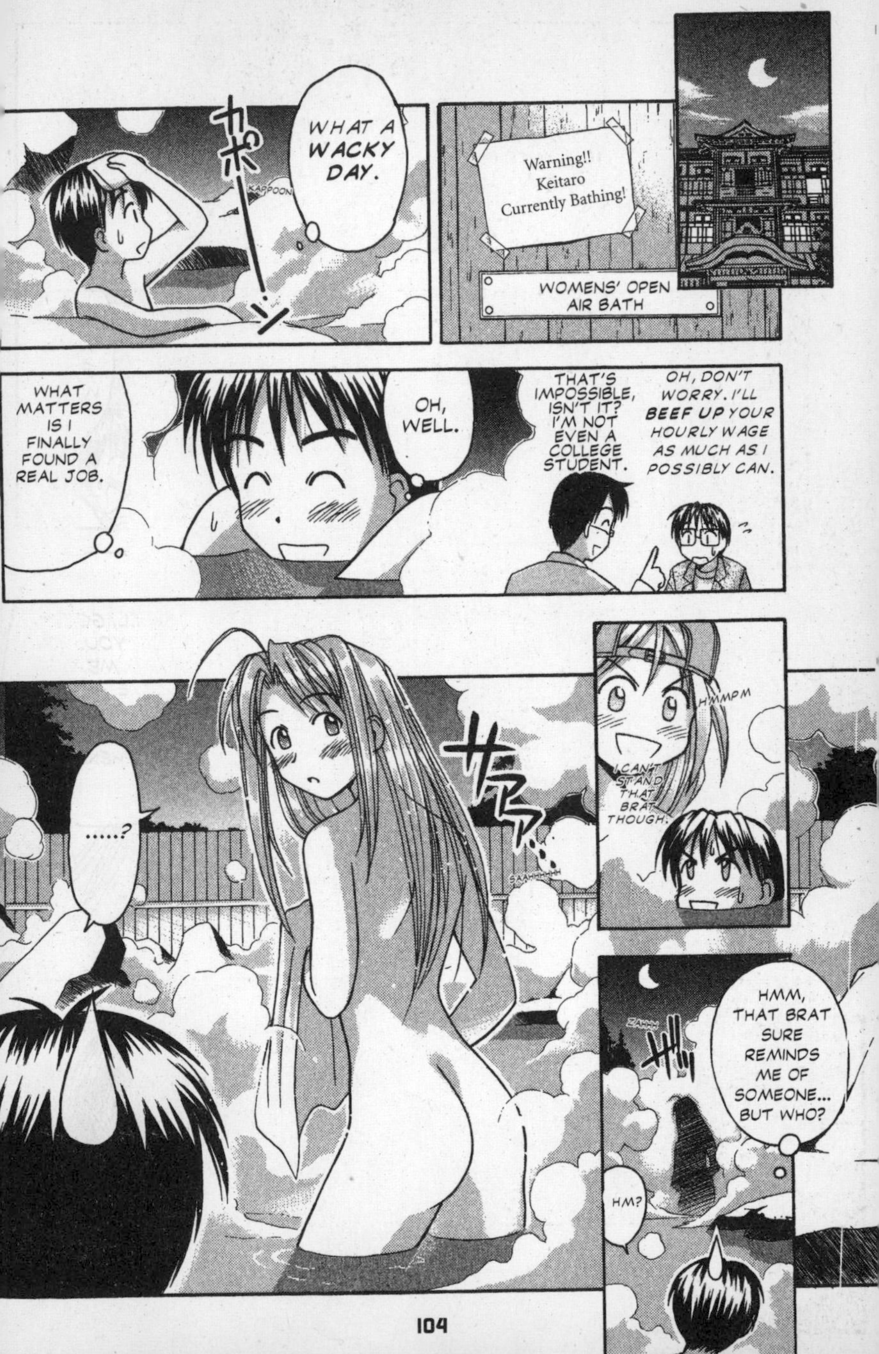
Warning!! Keitaro Currently Bathing!
WOMENS' OPEN AIR BATH
KAPPOON
WHAT A WACKY DAY.
OH, DON'T WORRY. I'LL BEEF UP YOUR HOURLY WAGE AS MUCH AS I POSSIBLY CAN.
THAT'S IMPOSSIBLE, ISN'T IT? I'M NOT EVEN A COLLEGE STUDENT.
OH, WELL.
WHAT MATTERS IS I FINALLY FOUND A REAL JOB.
HMMPM
I CAN'T STAND THAT BRAT THOUGH.
HMM, THAT BRAT SURE REMINDS ME OF SOMEONE... BUT WHO?
ZAHHH
HM?
SAAHHHHHH
......?

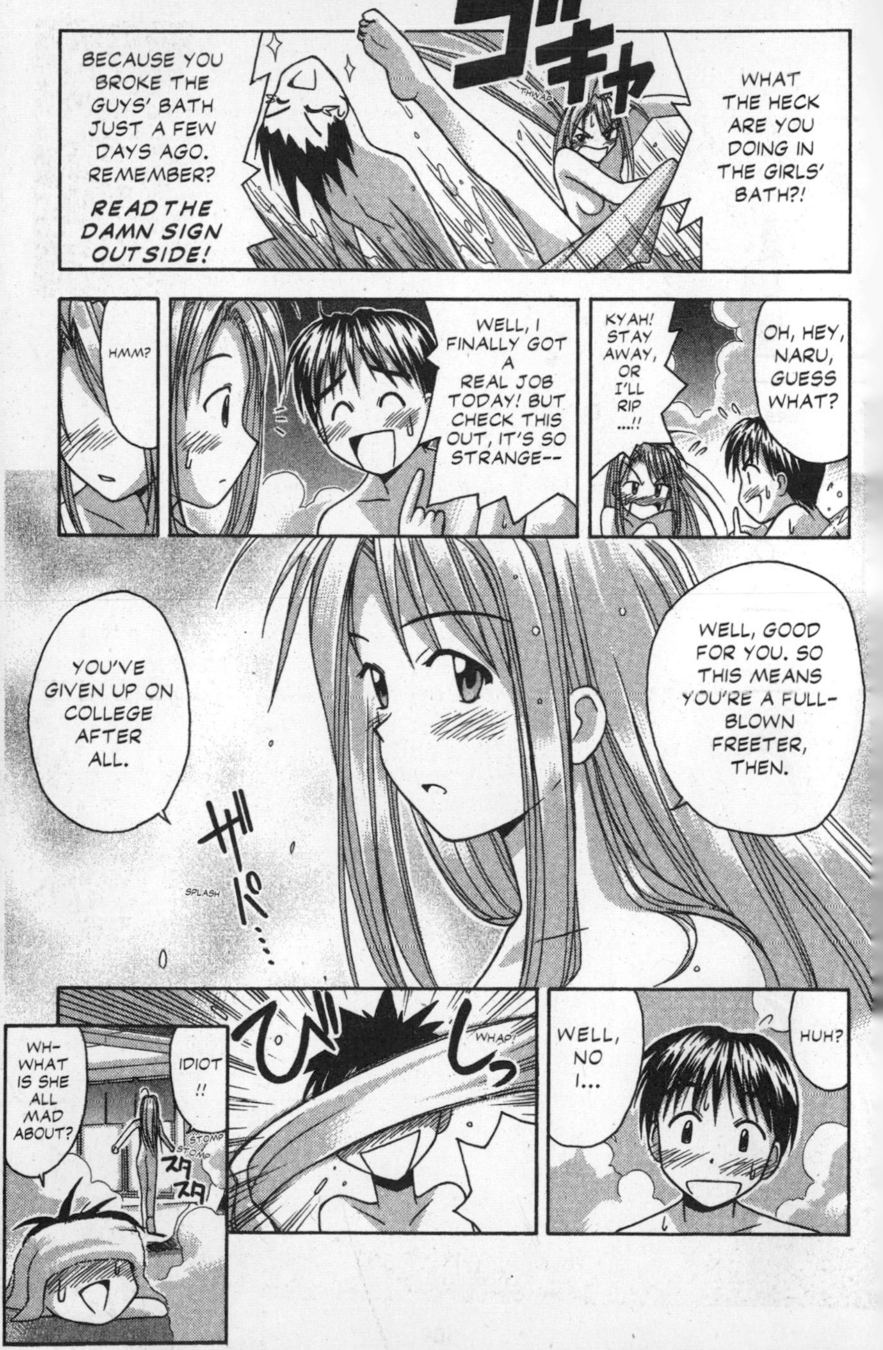
ゴキャ
THWAP
WHAT THE HECK ARE YOU DOING IN THE GIRLS' BATH?!
BECAUSE YOU BROKE THE GUYS' BATH JUST A FEW DAYS AGO. REMEMBER?
READ THE DAMN SIGN OUTSIDE!
OH, HEY, NARU, GUESS WHAT?
KYAH! STAY AWAY, OR I'LL RIP ...!!
WELL, I FINALLY GOT A REAL JOB TODAY! BUT CHECK THIS OUT, IT'S SO STRANGE--
HMM?
WELL, GOOD FOR YOU. SO THIS MEANS YOU'RE A FULL-BLOWN FREETER, THEN.
YOU'VE GIVEN UP ON COLLEGE AFTER ALL.
ザパ…
SPLASH
HUH?
WELL, NO I...
びしっ
WHAP!
IDIOT !!
スタスタ
STOMP STOMP
WH-WHAT IS SHE ALL MAD ABOUT?

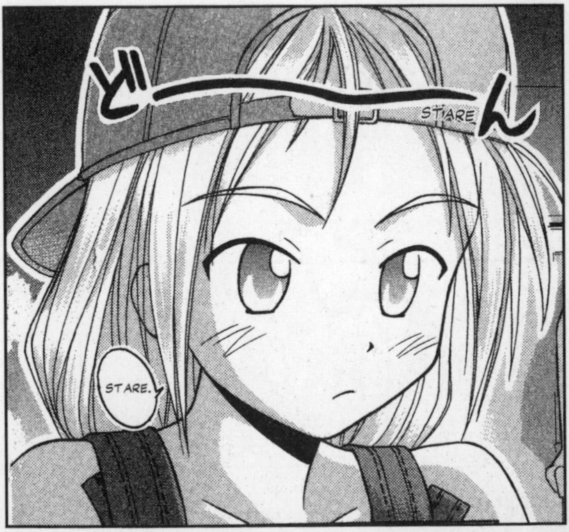
STARE
STARE.

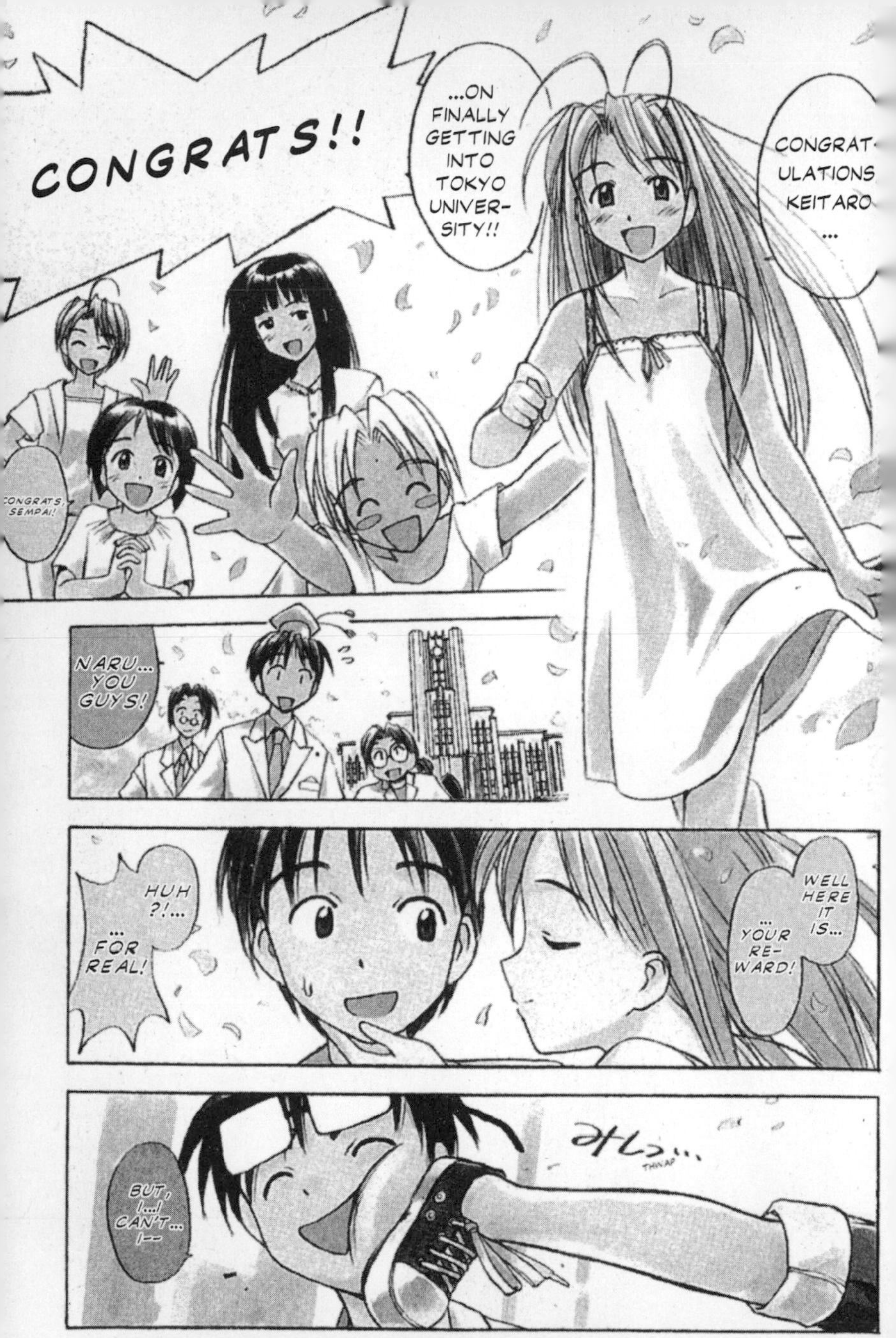
CONGRATULATIONS KEITARO ...
...ON FINALLY GETTING INTO TOKYO UNIVERSITY!!
CONGRATS!!
CONGRATS, SEMPAI!
NARU... YOU GUYS!
WELL HERE IT IS... ...YOUR REWARD!
HUH?!... ...FOR REAL!
THWAP
BUT, I...I CAN'T... I--

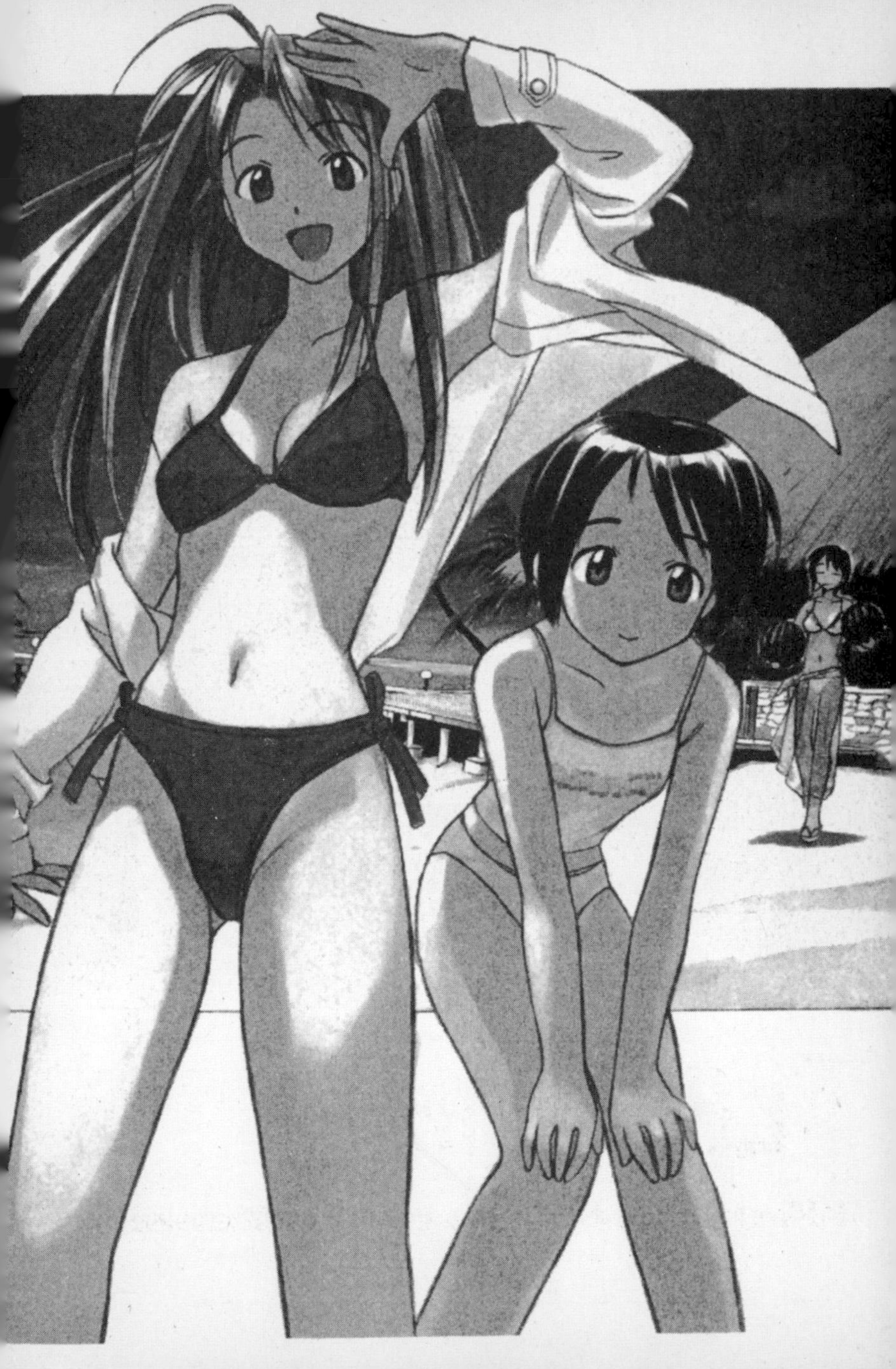

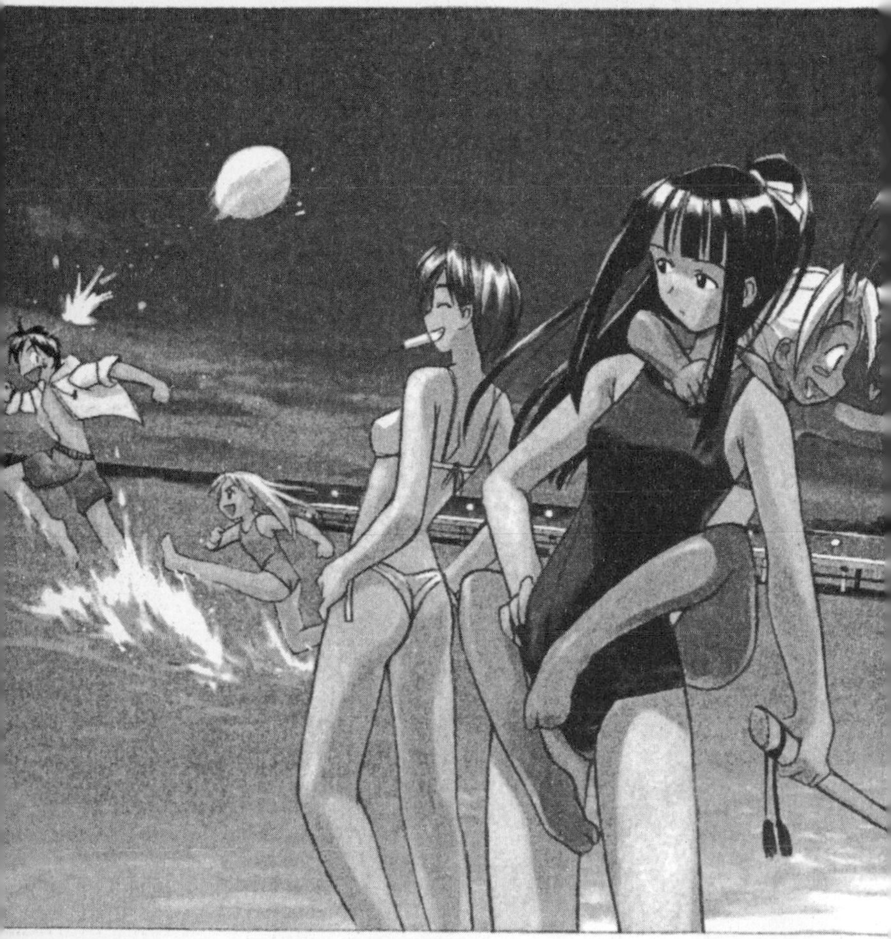

Love Hina

HINATA. 30 Battle! Print Club Man vs. Earthenware Girl

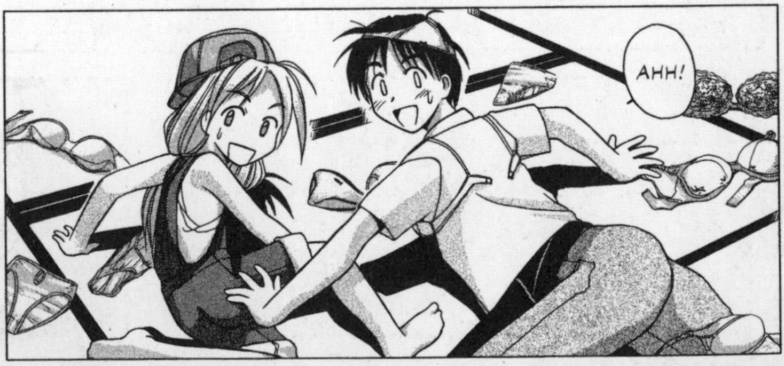
AHH!

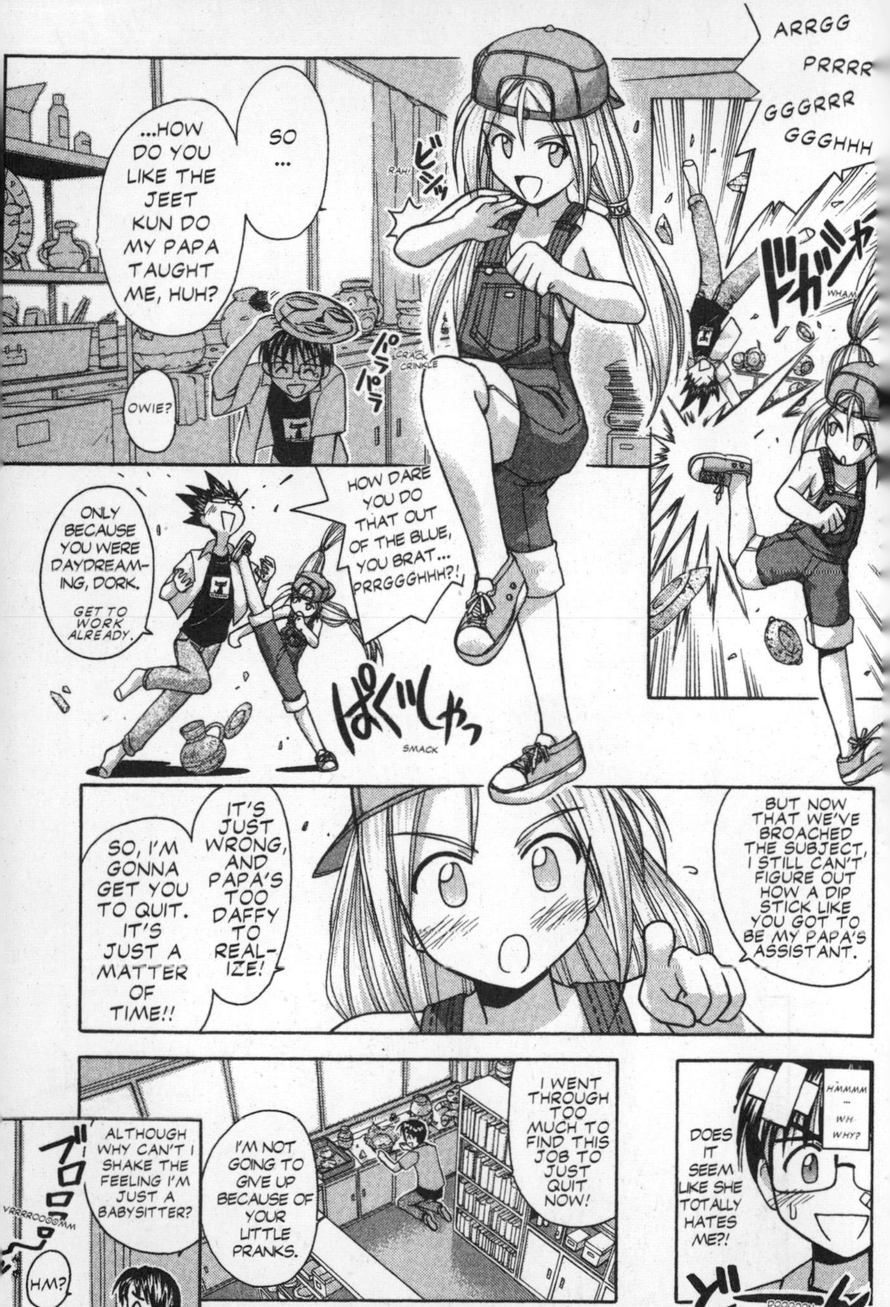
ARRGG
PRRRR
GGGRRR
GGGHHH
WHAM
SO ...
...HOW DO YOU LIKE THE JEET KUN DO MY PAPA TAUGHT ME, HUH?
RAH!
CRACK CRINKLE
OWIE?
HOW DARE YOU DO THAT OUT OF THE BLUE, YOU BRAT... PRRGGGHHH?!
ONLY BECAUSE YOU WERE DAYDREAMING, DORK.
GET TO WORK ALREADY.
SMACK
BUT NOW THAT WE'VE BROACHED THE SUBJECT, I STILL CAN'T FIGURE OUT HOW A DIP STICK LIKE YOU GOT TO BE MY PAPA'S ASSISTANT.
IT'S JUST WRONG, AND PAPA'S TOO DAFFY TO REALIZE!
SO, I'M GONNA GET YOU TO QUIT. IT'S JUST A MATTER OF TIME!!
HMMMM ...
WH WHY?
DOES IT SEEM LIKE SHE TOTALLY HATES ME?!
DOOOOON
I WENT THROUGH TOO MUCH TO FIND THIS JOB TO JUST QUIT NOW!
I'M NOT GOING TO GIVE UP BECAUSE OF YOUR LITTLE PRANKS.
ALTHOUGH WHY CAN'T I SHAKE THE FEELING I'M JUST A BABYSITTER?
VRRRROOOOMM
HM?

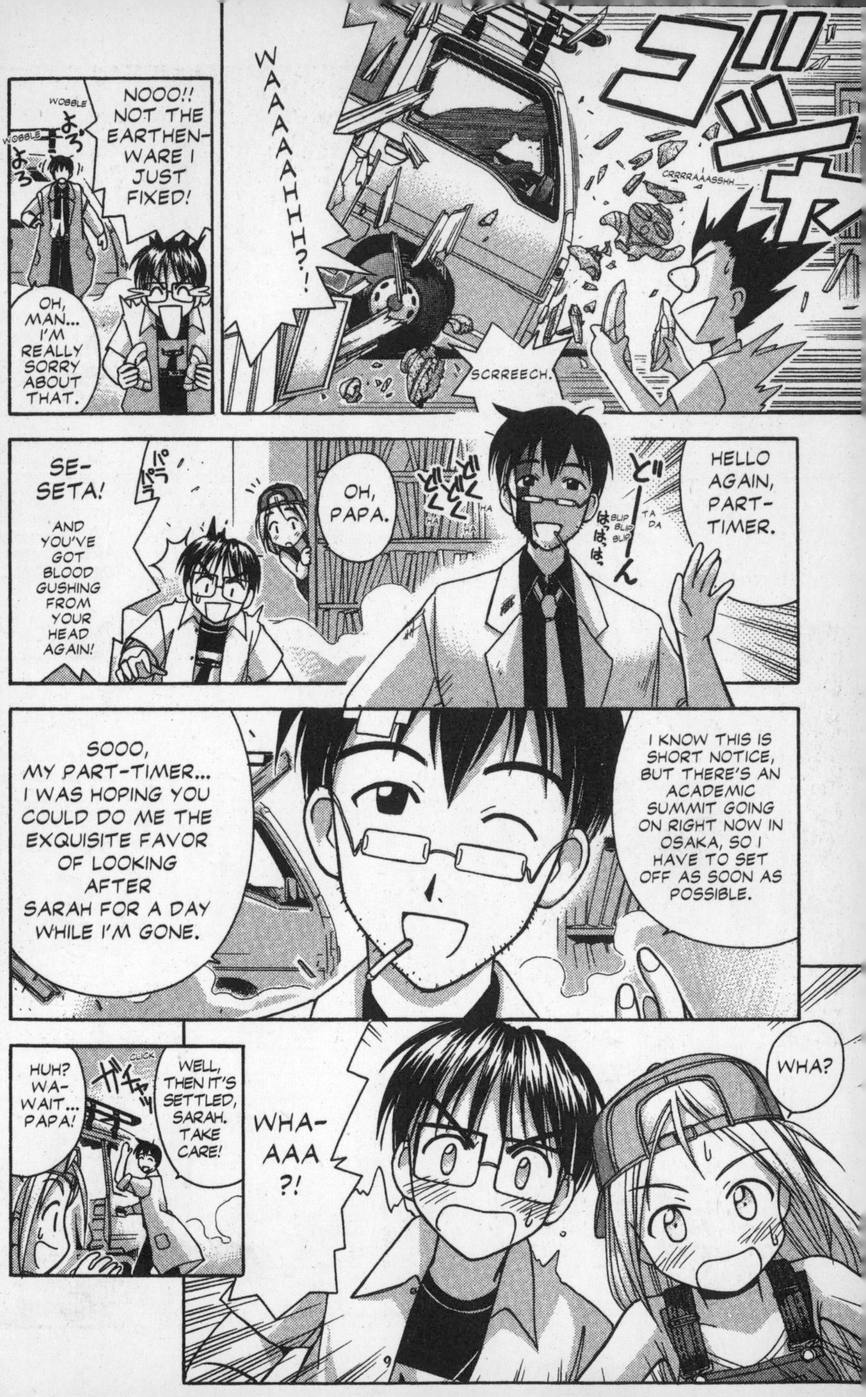
CRRRRAAASSHH
WAAAAAAHHH?!
SCRREECH.
NOOO!! NOT THE EARTHEN-WARE I JUST FIXED!
WOBBLE
WOBBLE
OH, MAN... I'M REALLY SORRY ABOUT THAT.
HELLO AGAIN, PART-TIMER.
TA DA
BLIP BLIP BLIP
HA HA HA
OH, PAPA.
SE-SETA!
AND YOU'VE GOT BLOOD GUSHING FROM YOUR HEAD AGAIN!
I KNOW THIS IS SHORT NOTICE, BUT THERE'S AN ACADEMIC SUMMIT GOING ON RIGHT NOW IN OSAKA, SO I HAVE TO SET OFF AS SOON AS POSSIBLE.
SOOO, MY PART-TIMER... I WAS HOPING YOU COULD DO ME THE EXQUISITE FAVOR OF LOOKING AFTER SARAH FOR A DAY WHILE I'M GONE.
WHA?
WHA-AAA?!
WELL, THEN IT'S SETTLED, SARAH. TAKE CARE!
CLICK
HUH? WA-WAIT... PAPA!

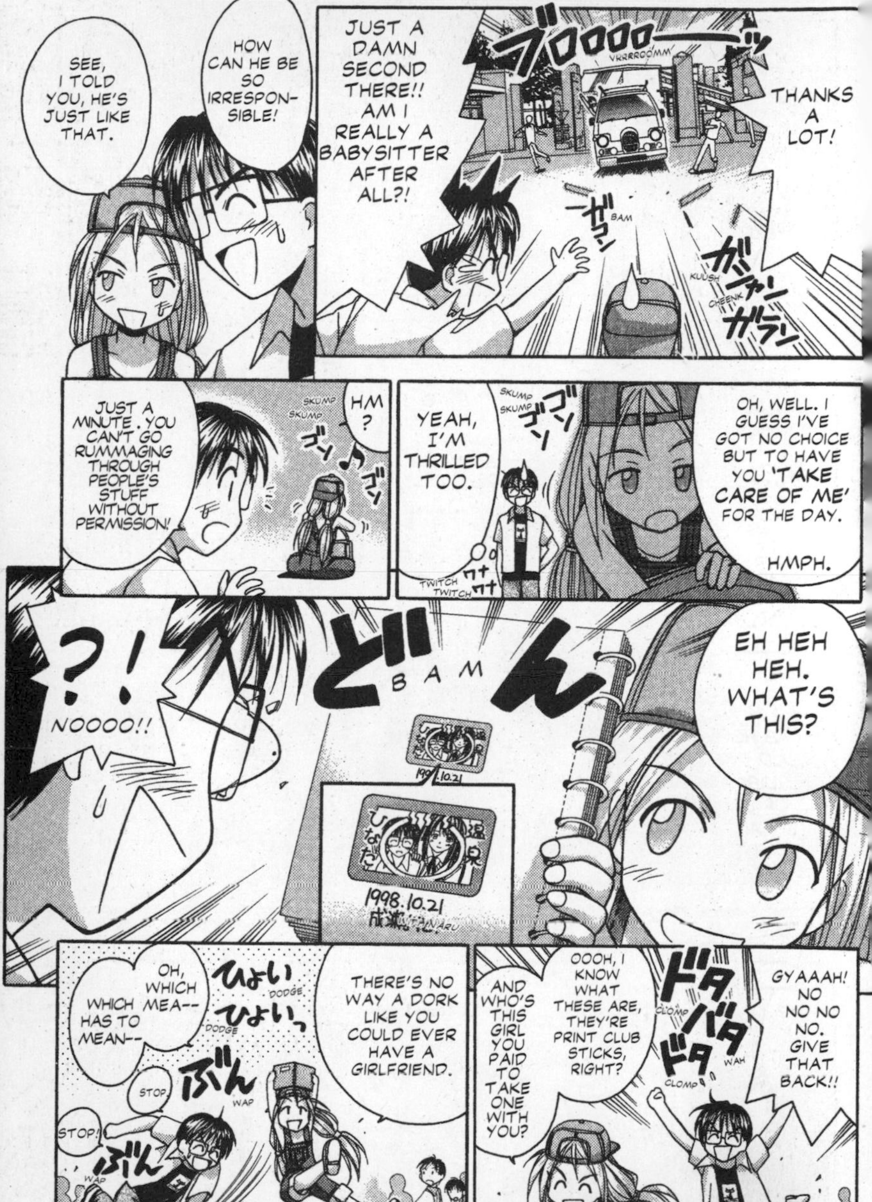
THANKS A LOT!
VKRRROOMM
JUST A DAMN SECOND THERE!! AM I REALLY A BABYSITTER AFTER ALL?!
BAM
KUUSH
CHEENK
HOW CAN HE BE SO IRRESPONSIBLE!
SEE, I TOLD YOU, HE'S JUST LIKE THAT.
OH, WELL. I GUESS I'VE GOT NO CHOICE BUT TO HAVE YOU 'TAKE CARE OF ME' FOR THE DAY.
HMPH.
SKUMP SKUMP
YEAH, I'M THRILLED TOO.
TWITCH TWITCH
HM?
SKUMP SKUMP
JUST A MINUTE. YOU CAN'T GO RUMMAGING THROUGH PEOPLE'S STUFF WITHOUT PERMISSION!
EH HEH HEH. WHAT'S THIS?
BAM
?!
NOOOO!!
1998.10.21
GYAAAH! NO NO NO. GIVE THAT BACK!!
CLOMP
WAH
CLOMP
OOOH, I KNOW WHAT THESE ARE, THEY'RE PRINT CLUB STICKS, RIGHT?
AND WHO'S THIS GIRL YOU PAID TO TAKE ONE WITH YOU?
THERE'S NO WAY A DORK LIKE YOU COULD EVER HAVE A GIRLFRIEND.
OH, WHICH MEA--
WHICH HAS TO MEAN--
DODGE
DODGE
WAP
STOP
STOP!
WAP

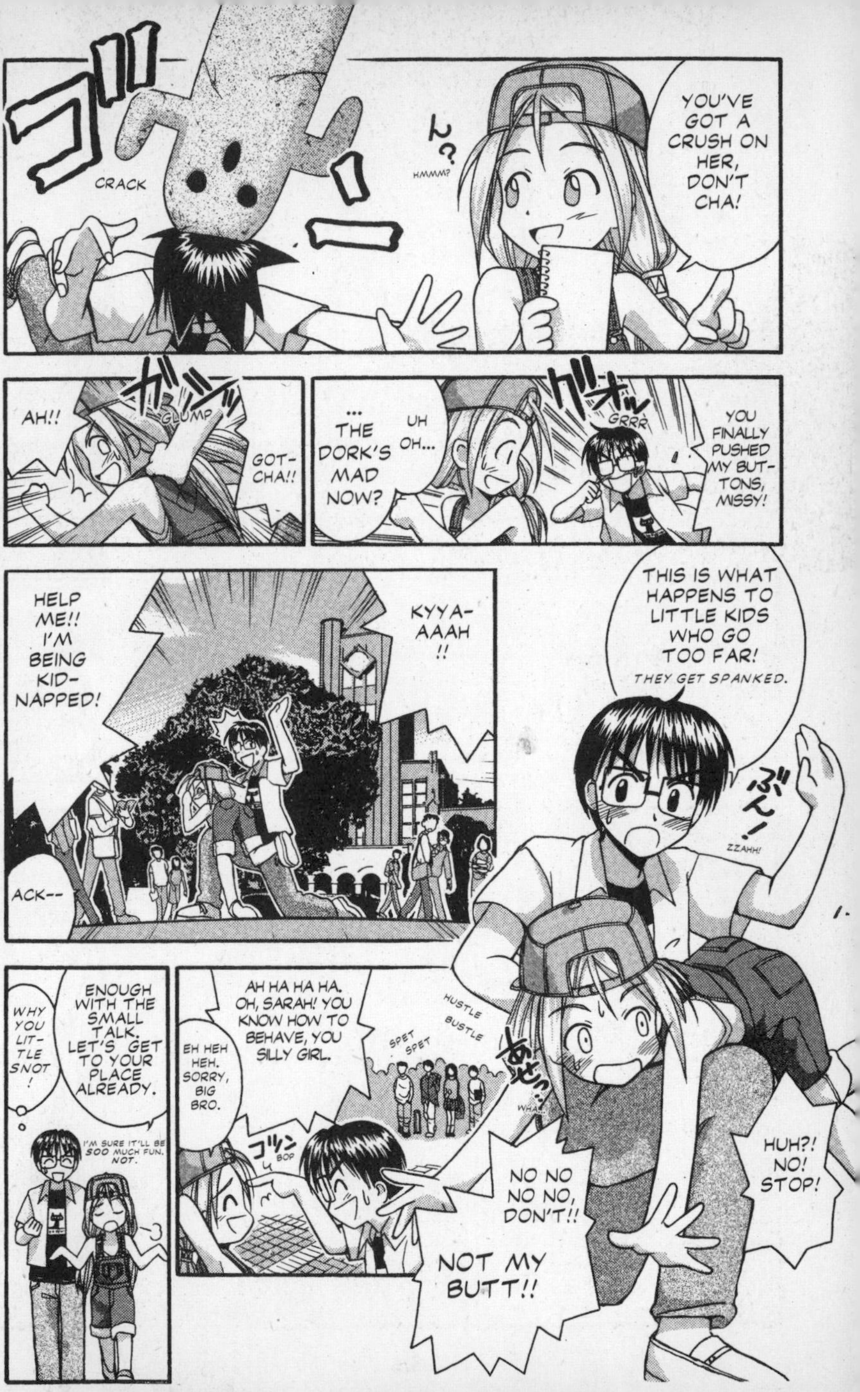

YOU'VE GOT A CRUSH ON HER, DON'T CHA!
HMMM?
CRACK
YOU FINALLY PUSHED MY BUT-TONS, MISSY!
GRRR
UH OH...
... THE DORK'S MAD NOW?
GOT-CHA!!
GLUMP
AH!!
THIS IS WHAT HAPPENS TO LITTLE KIDS WHO GO TOO FAR!
THEY GET SPANKED.
ZZAHH!
HUH?! NO! STOP!
WHA...
NO NO NO NO, DON'T!!
NOT MY BUTT!!
KYYA-AAAH !!
HELP ME!! I'M BEING KID-NAPPED!
ACK--
AH HA HA HA. OH, SARAH! YOU KNOW HOW TO BEHAVE, YOU SILLY GIRL.
HUSTLE BUSTLE
SPET SPET
EH HEH HEH. SORRY, BIG BRO.
BOP
ENOUGH WITH THE SMALL TALK. LET'S GET TO YOUR PLACE ALREADY.
WHY YOU LITTLE SNOT!
I'M SURE IT'LL BE SOO MUCH FUN. NOT.

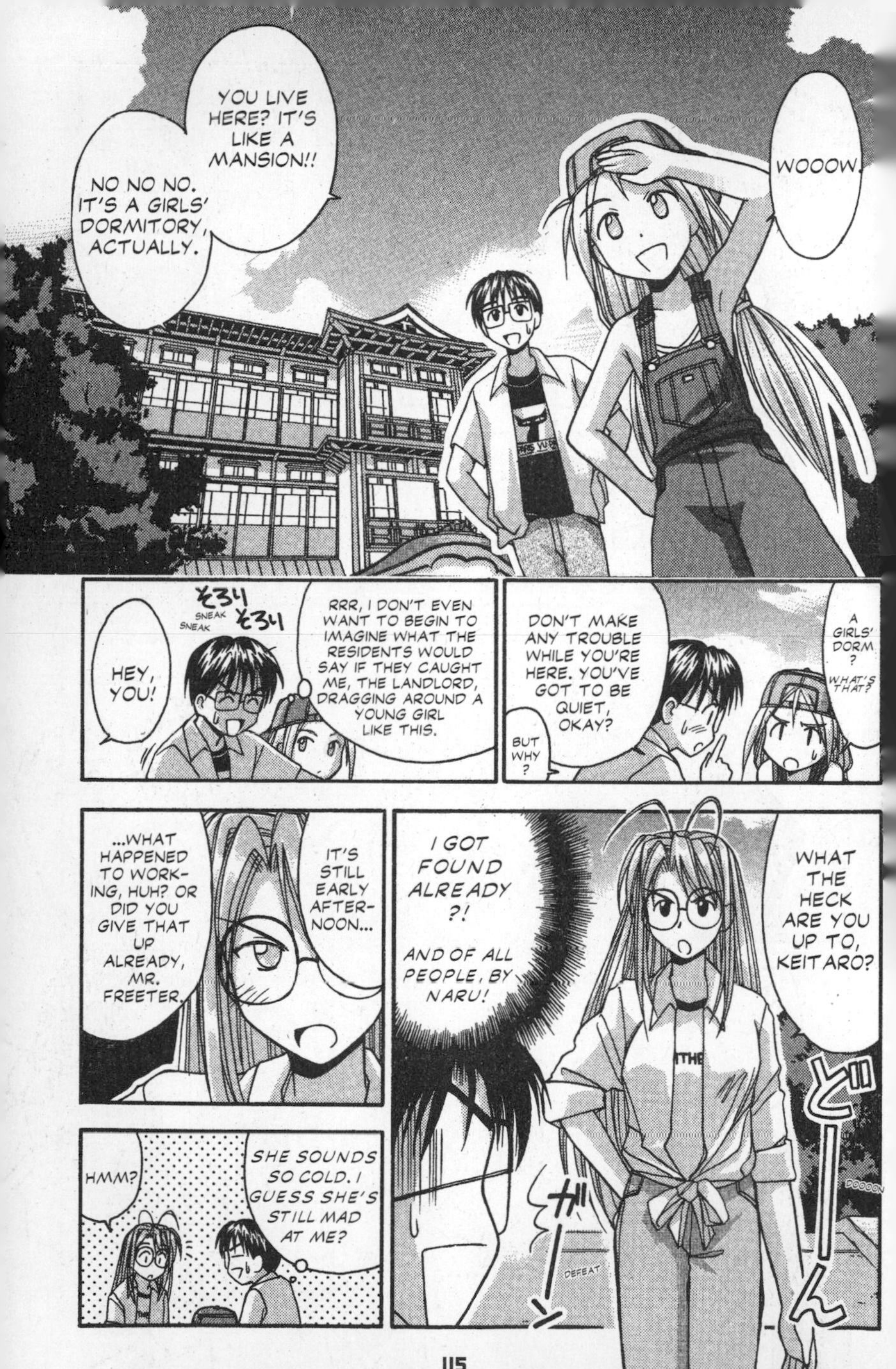
WOOOW.
YOU LIVE HERE? IT'S LIKE A MANSION!!
NO NO NO. IT'S A GIRLS' DORMITORY, ACTUALLY.
A GIRLS' DORM? WHAT'S THAT?
DON'T MAKE ANY TROUBLE WHILE YOU'RE HERE. YOU'VE GOT TO BE QUIET, OKAY?
BUT WHY?
RRR, I DON'T EVEN WANT TO BEGIN TO IMAGINE WHAT THE RESIDENTS WOULD SAY IF THEY CAUGHT ME, THE LANDLORD, DRAGGING AROUND A YOUNG GIRL LIKE THIS.
そろり そろり
SNEAK SNEAK
HEY, YOU!
WHAT THE HECK ARE YOU UP TO, KEITARO?
どーん
DOOOON
I GOT FOUND ALREADY?!
AND OF ALL PEOPLE, BY NARU!
ガー
DEFEAT
IT'S STILL EARLY AFTERNOON...
...WHAT HAPPENED TO WORKING, HUH? OR DID YOU GIVE THAT UP ALREADY, MR. FREETER.
SHE SOUNDS SO COLD. I GUESS SHE'S STILL MAD AT ME?
HMM?

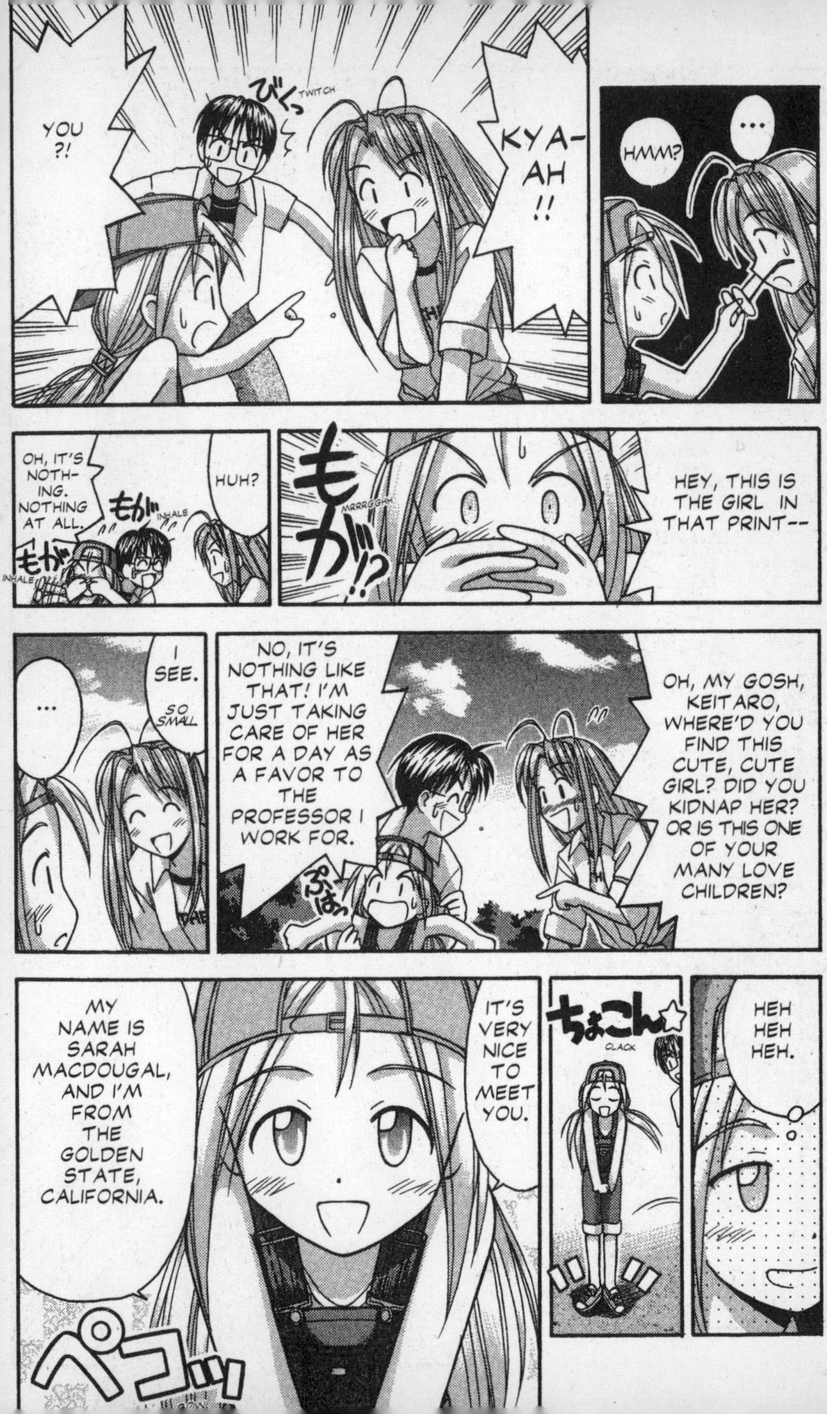
...
HMM?
KYA-AH!!
びくっ
TWITCH
YOU?!
HEY, THIS IS THE GIRL IN THAT PRINT--
もが!?
MRRRGGHH
HUH?
OH, IT'S NOTHING. NOTHING AT ALL.
もが
INHALE
もが
INHALE
OH, MY GOSH, KEITARO, WHERE'D YOU FIND THIS CUTE, CUTE GIRL? DID YOU KIDNAP HER? OR IS THIS ONE OF YOUR MANY LOVE CHILDREN?
NO, IT'S NOTHING LIKE THAT! I'M JUST TAKING CARE OF HER FOR A DAY AS A FAVOR TO THE PROFESSOR I WORK FOR.
ぷはっ
I SEE.
SO SMALL
...
HEH HEH HEH.
ちょこん☆
CLACK
IT'S VERY NICE TO MEET YOU.
MY NAME IS SARAH MACDOUGAL, AND I'M FROM THE GOLDEN STATE, CALIFORNIA.
ペコッ

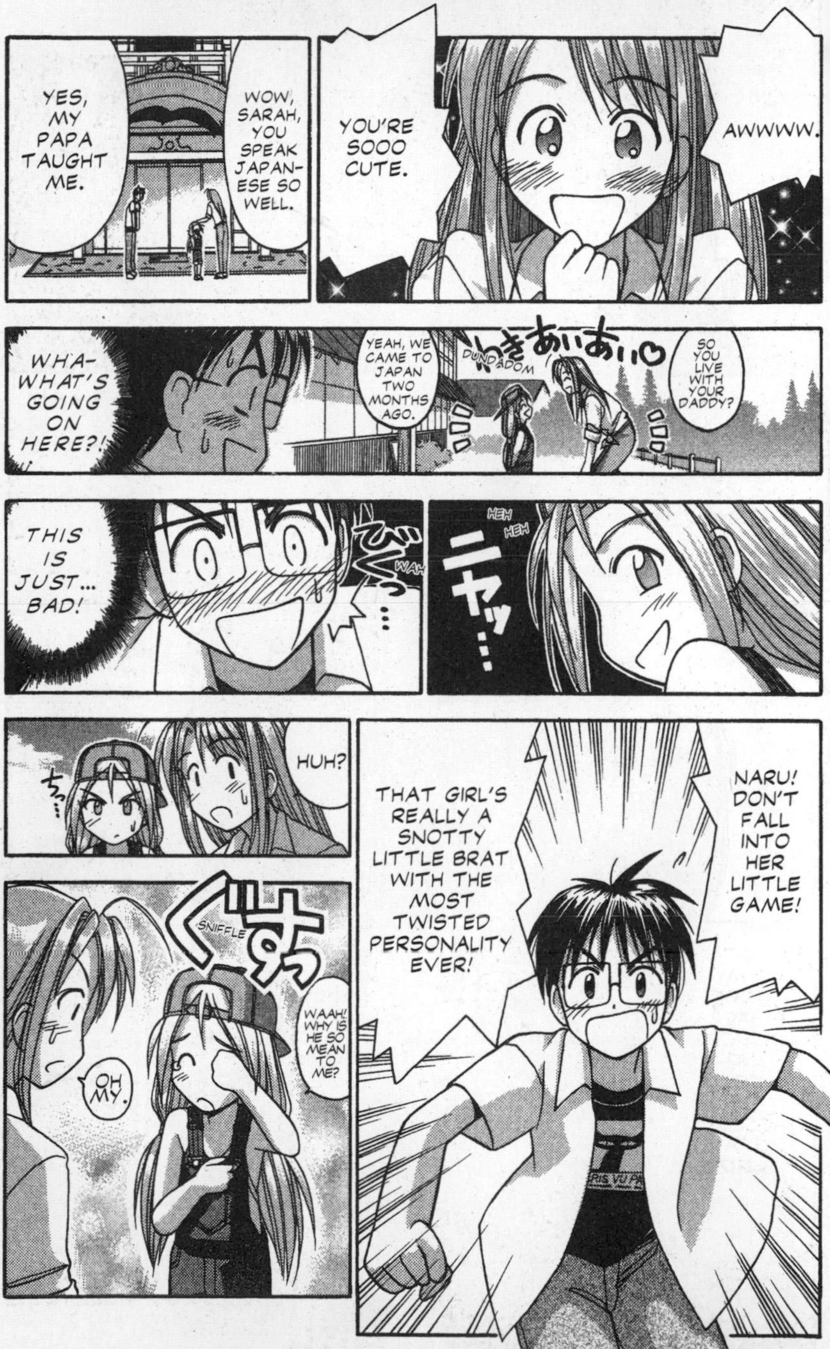
AWWWW.
YOU'RE SOOO CUTE.
WOW, SARAH, YOU SPEAK JAPANESE SO WELL.
YES, MY PAPA TAUGHT ME.
SO YOU LIVE WITH YOUR DADDY?
わきあいあい♡
DUNDADOM
YEAH, WE CAME TO JAPAN TWO MONTHS AGO.
WHA-WHAT'S GOING ON HERE?!
HEH HEH
ニヤッ…
びくっ
WAH
THIS IS JUST... BAD!
NARU! DON'T FALL INTO HER LITTLE GAME!
THAT GIRL'S REALLY A SNOTTY LITTLE BRAT WITH THE MOST TWISTED PERSONALITY EVER!
HUH?
WAAH! WHY IS HE SO MEAN TO ME?
ぐすっ
SNIFFLE
OH MY.

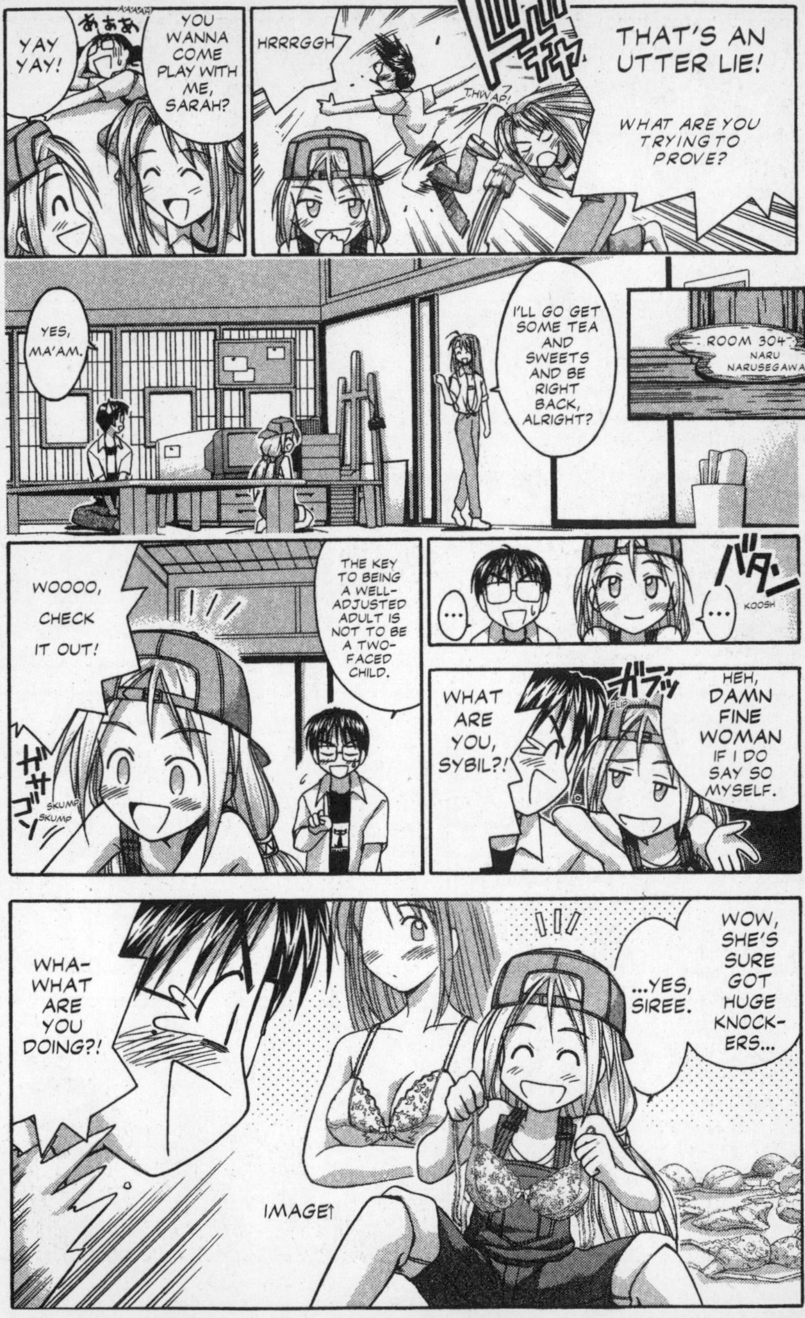
ドギャ
THAT'S AN UTTER LIE!
WHAT ARE YOU TRYING TO PROVE?
THWAP!
HRRRGGH
YOU WANNA COME PLAY WITH ME, SARAH?
あああ
AAAAAH
YAY YAY!
ROOM 304 NARU NARUSEGAWA
I'LL GO GET SOME TEA AND SWEETS AND BE RIGHT BACK, ALRIGHT?
YES, MA'AM.
バタン
KOOSH
...
...
ガラッ
FLIP
HEH, DAMN FINE WOMAN IF I DO SAY SO MYSELF.
WHAT ARE YOU, SYBIL?!
THE KEY TO BEING A WELL-ADJUSTED ADULT IS NOT TO BE A TWO-FACED CHILD.
WOOOO, CHECK IT OUT!
ガサゴソ
SKUMP SKUMP
WOW, SHE'S SURE GOT HUGE KNOCKERS...
...YES, SIREE.
WHA-WHAT ARE YOU DOING?!
IMAGE↑

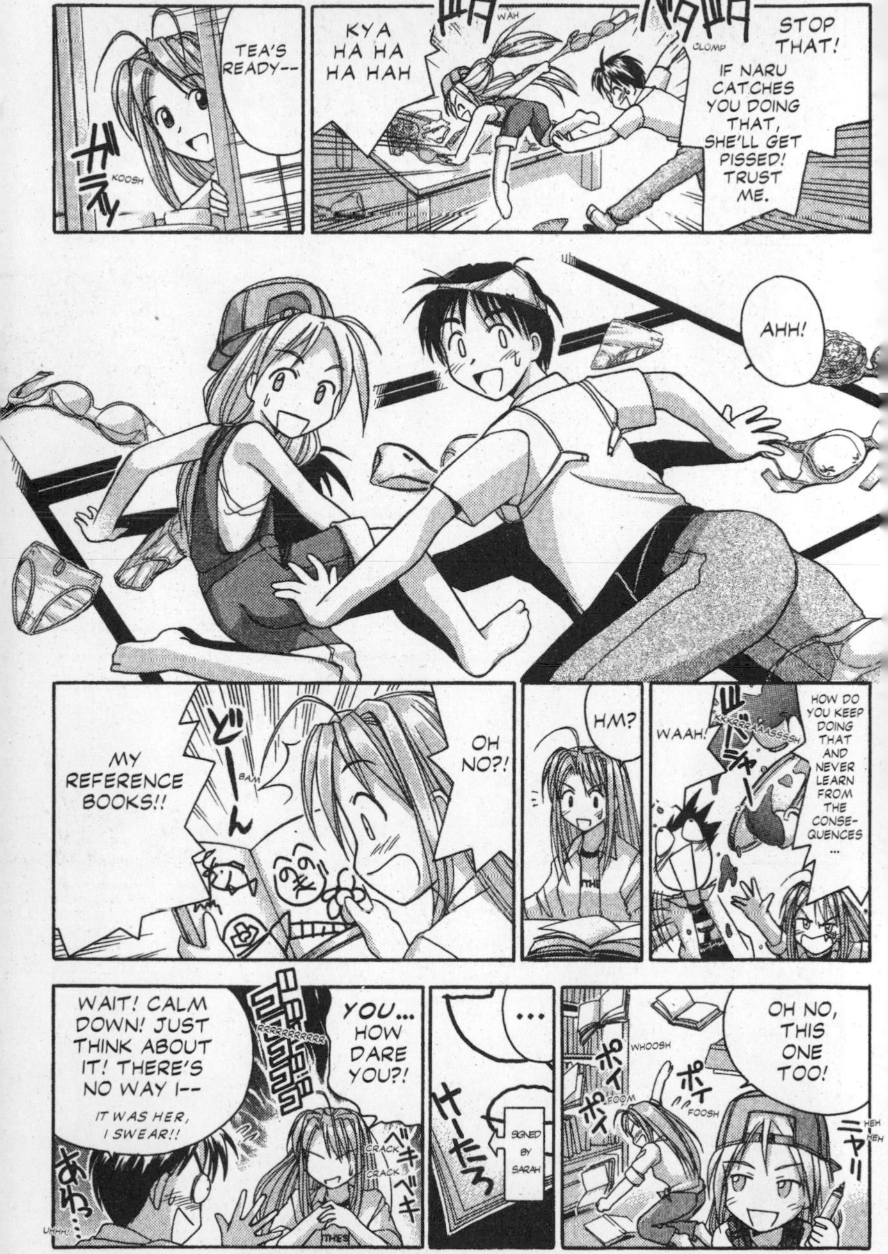
STOP THAT!
IF NARU CATCHES YOU DOING THAT, SHE'LL GET PISSED! TRUST ME.
CLOMP
WAH
KYA HA HA HA HAH
TEA'S READY--
KOOSH
AHH!
HOW DO YOU KEEP DOING THAT AND NEVER LEARN FROM THE CONSE-QUENCES ...
WAAH!
KKKRRRAAASSSSH
HM?
OH NO?!
BAM
MY REFERENCE BOOKS!!
OH NO, THIS ONE TOO!
HEH HEH
WHOOSH
FOOSH
FOOM
...
SIGNED BY SARAH
YOU... HOW DARE YOU?!
CRACK
CRACK
WAIT! CALM DOWN! JUST THINK ABOUT IT! THERE'S NO WAY I--
IT WAS HER, I SWEAR!!
UHHH!...

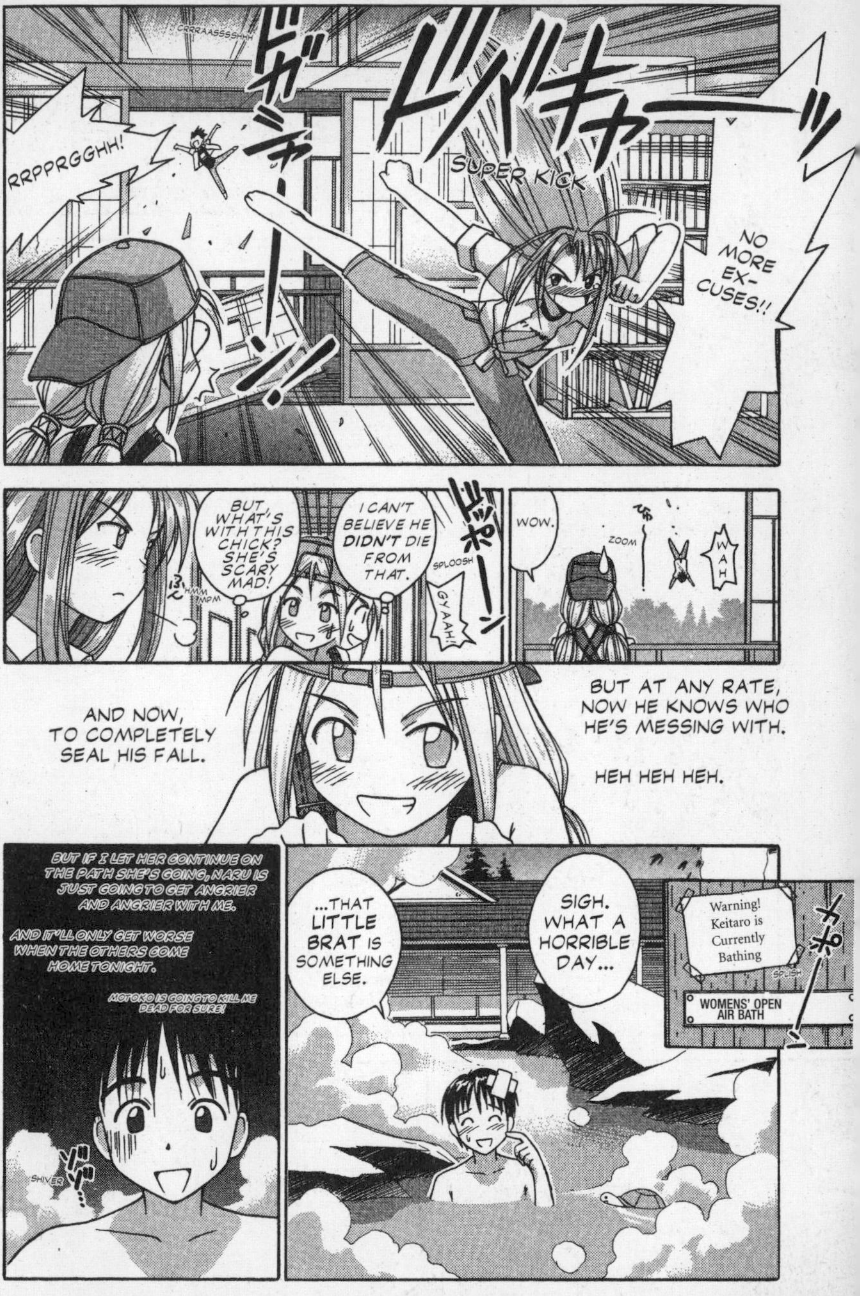
SUPER KICK
NO MORE EX-CUSES!!
CRRRAASSSSHHH
RRPPRGGHH!
WAH
ZOOM
WOW.
I CAN'T BELIEVE HE **DIDN'T** DIE FROM THAT.
SPLOOSH
GYAAH!
BUT, WHAT'S WITH THIS CHICK? SHE'S SCARY MAD!
HMM MPM
BUT AT ANY RATE, NOW HE KNOWS WHO HE'S MESSING WITH.
HEH HEH HEH.
AND NOW, TO COMPLETELY SEAL HIS FALL.
Warning! Keitaro is Currently Bathing
WOMENS' OPEN AIR BATH
SPLISH
SIGH. WHAT A HORRIBLE DAY...
...THAT **LITTLE BRAT** IS SOMETHING ELSE.
BUT IF I LET HER CONTINUE ON THE PATH SHE'S GOING, NARU IS JUST GOING TO GET ANGRIER AND ANGRIER WITH ME.
AND IT'LL ONLY GET WORSE WHEN THE OTHERS COME HOME TONIGHT.
MOTOKO IS GOING TO KILL ME DEAD FOR SURE!
SHIVER

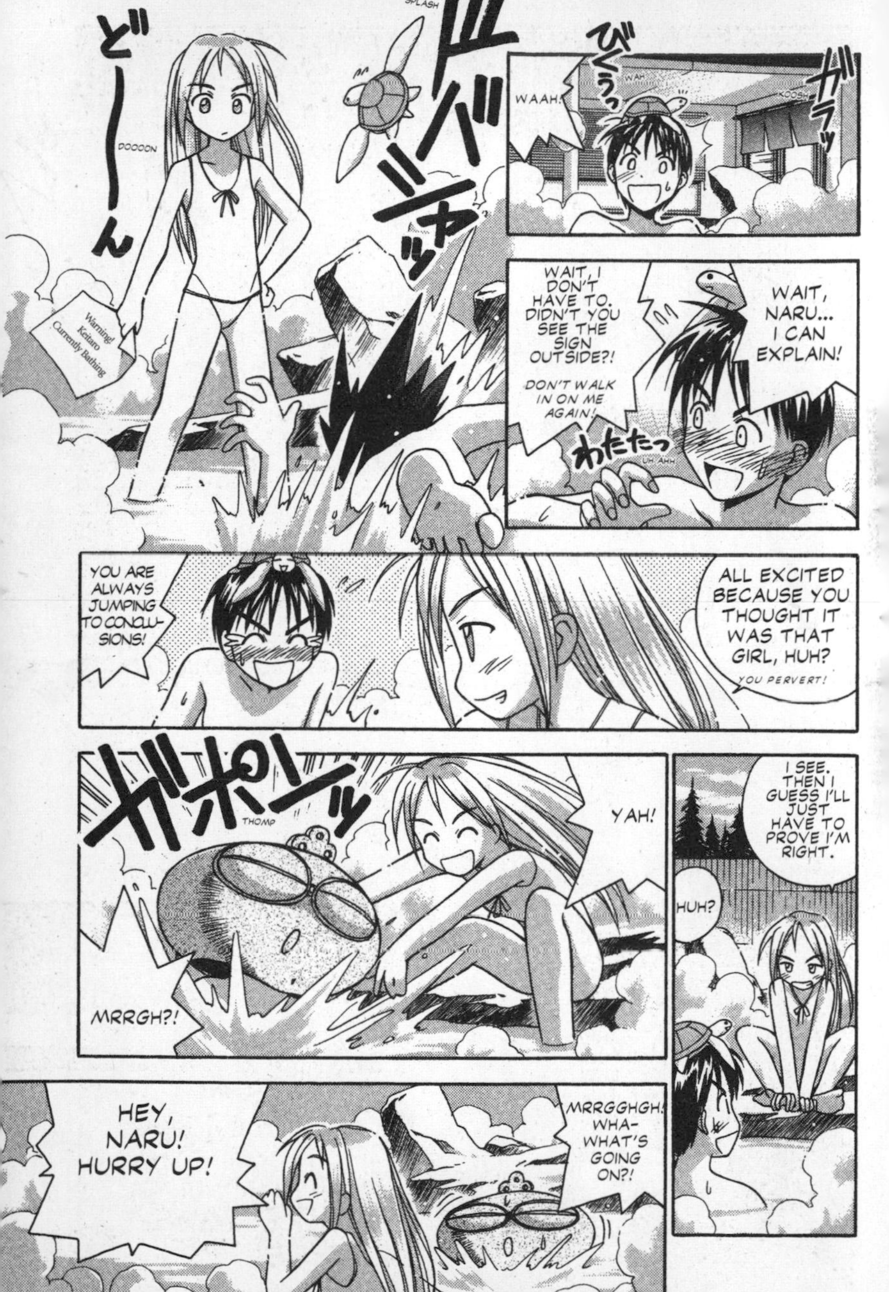
ガラッ
KOOSH
びくぅっ
WAH
WAAH!
WAIT, NARU... I CAN EXPLAIN!
WAIT, I DON'T HAVE TO. DIDN'T YOU SEE THE SIGN OUTSIDE?!
DON'T WALK IN ON ME AGAIN!
わたたっ
UH AHH
ドバシャッ
SPLASH
どーーーん
DOOOON
Warning! Keitaro Currently Bathing
ALL EXCITED BECAUSE YOU THOUGHT IT WAS THAT GIRL, HUH?
YOU PERVERT!
YOU ARE ALWAYS JUMPING TO CONCLU-SIONS!
I SEE. THEN I GUESS I'LL JUST HAVE TO PROVE I'M RIGHT.
HUH?
YAH!
ガポンッ
THOMP
MRRGH?!
MRRGGHGH! WHA-WHAT'S GOING ON?!
HEY, NARU! HURRY UP!

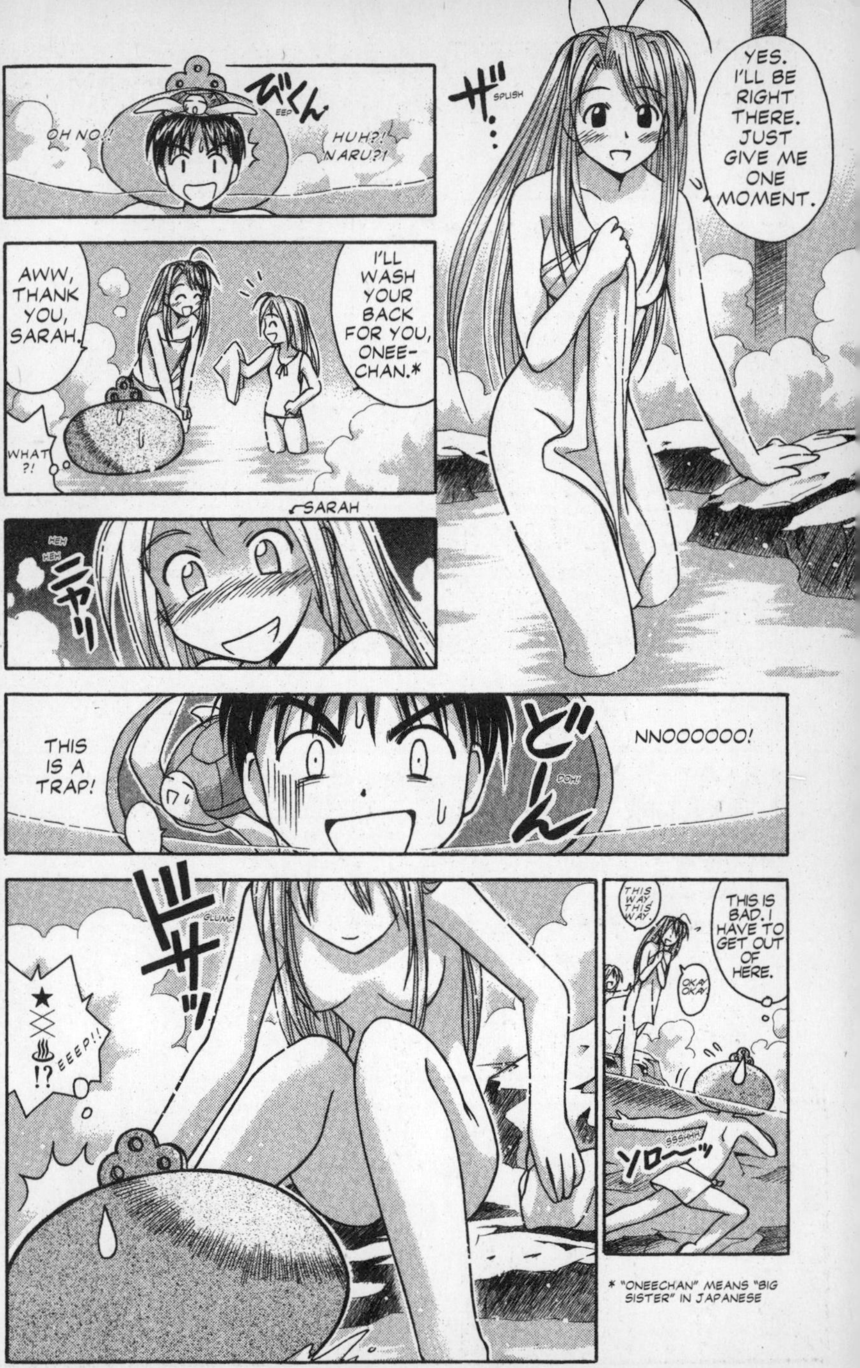
ザ
SPLISH
YES. I'LL BE RIGHT THERE. JUST GIVE ME ONE MOMENT.
びくん
EEP
HUH?! NARU?!
OH NO!!
I'LL WASH YOUR BACK FOR YOU, ONEE-CHAN.*
AWW, THANK YOU, SARAH.
WHAT?!
SARAH
ニヤリ
HEH HEH
NNOOOOOO!
どん
DOH!
THIS IS A TRAP!
THIS IS BAD. I HAVE TO GET OUT OF HERE.
OKAY OKAY.
THIS WAY, THIS WAY.
ソロ〜ッ
SSSHHH
ドサッ
GLUMP
EEEP!!
!?

* "ONEECHAN" MEANS "BIG SISTER" IN JAPANESE

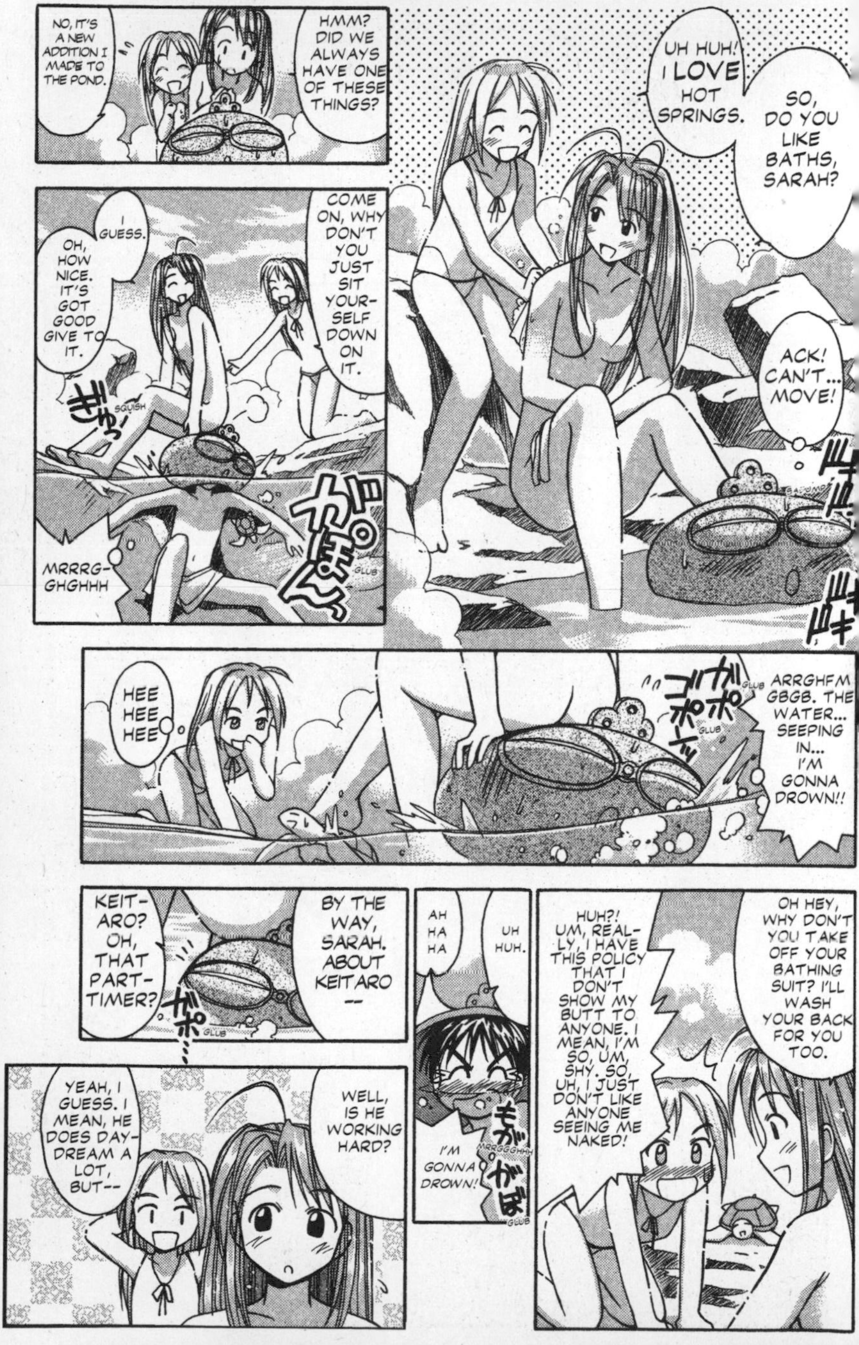
SO, DO YOU LIKE BATHS, SARAH?
UH HUH! I LOVE HOT SPRINGS.
ACK! CAN'T... MOVE!
BA-DUMP
HMM? DID WE ALWAYS HAVE ONE OF THESE THINGS?
NO, IT'S A NEW ADDITION I MADE TO THE POND.
COME ON, WHY DON'T YOU JUST SIT YOURSELF DOWN ON IT.
I GUESS.
OH, HOW NICE. IT'S GOT GOOD GIVE TO IT.
SQUISH
GLUB
MRRRG-GHGHHH
ARRGHFM GBGB. THE WATER... SEEPING IN... I'M GONNA DROWN!!
GLUB
GLUB
HEE HEE HEE
OH HEY, WHY DON'T YOU TAKE OFF YOUR BATHING SUIT? I'LL WASH YOUR BACK FOR YOU TOO.
HUH?! UM, REALLY, I HAVE THIS POLICY THAT I DON'T SHOW MY BUTT TO ANYONE. I MEAN, I'M SO, UM, SHY. SO, UH, I JUST DON'T LIKE ANYONE SEEING ME NAKED!
UH HUH.
AH HA HA
MRRGGGHHH
I'M GONNA DROWN!
GLUB
BY THE WAY, SARAH. ABOUT KEITARO --
KEITARO? OH, THAT PART-TIMER?
GLUB
WELL, IS HE WORKING HARD?
YEAH, I GUESS. I MEAN, HE DOES DAYDREAM A LOT, BUT--

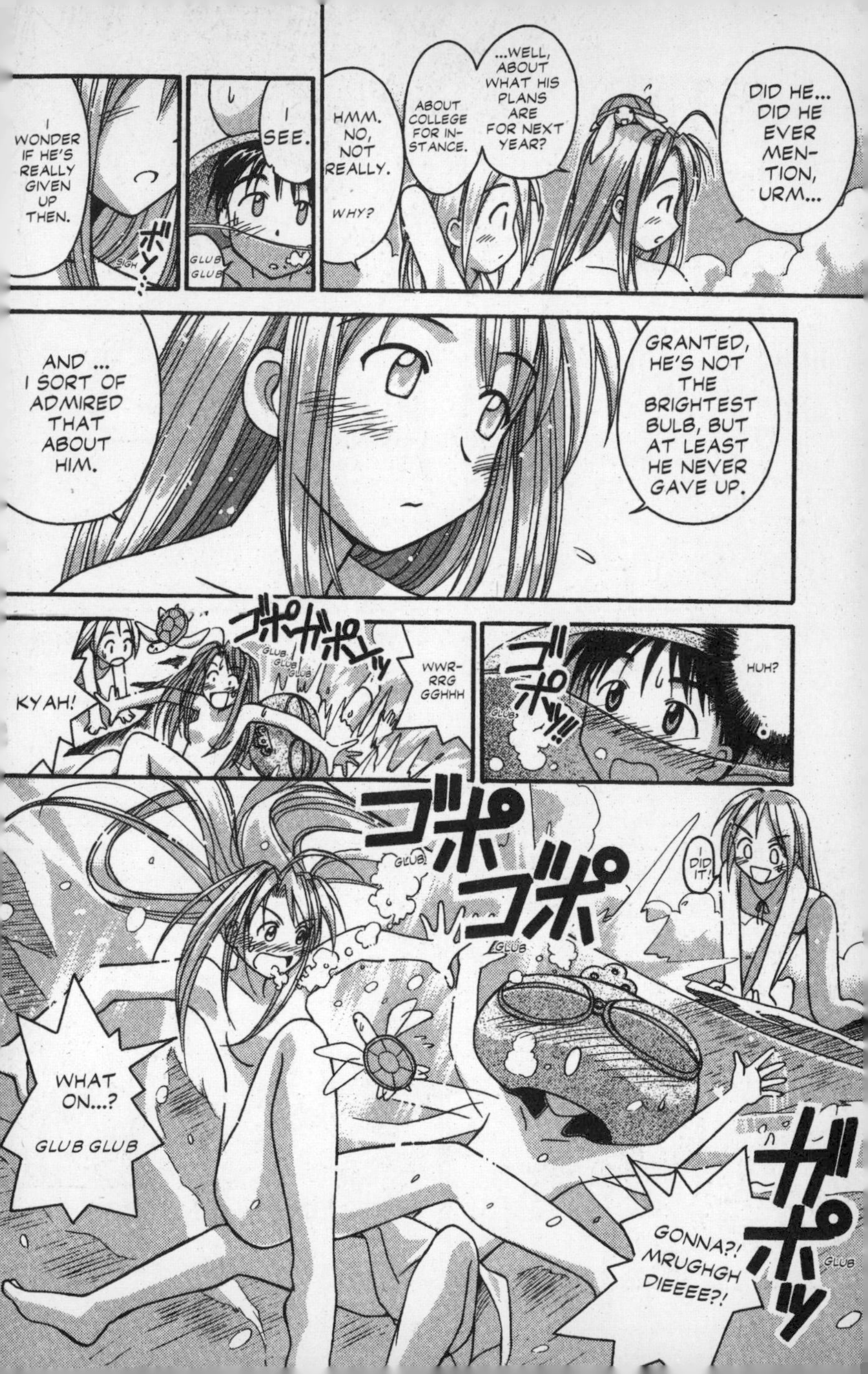
DID HE... DID HE EVER MENTION, URM...
...WELL, ABOUT WHAT HIS PLANS ARE FOR NEXT YEAR?
ABOUT COLLEGE FOR INSTANCE.
HMM. NO, NOT REALLY.
WHY?
I SEE.
GLUB GLUB
I WONDER IF HE'S REALLY GIVEN UP THEN.
ボソ…
SIGH
GRANTED, HE'S NOT THE BRIGHTEST BULB, BUT AT LEAST HE NEVER GAVE UP.
AND ... I SORT OF ADMIRED THAT ABOUT HIM.
HUH?
ゴポッ!!
GLUB
WWR-RRG GGHHH
ゴポガポュッ
GLUB GLUB GLUB
KYAH!
I DID IT!
ゴポゴポ
GLUB
GLUB
ガポッ
GLUB
GONNA?! MRUGHGH DIEEEE?!
WHAT ON...? GLUB GLUB

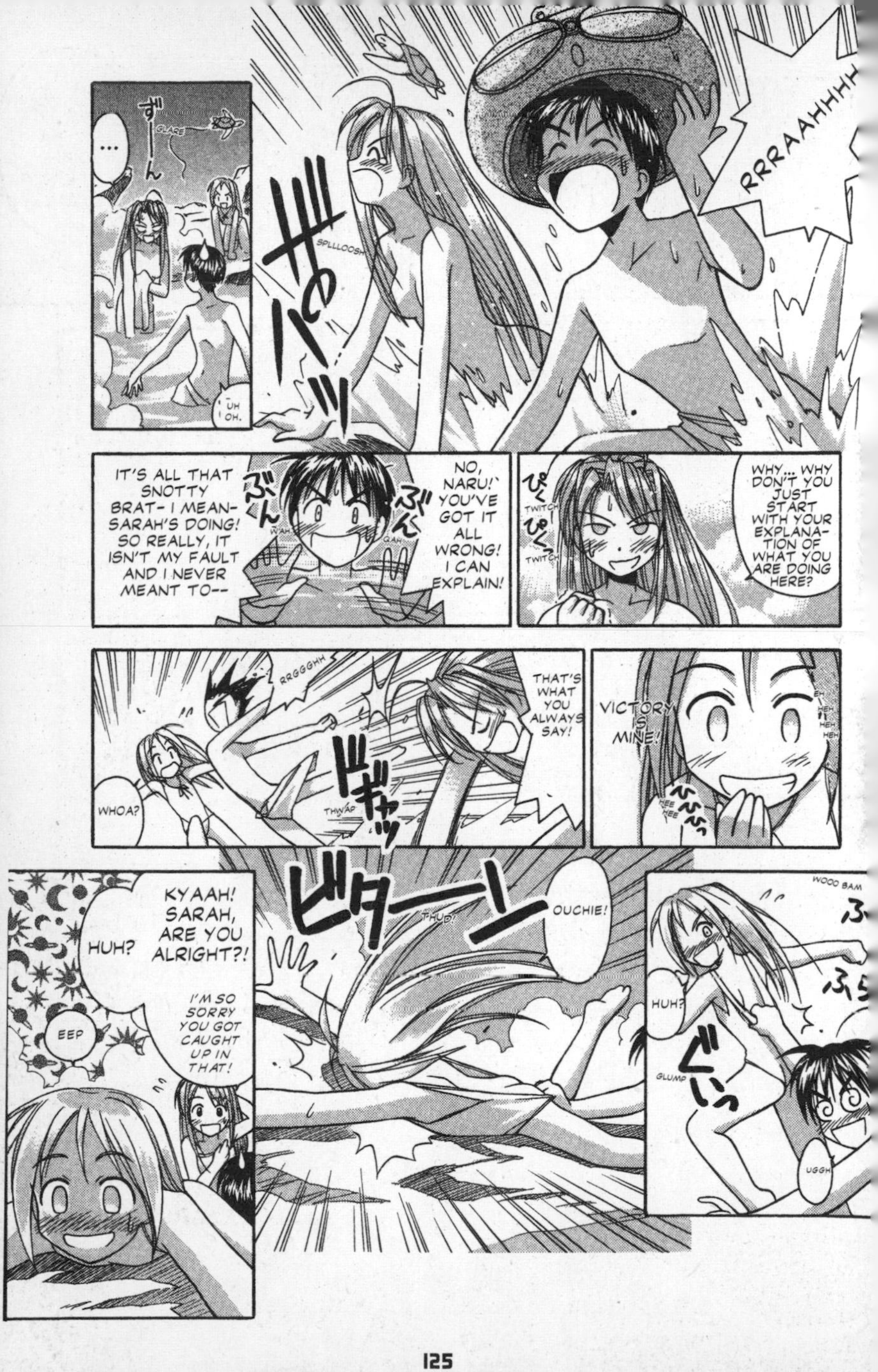
RRRAAHHHH
SPLLLOOSH
ずーん
GLARE
...
UH OH.
WHY... WHY DON'T YOU JUST START WITH YOUR EXPLANATION OF WHAT YOU ARE DOING HERE?
TWITCH
TWITCH
NO, NARU! YOU'VE GOT IT ALL WRONG! I CAN EXPLAIN!
IT'S ALL THAT SNOTTY BRAT- I MEAN- SARAH'S DOING! SO REALLY, IT ISN'T MY FAULT AND I NEVER MEANT TO--
WAH
GAH
VICTORY IS MINE!
EH HEH HEH HEH
HEE HEE
THAT'S WHAT YOU ALWAYS SAY!
RRGGGHH
THWAP
WHOA?
WOOO BAM
HUH?
GLUMP
UGGH
THUD!
OUCHIE!
KYAAH! SARAH, ARE YOU ALRIGHT?!
HUH?
I'M SO SORRY YOU GOT CAUGHT UP IN THAT!
EEP

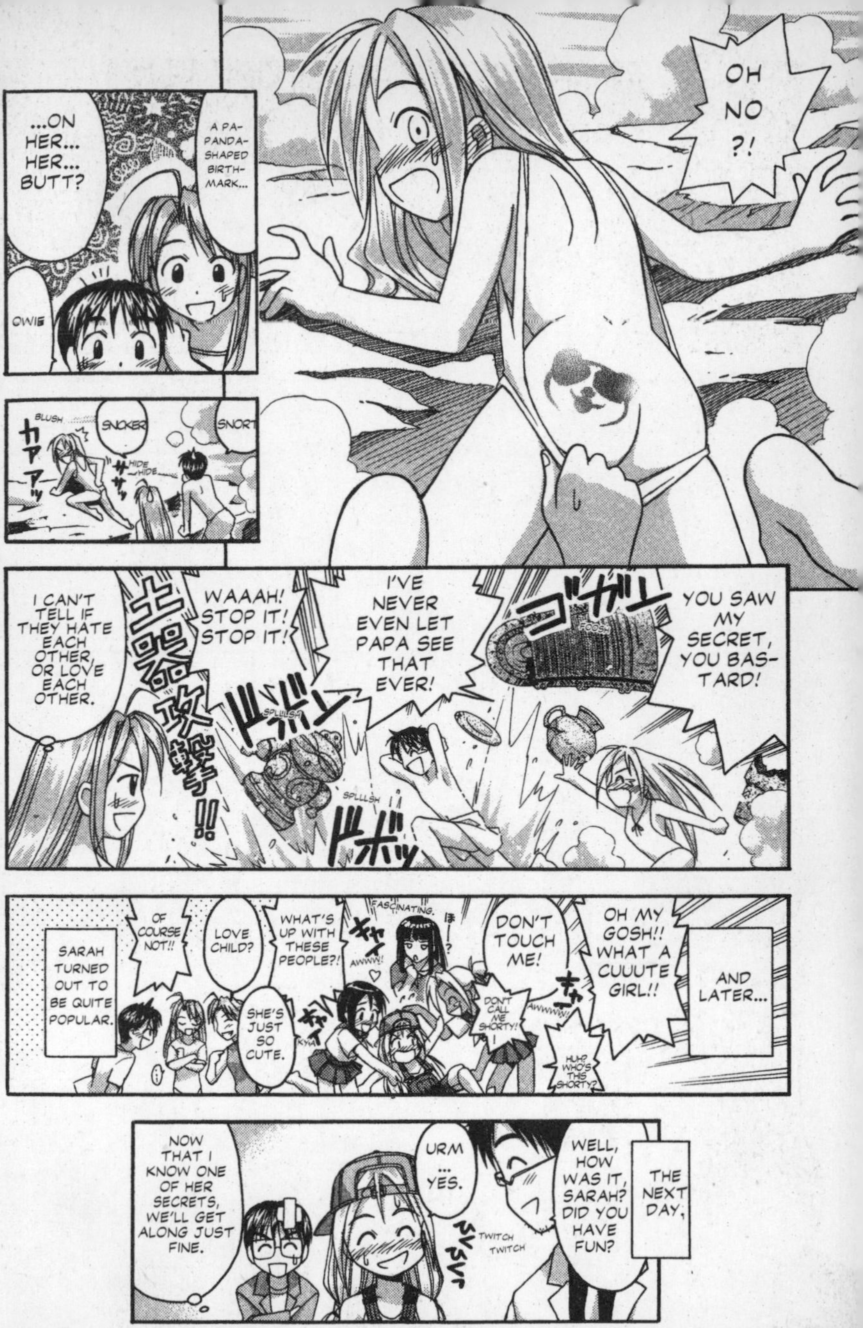
OH NO ?!
A PA-PANDA-SHAPED BIRTH-MARK...
...ON HER... HER... BUTT?
OWIE
SNORT
SNICKER
HIDE HIDE
BLUSH
YOU SAW MY SECRET, YOU BASTARD!
FOOSH
I'VE NEVER EVEN LET PAPA SEE THAT EVER!
SPLLLSH
WAAAH! STOP IT! STOP IT!
土器攻撃!!
SPLLLSH
I CAN'T TELL IF THEY HATE EACH OTHER, OR LOVE EACH OTHER.
AND LATER...
OH MY GOSH!! WHAT A CUUUTE GIRL!!
AWWWW!!
DON'T TOUCH ME!
HUH? WHO'S THIS SHORTY?
DON'T CALL ME SHORTY!!
FASCINATING.
WHAT'S UP WITH THESE PEOPLE?!
AWWW!
KYA
SHE'S JUST SO CUTE.
LOVE CHILD?
OF COURSE NOT!!
SARAH TURNED OUT TO BE QUITE POPULAR.
THE NEXT DAY,
WELL, HOW WAS IT, SARAH? DID YOU HAVE FUN?
URM... YES.
TWITCH TWITCH
NOW THAT I KNOW ONE OF HER SECRETS, WE'LL GET ALONG JUST FINE.

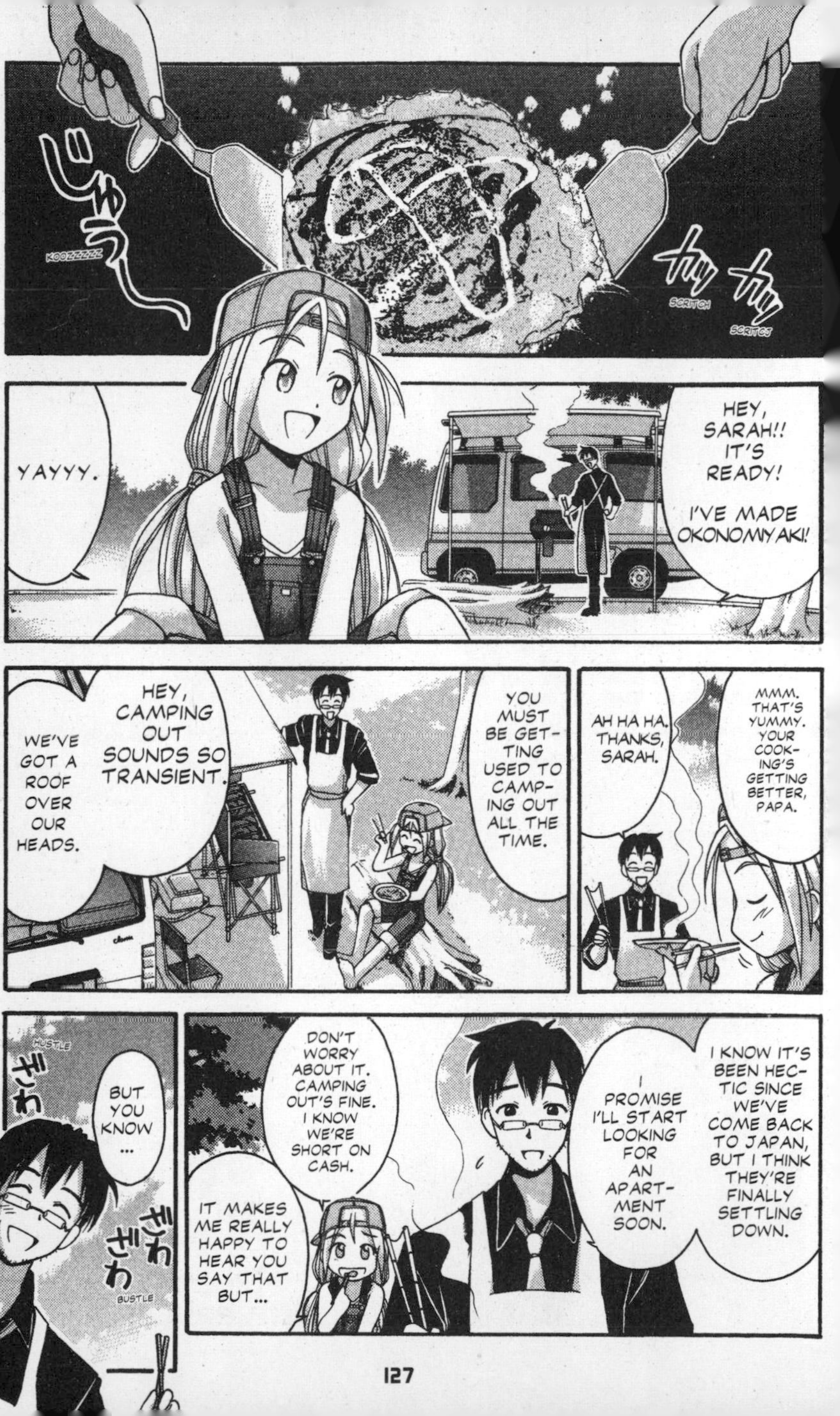

じゅう～
KOOZZZZZ
カッ カッ
SCRITCH
SCRITCJ
HEY, SARAH!! IT'S READY!
I'VE MADE OKONOMIYAKI!
YAYYY.
MMM. THAT'S YUMMY. YOUR COOKING'S GETTING BETTER, PAPA.
AH HA HA. THANKS, SARAH.
YOU MUST BE GETTING USED TO CAMPING OUT ALL THE TIME.
HEY, CAMPING OUT SOUNDS SO TRANSIENT.
WE'VE GOT A ROOF OVER OUR HEADS.
I KNOW IT'S BEEN HECTIC SINCE WE'VE COME BACK TO JAPAN, BUT I THINK THEY'RE FINALLY SETTLING DOWN.
I PROMISE I'LL START LOOKING FOR AN APARTMENT SOON.
DON'T WORRY ABOUT IT. CAMPING OUT'S FINE. I KNOW WE'RE SHORT ON CASH.
IT MAKES ME REALLY HAPPY TO HEAR YOU SAY THAT BUT...
HUSTLE
ざわ
BUT YOU KNOW...
ざわ ざわ
BUSTLE

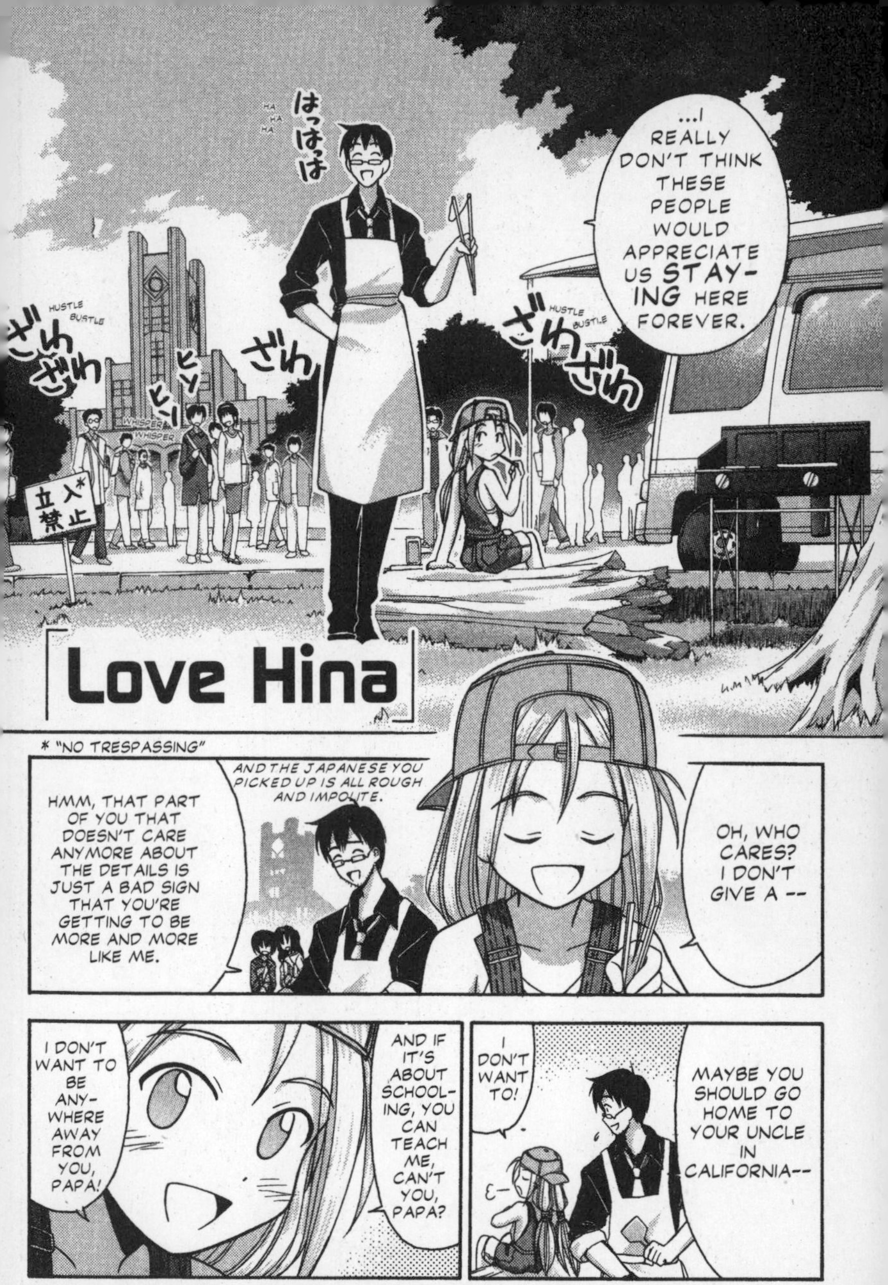
はっはっは
HA HA HA
...I REALLY DON'T THINK THESE PEOPLE WOULD APPRECIATE US STAYING HERE FOREVER.
ざわざわ
HUSTLE BUSTLE
ざわ
ヒソヒソ
WHISPER WHISPER
ざわざわ
HUSTLE BUSTLE
立入禁止*
Love Hina
* "NO TRESPASSING"
OH, WHO CARES? I DON'T GIVE A --
HMM, THAT PART OF YOU THAT DOESN'T CARE ANYMORE ABOUT THE DETAILS IS JUST A BAD SIGN THAT YOU'RE GETTING TO BE MORE AND MORE LIKE ME.
AND THE JAPANESE YOU PICKED UP IS ALL ROUGH AND IMPOLITE.
MAYBE YOU SHOULD GO HOME TO YOUR UNCLE IN CALIFORNIA--
I DON'T WANT TO!
ε—
AND IF IT'S ABOUT SCHOOLING, YOU CAN TEACH ME, CAN'T YOU, PAPA?
I DON'T WANT TO BE ANYWHERE AWAY FROM YOU, PAPA!

HINATA. 31 Missing You at Hinata House

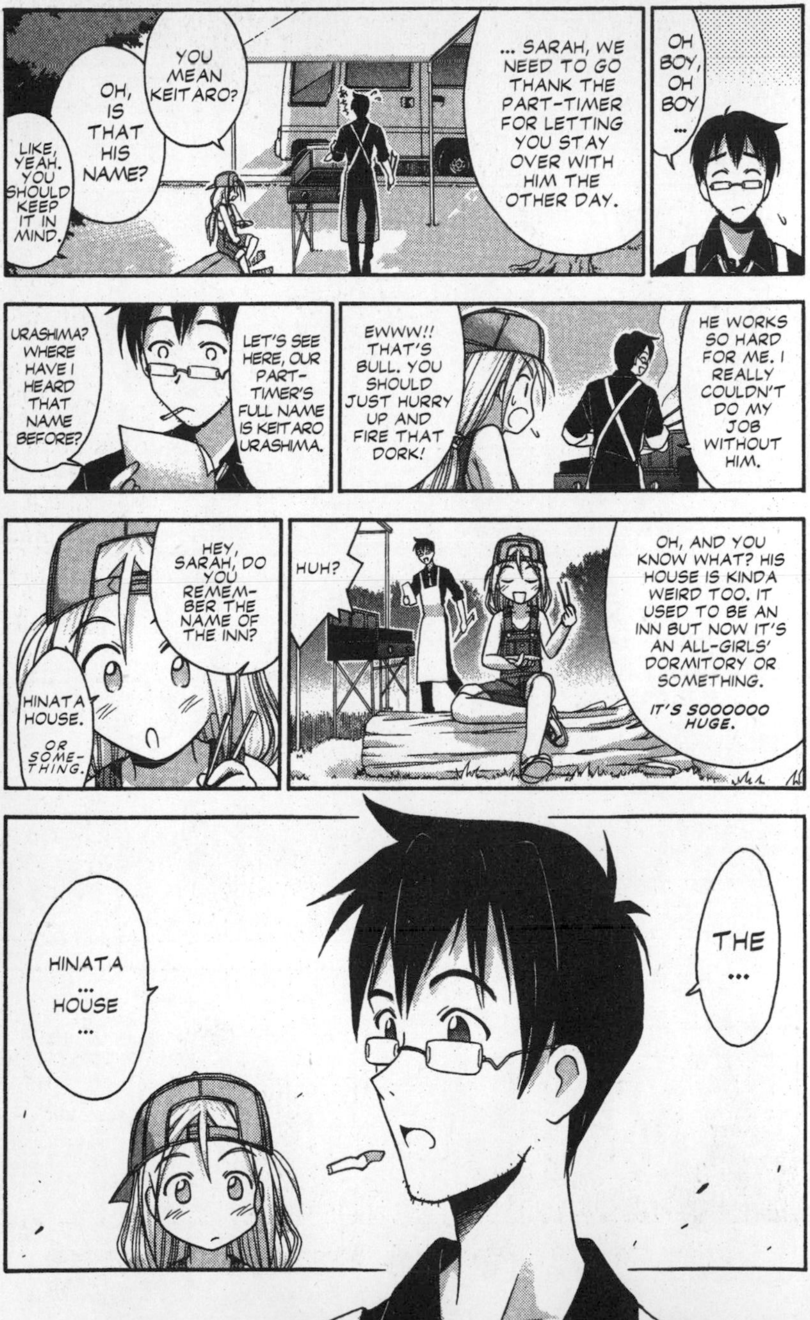
OH BOY, OH BOY ...
... SARAH, WE NEED TO GO THANK THE PART-TIMER FOR LETTING YOU STAY OVER WITH HIM THE OTHER DAY.
YOU MEAN KEITARO?
OH, IS THAT HIS NAME?
LIKE, YEAH. YOU SHOULD KEEP IT IN MIND.
HE WORKS SO HARD FOR ME. I REALLY COULDN'T DO MY JOB WITHOUT HIM.
EWWW!! THAT'S BULL. YOU SHOULD JUST HURRY UP AND FIRE THAT DORK!
LET'S SEE HERE, OUR PART-TIMER'S FULL NAME IS KEITARO URASHIMA.
URASHIMA? WHERE HAVE I HEARD THAT NAME BEFORE?
OH, AND YOU KNOW WHAT? HIS HOUSE IS KINDA WEIRD TOO. IT USED TO BE AN INN BUT NOW IT'S AN ALL-GIRLS' DORMITORY OR SOMETHING.
IT'S SOOOOOO HUGE.
HUH?
HEY, SARAH, DO YOU REMEMBER THE NAME OF THE INN?
HINATA HOUSE.
OR SOMETHING.
THE ...
HINATA ... HOUSE ...

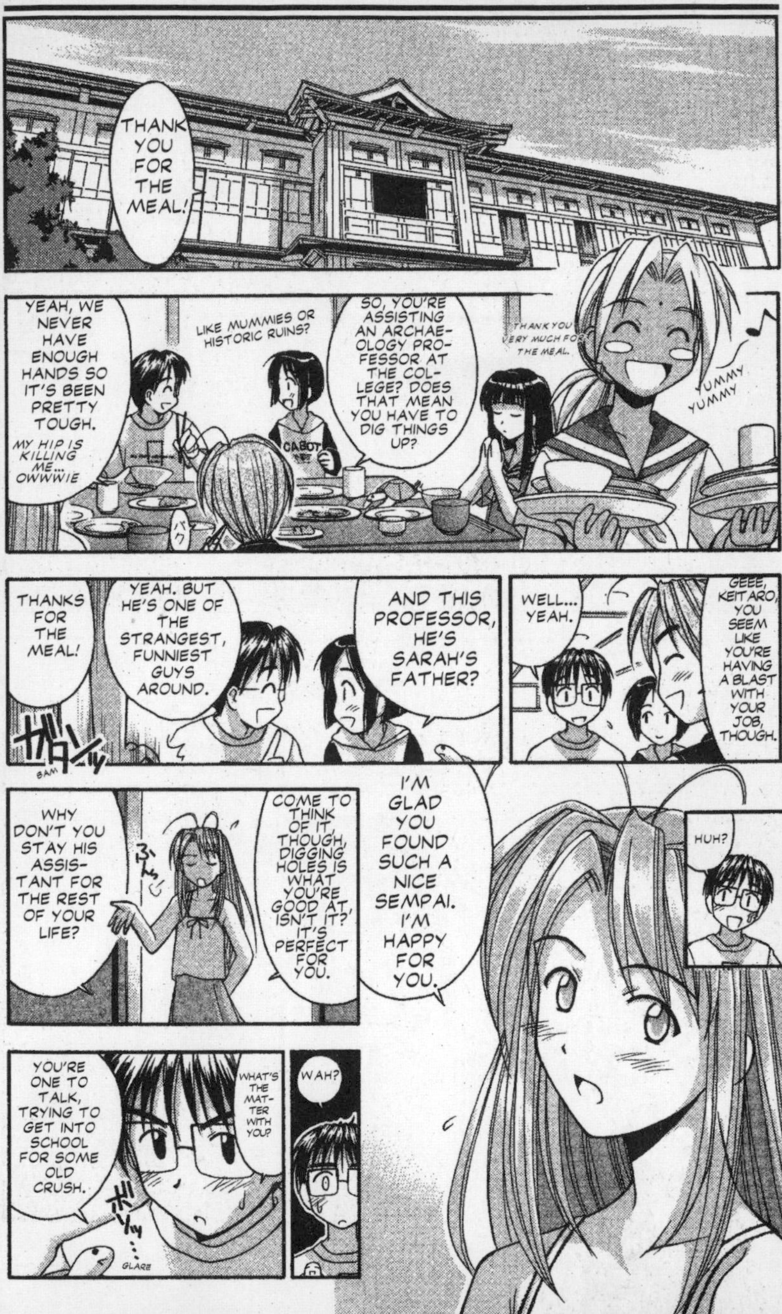
THANK YOU FOR THE MEAL!
YUMMY YUMMY
THANK YOU VERY MUCH FOR THE MEAL.
SO, YOU'RE ASSISTING AN ARCHAEOLOGY PROFESSOR AT THE COLLEGE? DOES THAT MEAN YOU HAVE TO DIG THINGS UP?
LIKE MUMMIES OR HISTORIC RUINS?
YEAH, WE NEVER HAVE ENOUGH HANDS SO IT'S BEEN PRETTY TOUGH.
MY HIP IS KILLING ME... OWWWIE
GEEE, KEITARO, YOU SEEM LIKE YOU'RE HAVING A BLAST WITH YOUR JOB, THOUGH.
WELL... YEAH.
AND THIS PROFESSOR, HE'S SARAH'S FATHER?
YEAH. BUT HE'S ONE OF THE STRANGEST, FUNNIEST GUYS AROUND.
THANKS FOR THE MEAL!
BAM
HUH?
I'M GLAD YOU FOUND SUCH A NICE SEMPAI. I'M HAPPY FOR YOU.
COME TO THINK OF IT, THOUGH, DIGGING HOLES IS WHAT YOU'RE GOOD AT, ISN'T IT? IT'S PERFECT FOR YOU.
WHY DON'T YOU STAY HIS ASSISTANT FOR THE REST OF YOUR LIFE?
WAH?
WHAT'S THE MATTER WITH YOU?
YOU'RE ONE TO TALK, TRYING TO GET INTO SCHOOL FOR SOME OLD CRUSH.
GLARE

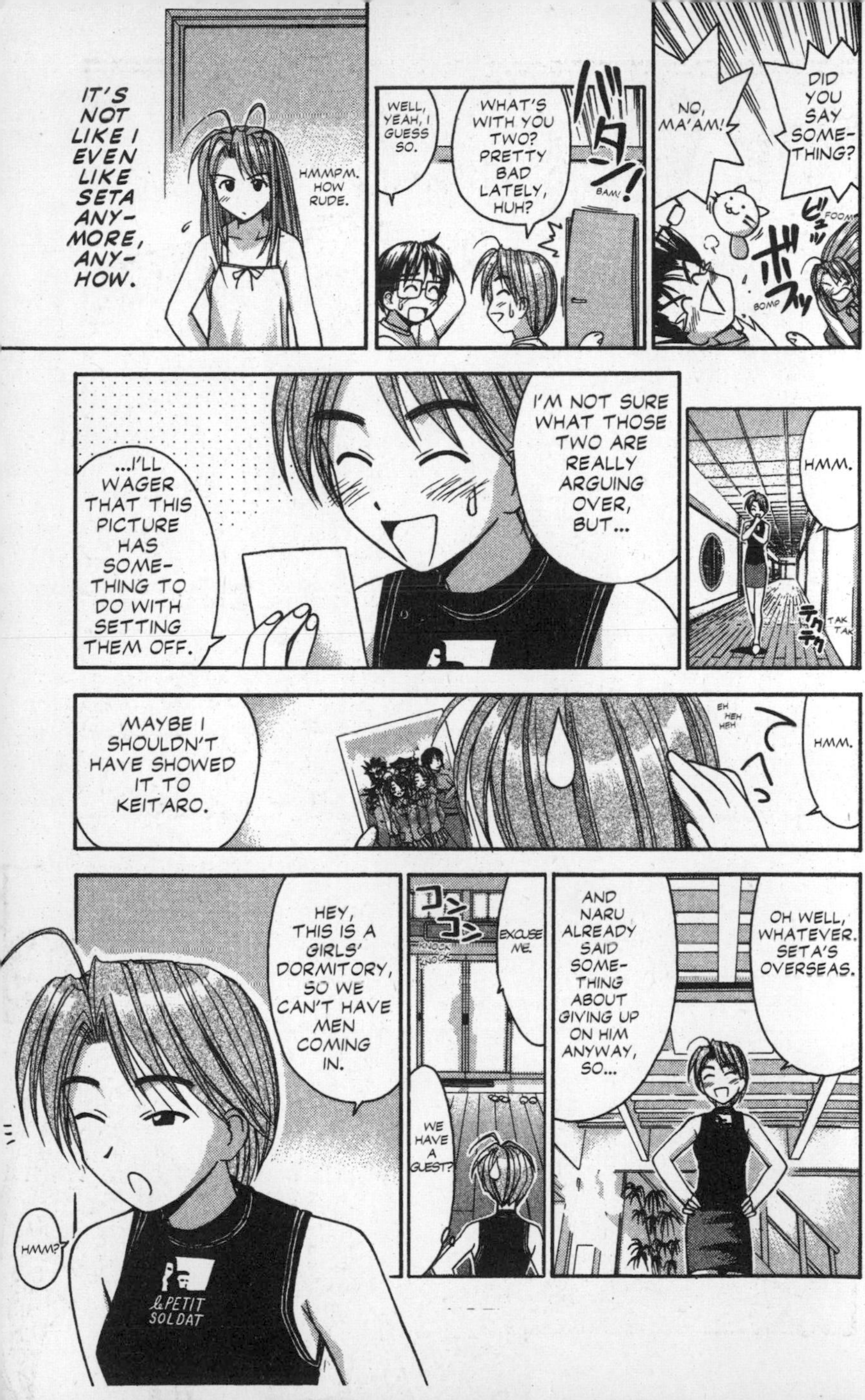
DID YOU SAY SOMETHING?
NO, MA'AM!
FOOM
BOMP
WHAT'S WITH YOU TWO? PRETTY BAD LATELY, HUH?
BAM!
WELL, YEAH, I GUESS SO.
HMMPM. HOW RUDE.
IT'S NOT LIKE I EVEN LIKE SETA ANYMORE, ANYHOW.
HMM.
TAK TAK
I'M NOT SURE WHAT THOSE TWO ARE REALLY ARGUING OVER, BUT...
...I'LL WAGER THAT THIS PICTURE HAS SOMETHING TO DO WITH SETTING THEM OFF.
HMM.
EH HEH HEH
MAYBE I SHOULDN'T HAVE SHOWED IT TO KEITARO.
OH WELL, WHATEVER. SETA'S OVERSEAS.
AND NARU ALREADY SAID SOMETHING ABOUT GIVING UP ON HIM ANYWAY, SO...
EXCUSE ME.
KNOCK KNOCK
WE HAVE A GUEST?
HEY, THIS IS A GIRLS' DORMITORY, SO WE CAN'T HAVE MEN COMING IN.
le PETIT SOLDAT
HMM?

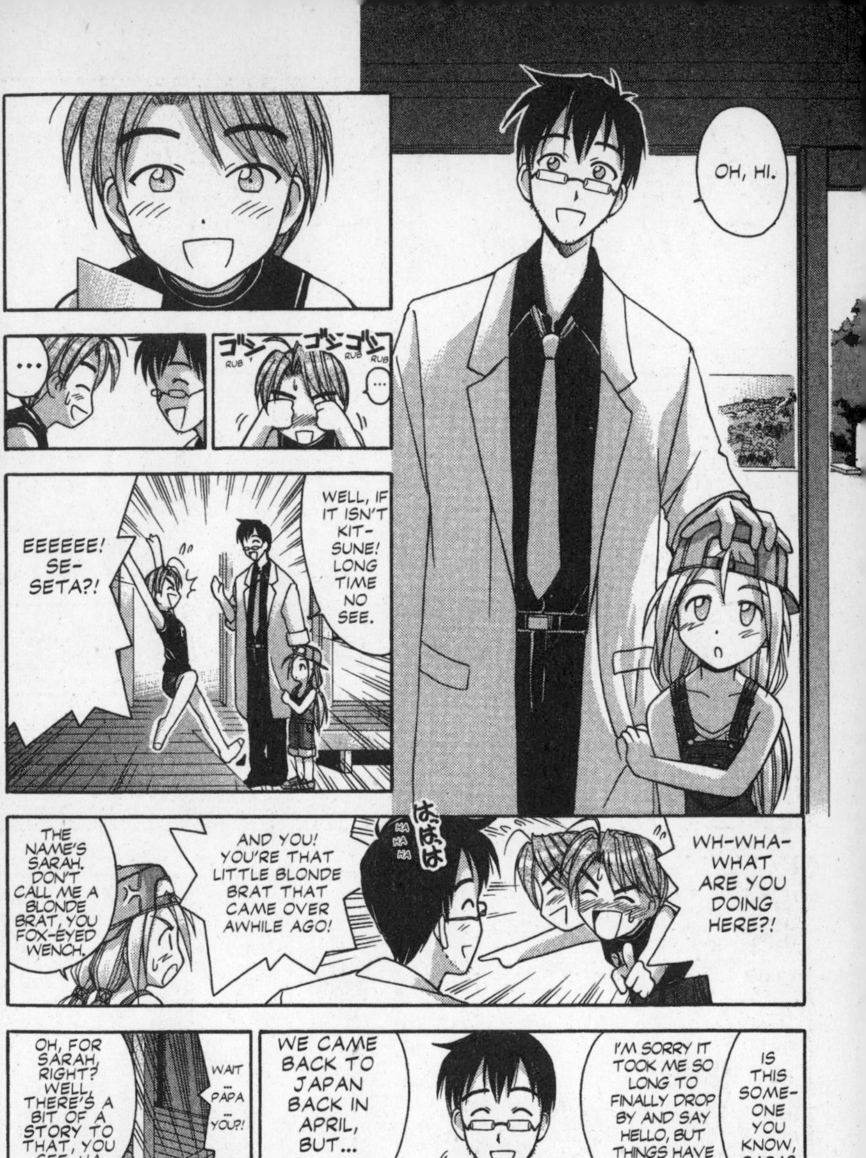
OH, HI.
ゴシゴシゴシ
RUB RUB RUB
...
...
WELL, IF IT ISN'T KIT-SUNE! LONG TIME NO SEE.
EEEEEE! SE-SETA?!
WH-WHA-WHAT ARE YOU DOING HERE?!
はっはっは
HA HA HA
AND YOU! YOU'RE THAT LITTLE BLONDE BRAT THAT CAME OVER AWHILE AGO!
THE NAME'S SARAH. DON'T CALL ME A BLONDE BRAT, YOU FOX-EYED WENCH.
IS THIS SOME-ONE YOU KNOW, PAPA?
I'M SORRY IT TOOK ME SO LONG TO FINALLY DROP BY AND SAY HELLO, BUT THINGS HAVE BEEN SO HECTIC.
WE CAME BACK TO JAPAN BACK IN APRIL, BUT...
WHEN I FIRST VISITED, NO ONE WAS AROUND.
WAIT ... PAPA ... YOU?!
OH, FOR SARAH, RIGHT? WELL, THERE'S A BIT OF A STORY TO THAT, YOU SEE. HA HA HA.

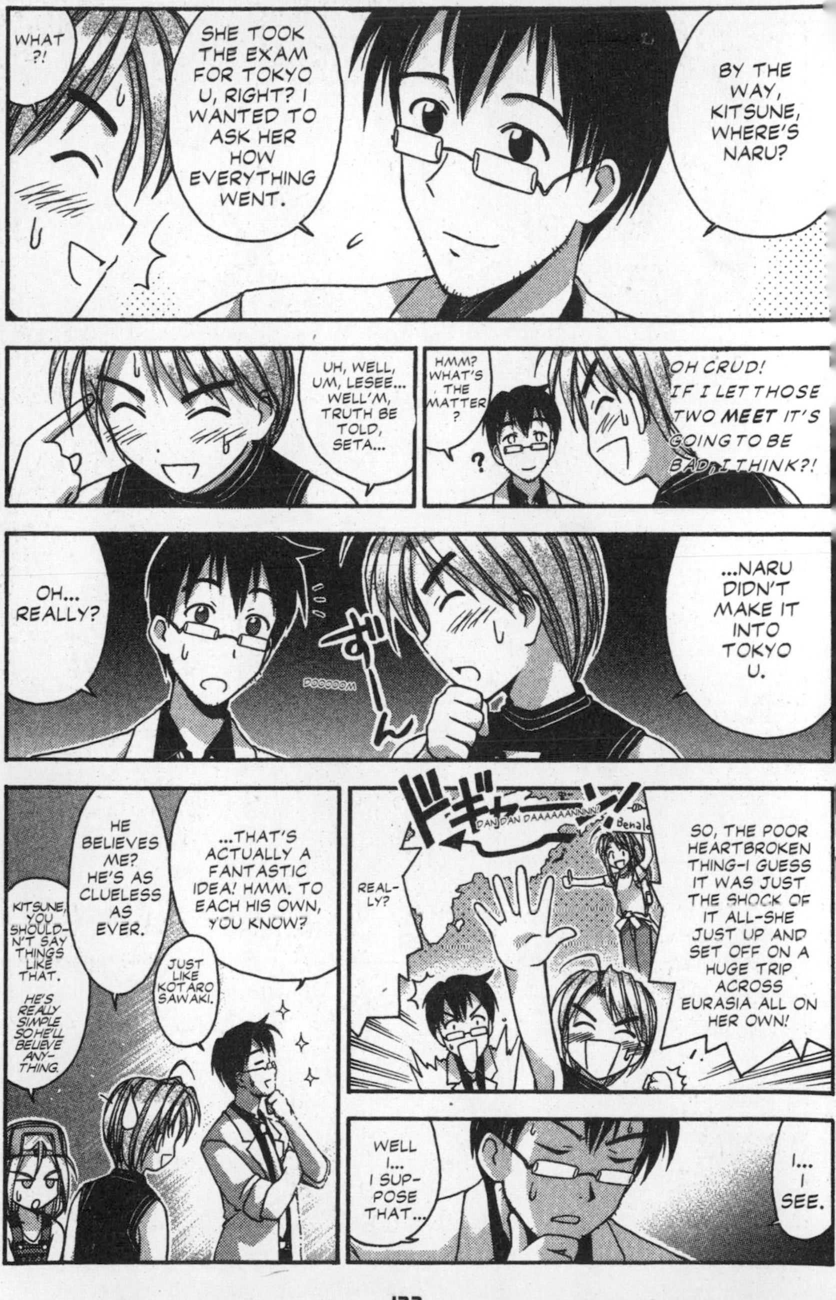
BY THE WAY, KITSUNE, WHERE'S NARU?
SHE TOOK THE EXAM FOR TOKYO U, RIGHT? I WANTED TO ASK HER HOW EVERYTHING WENT.
WHAT?!
OH CRUD! IF I LET THOSE TWO **MEET** IT'S GOING TO BE BAD, I THINK?!
HMM? WHAT'S THE MATTER?
?
UH, WELL, UM, LESEE... WELL'M, TRUTH BE TOLD, SETA...
...NARU DIDN'T MAKE IT INTO TOKYO U.
DOOOOOM
OH... REALLY?
DAN DAN DAAAAAAANNNN!
SO, THE POOR HEARTBROKEN THING-I GUESS IT WAS JUST THE SHOCK OF IT ALL-SHE JUST UP AND SET OFF ON A HUGE TRIP ACROSS EURASIA ALL ON HER OWN!
REAL-LY?
I... I SEE.
WELL I... I SUPPOSE THAT...
...THAT'S ACTUALLY A FANTASTIC IDEA! HMM. TO EACH HIS OWN, YOU KNOW?
JUST LIKE KOTARO SAWAKI.
HE BELIEVES ME? HE'S AS CLUELESS AS EVER.
KITSUNE, YOU SHOULDN'T SAY THINGS LIKE THAT.
HE'S REALLY SIMPLE SO HE'LL BELIEVE ANYTHING.

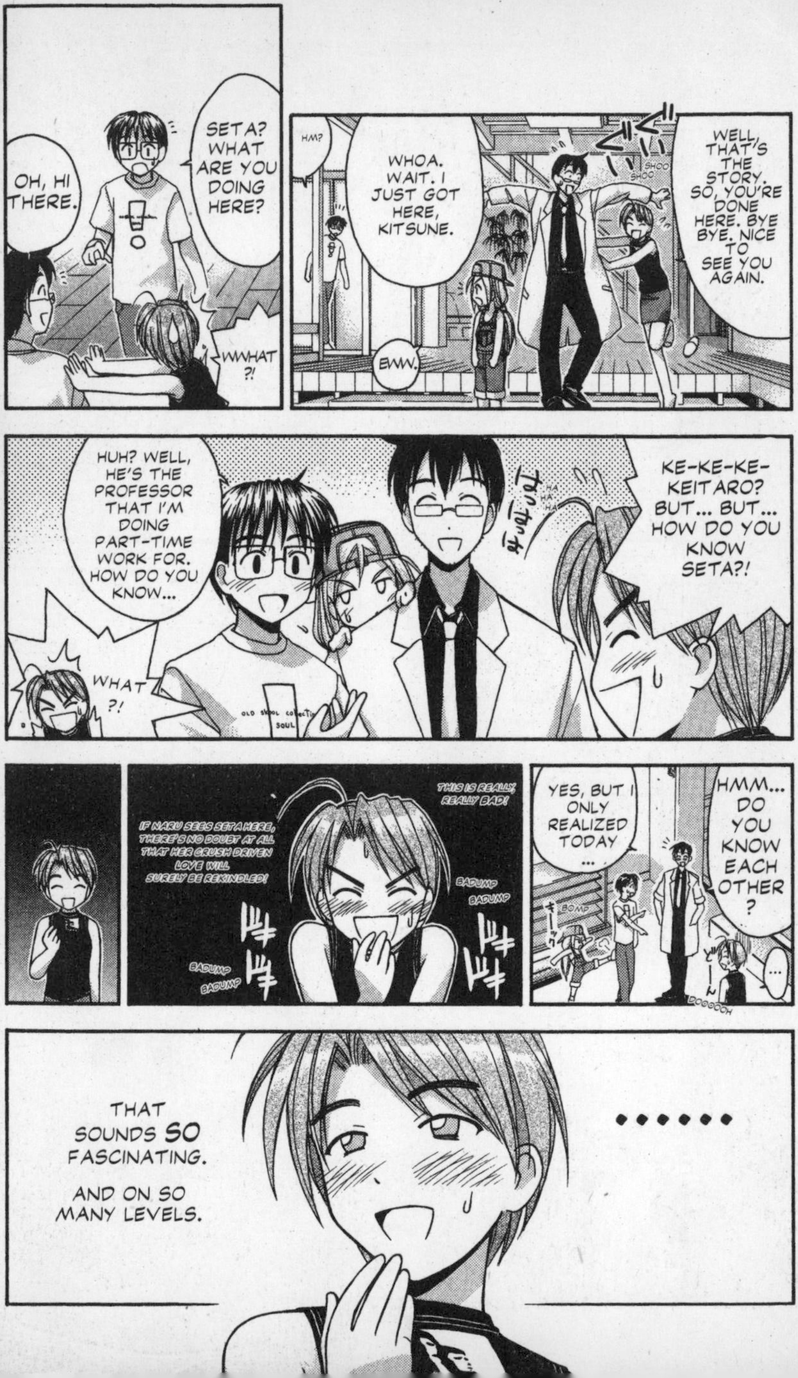
WELL, THAT'S THE STORY. SO, YOU'RE DONE HERE. BYE BYE. NICE TO SEE YOU AGAIN.
SHOO SHOO
WHOA. WAIT. I JUST GOT HERE, KITSUNE.
HM?
EWW.
SETA? WHAT ARE YOU DOING HERE?
OH, HI THERE.
WWHAT ?!
KE-KE-KE-KEITARO? BUT... BUT... HOW DO YOU KNOW SETA?!
HA HA HA
HUH? WELL, HE'S THE PROFESSOR THAT I'M DOING PART-TIME WORK FOR. HOW DO YOU KNOW...
WHAT ?!
HMM... DO YOU KNOW EACH OTHER ?
YES, BUT I ONLY REALIZED TODAY ...
BOMP
DOOOOOOH
...
THIS IS REALLY, REALLY BAD!
IF NARU SEES SETA HERE, THERE'S NO DOUBT AT ALL THAT HER CRUSH DRIVEN LOVE WILL SURELY BE REKINDLED!
BADUMP BADUMP
BADUMP BADUMP
••••••
THAT SOUNDS SO FASCINATING.
AND ON SO MANY LEVELS.

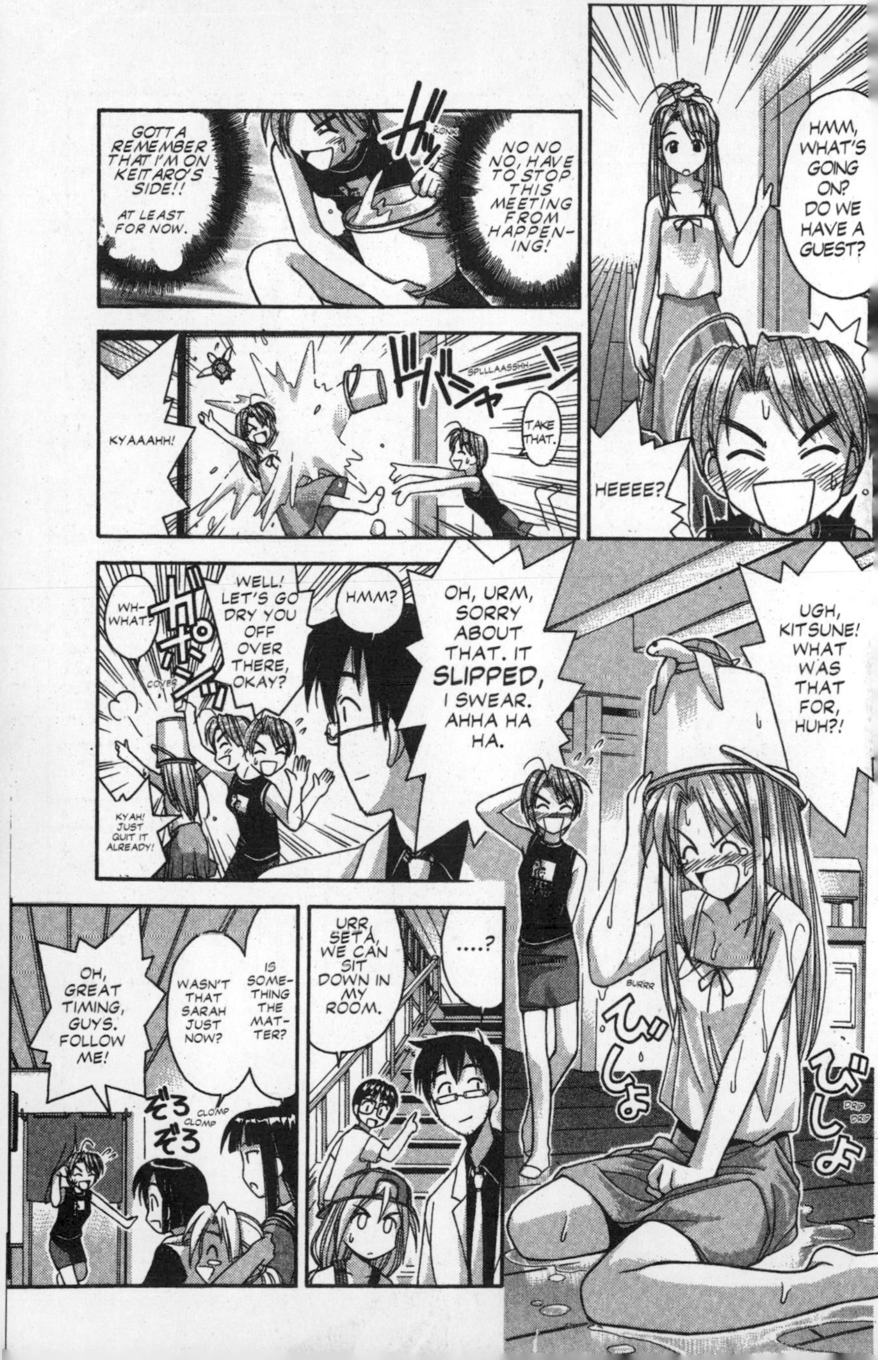
HMM, WHAT'S GOING ON? DO WE HAVE A GUEST?
HEEEE?
NO NO NO, HAVE TO STOP THIS MEETING FROM HAPPENING!
RONK
GOTTA REMEMBER THAT I'M ON KEITARO'S SIDE!!
AT LEAST FOR NOW.
SPLLLAASSHH
TAKE THAT.
KYAAAHH!
UGH, KITSUNE! WHAT WAS THAT FOR, HUH?!
DRIP DRIP
BURRR
OH, URM, SORRY ABOUT THAT. IT SLIPPED, I SWEAR. AHHA HA HA.
HMM?
WELL! LET'S GO DRY YOU OFF OVER THERE, OKAY?
WH-WHAT?
COVER
KYAH! JUST QUIT IT ALREADY!
....?
URR, SETA, WE CAN SIT DOWN IN MY ROOM.
IS SOMETHING THE MATTER?
WASN'T THAT SARAH JUST NOW?
OH, GREAT TIMING, GUYS. FOLLOW ME!
CLOMP CLOMP

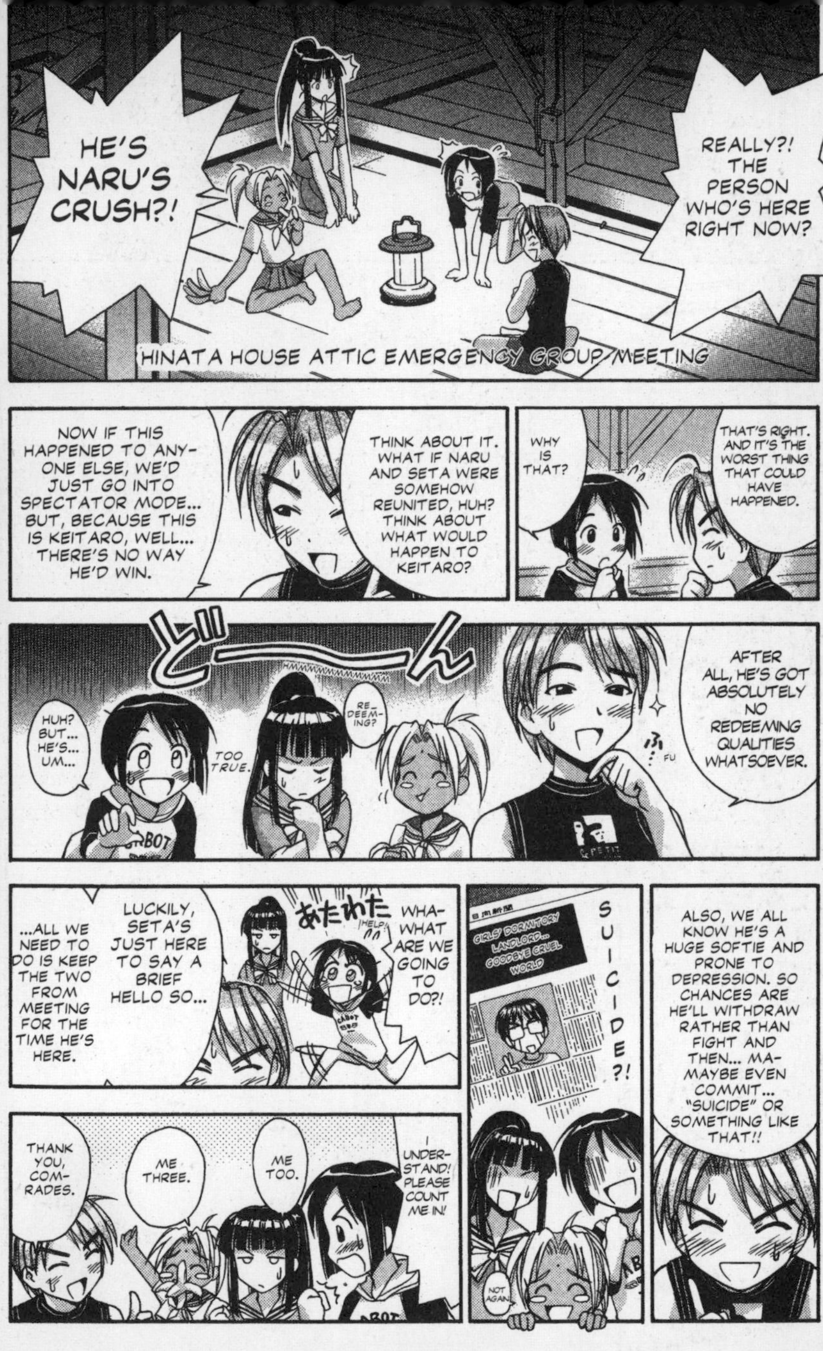
REALLY?! THE PERSON WHO'S HERE RIGHT NOW?
HE'S NARU'S CRUSH?!
HINATA HOUSE ATTIC EMERGENCY GROUP MEETING
THAT'S RIGHT. AND IT'S THE WORST THING THAT COULD HAVE HAPPENED.
WHY IS THAT?
THINK ABOUT IT. WHAT IF NARU AND SETA WERE SOMEHOW REUNITED, HUH? THINK ABOUT WHAT WOULD HAPPEN TO KEITARO?
NOW IF THIS HAPPENED TO ANY-ONE ELSE, WE'D JUST GO INTO SPECTATOR MODE... BUT, BECAUSE THIS IS KEITARO, WELL... THERE'S NO WAY HE'D WIN.
AFTER ALL, HE'S GOT ABSOLUTELY NO REDEEMING QUALITIES WHATSOEVER.
ふ
FU
どーーん
HMMMMMMMMMMMMMMMM
RE-DEEMING?
TOO TRUE.
HUH? BUT... HE'S... UM...
ALSO, WE ALL KNOW HE'S A HUGE SOFTIE AND PRONE TO DEPRESSION. SO CHANCES ARE HE'LL WITHDRAW RATHER THAN FIGHT AND THEN... MA-MAYBE EVEN COMMIT... "SUICIDE" OR SOMETHING LIKE THAT!!
SUICIDE?!
GIRLS' DORMITORY LANDLORD... GOODBYE CRUEL WORLD
NOT AGAIN.
WHA-WHAT ARE WE GOING TO DO?!
HELP!
LUCKILY, SETA'S JUST HERE TO SAY A BRIEF HELLO SO...
...ALL WE NEED TO DO IS KEEP THE TWO FROM MEETING FOR THE TIME HE'S HERE.
I UNDERSTAND! PLEASE COUNT ME IN!
ME TOO.
ME THREE.
THANK YOU, COMRADES.

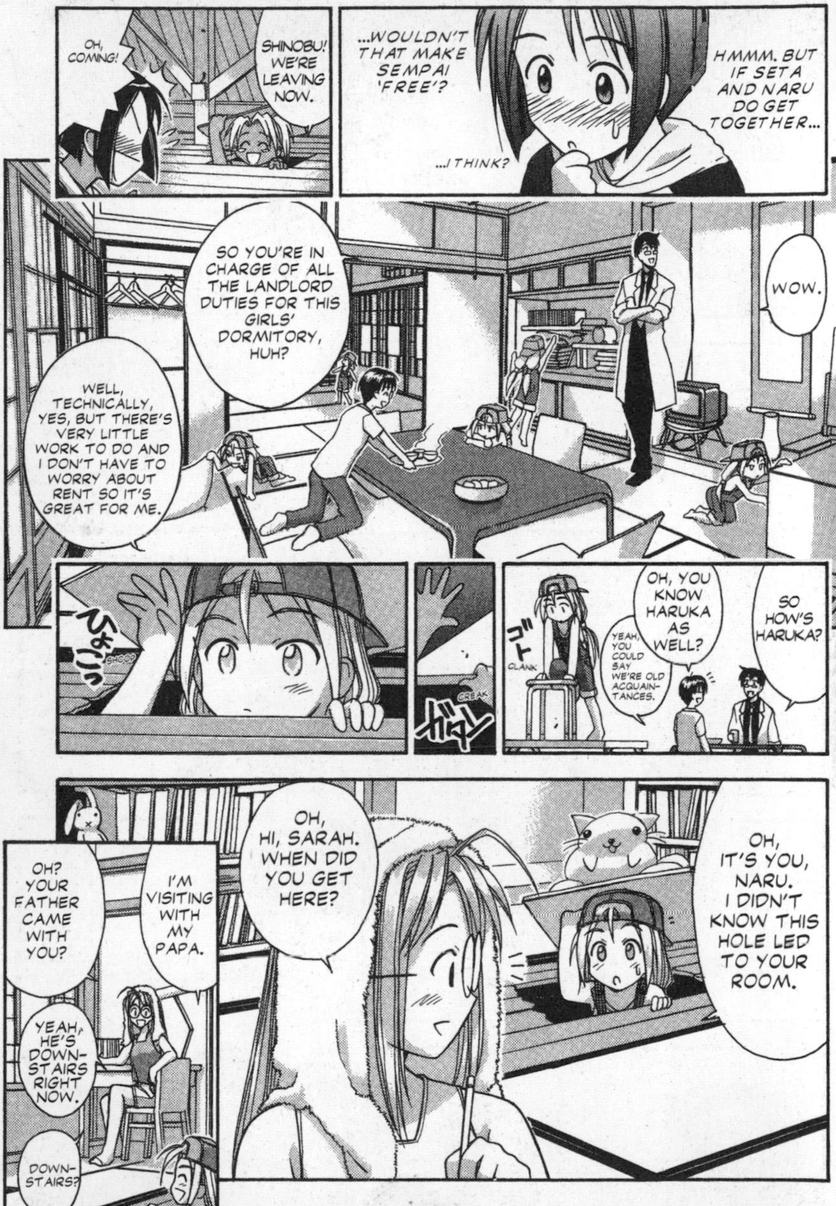

HMMM. BUT IF SETA AND NARU DO GET TOGETHER...
...WOULDN'T THAT MAKE SEMPAI 'FREE'?
...I THINK?
SHINOBU! WE'RE LEAVING NOW.
OH, COMING!
WOW.
SO YOU'RE IN CHARGE OF ALL THE LANDLORD DUTIES FOR THIS GIRLS' DORMITORY, HUH?
WELL, TECHNICALLY, YES, BUT THERE'S VERY LITTLE WORK TO DO AND I DON'T HAVE TO WORRY ABOUT RENT SO IT'S GREAT FOR ME.
SO HOW'S HARUKA?
OH, YOU KNOW HARUKA AS WELL?
YEAH, YOU COULD SAY WE'RE OLD ACQUAINTANCES.
ゴト
CLANK
CREAK
ひょこっ
SHOOP
OH, IT'S YOU, NARU. I DIDN'T KNOW THIS HOLE LED TO YOUR ROOM.
OH, HI, SARAH. WHEN DID YOU GET HERE?
I'M VISITING WITH MY PAPA.
OH? YOUR FATHER CAME WITH YOU?
YEAH, HE'S DOWNSTAIRS RIGHT NOW.
DOWNSTAIRS?

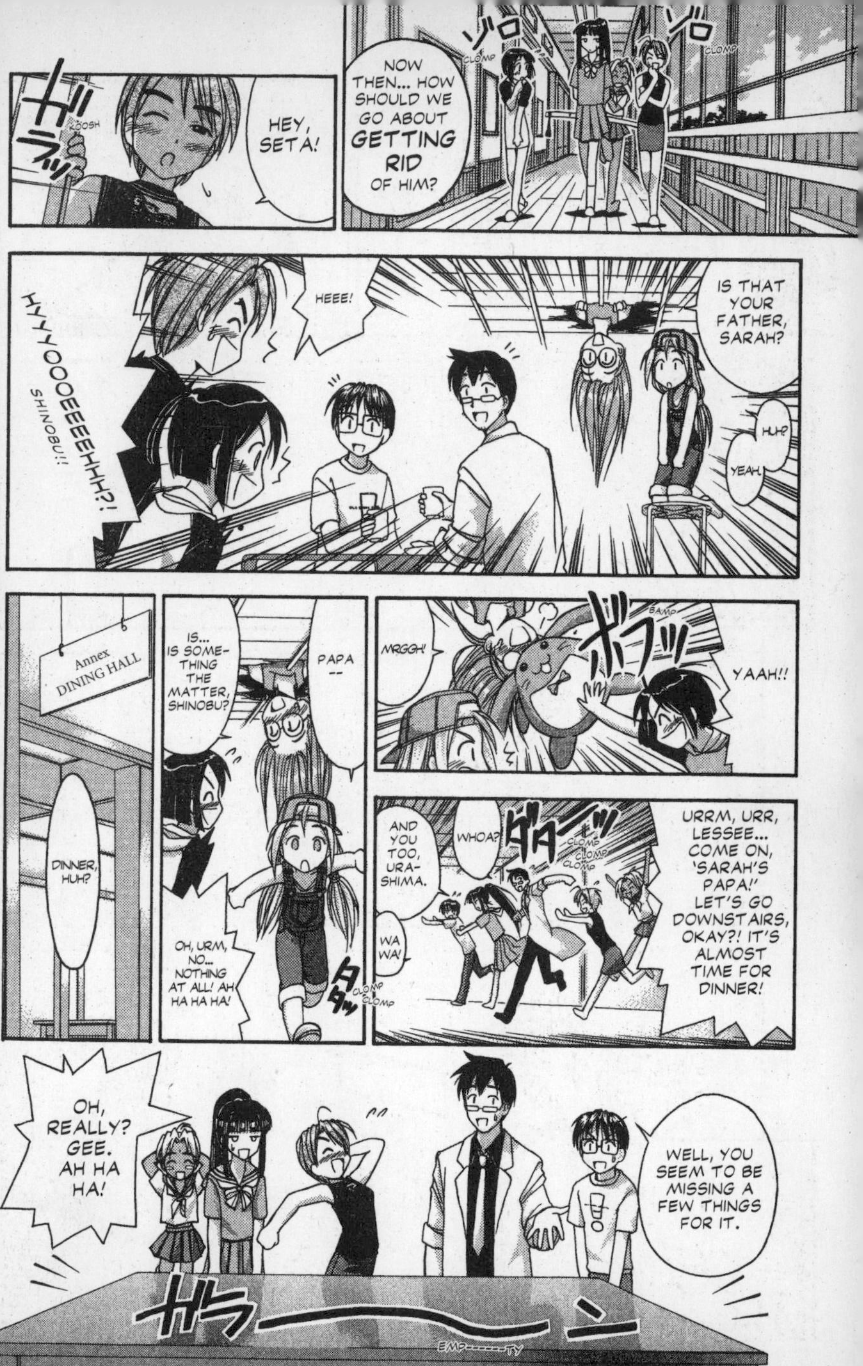
ゾロ
CLOMP
ゾロ
CLOMP
NOW THEN... HOW SHOULD WE GO ABOUT GETTING RID OF HIM?
HEY, SETA!
ガラッ
KOOSH
IS THAT YOUR FATHER, SARAH?
HUH?
YEAH.
HEEE!
HYYYOOOEEEEHHH?!
SHINOBU!!
YAAH!!
ボフッ
BAMP
MRGGH!
URRM, URR, LESSEE... COME ON, 'SARAH'S PAPA!' LET'S GO DOWNSTAIRS, OKAY?! IT'S ALMOST TIME FOR DINNER!
ダダーッ
CLOMP
CLOMP
CLOMP
WHOA?
AND YOU TOO, URA-SHIMA.
WA WA!
PAPA --
IS... IS SOMETHING THE MATTER, SHINOBU?
OH, URM, NO... NOTHING AT ALL! AH HA HA HA!
タタッ
CLOMP
CLOMP
Annex
DINING HALL
DINNER, HUH?
WELL, YOU SEEM TO BE MISSING A FEW THINGS FOR IT.
OH, REALLY? GEE. AH HA HA!
ガラ～ン
EMP------TY

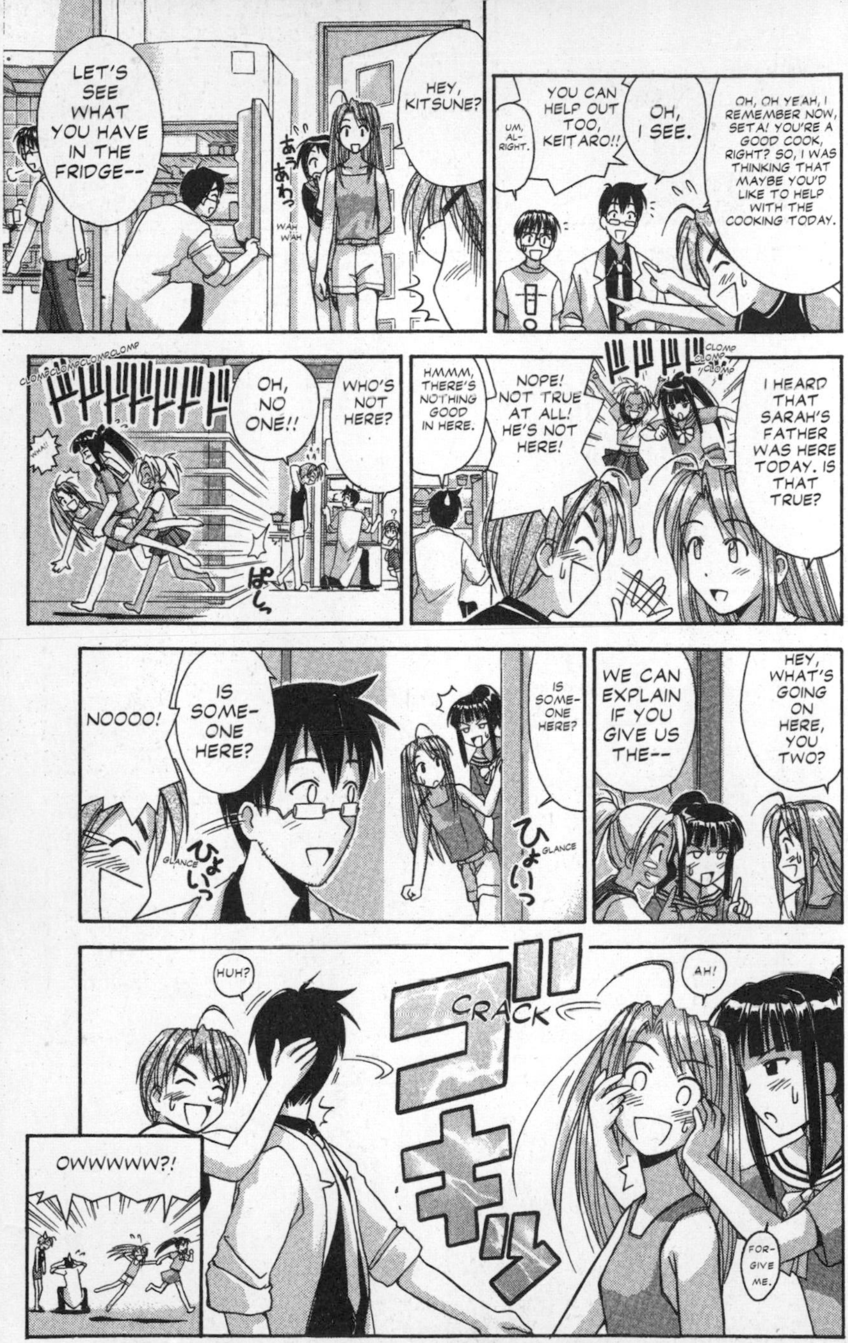
OH, OH YEAH, I REMEMBER NOW, SETA! YOU'RE A GOOD COOK, RIGHT? SO, I WAS THINKING THAT MAYBE YOU'D LIKE TO HELP WITH THE COOKING TODAY.
OH, I SEE.
YOU CAN HELP OUT TOO, KEITARO!!
UM, AL-RIGHT.
HEY, KITSUNE?
WAH WAH
LET'S SEE WHAT YOU HAVE IN THE FRIDGE--
CLOMP CLOMP CLOMP
I HEARD THAT SARAH'S FATHER WAS HERE TODAY. IS THAT TRUE?
NOPE! NOT TRUE AT ALL! HE'S NOT HERE!
HMMM, THERE'S NOTHING GOOD IN HERE.
WHO'S NOT HERE?
OH, NO ONE!!
CLOMPCLOMPCLOMPCLOMP
WHA!!
HEY, WHAT'S GOING ON HERE, YOU TWO?
WE CAN EXPLAIN IF YOU GIVE US THE--
IS SOME-ONE HERE?
GLANCE
IS SOME-ONE HERE?
NOOOO!
GLANCE
FOR-GIVE ME.
AH!
CRACK
HUH?
OWWWWW?!

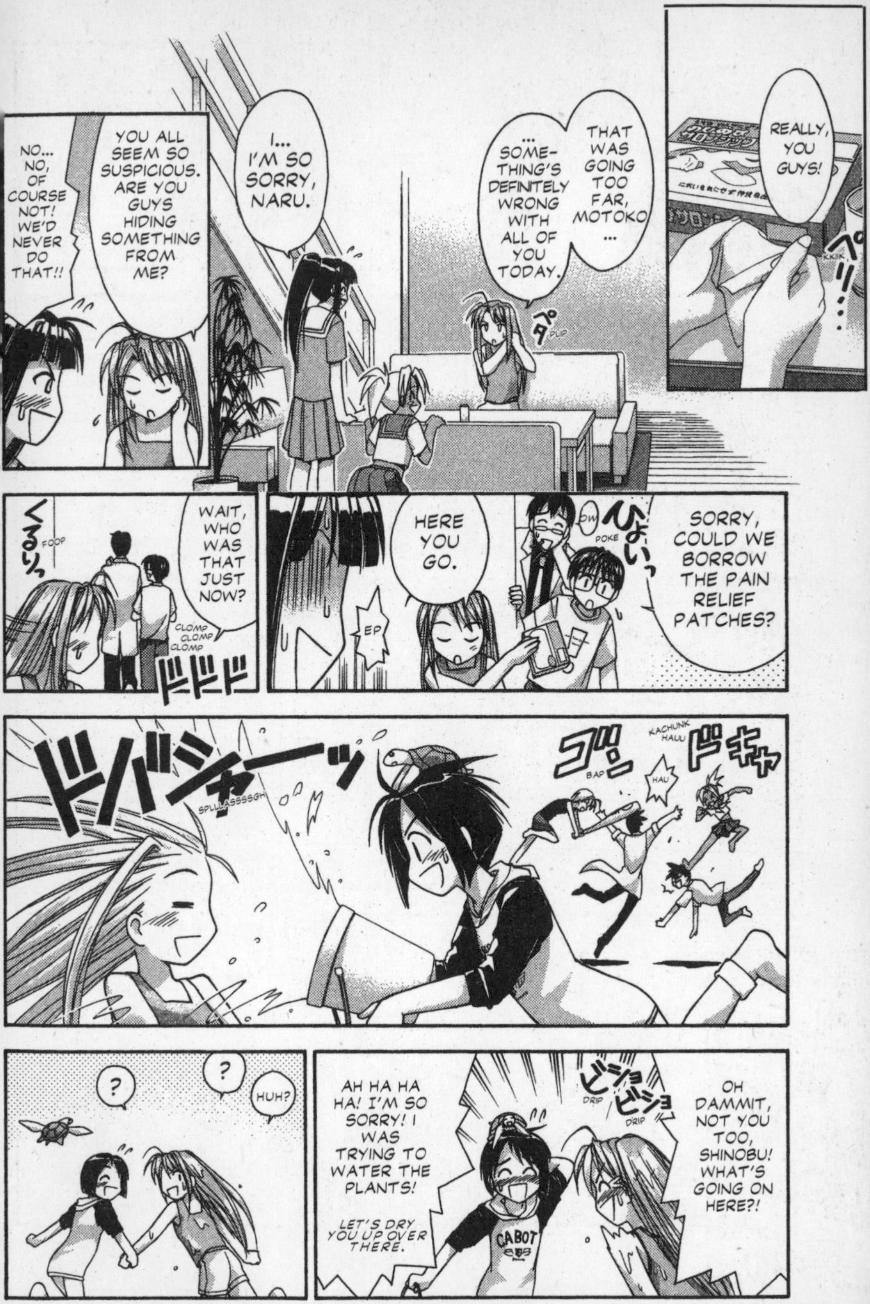
REALLY, YOU GUYS!
KKIIK
THAT WAS GOING TOO FAR, MOTOKO...
...SOMETHING'S DEFINITELY WRONG WITH ALL OF YOU TODAY.
PLIP
I... I'M SO SORRY, NARU.
YOU ALL SEEM SO SUSPICIOUS. ARE YOU GUYS HIDING SOMETHING FROM ME?
NO... NO, OF COURSE NOT! WE'D NEVER DO THAT!!
SORRY, COULD WE BORROW THE PAIN RELIEF PATCHES?
POKE
OW
HERE YOU GO.
EP
WAIT, WHO WAS THAT JUST NOW?
FOOP
CLOMP CLOMP CLOMP
KACHUNK HAUU
HAU
BAP
SPLLLASSSSGH
OH DAMMIT, NOT YOU TOO, SHINOBU! WHAT'S GOING ON HERE?!
DRIP
DRIP
AH HA HA HA! I'M SO SORRY! I WAS TRYING TO WATER THE PLANTS!
LET'S DRY YOU UP OVER THERE.
CABOT
HUH?
?
?

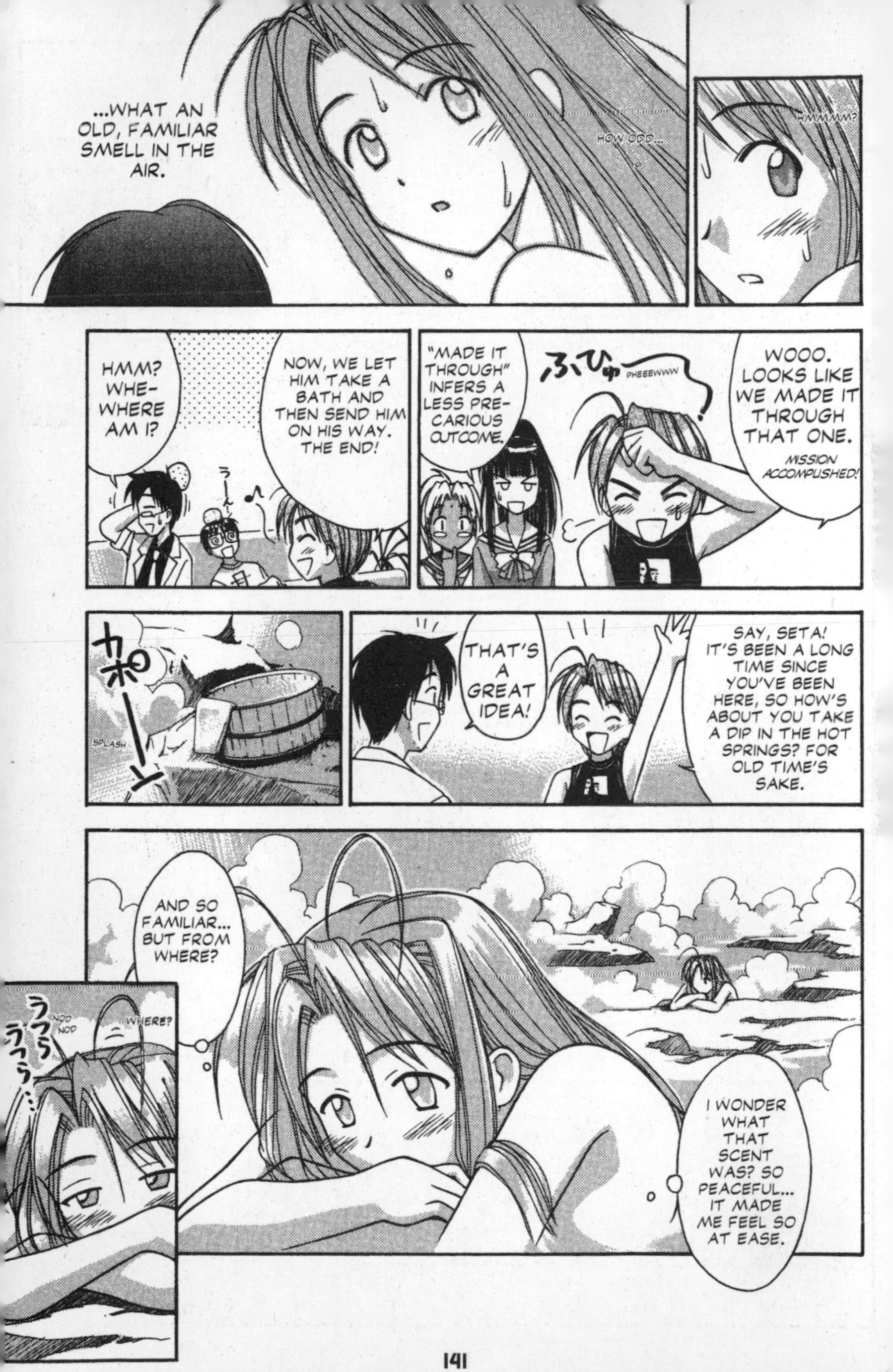
HMMMM?
HOW ODD...
...WHAT AN OLD, FAMILIAR SMELL IN THE AIR.
WOOO. LOOKS LIKE WE MADE IT THROUGH THAT ONE.
MISSION ACCOMPLISHED!
ふひゅ PHEEEWWW
"MADE IT THROUGH" INFERS A LESS PRE-CARIOUS OUTCOME.
NOW, WE LET HIM TAKE A BATH AND THEN SEND HIM ON HIS WAY. THE END!
うーん
HMM? WHE- WHERE AM I?
SAY, SETA! IT'S BEEN A LONG TIME SINCE YOU'VE BEEN HERE, SO HOW'S ABOUT YOU TAKE A DIP IN THE HOT SPRINGS? FOR OLD TIME'S SAKE.
THAT'S A GREAT IDEA!
カポーン
SPLASH
I WONDER WHAT THAT SCENT WAS? SO PEACEFUL... IT MADE ME FEEL SO AT EASE.
AND SO FAMILIAR... BUT FROM WHERE?
WHERE?
NOD NOD
うつらうつら...

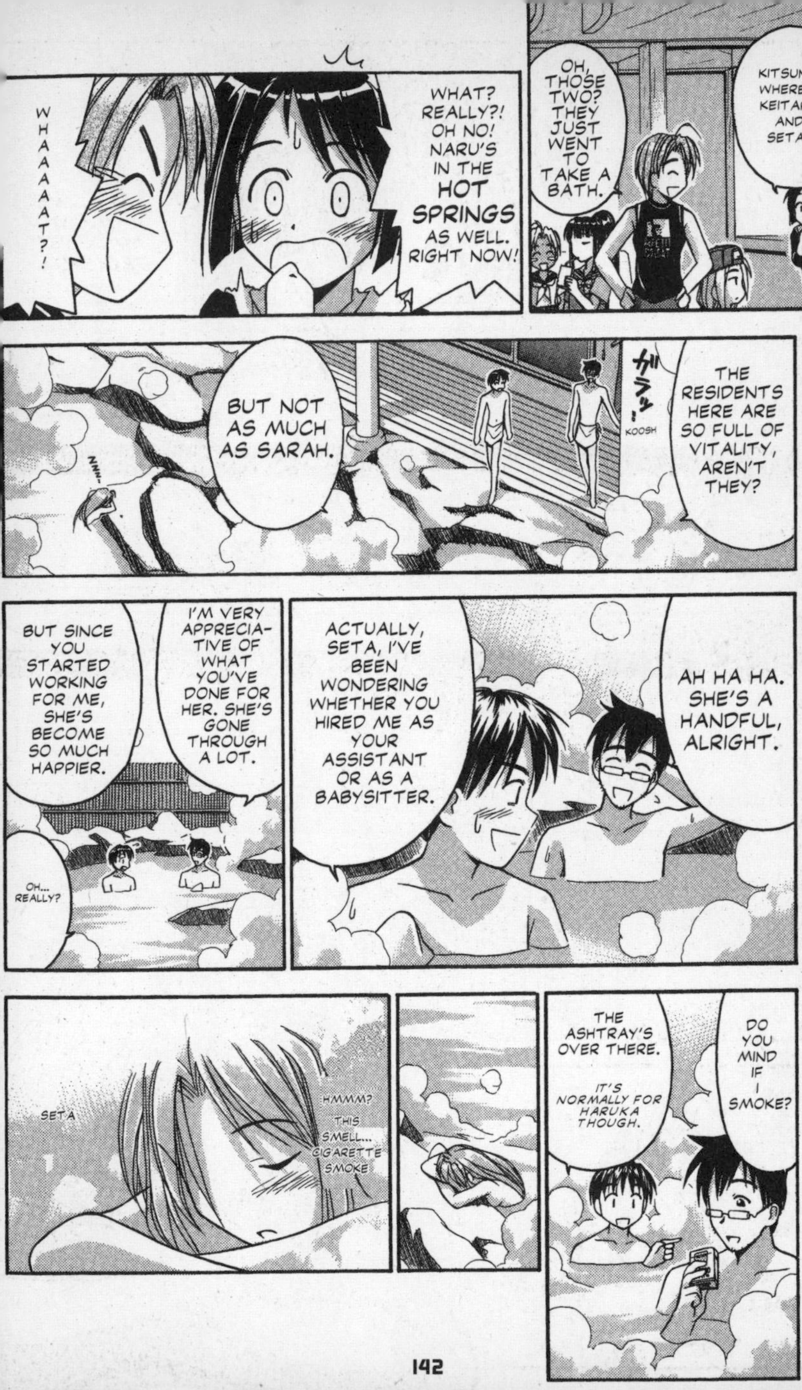

KITSUNE. WHERE'S KEITARO AND SETA?
OH, THOSE TWO? THEY JUST WENT TO TAKE A BATH.
WHAT? REALLY?! OH NO! NARU'S IN THE HOT SPRINGS AS WELL. RIGHT NOW!
WHAAAAAAAT?!
KOOSH
THE RESIDENTS HERE ARE SO FULL OF VITALITY, AREN'T THEY?
BUT NOT AS MUCH AS SARAH.
AH HA HA. SHE'S A HANDFUL, ALRIGHT.
ACTUALLY, SETA, I'VE BEEN WONDERING WHETHER YOU HIRED ME AS YOUR ASSISTANT OR AS A BABYSITTER.
I'M VERY APPRECIATIVE OF WHAT YOU'VE DONE FOR HER. SHE'S GONE THROUGH A LOT.
BUT SINCE YOU STARTED WORKING FOR ME, SHE'S BECOME SO MUCH HAPPIER.
OH... REALLY?
DO YOU MIND IF I SMOKE?
THE ASHTRAY'S OVER THERE.
IT'S NORMALLY FOR HARUKA THOUGH.
HMMM? THIS SMELL... CIGARETTE SMOKE
SETA

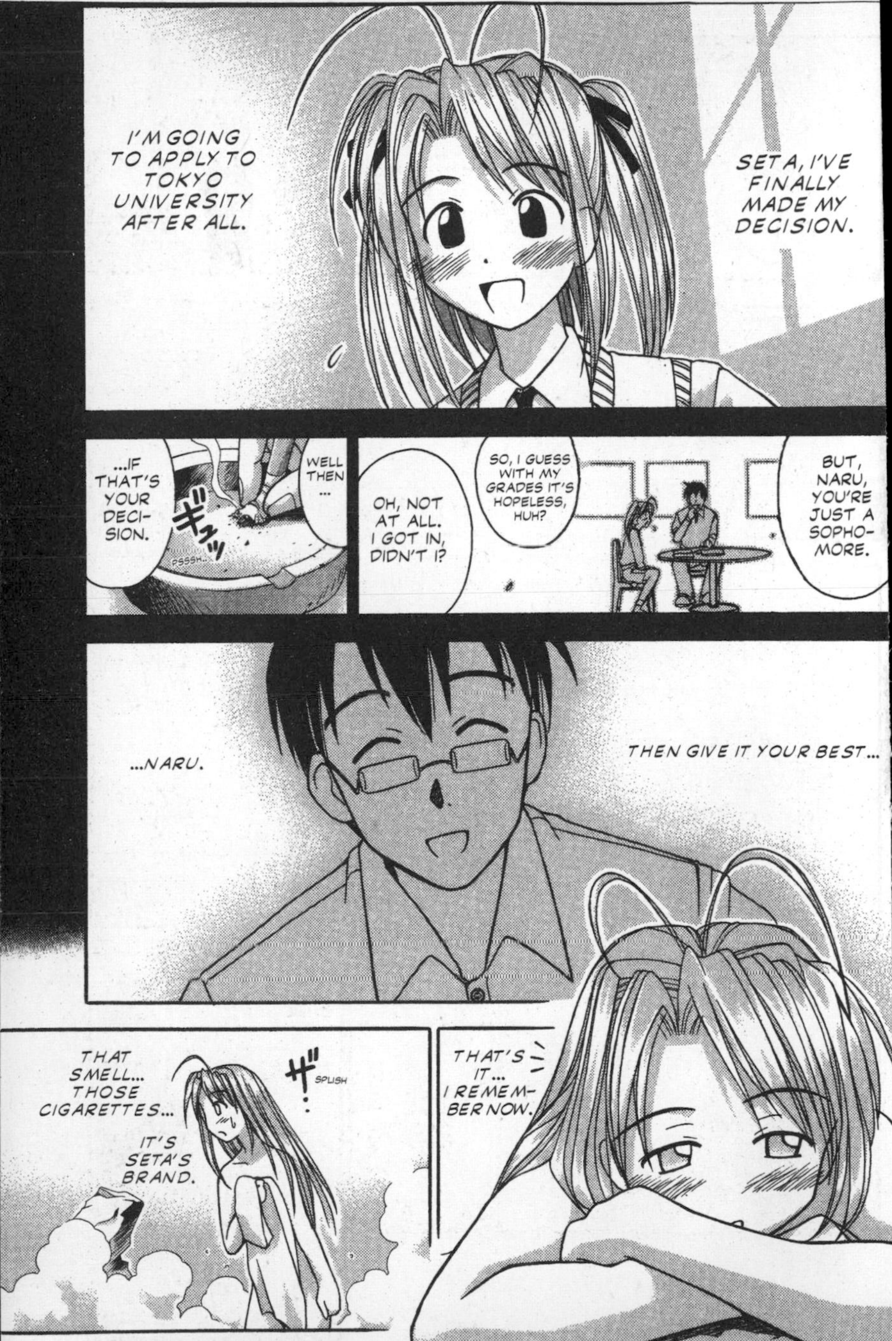
SETA, I'VE FINALLY MADE MY DECISION.
I'M GOING TO APPLY TO TOKYO UNIVERSITY AFTER ALL.
BUT, NARU, YOU'RE JUST A SOPHOMORE.
SO, I GUESS WITH MY GRADES IT'S HOPELESS, HUH?
OH, NOT AT ALL. I GOT IN, DIDN'T I?
WELL THEN ...
...IF THAT'S YOUR DECISION.
ギュッ
PSSSH...
THEN GIVE IT YOUR BEST...
...NARU.
THAT'S IT... I REMEMBER NOW.
THAT SMELL... THOSE CIGARETTES...
ザ
SPLISH
IT'S SETA'S BRAND.

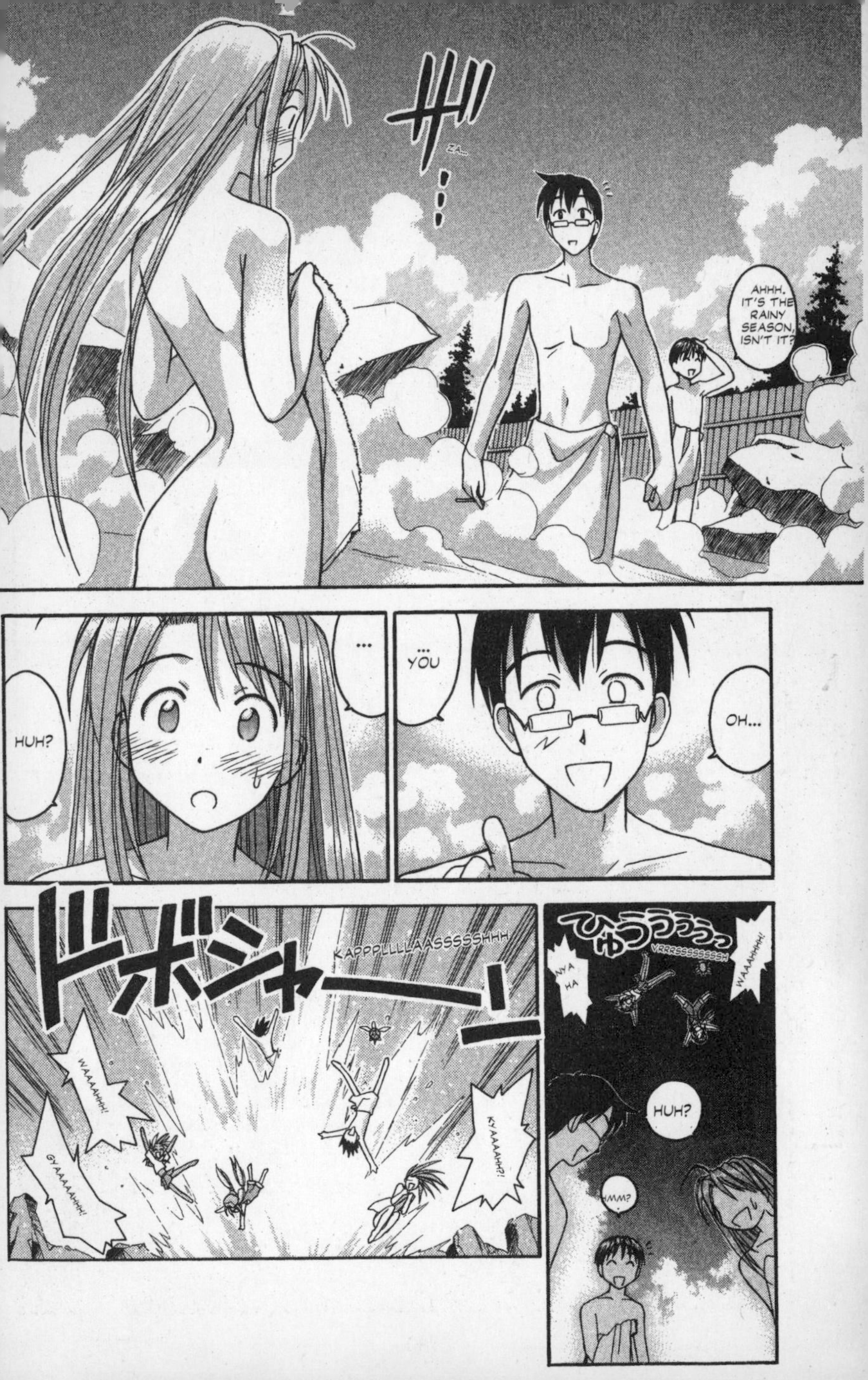
ザ
ZA...
AHHH. IT'S THE RAINY SEASON, ISN'T IT?
OH...
... YOU
...
HUH?
ひゅうううううっ
VRRRSSSSSSSSSSH
WAAAHHHH!
NYA HA
HUH?
HMM?
ドボシャーーー
KAPPPLLLLAASSSSSHHH
KYAAAAAHH?!
WAAAAAHHH!
GYAAAAAAHHH!

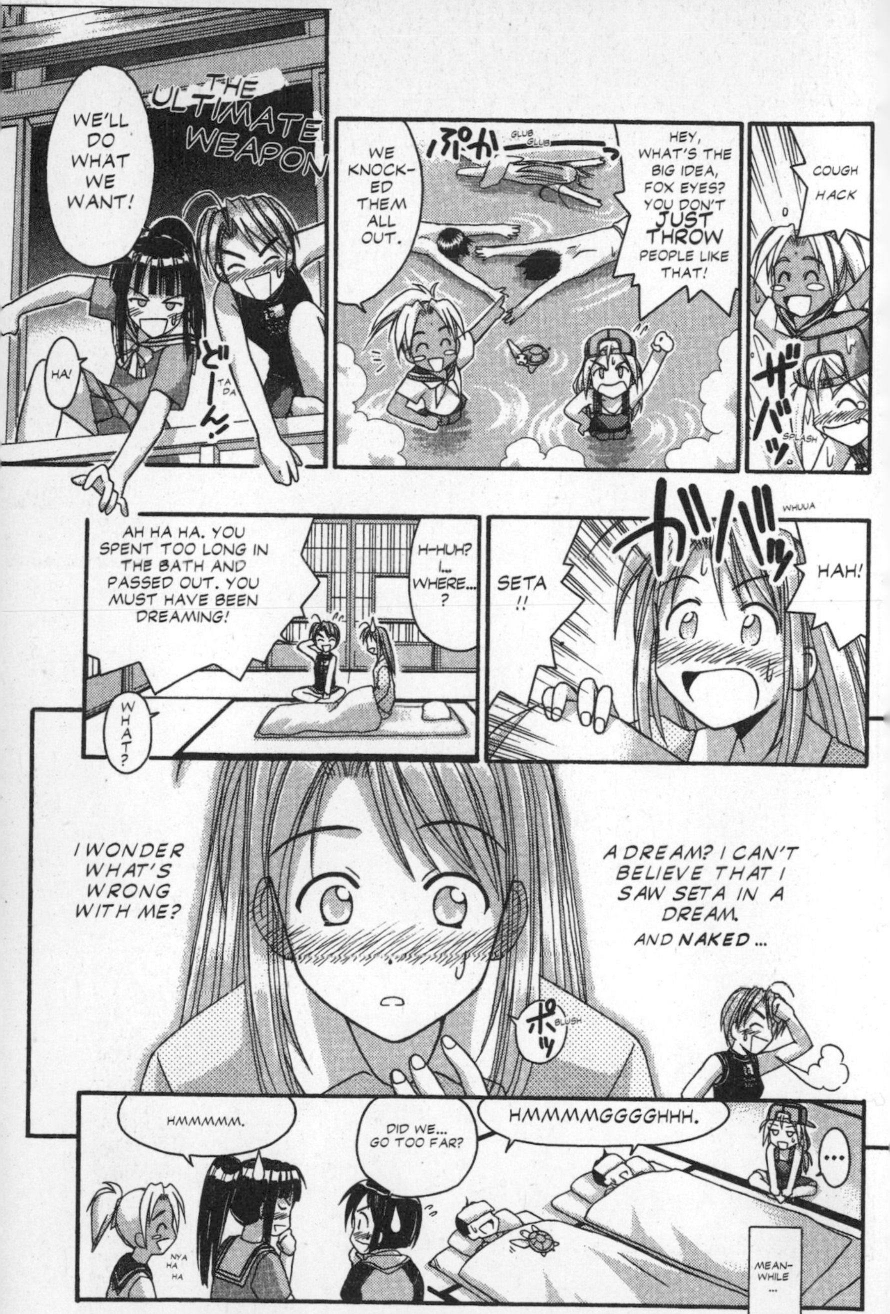
COUGH
HACK
ザバッ。
SPLASH
HEY, WHAT'S THE BIG IDEA, FOX EYES? YOU DON'T JUST THROW PEOPLE LIKE THAT!
ぷかー
GLUB GLUB
WE KNOCKED THEM ALL OUT.
THE ULTIMATE WEAPON
WE'LL DO WHAT WE WANT!
どーん!
TA DA
HA!
がバッ
WHUUA
HAH!
SETA !!
H-HUH? I... WHERE...?
AH HA HA. YOU SPENT TOO LONG IN THE BATH AND PASSED OUT. YOU MUST HAVE BEEN DREAMING!
WHAT?
A DREAM? I CAN'T BELIEVE THAT I SAW SETA IN A DREAM.
AND NAKED...
I WONDER WHAT'S WRONG WITH ME?
ポッ
BLUSH
MEAN-WHILE...
...
HMMMMGGGGHHH.
DID WE... GO TOO FAR?
HMMMMM.
NYA HA HA

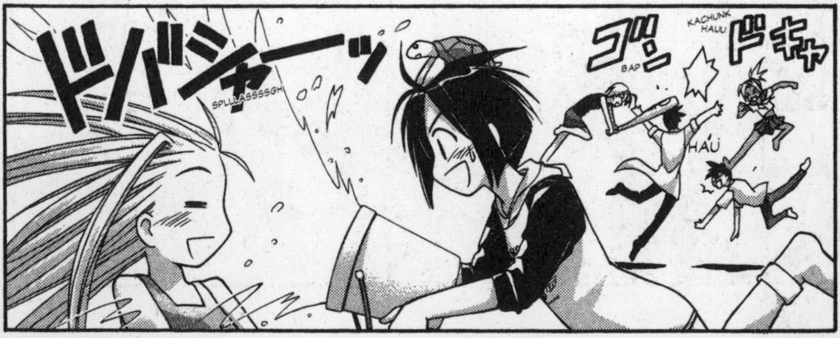
ドキャ
KACHUNK
HAUU
ゴン
BAP
HAU
ドバシャーッ
SPLLLASSSSGH

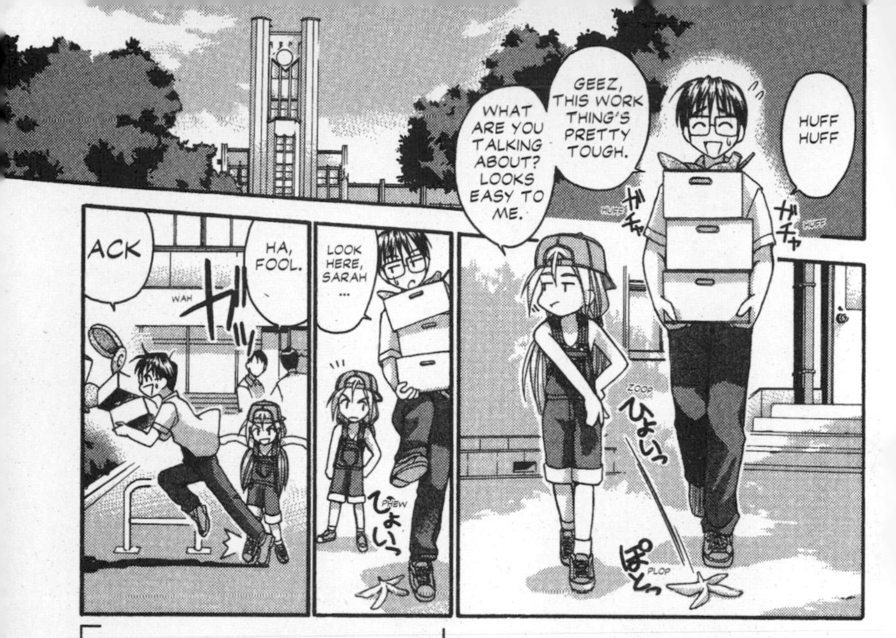
HUFF HUFF
HUFF
HUFF
GEEZ, THIS WORK THING'S PRETTY TOUGH.
WHAT ARE YOU TALKING ABOUT? LOOKS EASY TO ME.
ZOOP
PLOP
LOOK HERE, SARAH ...
PHEW
HA, FOOL.
ACK
WAH

Love Hina

HINATA. 32 A Sudden Resume

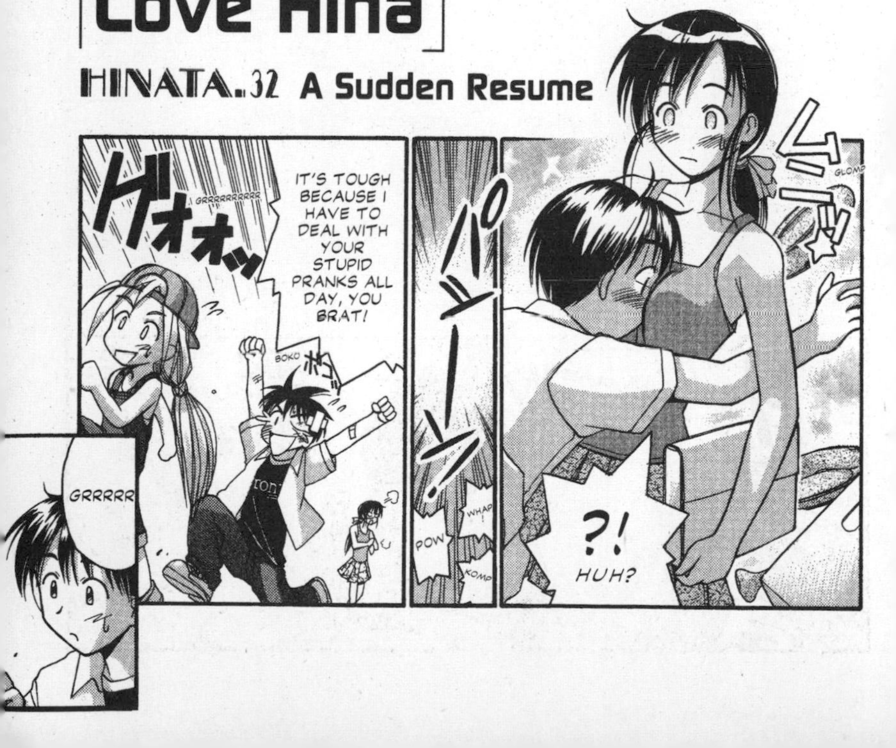
GLOMP
?! HUH?
WHAP
POW
KOMP
GRRRRRRRRRR
IT'S TOUGH BECAUSE I HAVE TO DEAL WITH YOUR STUPID PRANKS ALL DAY, YOU BRAT!
BOKO
GRRRRR

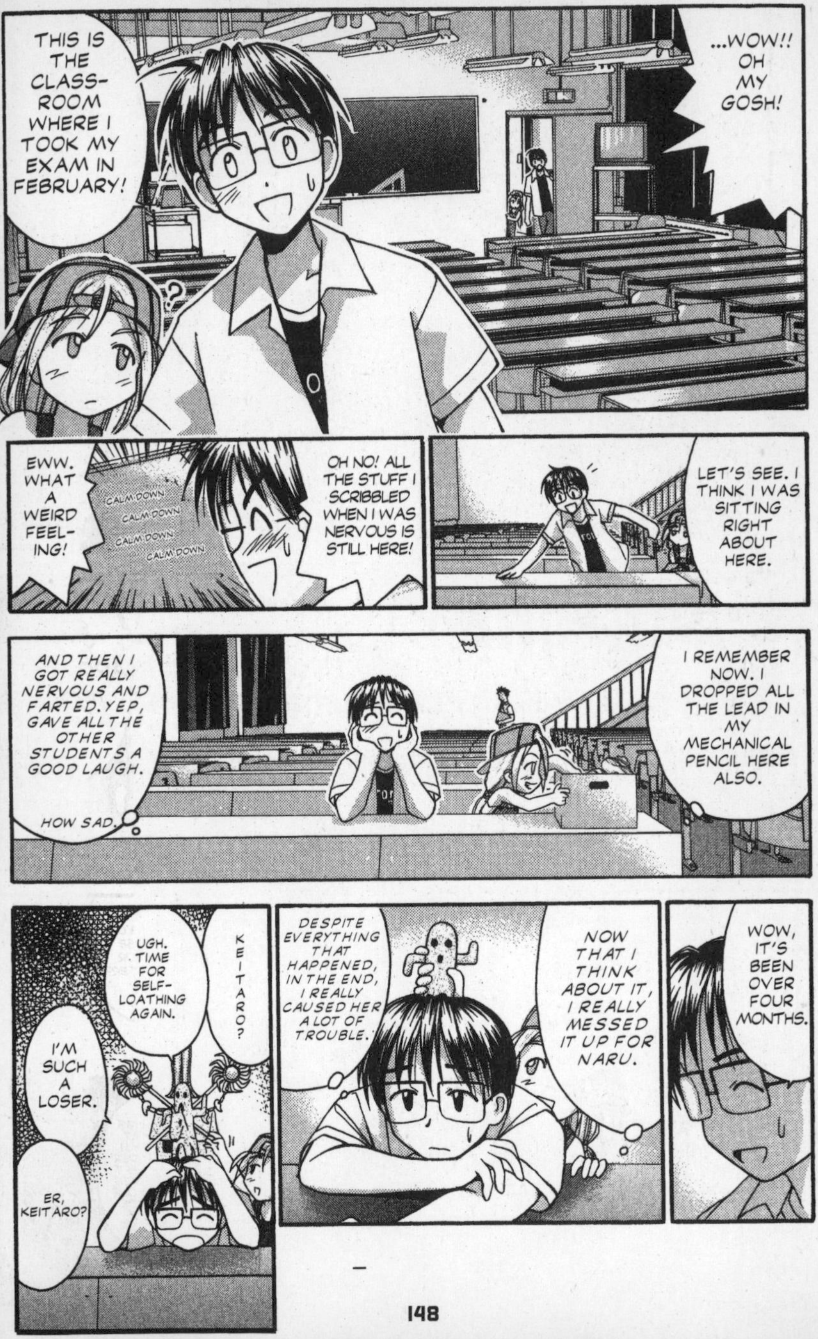
...WOW!! OH MY GOSH!
THIS IS THE CLASS-ROOM WHERE I TOOK MY EXAM IN FEBRUARY!
?
LET'S SEE. I THINK I WAS SITTING RIGHT ABOUT HERE.
OH NO! ALL THE STUFF I SCRIBBLED WHEN I WAS NERVOUS IS STILL HERE!
CALM DOWN
CALM DOWN
CALM DOWN
CALM DOWN
EWW. WHAT A WEIRD FEEL-ING!
I REMEMBER NOW. I DROPPED ALL THE LEAD IN MY MECHANICAL PENCIL HERE ALSO.
AND THEN I GOT REALLY NERVOUS AND FARTED. YEP, GAVE ALL THE OTHER STUDENTS A GOOD LAUGH.
HOW SAD.
WOW, IT'S BEEN OVER FOUR MONTHS.
NOW THAT I THINK ABOUT IT, I REALLY MESSED IT UP FOR NARU.
DESPITE EVERYTHING THAT HAPPENED, IN THE END, I REALLY CAUSED HER A LOT OF TROUBLE.
KEITARO?
UGH. TIME FOR SELF-LOATHING AGAIN.
I'M SUCH A LOSER.
ER, KEITARO?

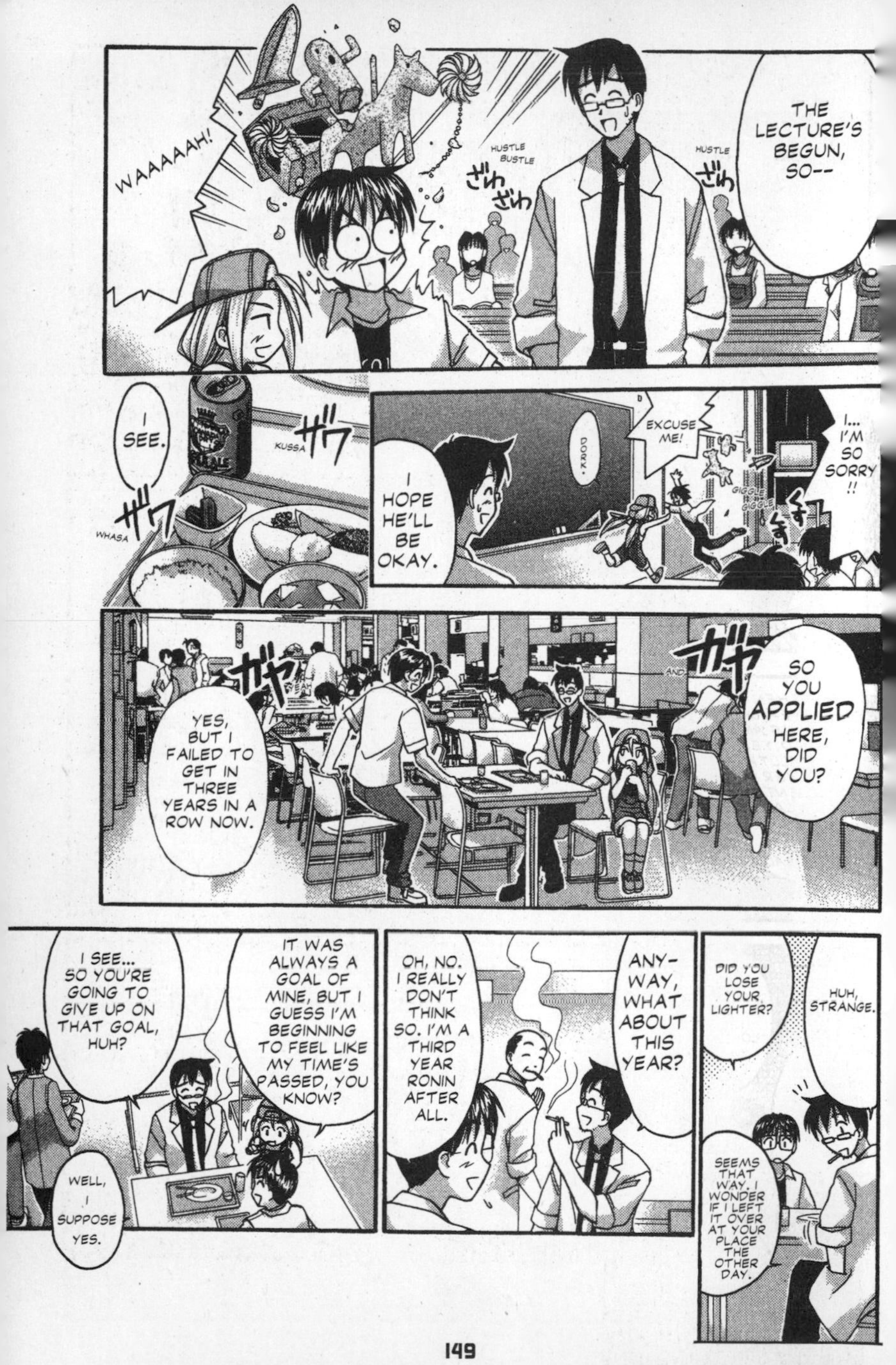
THE LECTURE'S BEGUN, SO--
HUSTLE ざわ
HUSTLE BUSTLE ざわ ざわ
WAAAAAH!
I... I'M SO SORRY!!
GIGGLE GIGGLE くすくす
EXCUSE ME!
DORK.
I HOPE HE'LL BE OKAY.
KUSSA ザワ
I SEE.
WHASA ザワ
SO YOU APPLIED HERE, DID YOU?
AND ガヤ
ガヤ
YES, BUT I FAILED TO GET IN THREE YEARS IN A ROW NOW.
HUH, STRANGE.
DID YOU LOSE YOUR LIGHTER?
SEEMS THAT WAY. I WONDER IF I LEFT IT OVER AT YOUR PLACE THE OTHER DAY.
ANY-WAY, WHAT ABOUT THIS YEAR?
OH, NO. I REALLY DON'T THINK SO. I'M A THIRD YEAR RONIN AFTER ALL.
IT WAS ALWAYS A GOAL OF MINE, BUT I GUESS I'M BEGINNING TO FEEL LIKE MY TIME'S PASSED, YOU KNOW?
I SEE... SO YOU'RE GOING TO GIVE UP ON THAT GOAL, HUH?
WELL, I SUPPOSE YES.

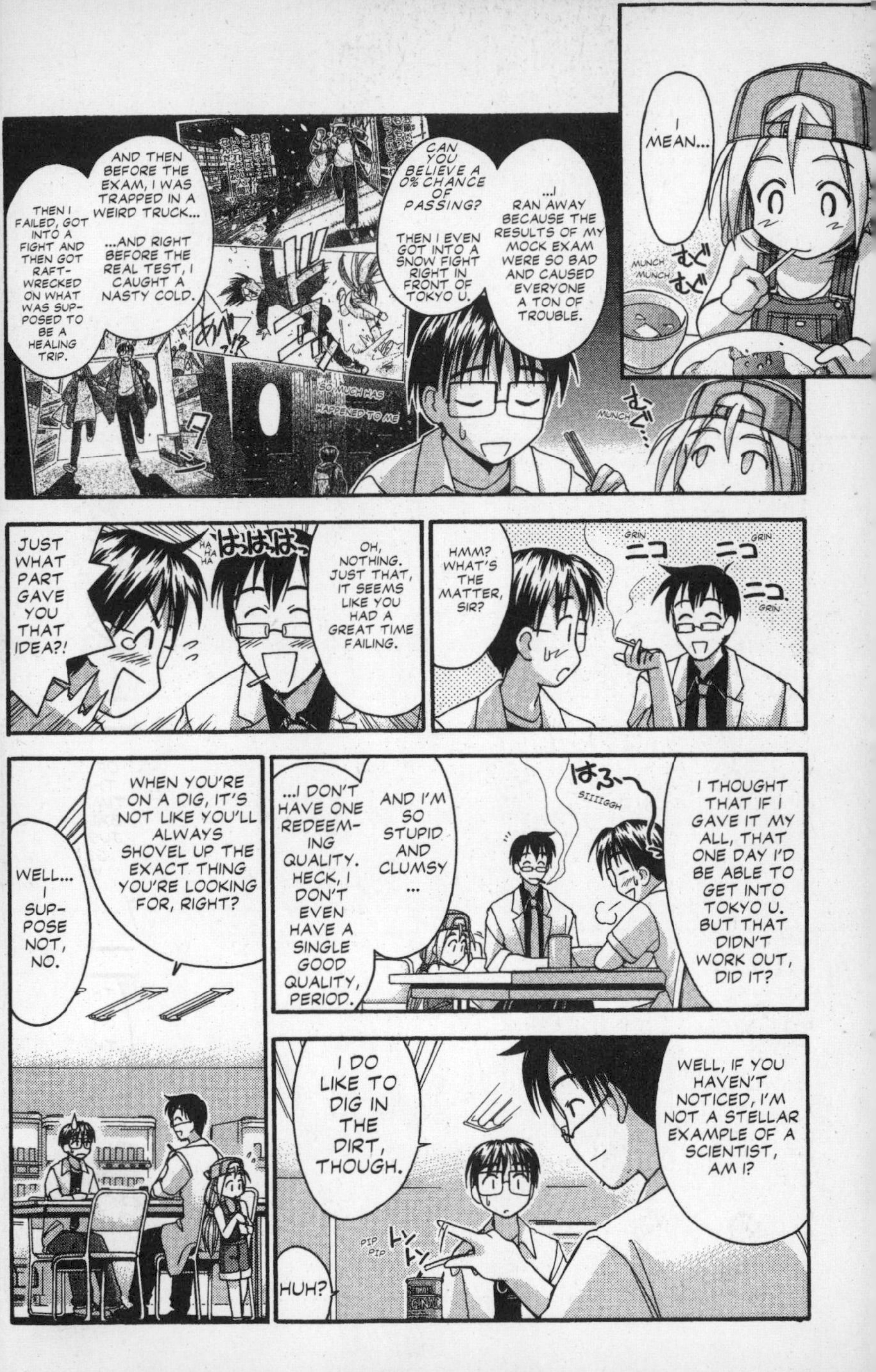
I MEAN...
むぐむぐ
MUNCH MUNCH
...I RAN AWAY BECAUSE THE RESULTS OF MY MOCK EXAM WERE SO BAD AND CAUSED EVERYONE A TON OF TROUBLE.
CAN YOU BELIEVE A 0% CHANCE OF PASSING?
THEN I EVEN GOT INTO A SNOW FIGHT RIGHT IN FRONT OF TOKYO U.
AND THEN BEFORE THE EXAM, I WAS TRAPPED IN A WEIRD TRUCK...
...AND RIGHT BEFORE THE REAL TEST, I CAUGHT A NASTY COLD.
THEN I FAILED, GOT INTO A FIGHT AND THEN GOT RAFT-WRECKED ON WHAT WAS SUPPOSED TO BE A HEALING TRIP.
SO MUCH HAS HAPPENED TO ME
むぐ...
MUNCH
ニコ
GRIN
ニコ
GRIN
ニコ
GRIN
HMM? WHAT'S THE MATTER, SIR?
OH, NOTHING. JUST THAT, IT SEEMS LIKE YOU HAD A GREAT TIME FAILING.
はっはっはっ
HA HA HA
JUST WHAT PART GAVE YOU THAT IDEA?!
I THOUGHT THAT IF I GAVE IT MY ALL, THAT ONE DAY I'D BE ABLE TO GET INTO TOKYO U. BUT THAT DIDN'T WORK OUT, DID IT?
はふ~
SIIIIGGH
AND I'M SO STUPID AND CLUMSY...
...I DON'T HAVE ONE REDEEMING QUALITY. HECK, I DON'T EVEN HAVE A SINGLE GOOD QUALITY, PERIOD.
WELL, IF YOU HAVEN'T NOTICED, I'M NOT A STELLAR EXAMPLE OF A SCIENTIST, AM I?
I DO LIKE TO DIG IN THE DIRT, THOUGH.
トントン
PIP PIP
HUH?
WHEN YOU'RE ON A DIG, IT'S NOT LIKE YOU'LL ALWAYS SHOVEL UP THE EXACT THING YOU'RE LOOKING FOR, RIGHT?
WELL... I SUPPOSE NOT, NO.

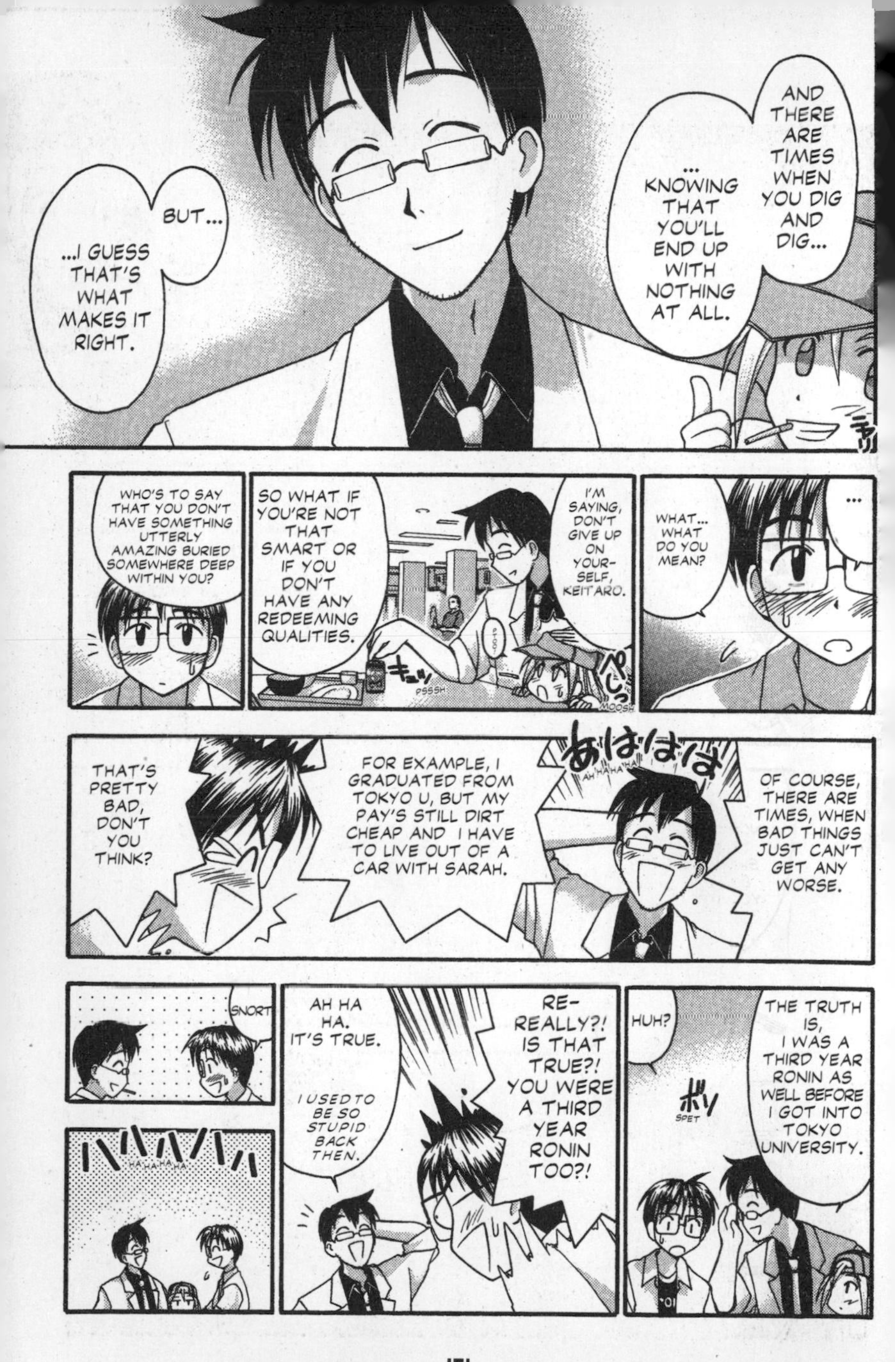
AND THERE ARE TIMES WHEN YOU DIG AND DIG...
...KNOWING THAT YOU'LL END UP WITH NOTHING AT ALL.
BUT...
...I GUESS THAT'S WHAT MAKES IT RIGHT.
...
WHAT... WHAT DO YOU MEAN?
I'M SAYING, DON'T GIVE UP ON YOURSELF, KEITARO.
MOOSH
SO WHAT IF YOU'RE NOT THAT SMART OR IF YOU DON'T HAVE ANY REDEEMING QUALITIES.
PSSSH
WHO'S TO SAY THAT YOU DON'T HAVE SOMETHING UTTERLY AMAZING BURIED SOMEWHERE DEEP WITHIN YOU?
OF COURSE, THERE ARE TIMES, WHEN BAD THINGS JUST CAN'T GET ANY WORSE.
あははは
AH HA HA HA
FOR EXAMPLE, I GRADUATED FROM TOKYO U, BUT MY PAY'S STILL DIRT CHEAP AND I HAVE TO LIVE OUT OF A CAR WITH SARAH.
THAT'S PRETTY BAD, DON'T YOU THINK?
THE TRUTH IS, I WAS A THIRD YEAR RONIN AS WELL BEFORE I GOT INTO TOKYO UNIVERSITY.
HUH?
SPET
RE-REALLY?! IS THAT TRUE?! YOU WERE A THIRD YEAR RONIN TOO?!
AH HA HA. IT'S TRUE.
I USED TO BE SO STUPID BACK THEN.
SNORT
ハハハハ
HA HA HA HA

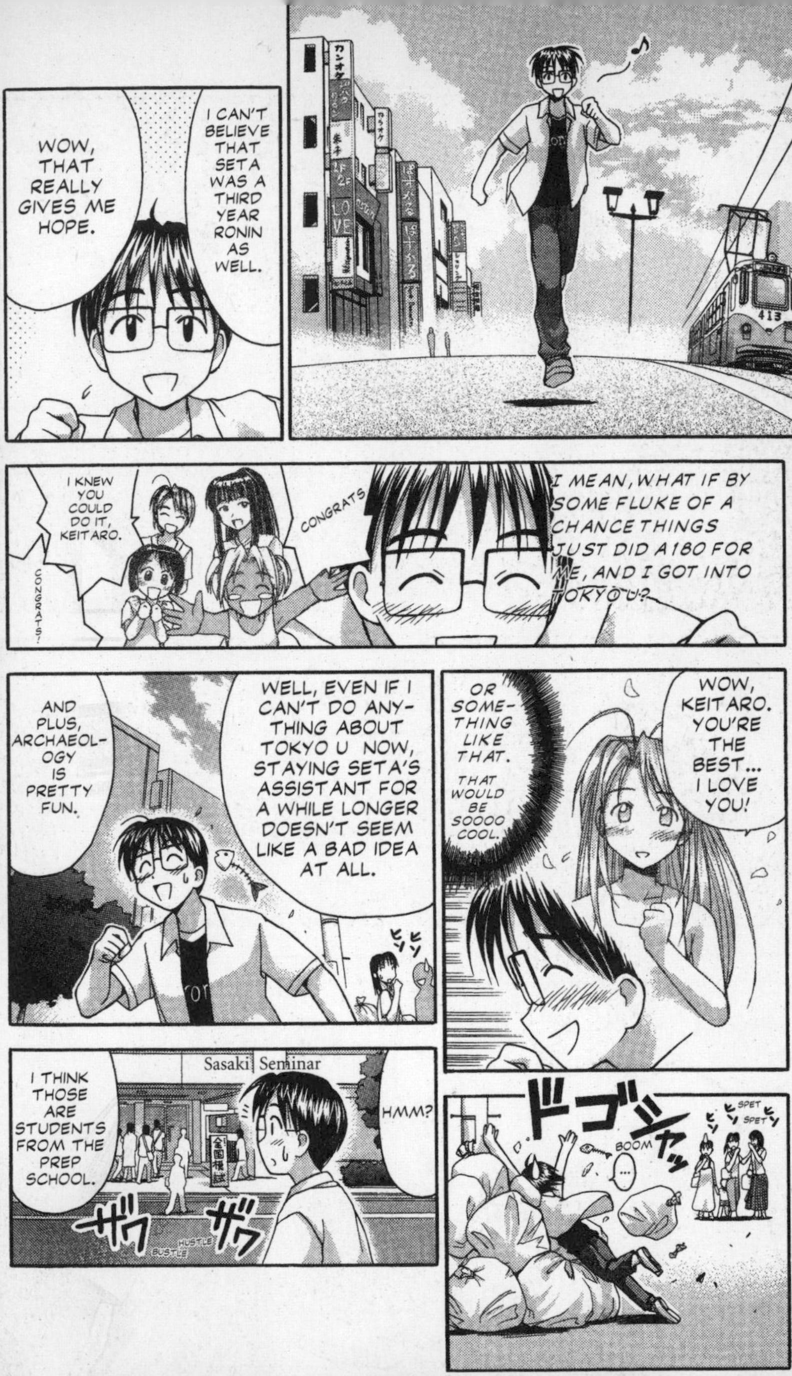
I CAN'T BELIEVE THAT SETA WAS A THIRD YEAR RONIN AS WELL.
WOW, THAT REALLY GIVES ME HOPE.
I MEAN, WHAT IF BY SOME FLUKE OF A CHANCE THINGS JUST DID A180 FOR ME, AND I GOT INTO TOKYO U?
CONGRATS
I KNEW YOU COULD DO IT, KEITARO.
CONGRATS!
WOW, KEITARO. YOU'RE THE BEST... I LOVE YOU!
OR SOMETHING LIKE THAT.
THAT WOULD BE SOOOO COOL.
WELL, EVEN IF I CAN'T DO ANYTHING ABOUT TOKYO U NOW, STAYING SETA'S ASSISTANT FOR A WHILE LONGER DOESN'T SEEM LIKE A BAD IDEA AT ALL.
AND PLUS, ARCHAEOLOGY IS PRETTY FUN.
ヒソ ヒソ
HMM?
Sasaki Seminar
I THINK THOSE ARE STUDENTS FROM THE PREP SCHOOL.
全国模試
ザワ ザワ
HUSTLE BUSTLE
ドゴシャッ
BOOM
...
ヒソ SPET ヒソ SPET

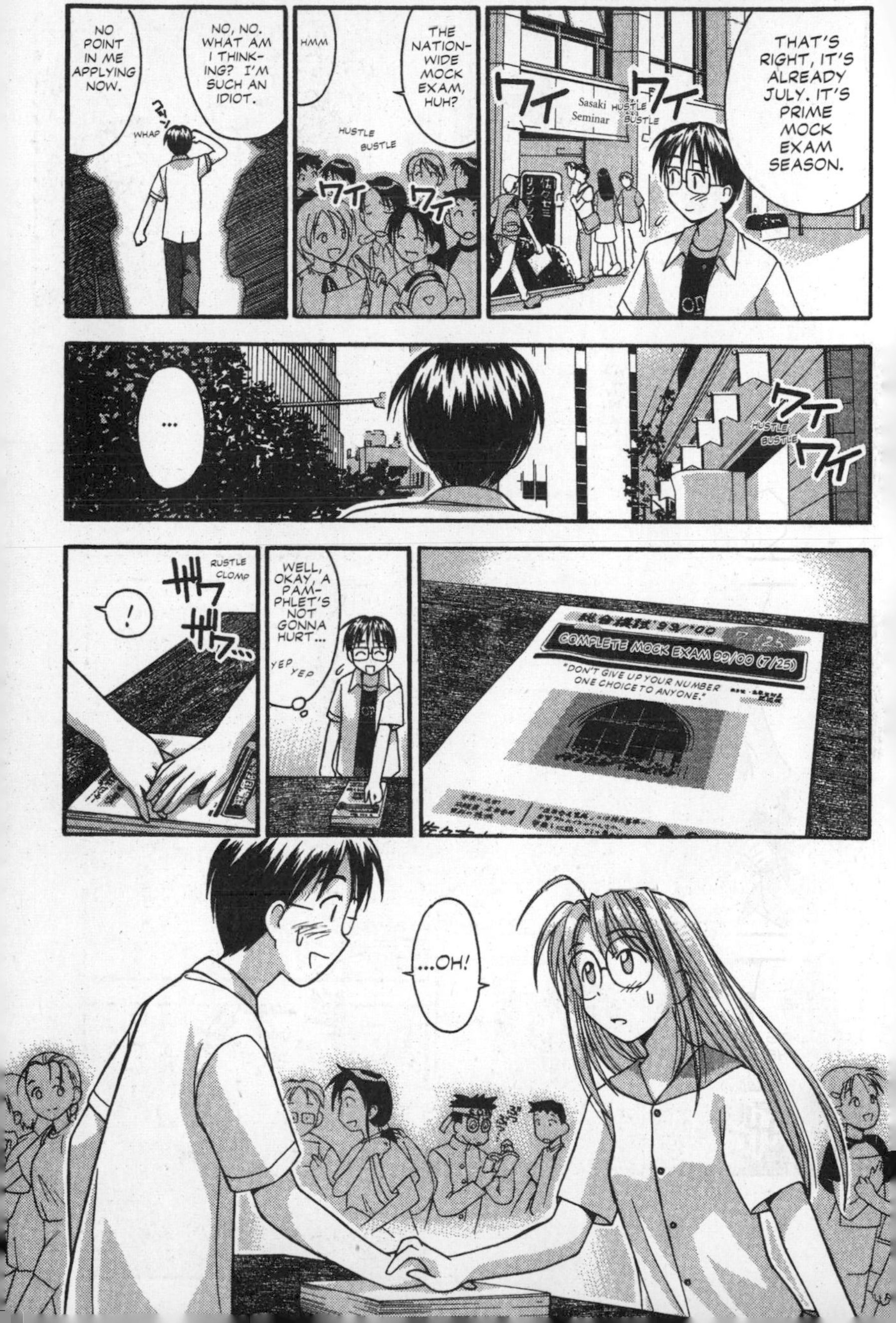
THAT'S RIGHT, IT'S ALREADY JULY. IT'S PRIME MOCK EXAM SEASON.
Sasaki Seminar
HUSTLE BUSTLE
THE NATION-WIDE MOCK EXAM, HUH?
HMM
HUSTLE BUSTLE
NO, NO. WHAT AM I THINKING? I'M SUCH AN IDIOT.
NO POINT IN ME APPLYING NOW.
WHAP
HUSTLE BUSTLE
...
COMPLETE MOCK EXAM 99/00 (7/25)
"DON'T GIVE UP YOUR NUMBER ONE CHOICE TO ANYONE."
WELL, OKAY, A PAMPHLET'S NOT GONNA HURT...
YEP YEP
RUSTLE CLOMP
!
...OH!

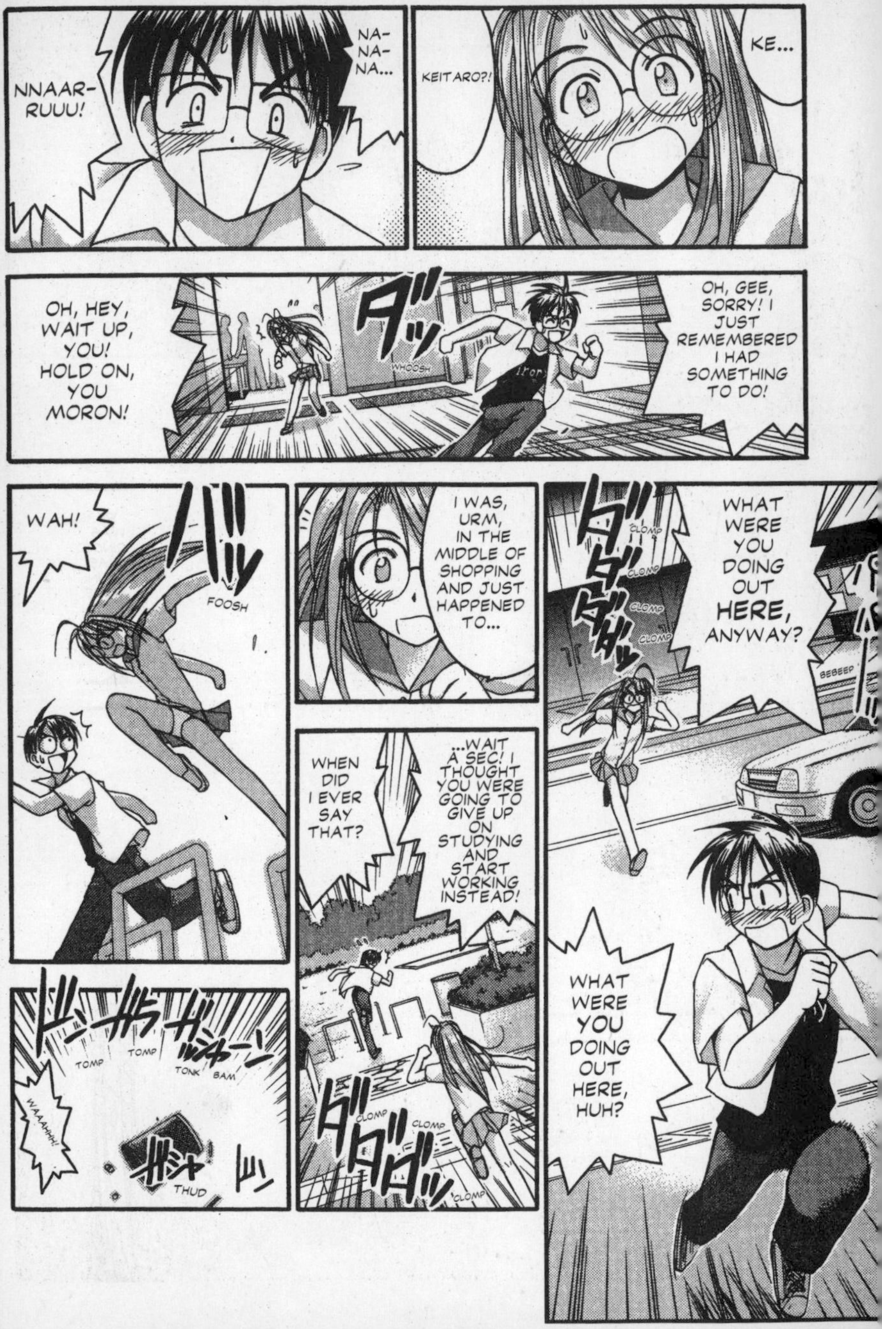
KE...
KEITARO?!
NA-NA-NA...
NNAAR-RUUU!
OH, GEE, SORRY! I JUST REMEMBERED I HAD SOMETHING TO DO!
WHOOSH
OH, HEY, WAIT UP, YOU! HOLD ON, YOU MORON!
WHAT WERE YOU DOING OUT HERE, ANYWAY?
BEBEEP
CLOMP
CLOMP
CLOMP
CLOMP
WHAT WERE YOU DOING OUT HERE, HUH?
I WAS, URM, IN THE MIDDLE OF SHOPPING AND JUST HAPPENED TO...
...WAIT A SEC! I THOUGHT YOU WERE GOING TO GIVE UP ON STUDYING AND START WORKING INSTEAD!
WHEN DID I EVER SAY THAT?
CLOMP
CLOMP
CLOMP
WAH!
FOOSH
TOMP
TOMP
TONK
BAM
WAAAHHH!
THUD

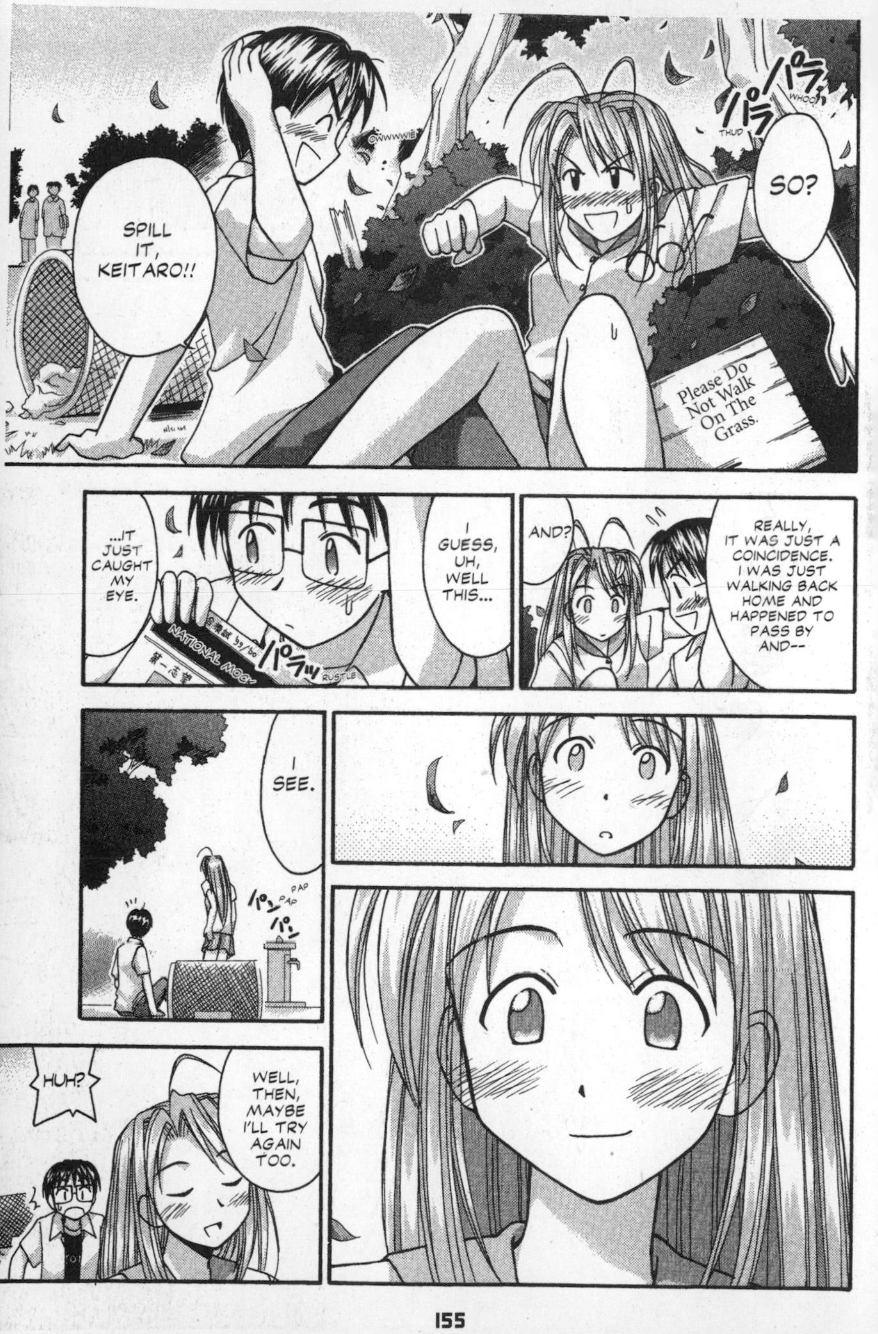
WHOOO...
THUD
SO?
SPILL IT, KEITARO!!
Please Do Not Walk On The Grass.
REALLY, IT WAS JUST A COINCIDENCE. I WAS JUST WALKING BACK HOME AND HAPPENED TO PASS BY AND--
AND?
I GUESS, UH, WELL THIS...
...IT JUST CAUGHT MY EYE.
NATIONAL MOCK
RUSTLE
I SEE.
PAP PAP
WELL, THEN, MAYBE I'LL TRY AGAIN TOO.
HUH?

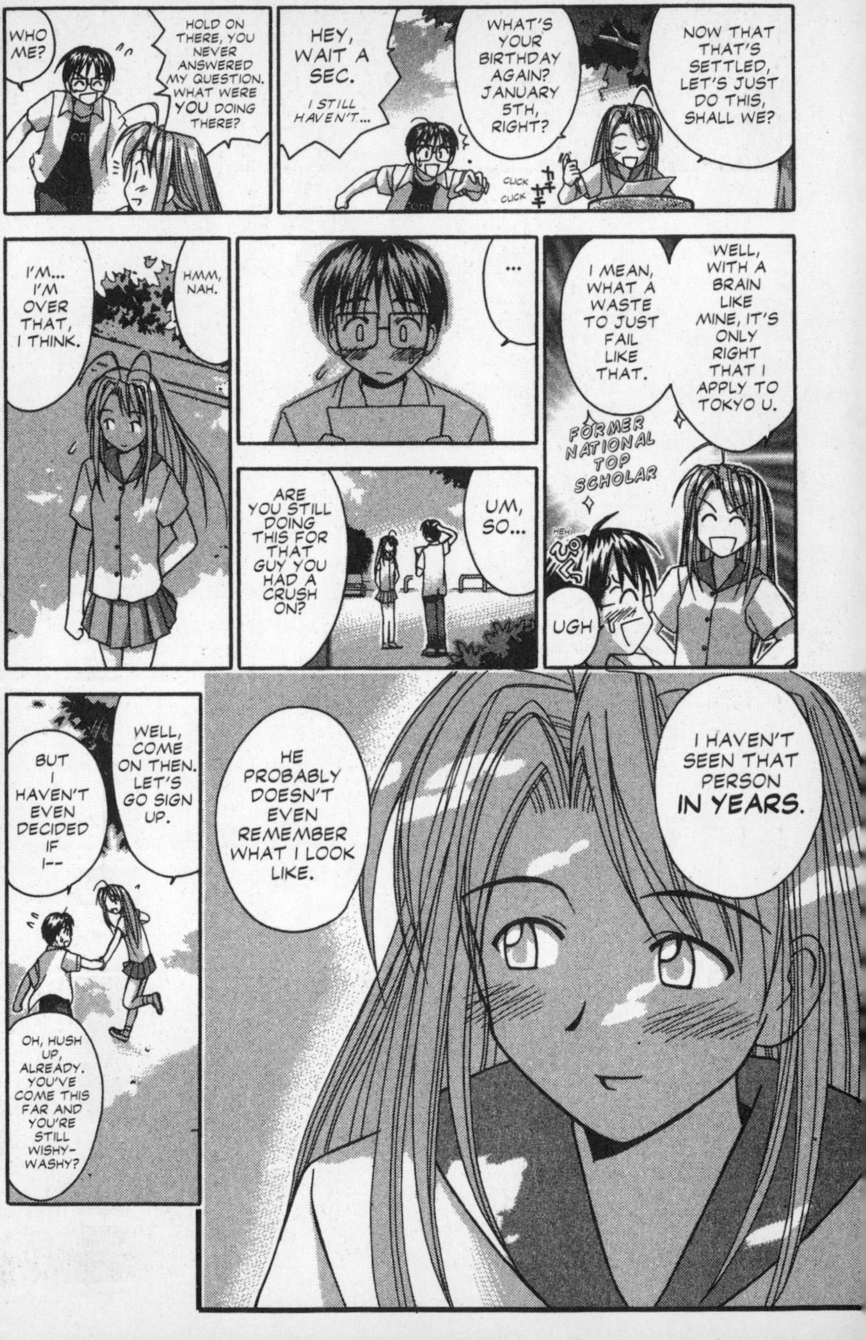
NOW THAT THAT'S SETTLED, LET'S JUST DO THIS, SHALL WE?
WHAT'S YOUR BIRTHDAY AGAIN? JANUARY 5TH, RIGHT?
CLICK CLICK
HEY, WAIT A SEC.
I STILL HAVEN'T...
HOLD ON THERE, YOU NEVER ANSWERED MY QUESTION. WHAT WERE YOU DOING THERE?
WHO ME?
WELL, WITH A BRAIN LIKE MINE, IT'S ONLY RIGHT THAT I APPLY TO TOKYO U.
I MEAN, WHAT A WASTE TO JUST FAIL LIKE THAT.
FORMER NATIONAL TOP SCHOLAR
HEH
UGH
...
UM, SO...
ARE YOU STILL DOING THIS FOR THAT GUY YOU HAD A CRUSH ON?
HMM, NAH.
I'M... I'M OVER THAT, I THINK.
I HAVEN'T SEEN THAT PERSON IN YEARS.
HE PROBABLY DOESN'T EVEN REMEMBER WHAT I LOOK LIKE.
WELL, COME ON THEN. LET'S GO SIGN UP.
BUT I HAVEN'T EVEN DECIDED IF I--
OH, HUSH UP, ALREADY. YOU'VE COME THIS FAR AND YOU'RE STILL WISHY-WASHY?

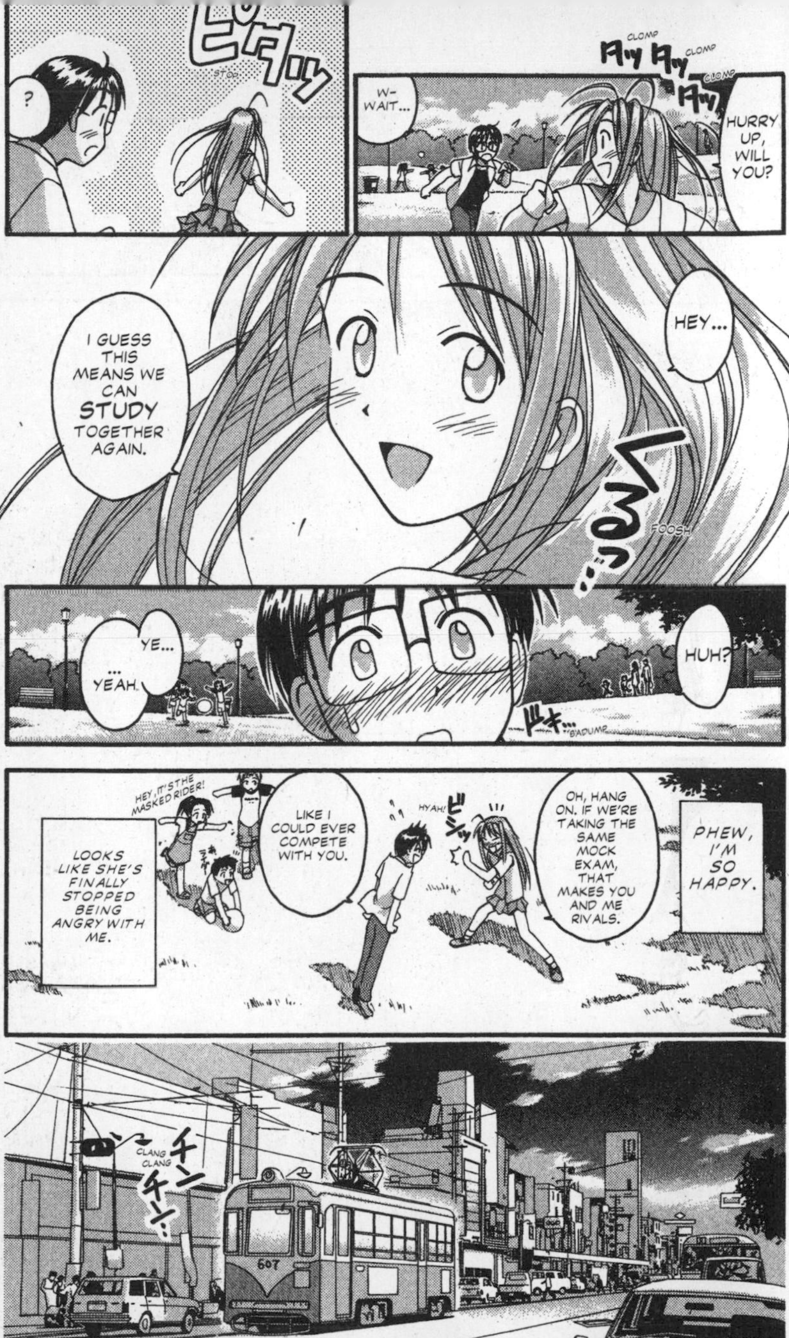
CLOMP
CLOMP
CLOMP
HURRY UP, WILL YOU?
W-WAIT...
STOP
?
HEY...
FOOSH
I GUESS THIS MEANS WE CAN STUDY TOGETHER AGAIN.
HUH?
BADUMP
YE... ...YEAH.
PHEW, I'M SO HAPPY.
OH, HANG ON. IF WE'RE TAKING THE SAME MOCK EXAM, THAT MAKES YOU AND ME RIVALS.
HYAH!
LIKE I COULD EVER COMPETE WITH YOU.
HEY, IT'S THE MASKED RIDER!
LOOKS LIKE SHE'S FINALLY STOPPED BEING ANGRY WITH ME.
CLANG CLANG

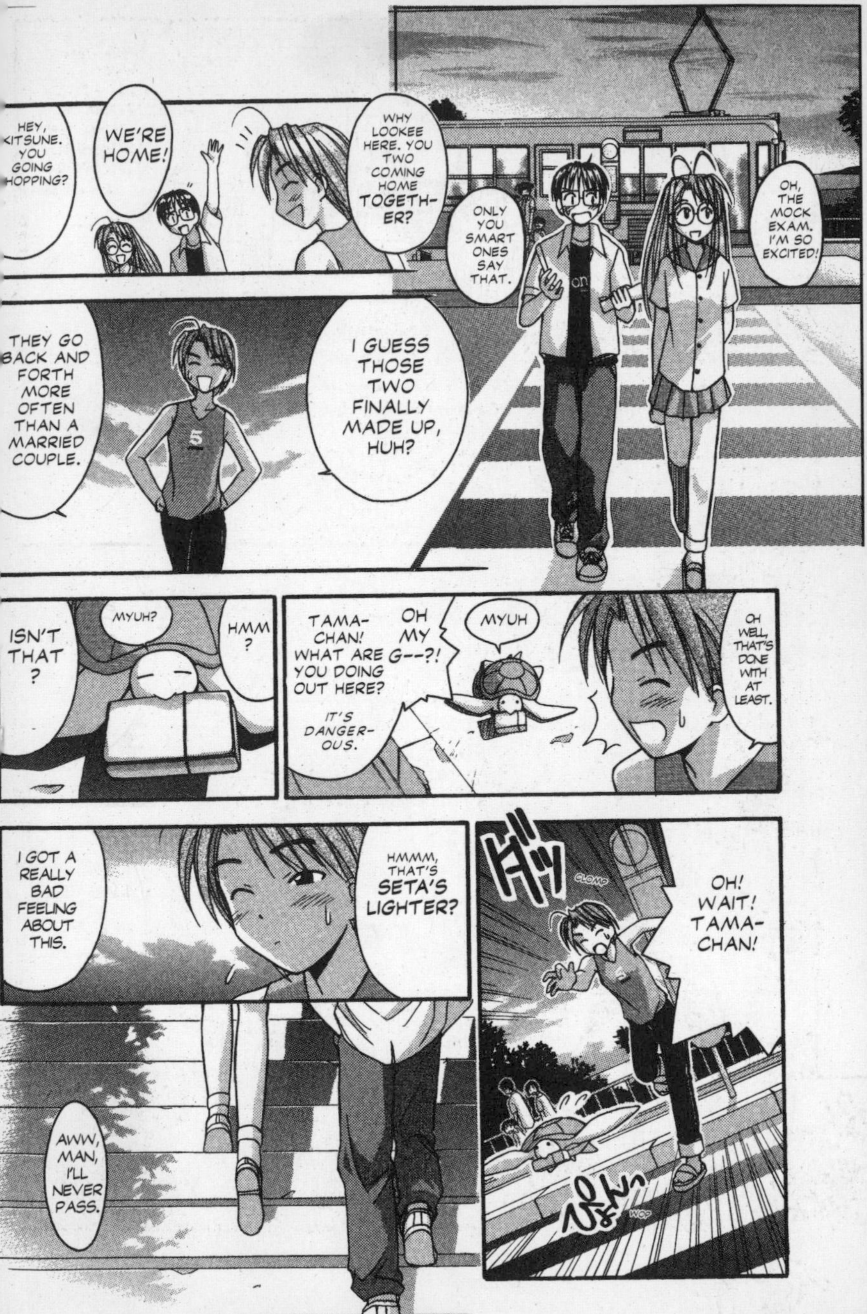
OH, THE MOCK EXAM. I'M SO EXCITED!
ONLY YOU SMART ONES SAY THAT.
WHY LOOKEE HERE. YOU TWO COMING HOME TOGETHER?
WE'RE HOME!
HEY, KITSUNE. YOU GOING SHOPPING?
I GUESS THOSE TWO FINALLY MADE UP, HUH?
THEY GO BACK AND FORTH MORE OFTEN THAN A MARRIED COUPLE.
OH WELL, THAT'S DONE WITH AT LEAST.
MYUH
OH MY G--?!
TAMA-CHAN! WHAT ARE YOU DOING OUT HERE?
IT'S DANGEROUS.
HMM?
MYUH?
ISN'T THAT?
OH! WAIT! TAMA-CHAN!
CLOMP
WOP
HMMM, THAT'S SETA'S LIGHTER?
I GOT A REALLY BAD FEELING ABOUT THIS.
AWW, MAN, I'LL NEVER PASS.

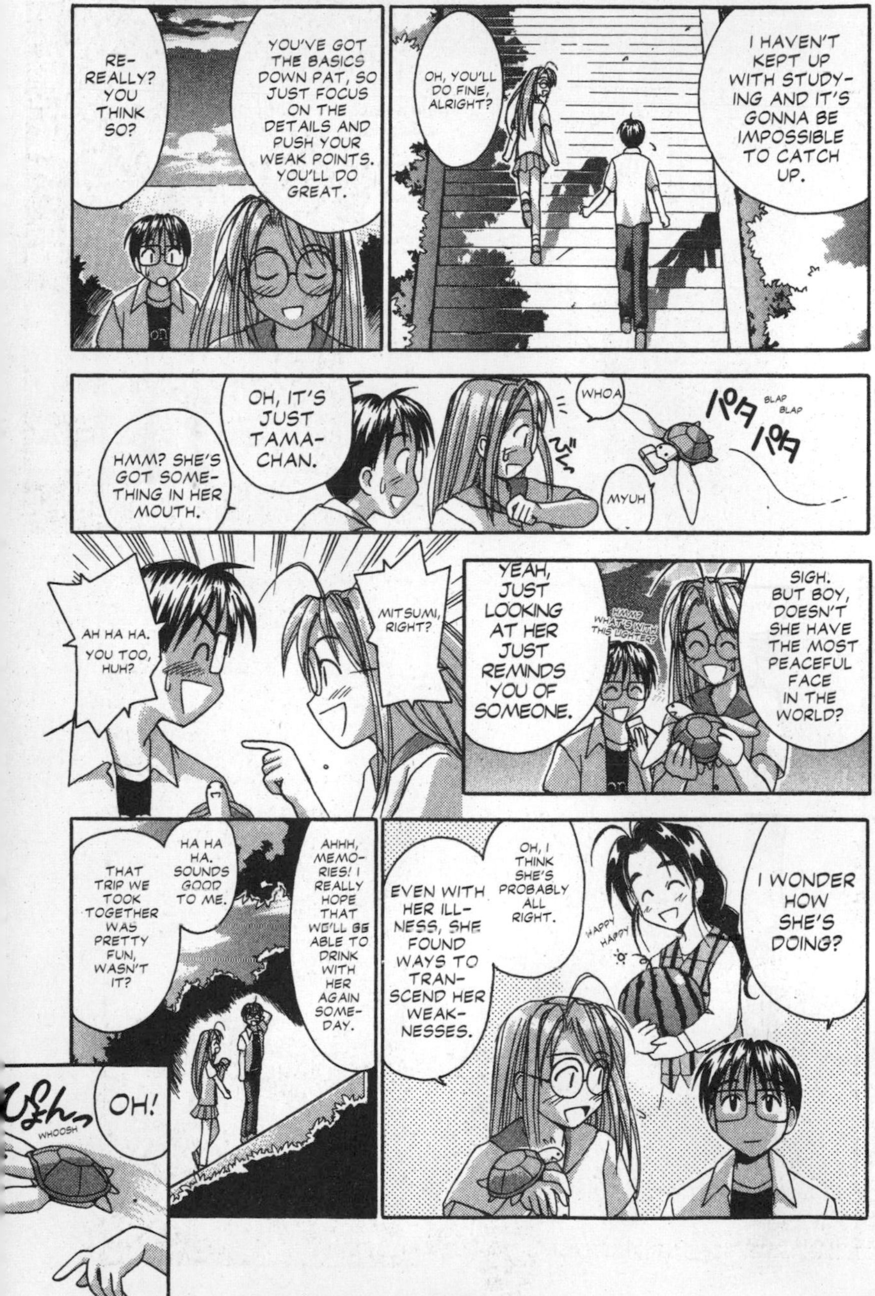
I HAVEN'T KEPT UP WITH STUDYING AND IT'S GONNA BE IMPOSSIBLE TO CATCH UP.
OH, YOU'LL DO FINE, ALRIGHT?
YOU'VE GOT THE BASICS DOWN PAT, SO JUST FOCUS ON THE DETAILS AND PUSH YOUR WEAK POINTS. YOU'LL DO GREAT.
RE-REALLY? YOU THINK SO?
パタ パタ
BLAP BLAP
WHOA
MYUH
OH, IT'S JUST TAMA-CHAN.
HMM? SHE'S GOT SOMETHING IN HER MOUTH.
SIGH. BUT BOY, DOESN'T SHE HAVE THE MOST PEACEFUL FACE IN THE WORLD?
HMM? WHAT'S WITH THIS LIGHTER?
YEAH, JUST LOOKING AT HER JUST REMINDS YOU OF SOMEONE.
MITSUMI, RIGHT?
AH HA HA. YOU TOO, HUH?
I WONDER HOW SHE'S DOING?
HAPPY HAPPY
OH, I THINK SHE'S PROBABLY ALL RIGHT.
EVEN WITH HER ILLNESS, SHE FOUND WAYS TO TRANSCEND HER WEAKNESSES.
AHHH, MEMORIES! I REALLY HOPE THAT WE'LL BE ABLE TO DRINK WITH HER AGAIN SOMEDAY.
HA HA HA. SOUNDS GOOD TO ME.
THAT TRIP WE TOOK TOGETHER WAS PRETTY FUN, WASN'T IT?
OH!
WHOOSH

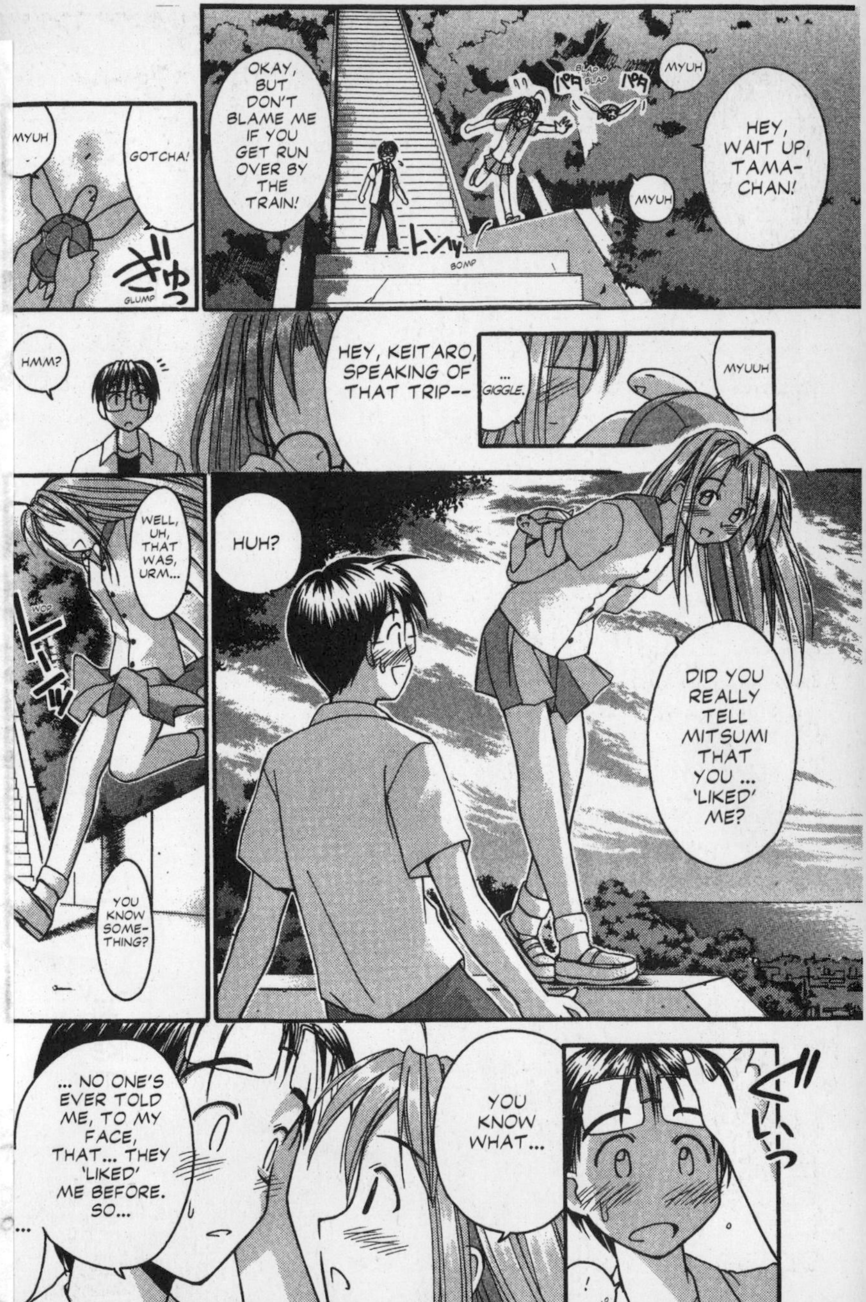
MYUH
HEY, WAIT UP, TAMA-CHAN!
BLAP BLAP
MYUH
OKAY, BUT DON'T BLAME ME IF YOU GET RUN OVER BY THE TRAIN!
BOMP
GOTCHA!
MYUH
GLUMP
MYUUH
... GIGGLE.
HEY, KEITARO, SPEAKING OF THAT TRIP--
HMM?
DID YOU REALLY TELL MITSUMI THAT YOU ... 'LIKED' ME?
HUH?
WELL, UH, THAT WAS, URM...
WOP
YOU KNOW SOMETHING?
!
BADUMP
YOU KNOW WHAT...
... NO ONE'S EVER TOLD ME, TO MY FACE, THAT... THEY 'LIKED' ME BEFORE. SO...
SO...

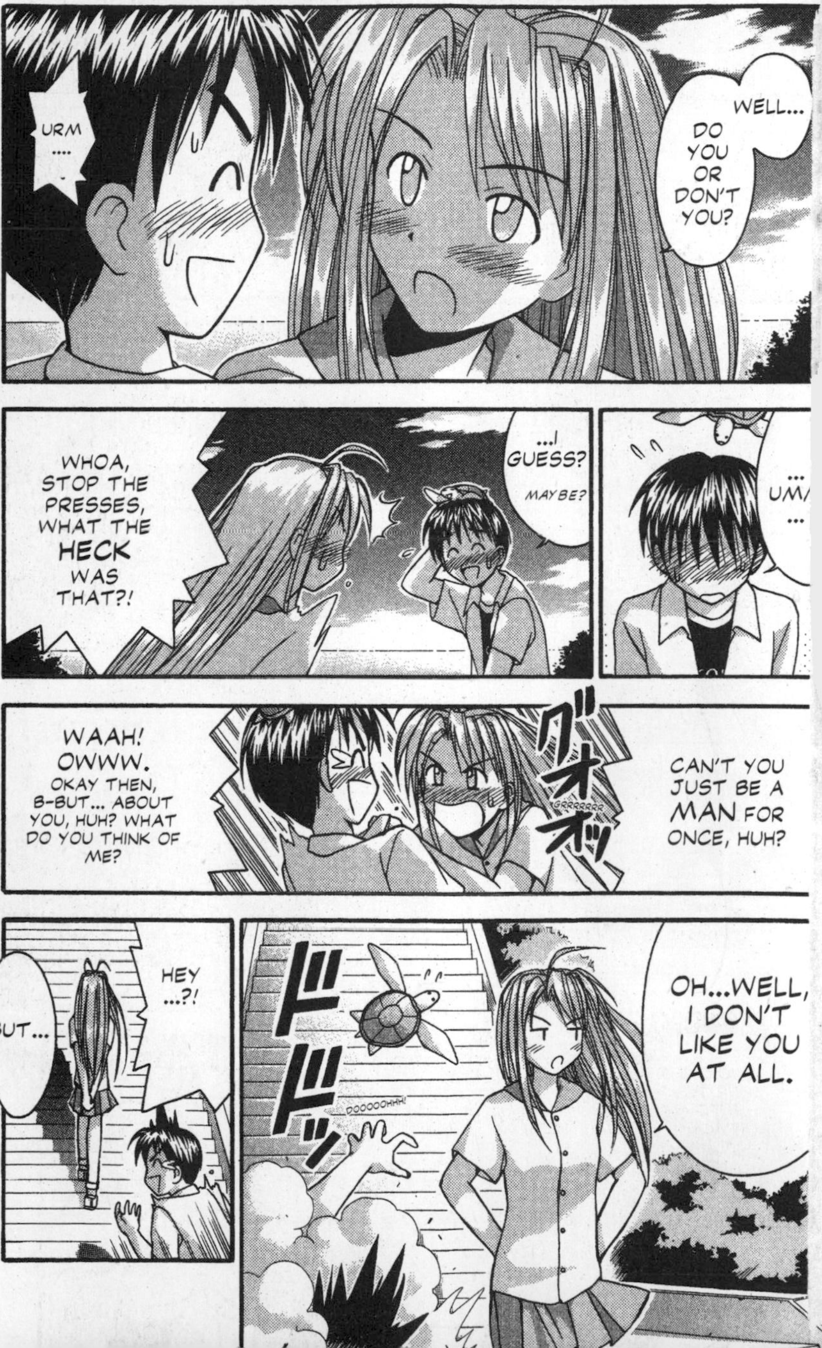
WELL... DO YOU OR DON'T YOU?
URM ....
... UM
...
...I GUESS? MAYBE?
WHOA, STOP THE PRESSES, WHAT THE HECK WAS THAT?!
CAN'T YOU JUST BE A MAN FOR ONCE, HUH?
グオオッ
GRRRRRRR
WAAH! OWWW. OKAY THEN, B-BUT... ABOUT YOU, HUH? WHAT DO YOU THINK OF ME?
OH...WELL, I DON'T LIKE YOU AT ALL.
ドドドッ
DOOOOOHHH!
HEY ...?!
BUT...

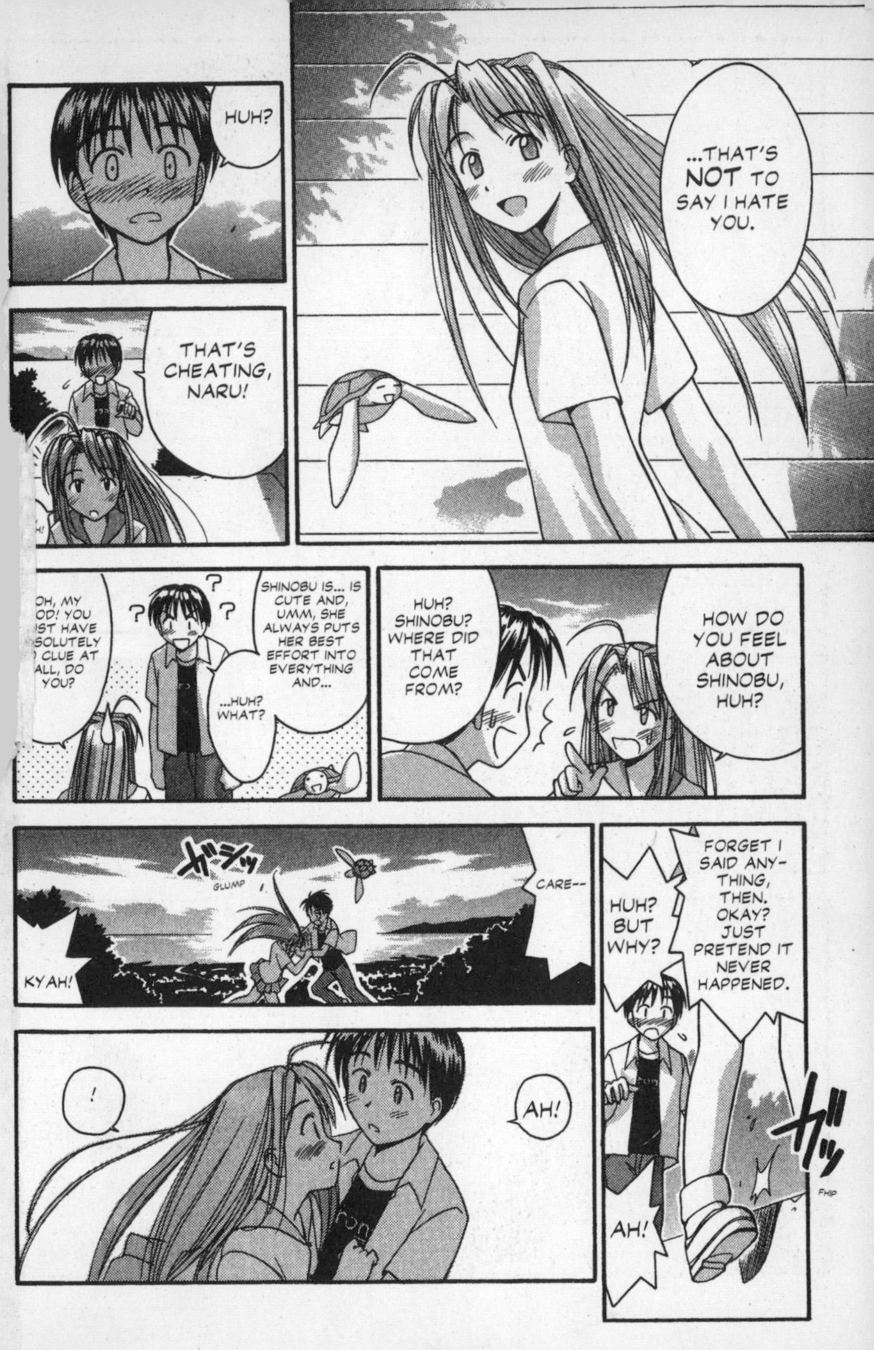
...THAT'S NOT TO SAY I HATE YOU.
HUH?
THAT'S CHEATING, NARU!
HOW DO YOU FEEL ABOUT SHINOBU, HUH?
HUH? SHINOBU? WHERE DID THAT COME FROM?
SHINOBU IS... IS CUTE AND, UMM, SHE ALWAYS PUTS HER BEST EFFORT INTO EVERYTHING AND...
...HUH? WHAT?
OH, MY OD! YOU IST HAVE SOLUTELY O CLUE AT ALL, DO YOU?
FORGET I SAID ANY-THING, THEN. OKAY? JUST PRETEND IT NEVER HAPPENED.
HUH? BUT WHY?
FHIP
AH!
CARE--
GLUMP
KYAH!
AH!
!

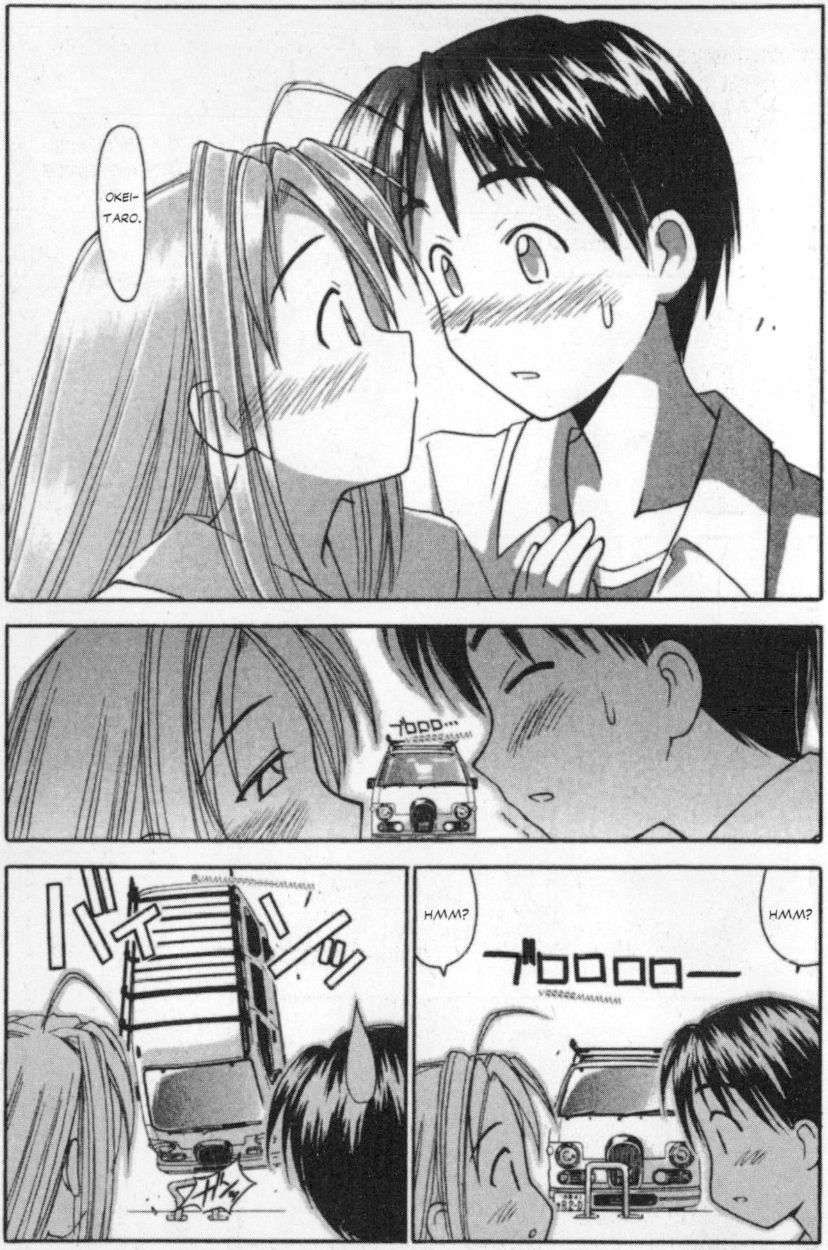
OKEI-TARO.
ブロロ…
HMM?
HMM?
ブロロロロー
バイーン

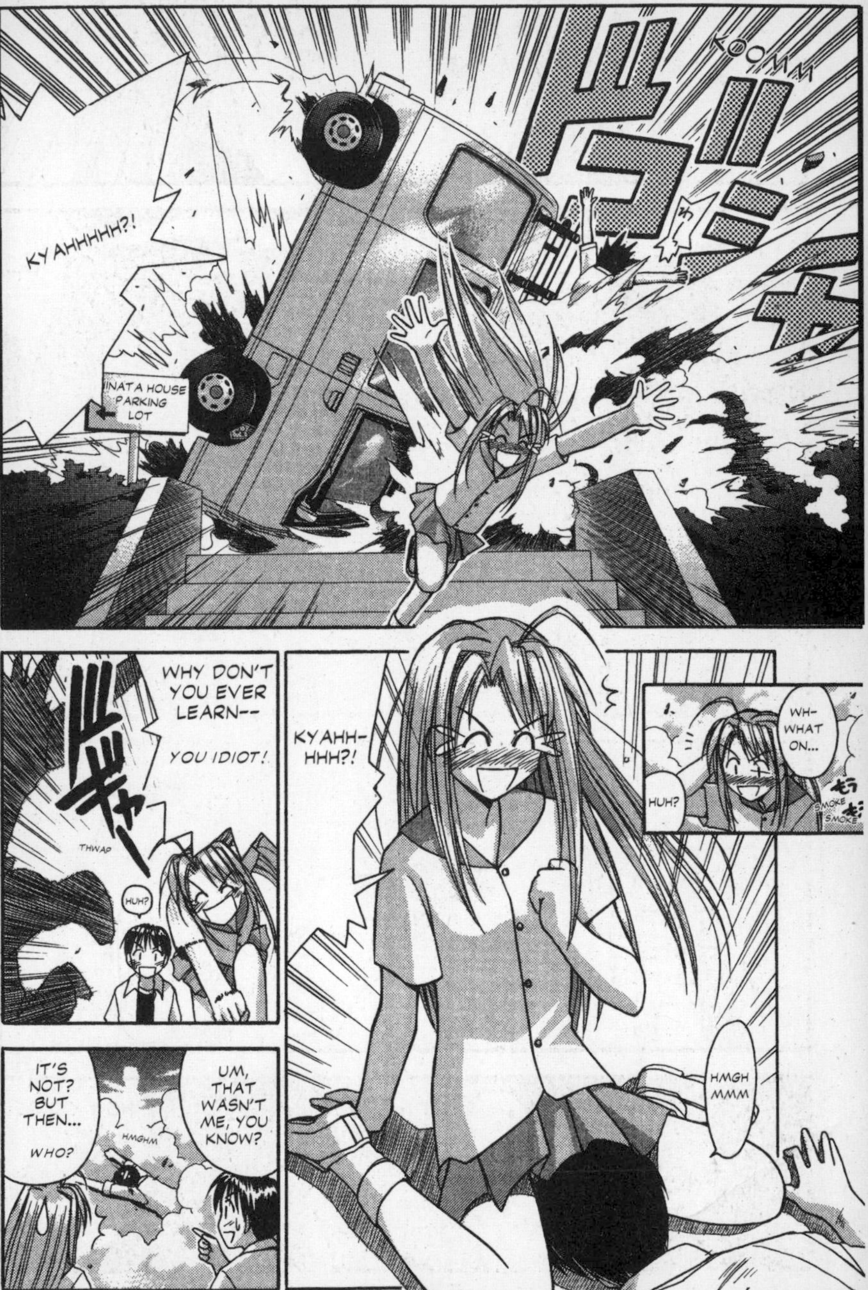
KOOMM
KYAHHHHH?!
INATA HOUSE PARKING LOT
WH- WHAT ON...
HUH?
SMOKE SMOKE
KYAHH- HHH?!
HMGH MMM
WHY DON'T YOU EVER LEARN--
YOU IDIOT!
THWAP
HUH?
UM, THAT WASN'T ME, YOU KNOW?
IT'S NOT? BUT THEN...
WHO?
HMGHM

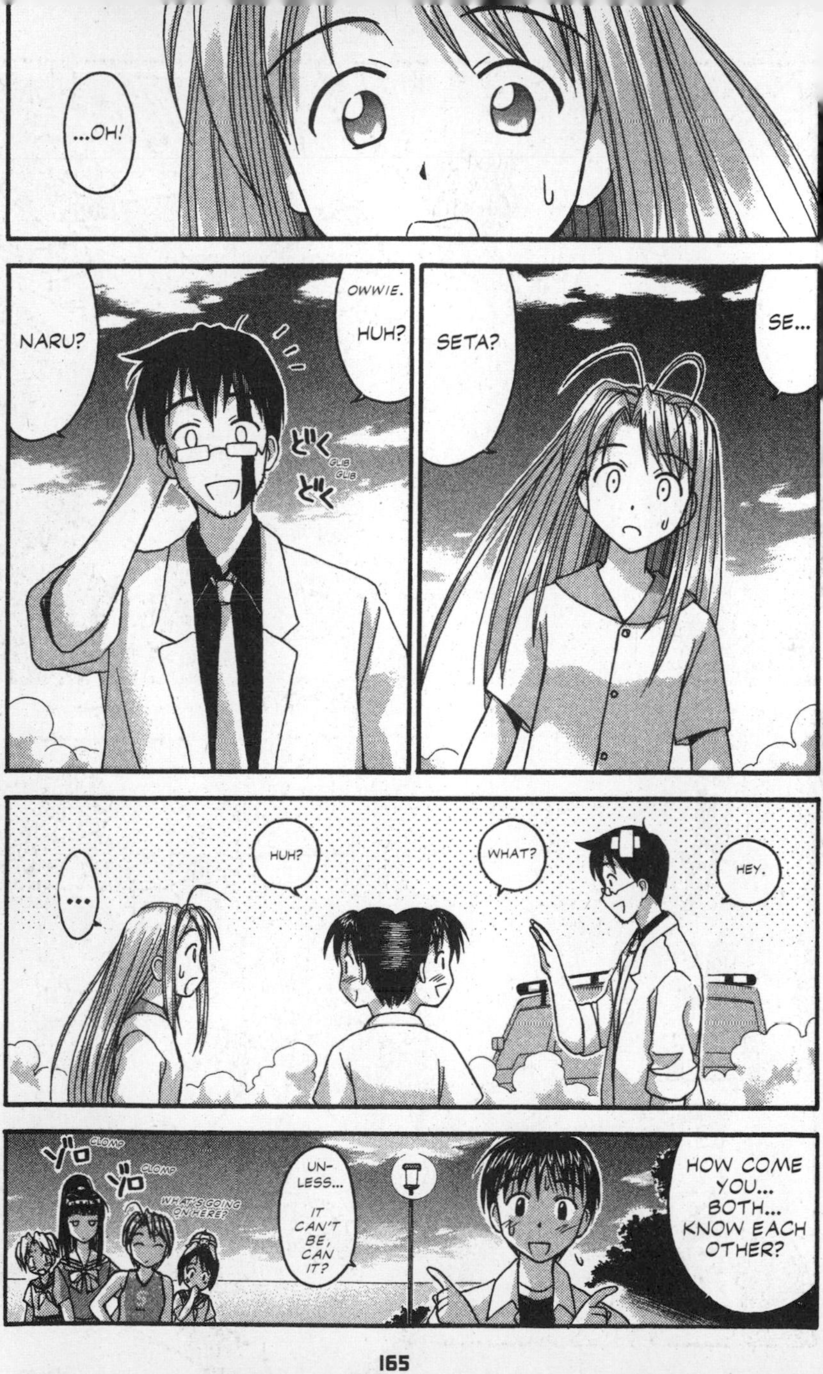
...OH!
SE...
SETA?
OWWIE.
HUH?
NARU?
どく
GLIB
GLIB
どく
HEY.
WHAT?
HUH?
...
HOW COME YOU... BOTH... KNOW EACH OTHER?
UN-LESS...
IT CAN'T BE, CAN IT?
WHAT'S GOING ON HERE?
ゾロ
CLOMP
ゾロ
CLOMP

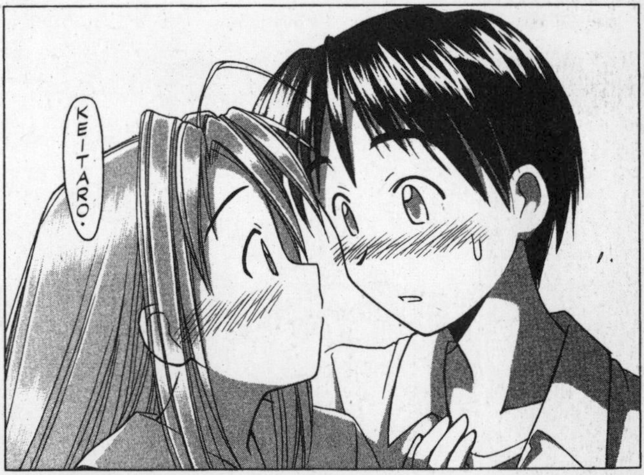
KEITARO.

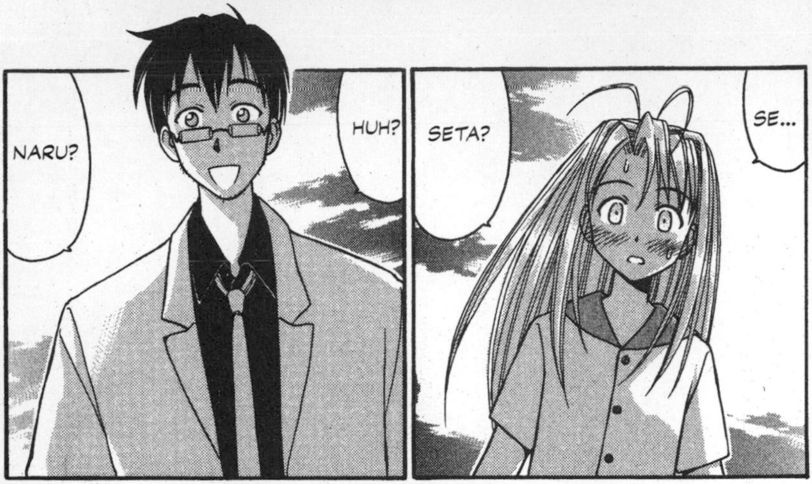
SE...
SETA?
HUH?
NARU?

Love Hina

HINATA..33 I Love You, Sempai!

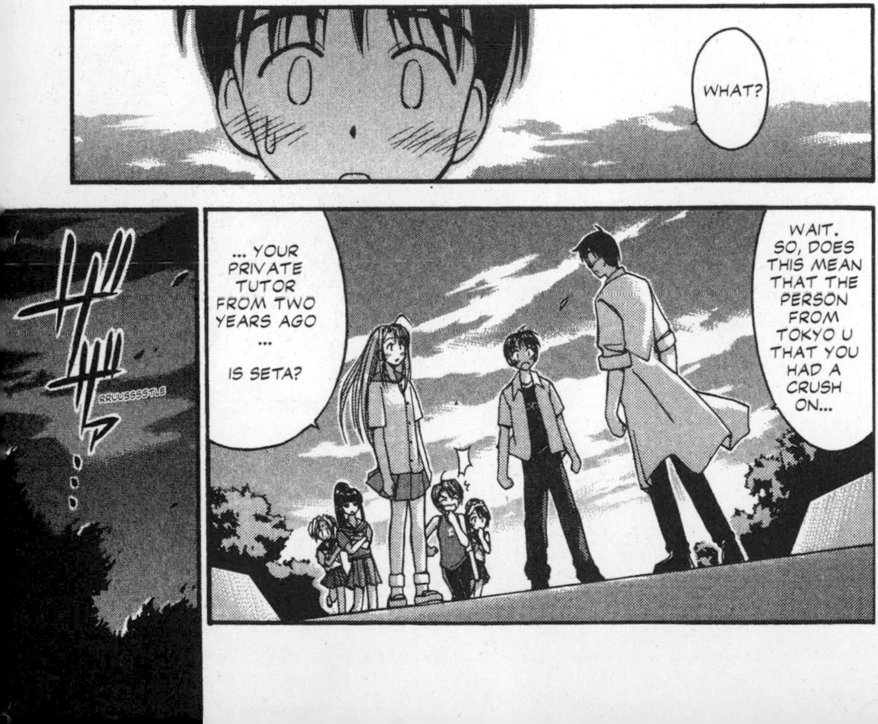
WHAT?
WAIT. SO, DOES THIS MEAN THAT THE PERSON FROM TOKYO U THAT YOU HAD A CRUSH ON...
... YOUR PRIVATE TUTOR FROM TWO YEARS AGO ... IS SETA?
RRUUSSSSTLE

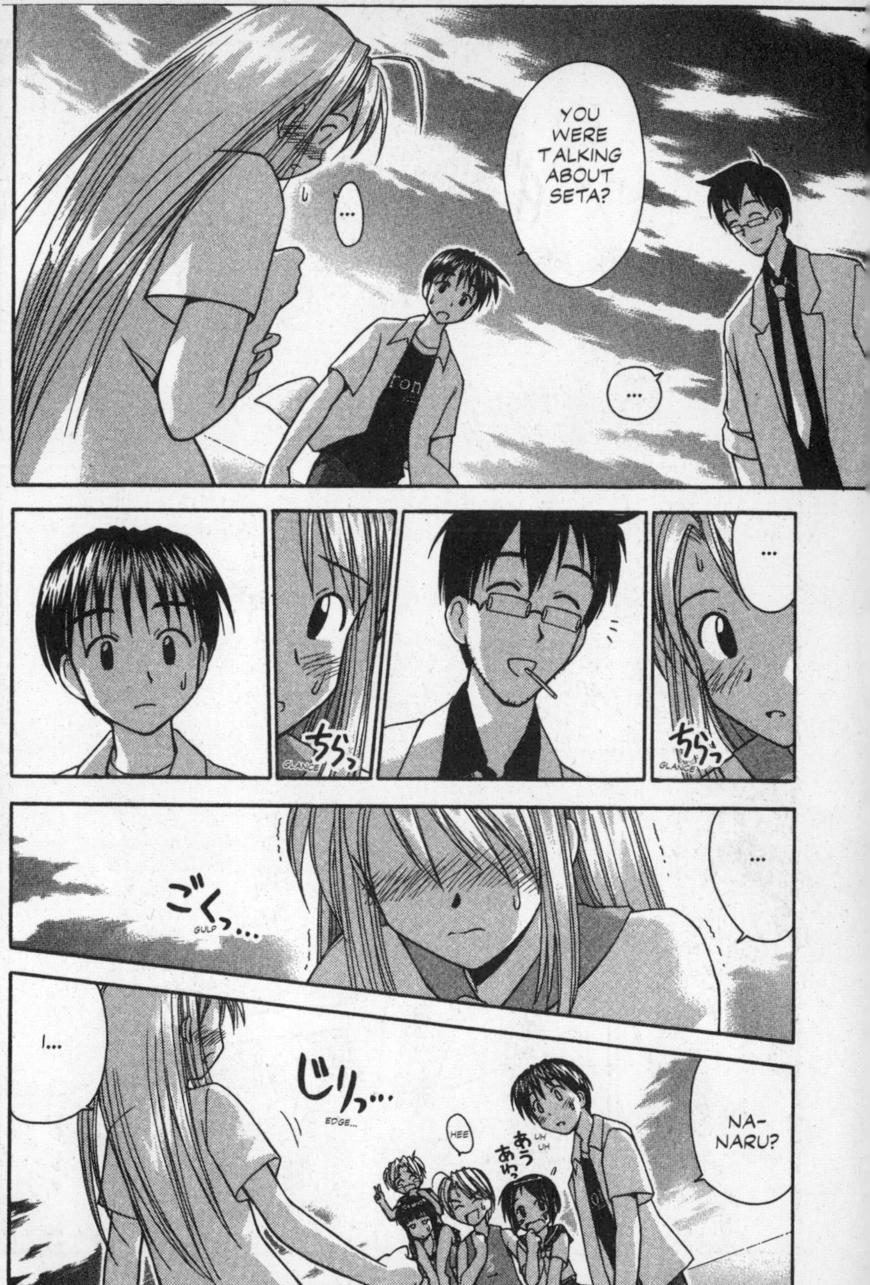
YOU WERE TALKING ABOUT SETA?
...
...
...
ちらっ
GLANCE
ちらっ
GLANCE
...
ごくっ...
GULP
NA-NARU?
あう あわっ
UH UH
HEE
じりっ...
EDGE...
I...

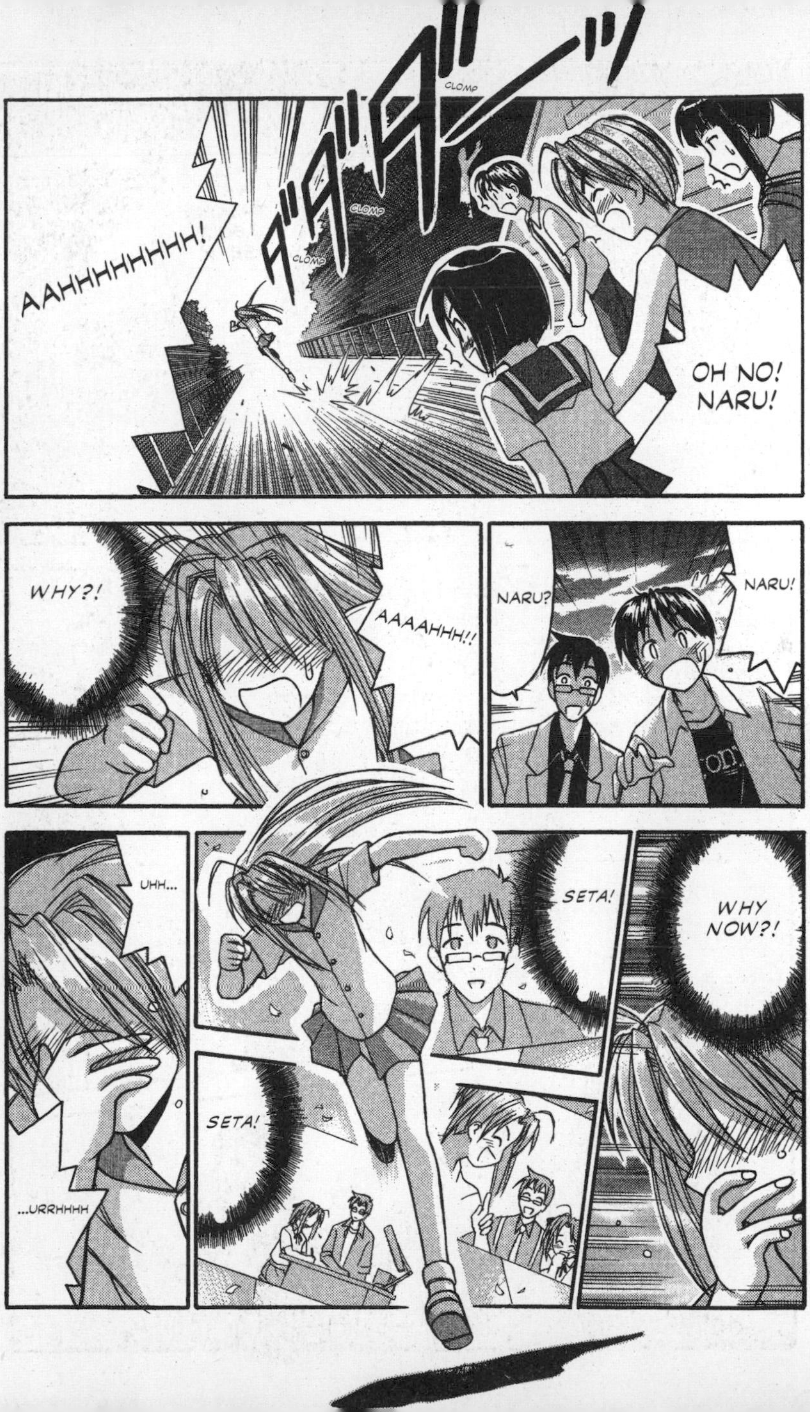
CLOMP
CLOMP
CLOMP
OH NO! NARU!
AAHHHHHHHHH!
NARU!
NARU?
AAAAHHH!!
WHY?!
WHY NOW?!
SETA!
SETA!
UHH...
...URRHHHH

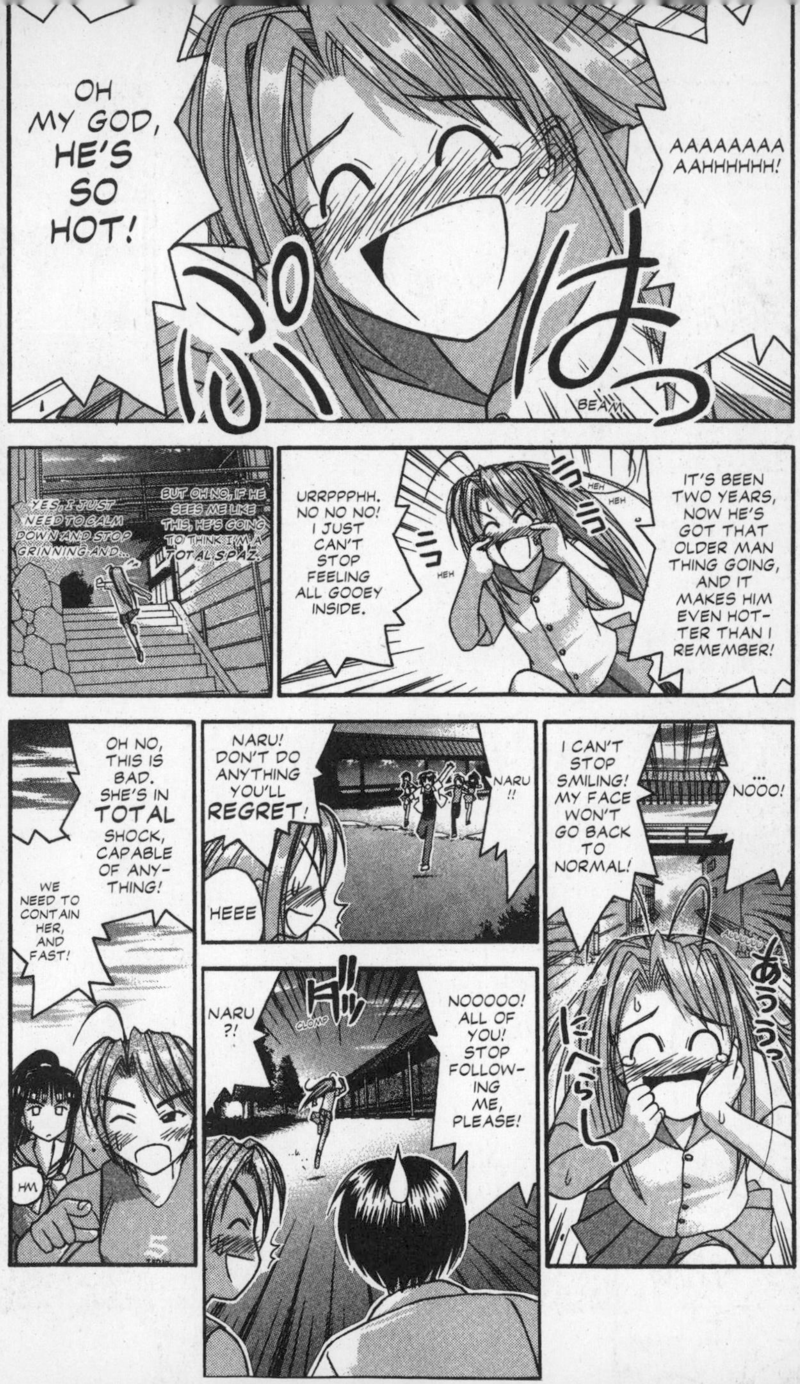
AAAAAAAA AAHHHHHH!
OH MY GOD, HE'S SO HOT!
BEAM
IT'S BEEN TWO YEARS, NOW HE'S GOT THAT OLDER MAN THING GOING, AND IT MAKES HIM EVEN HOTTER THAN I REMEMBER!
HEH
HEH
URRPPPHH. NO NO NO! I JUST CAN'T STOP FEELING ALL GOOEY INSIDE.
HEH
BUT OH NO, IF HE SEES ME LIKE THIS, HE'S GOING TO THINK I'M A TOTAL SPAZ.
YES, I JUST NEED TO CALM DOWN AND STOP GRINNING AND...
... NOOO!
I CAN'T STOP SMILING! MY FACE WON'T GO BACK TO NORMAL!
NARU !!
NARU! DON'T DO ANYTHING YOU'LL REGRET!
HEEE
NOOOOO! ALL OF YOU! STOP FOLLOWING ME, PLEASE!
NARU ?!
CLOMP
OH NO, THIS IS BAD. SHE'S IN TOTAL SHOCK, CAPABLE OF ANYTHING!
WE NEED TO CONTAIN HER, AND FAST!
HM

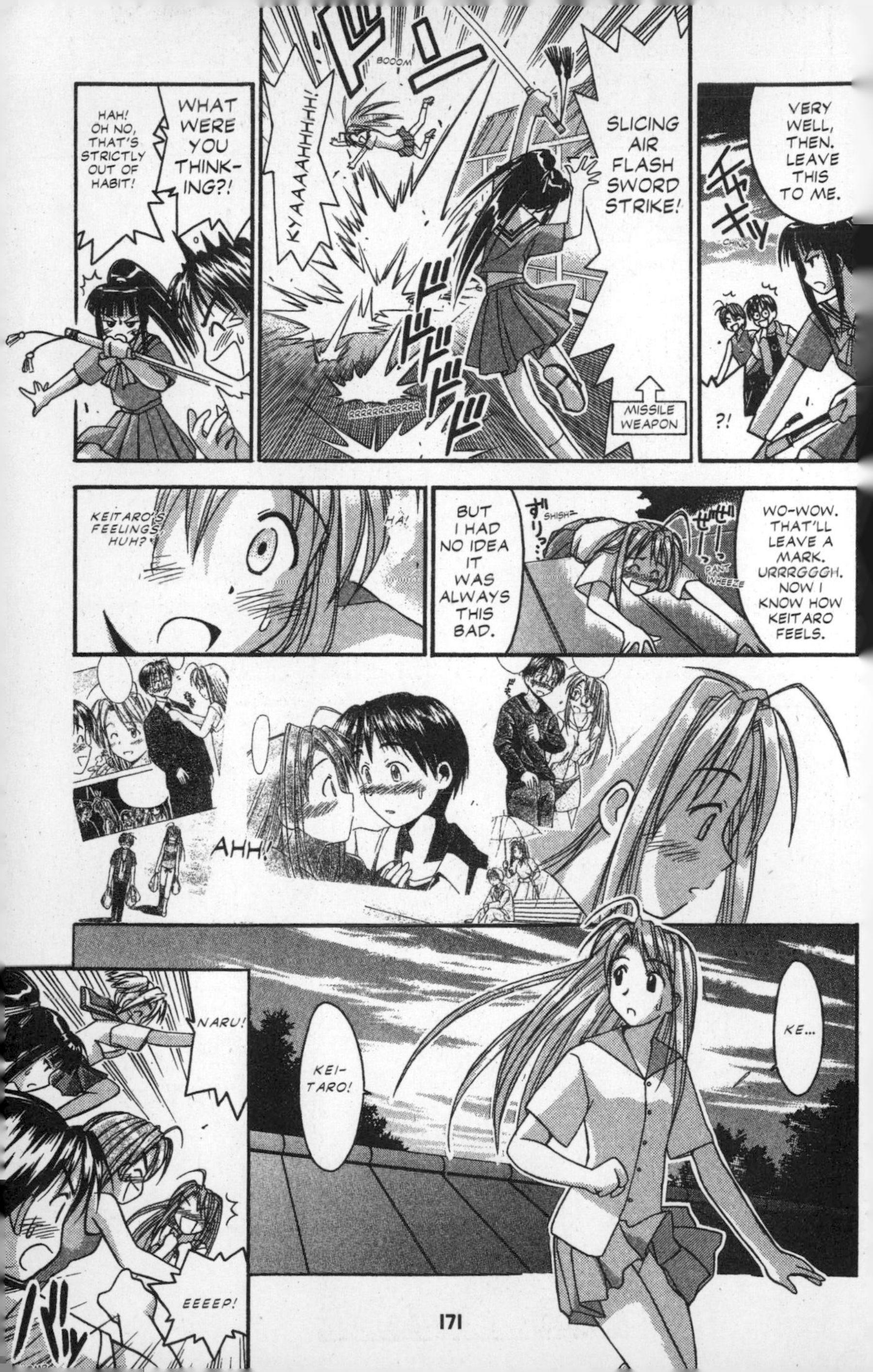
VERY WELL, THEN. LEAVE THIS TO ME.
CHINK
?!
BOOOM
SLICING AIR FLASH SWORD STRIKE!
KYAAAAHHHH!
MISSILE WEAPON
WHAT WERE YOU THINKING?!
HAH! OH NO, THAT'S STRICTLY OUT OF HABIT!
WO-WOW. THAT'LL LEAVE A MARK. URRRGGGH. NOW I KNOW HOW KEITARO FEELS.
PANT WHEEZE
SHISH
BUT I HAD NO IDEA IT WAS ALWAYS THIS BAD.
HA!
KEITARO'S FEELINGS, HUH?
AHH!
KE...
KEI-TARO!
NARU!
EEEEP!

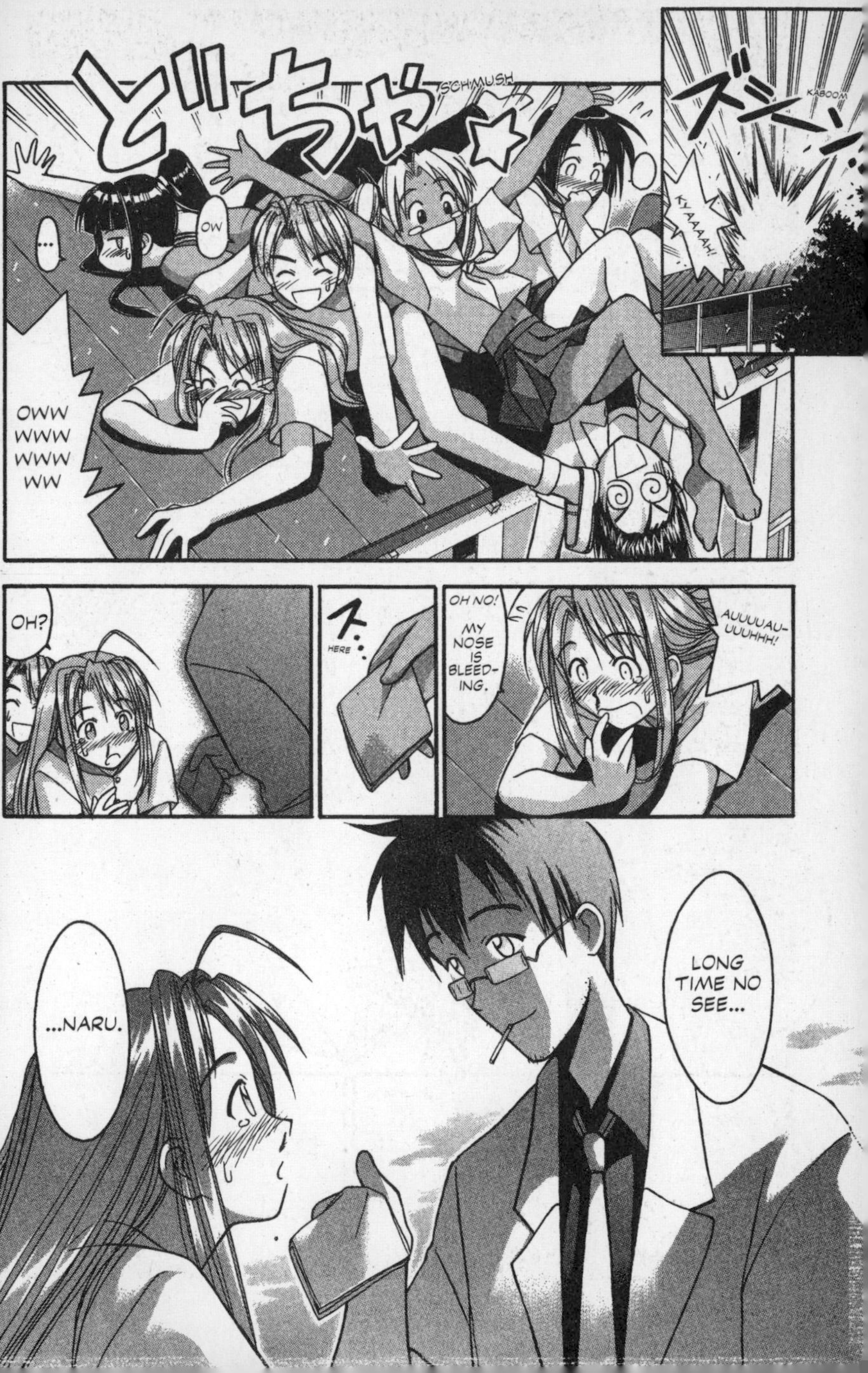

ズシーン
KABOOM
KYAAAAH!
どちゃ
SCHMUSH
OW
...
OWWWWWWWWWWWWW
AUUUUAU-UUUHHH!
OH NO! MY NOSE IS BLEEDING.
ス
HERE
OH?
LONG TIME NO SEE...
...NARU.

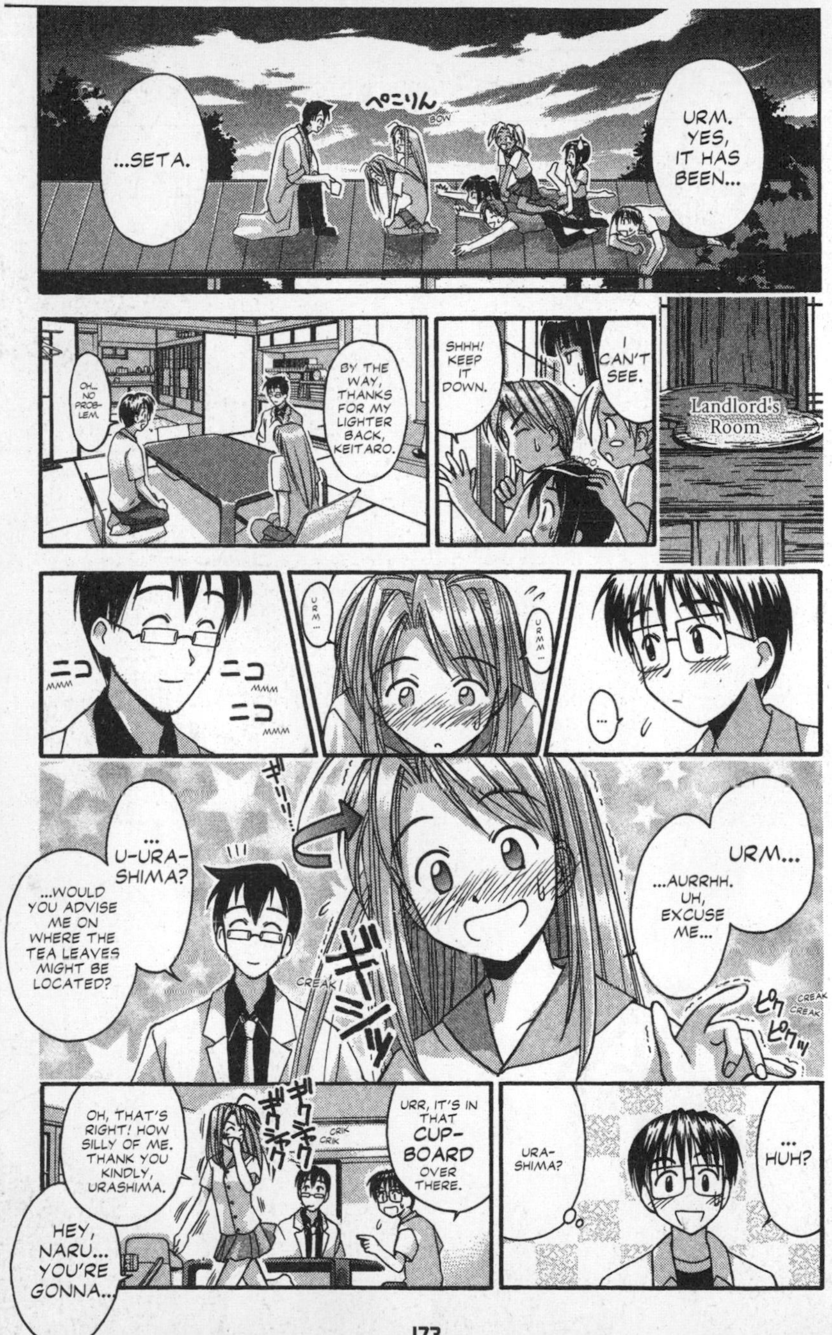
URM. YES, IT HAS BEEN...
ぺこりん
BOW
...SETA.
Landlord's Room
I CAN'T SEE.
SHHH! KEEP IT DOWN.
BY THE WAY, THANKS FOR MY LIGHTER BACK, KEITARO.
OH... NO PROBLEM.
...
URMM...
URM...
ニコ MMM
ニコ MMM
ニコ MMM
URM...
...AURRHH. UH, EXCUSE ME...
CREAK CREAK
ギシッ
CREAK
...U-URASHIMA?
...WOULD YOU ADVISE ME ON WHERE THE TEA LEAVES MIGHT BE LOCATED?
...HUH?
URASHIMA?
URR, IT'S IN THAT CUPBOARD OVER THERE.
CRIK CRIK
OH, THAT'S RIGHT! HOW SILLY OF ME. THANK YOU KINDLY, URASHIMA.
HEY, NARU... YOU'RE GONNA...

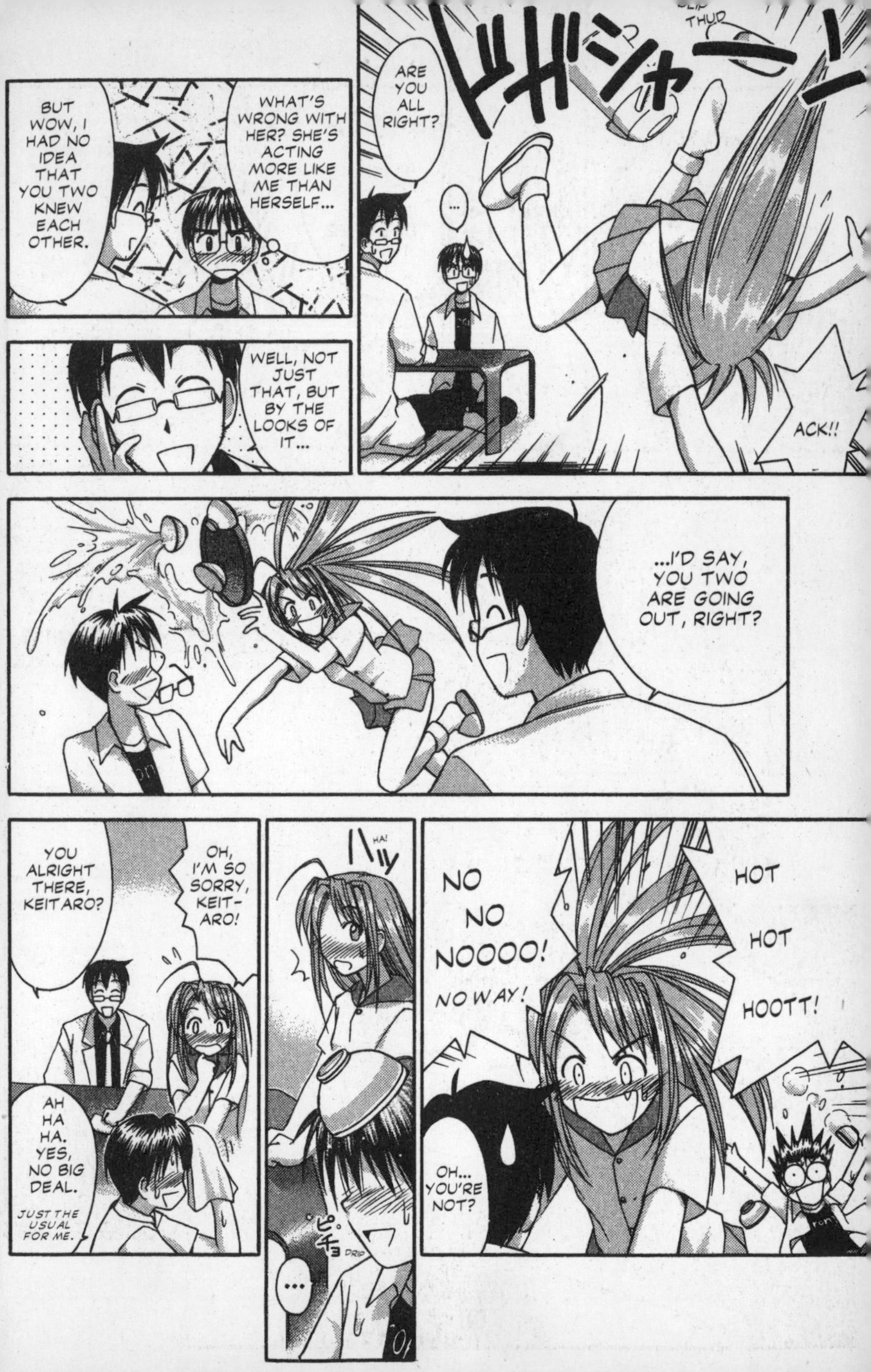
ドガシャーン
THUD
ARE YOU ALL RIGHT?
...
ACK!!
WHAT'S WRONG WITH HER? SHE'S ACTING MORE LIKE ME THAN HERSELF...
BUT WOW, I HAD NO IDEA THAT YOU TWO KNEW EACH OTHER.
WELL, NOT JUST THAT, BUT BY THE LOOKS OF IT...
...I'D SAY, YOU TWO ARE GOING OUT, RIGHT?
HOT HOT HOOTT!
NO NO NOOOO!
NO WAY!
OH... YOU'RE NOT?
ハッ HA!
ピチョ DRIP
...
OH, I'M SO SORRY, KEIT-ARO!
YOU ALRIGHT THERE, KEITARO?
AH HA HA. YES, NO BIG DEAL.
JUST THE USUAL FOR ME.

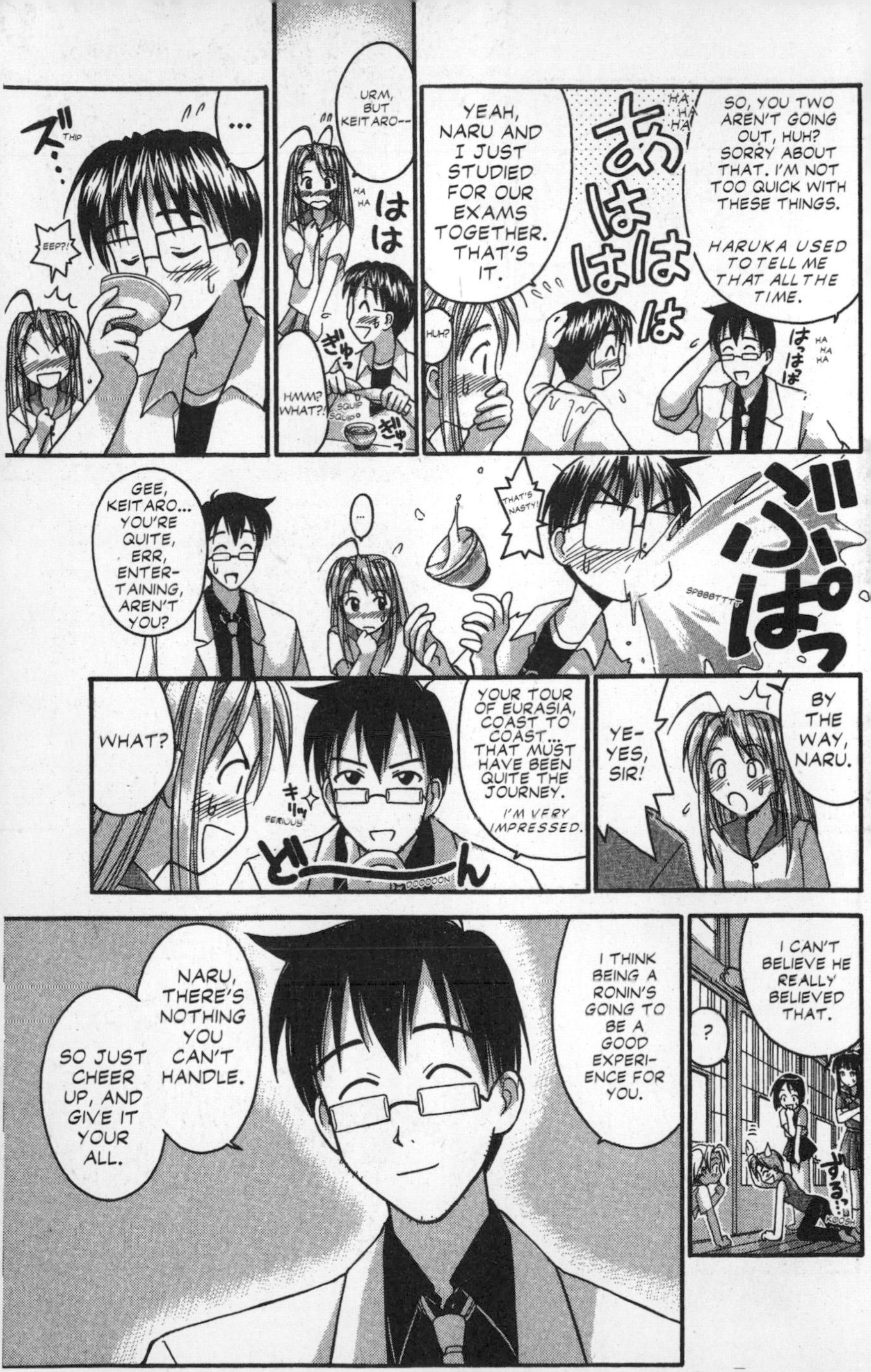
SO, YOU TWO AREN'T GOING OUT, HUH? SORRY ABOUT THAT. I'M NOT TOO QUICK WITH THESE THINGS.
HARUKA USED TO TELL ME THAT ALL THE TIME.
はっはっは
HA HA HA
YEAH, NARU AND I JUST STUDIED FOR OUR EXAMS TOGETHER. THAT'S IT.
あははは
HA HA HA
HUH?
URM, BUT KEITARO--
はは
HA HA
HMM? WHAT?!
ぎゅっ
SQUIP SQUIP
...
ズ…
THIP
EEP?!
ぶぱっ
SPBBBTTTT
THAT'S NASTY!
...
GEE, KEITARO... YOU'RE QUITE, ERR, ENTERTAINING, AREN'T YOU?
BY THE WAY, NARU.
YE-YES, SIR!
YOUR TOUR OF EURASIA, COAST TO COAST... THAT MUST HAVE BEEN QUITE THE JOURNEY.
I'M VERY IMPRESSED.
WHAT?
キリッ
SERIOUS
どーん
DOOOOON
I CAN'T BELIEVE HE REALLY BELIEVED THAT.
?
ずる…
KOOSH
I THINK BEING A RONIN'S GOING TO BE A GOOD EXPERIENCE FOR YOU.
NARU, THERE'S NOTHING YOU CAN'T HANDLE.
SO JUST CHEER UP, AND GIVE IT YOUR ALL.

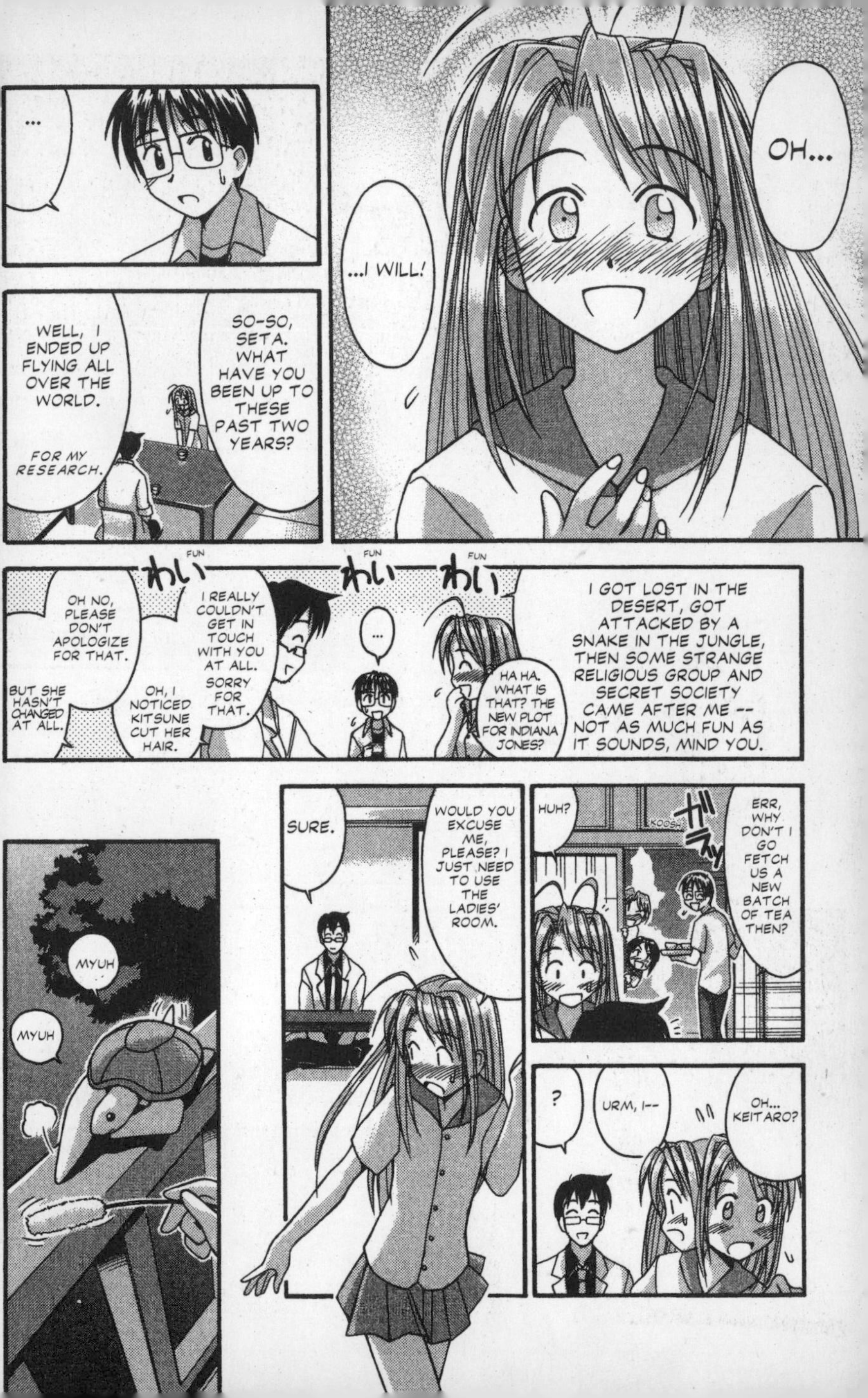
OH...
...I WILL!
...
SO-SO, SETA. WHAT HAVE YOU BEEN UP TO THESE PAST TWO YEARS?
WELL, I ENDED UP FLYING ALL OVER THE WORLD.
FOR MY RESEARCH.
I GOT LOST IN THE DESERT, GOT ATTACKED BY A SNAKE IN THE JUNGLE, THEN SOME STRANGE RELIGIOUS GROUP AND SECRET SOCIETY CAME AFTER ME -- NOT AS MUCH FUN AS IT SOUNDS, MIND YOU.
FUN
わい
HA HA. WHAT IS THAT? THE NEW PLOT FOR INDIANA JONES?
FUN
わい
...
FUN
わい
I REALLY COULDN'T GET IN TOUCH WITH YOU AT ALL. SORRY FOR THAT.
OH, I NOTICED KITSUNE CUT HER HAIR.
OH NO, PLEASE DON'T APOLOGIZE FOR THAT.
BUT SHE HASN'T CHANGED AT ALL.
ERR, WHY DON'T I GO FETCH US A NEW BATCH OF TEA THEN?
KOOSH
HUH?
OH... KEITARO?
URM, I--
?
WOULD YOU EXCUSE ME, PLEASE? I JUST NEED TO USE THE LADIES' ROOM.
SURE.
MYUH
MYUH

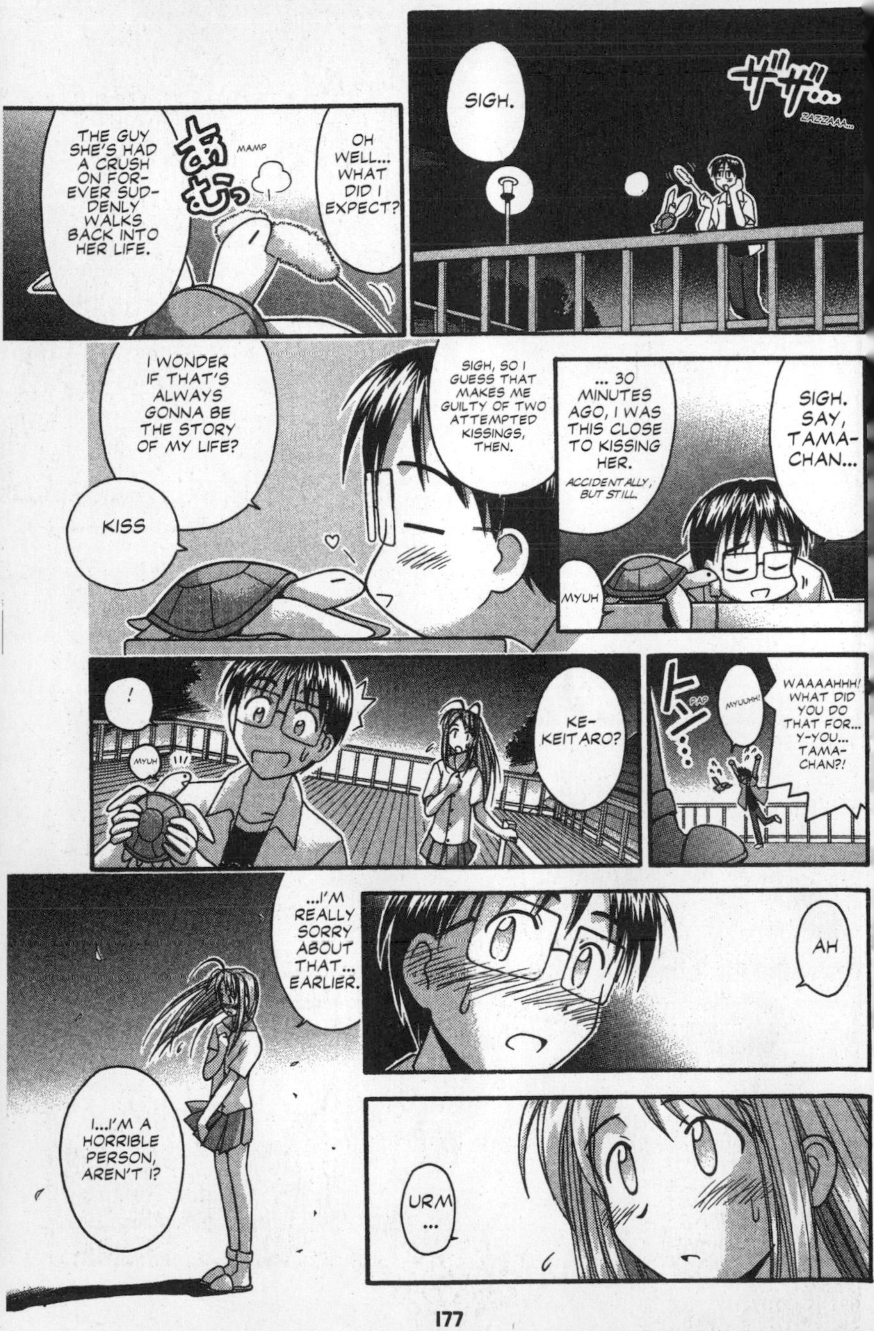
SIGH.
ザザ…
ZAZZAAA...
OH WELL... WHAT DID I EXPECT?
あむっ
MAMP
THE GUY SHE'S HAD A CRUSH ON FOR-EVER SUD-DENLY WALKS BACK INTO HER LIFE.
SIGH. SAY, TAMA-CHAN...
... 30 MINUTES AGO, I WAS THIS CLOSE TO KISSING HER.
ACCIDENTALLY, BUT STILL.
MYUH
SIGH, SO I GUESS THAT MAKES ME GUILTY OF TWO ATTEMPTED KISSINGS, THEN.
I WONDER IF THAT'S ALWAYS GONNA BE THE STORY OF MY LIFE?
KISS
WAAAAHHH! WHAT DID YOU DO THAT FOR... Y-YOU... TAMA-CHAN?!
MYUUHH!
PAP
KE-KEITARO?
!
MYUH
AH
...I'M REALLY SORRY ABOUT THAT... EARLIER.
URM ...
I...I'M A HORRIBLE PERSON, AREN'T I?

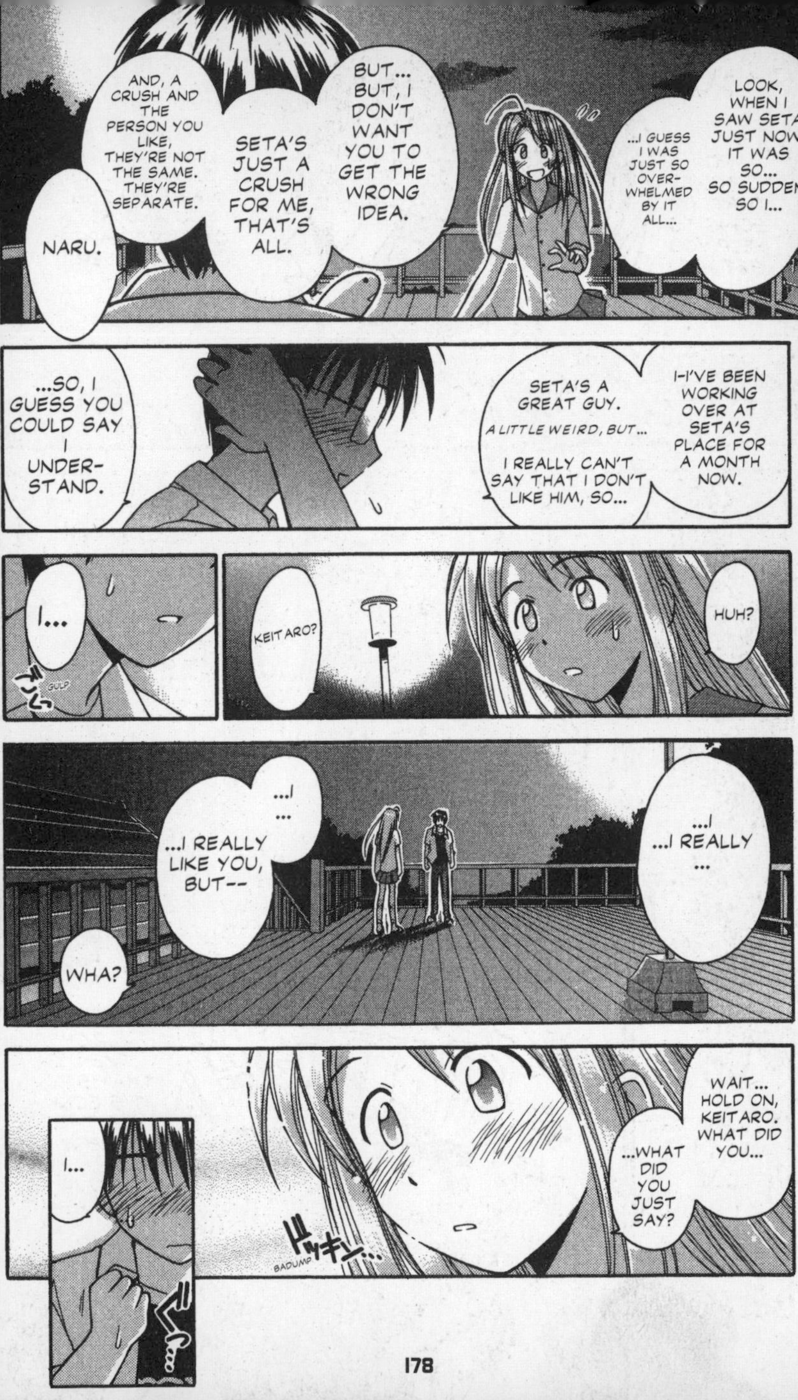
LOOK, WHEN I SAW SETA JUST NOW, IT WAS SO... SO SUDDEN, SO I...
...I GUESS I WAS JUST SO OVER-WHELMED BY IT ALL...
BUT... BUT, I DON'T WANT YOU TO GET THE WRONG IDEA.
SETA'S JUST A CRUSH FOR ME, THAT'S ALL.
AND, A CRUSH AND THE PERSON YOU LIKE, THEY'RE NOT THE SAME. THEY'RE SEPARATE.
NARU.
I-I'VE BEEN WORKING OVER AT SETA'S PLACE FOR A MONTH NOW.
SETA'S A GREAT GUY.
A LITTLE WEIRD, BUT...
I REALLY CAN'T SAY THAT I DON'T LIKE HIM, SO...
...SO, I GUESS YOU COULD SAY I UNDER-STAND.
HUH?
KEITARO?
I...
GULP
...I
...I REALLY
...
...I
...
...I REALLY LIKE YOU, BUT--
WHA?
WAIT... HOLD ON, KEITARO. WHAT DID YOU...
...WHAT DID YOU JUST SAY?
BADUMP
I...

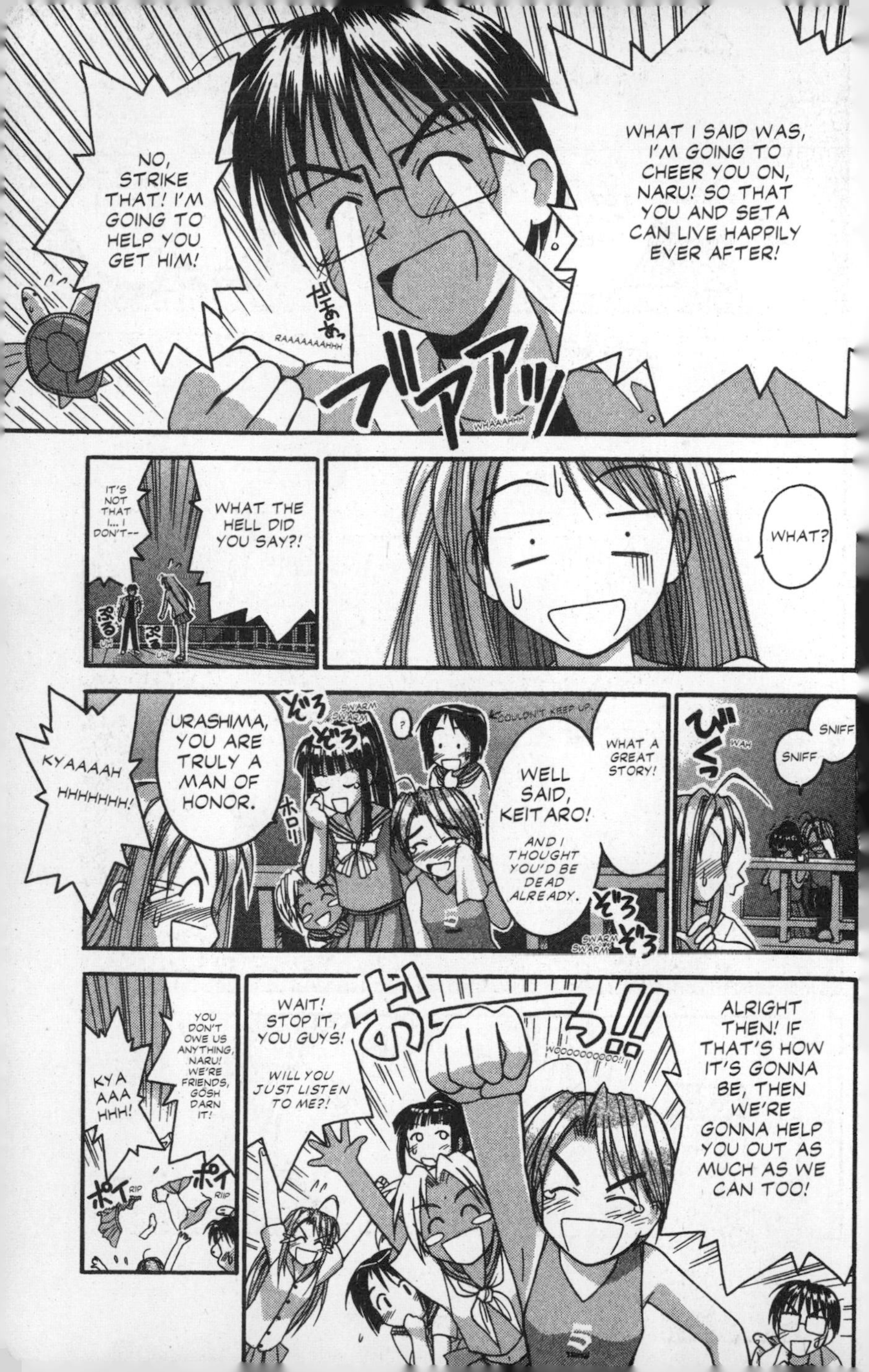
WHAT I SAID WAS, I'M GOING TO CHEER YOU ON, NARU! SO THAT YOU AND SETA CAN LIVE HAPPILY EVER AFTER!
NO, STRIKE THAT! I'M GOING TO HELP YOU GET HIM!
RAAAAAAAHHH
WHAAAHHH
WHAT?
WHAT THE HELL DID YOU SAY?!
IT'S NOT THAT I... I DON'T--
UH
UH
SNIFF
SNIFF
WAH
WHAT A GREAT STORY!
WELL SAID, KEITARO!
AND I THOUGHT YOU'D BE DEAD ALREADY.
COULDN'T KEEP UP.
?
SWARM SWARM
URASHIMA, YOU ARE TRULY A MAN OF HONOR.
SWARM SWARM
KYAAAAH HHHHHHH!
ALRIGHT THEN! IF THAT'S HOW IT'S GONNA BE, THEN WE'RE GONNA HELP YOU OUT AS MUCH AS WE CAN TOO!
WOOOOOOOOOOO!!
WAIT! STOP IT, YOU GUYS!
WILL YOU JUST LISTEN TO ME?!
YOU DON'T OWE US ANYTHING, NARU! WE'RE FRIENDS, GOSH DARN IT!
KYA AAA HHH!
RIP
RIP

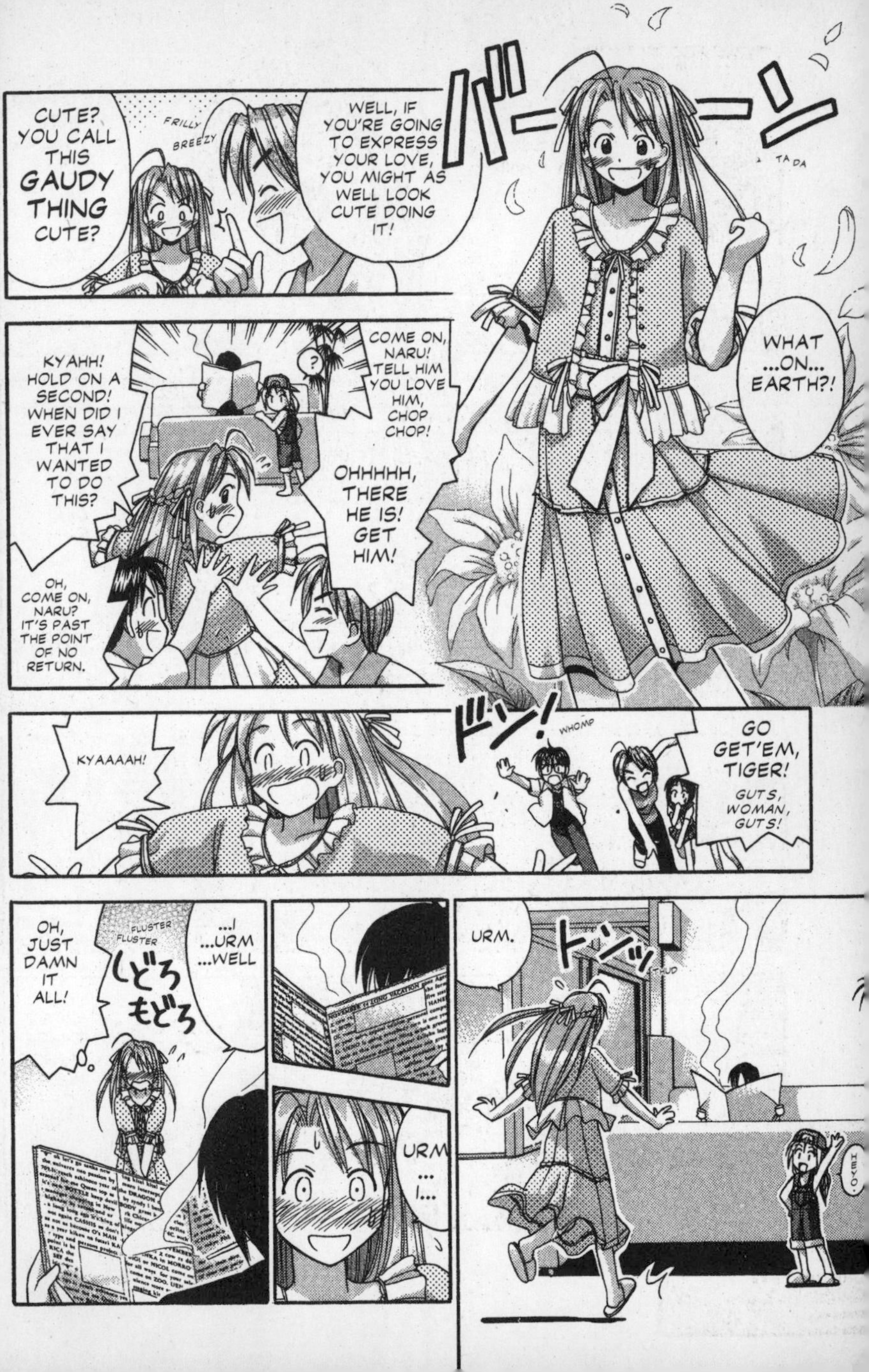
バーーン
TA DA
WHAT ...ON... EARTH?!
WELL, IF YOU'RE GOING TO EXPRESS YOUR LOVE, YOU MIGHT AS WELL LOOK CUTE DOING IT!
FRILLY
BREEZY
CUTE? YOU CALL THIS GAUDY THING CUTE?
COME ON, NARU! TELL HIM YOU LOVE HIM, CHOP CHOP!
KYAHH! HOLD ON A SECOND! WHEN DID I EVER SAY THAT I WANTED TO DO THIS?
OHHHHH, THERE HE IS! GET HIM!
OH, COME ON, NARU? IT'S PAST THE POINT OF NO RETURN.
GO GET'EM, TIGER!
GUTS, WOMAN, GUTS!
ドン!
WHOMP
KYAAAAH!
URM.
トンッ
THUD
HEYO.
URM ... I...
...I ...URM ...WELL
FLUSTER
FLUSTER
しどろもどろ
OH, JUST DAMN IT ALL!

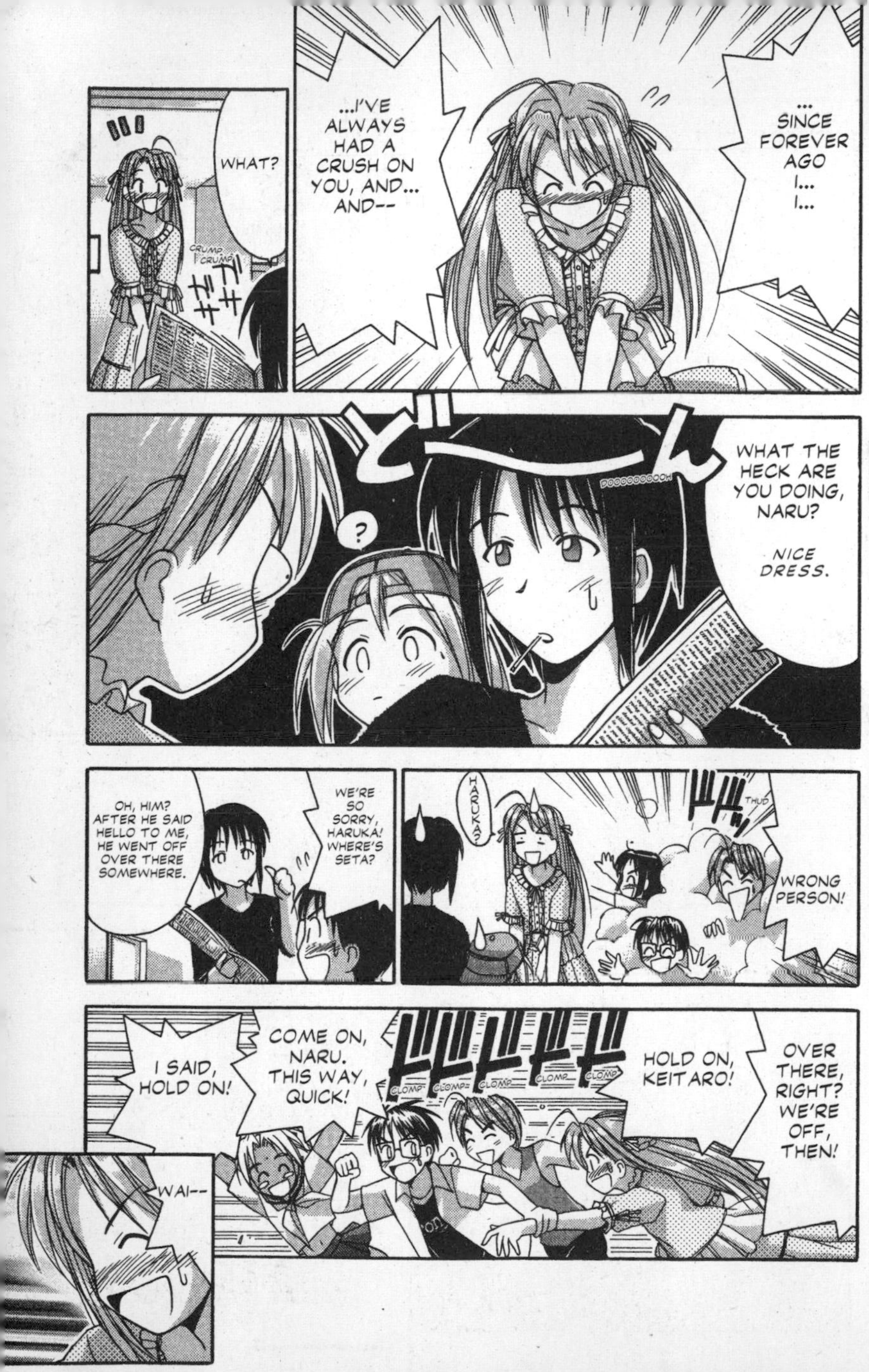
...SINCE FOREVER AGO I... I...
...I'VE ALWAYS HAD A CRUSH ON YOU, AND... AND--
WHAT?
CRUMP CRUMP
DOOOOOOOOOH
WHAT THE HECK ARE YOU DOING, NARU?
NICE DRESS.
?
THUD
HARUKA?
WRONG PERSON!
WE'RE SO SORRY, HARUKA! WHERE'S SETA?
OH, HIM? AFTER HE SAID HELLO TO ME, HE WENT OFF OVER THERE SOMEWHERE.
OVER THERE, RIGHT? WE'RE OFF, THEN!
HOLD ON, KEITARO!
CLOMP CLOMP CLOMP CLOMP CLOMP
COME ON, NARU. THIS WAY, QUICK!
I SAID, HOLD ON!
WAI--

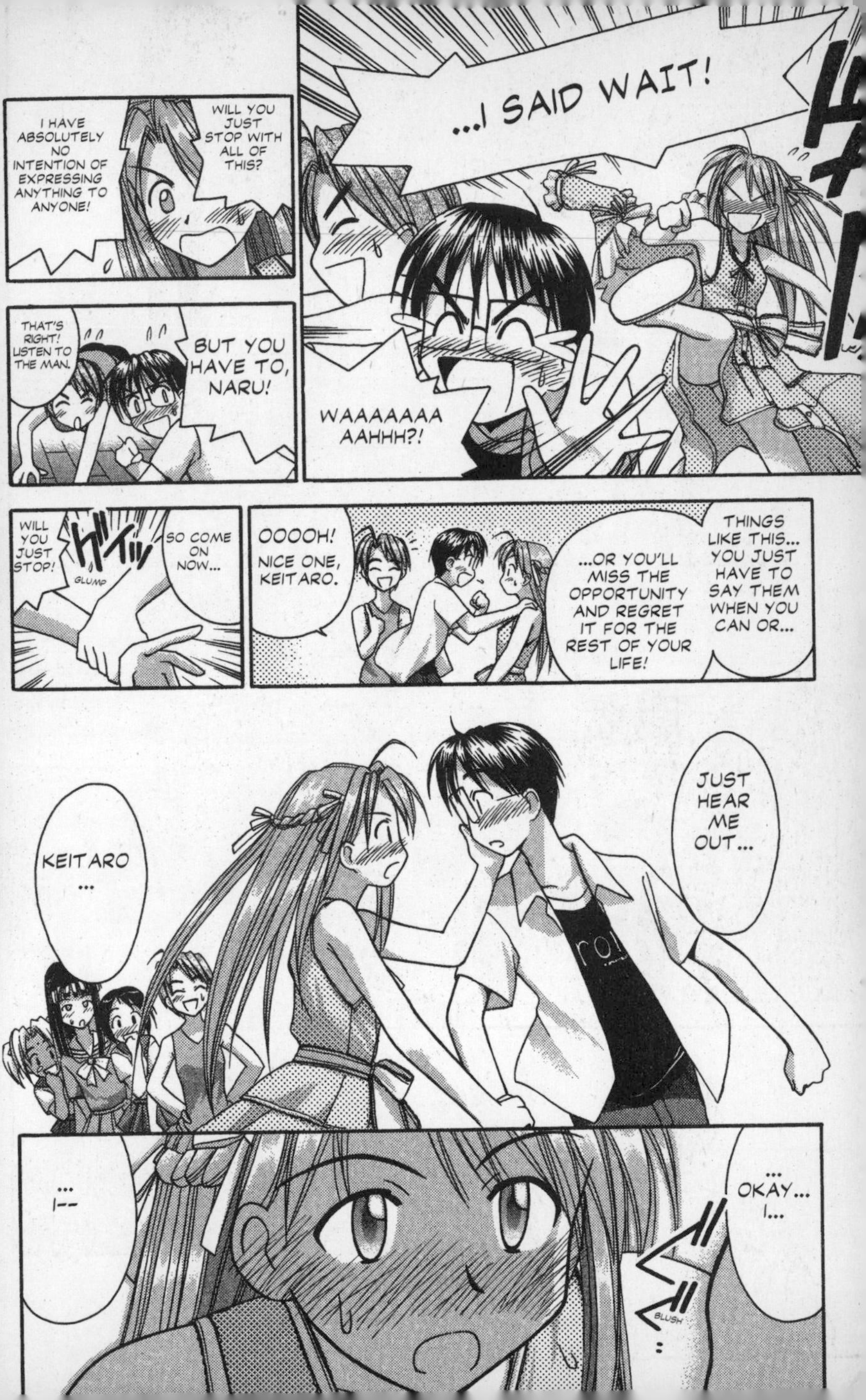
...I SAID WAIT!
WAAAAAAA AAHHH?!
WILL YOU JUST STOP WITH ALL OF THIS?
I HAVE ABSOLUTELY NO INTENTION OF EXPRESSING ANYTHING TO ANYONE!
BUT YOU HAVE TO, NARU!
THAT'S RIGHT! LISTEN TO THE MAN.
THINGS LIKE THIS... YOU JUST HAVE TO SAY THEM WHEN YOU CAN OR...
...OR YOU'LL MISS THE OPPORTUNITY AND REGRET IT FOR THE REST OF YOUR LIFE!
OOOOH! NICE ONE, KEITARO.
SO COME ON NOW...
GLUMP
WILL YOU JUST STOP!
JUST HEAR ME OUT...
KEITARO ...
... OKAY... I...
BLUSH
... I--

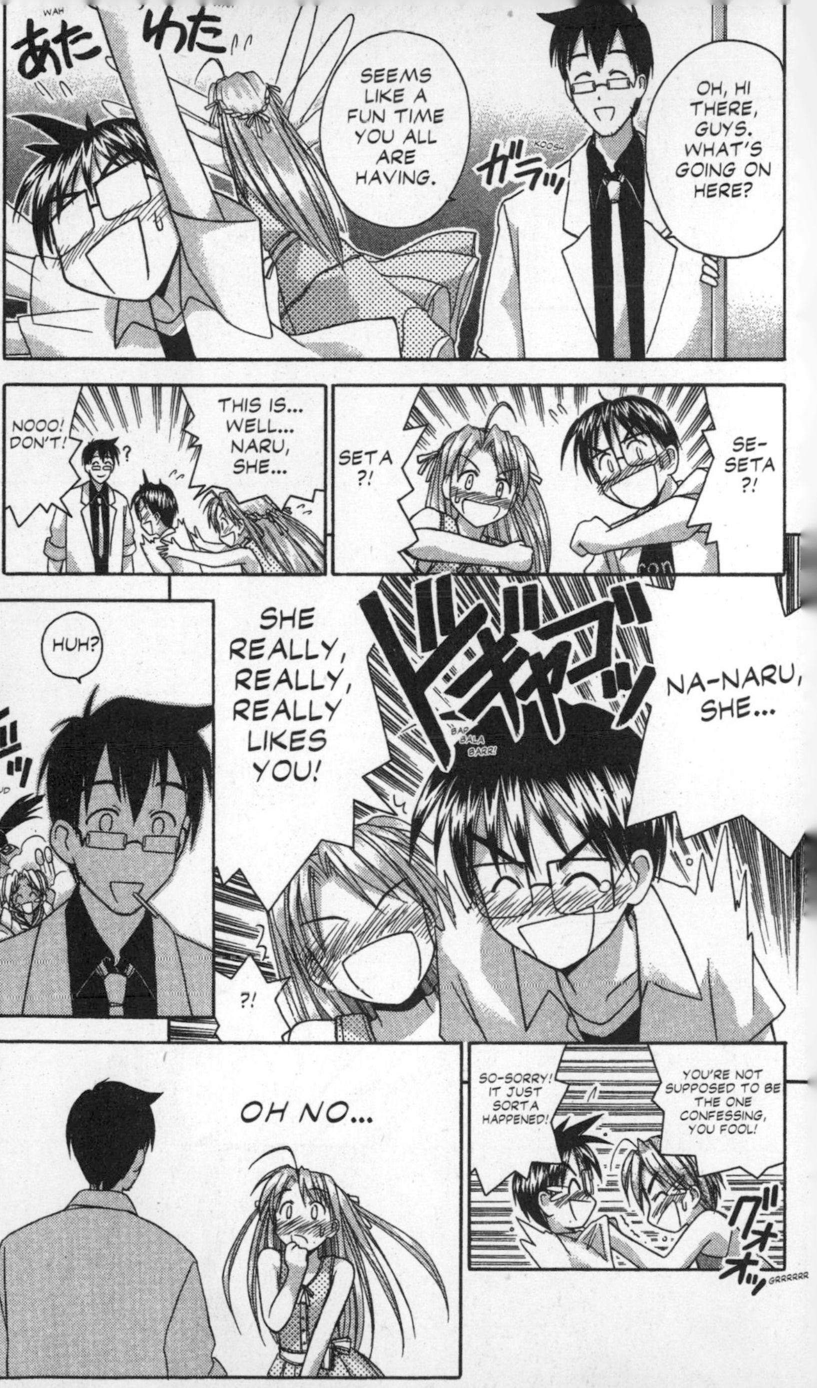
OH, HI THERE, GUYS. WHAT'S GOING ON HERE?
KOOSH
SEEMS LIKE A FUN TIME YOU ALL ARE HAVING.
WAH
SE- SETA ?!
SETA ?!
THIS IS... WELL... NARU, SHE...
NOOO! DON'T!
?
NA-NARU, SHE...
SHE REALLY, REALLY, REALLY LIKES YOU!
BAP BALA BARR!
?!
HUH?
KLUUUUUD
YOU'RE NOT SUPPOSED TO BE THE ONE CONFESSING, YOU FOOL!
SO-SORRY! IT JUST SORTA HAPPENED!
GRRRRRR
OH NO...

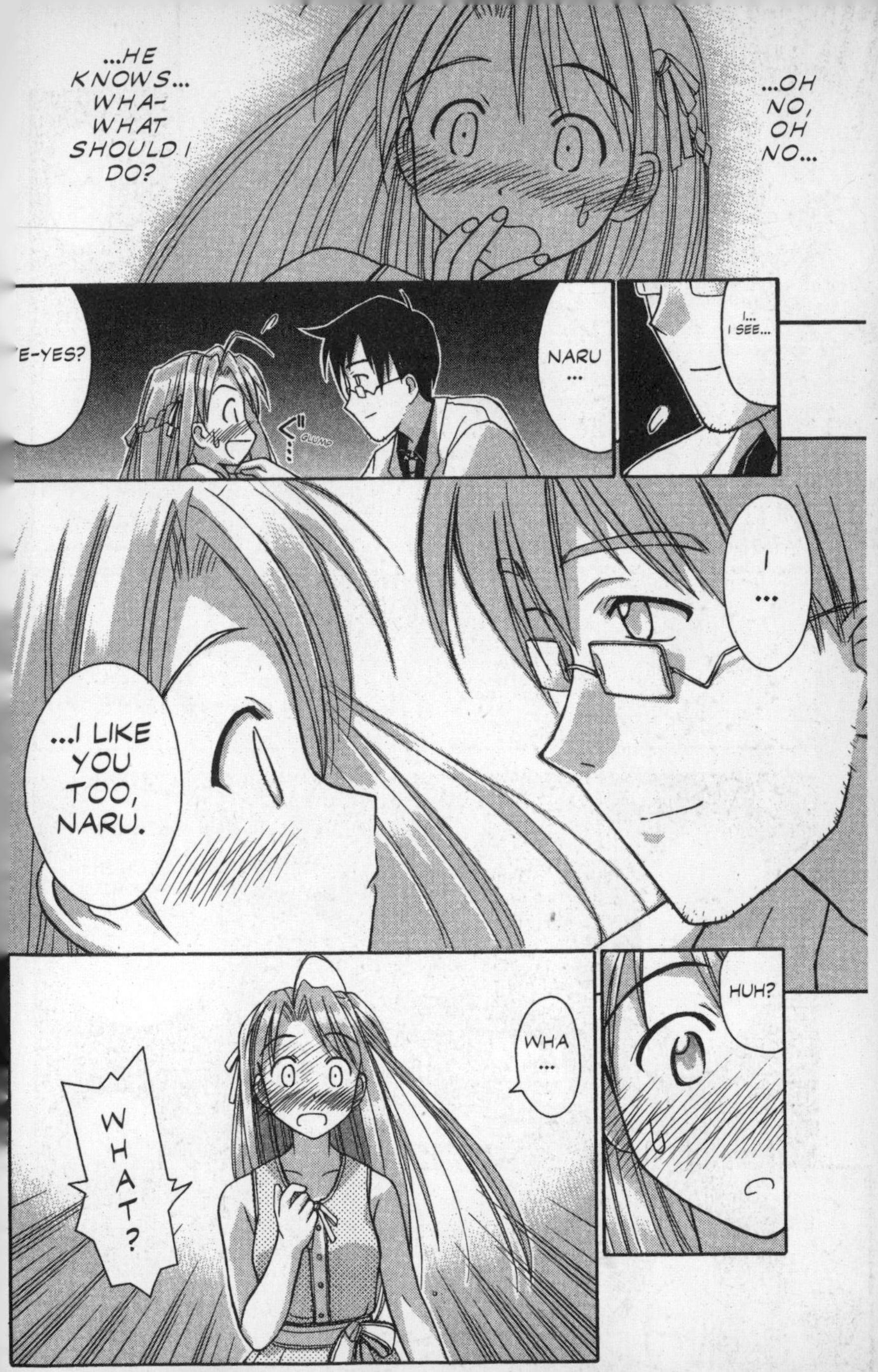
...OH NO, OH NO...
...HE KNOWS... WHA-WHAT SHOULD I DO?
I... I SEE...
NARU ...
E-YES?
GLUMP
I ...
...I LIKE YOU TOO, NARU.
HUH?
WHA ...
WHAT?

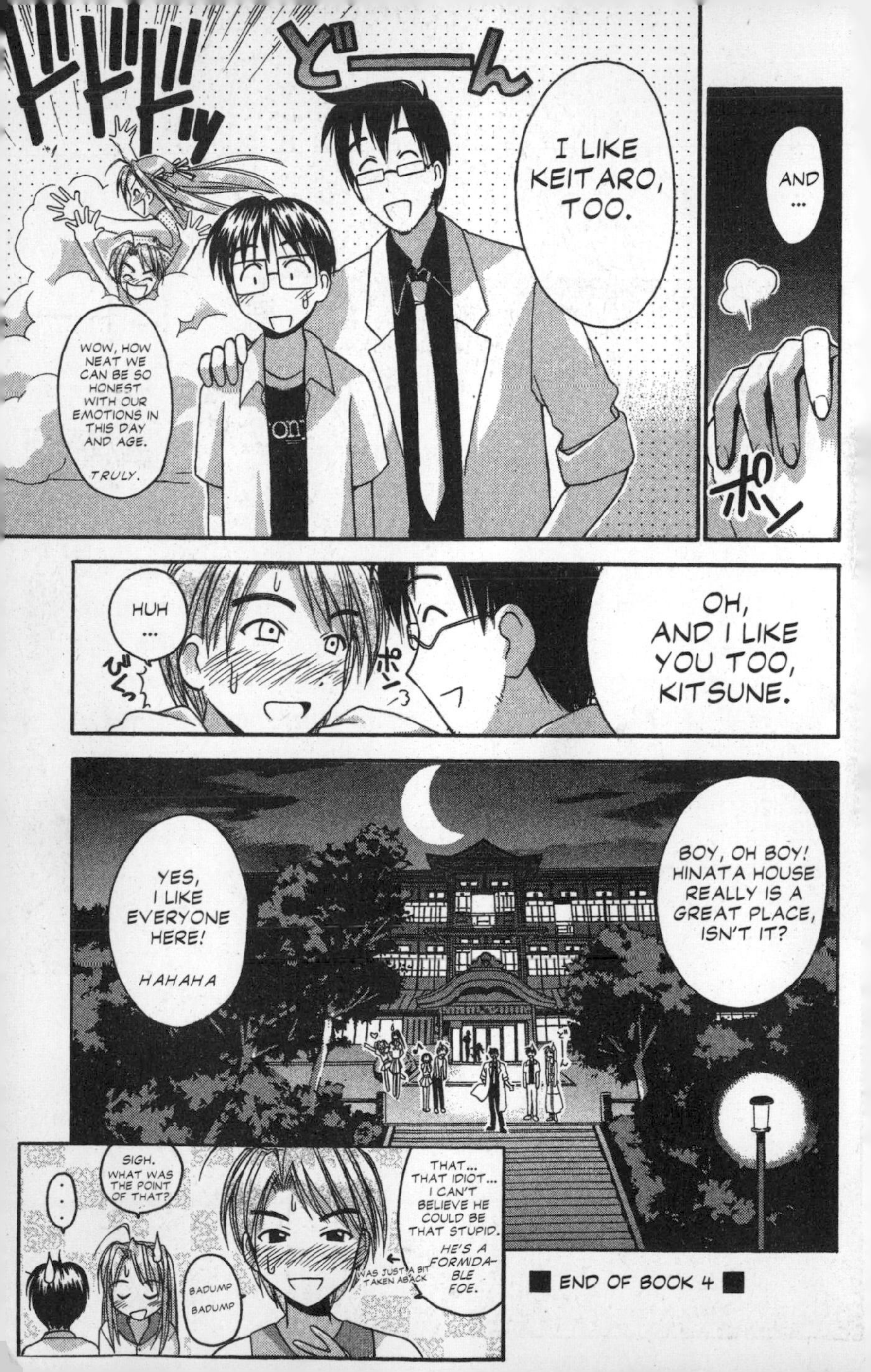
AND ...
ポン
どーん
I LIKE KEITARO, TOO.
WOW, HOW NEAT WE CAN BE SO HONEST WITH OUR EMOTIONS IN THIS DAY AND AGE.
TRULY.
OH, AND I LIKE YOU TOO, KITSUNE.
HUH ...
BOY, OH BOY! HINATA HOUSE REALLY IS A GREAT PLACE, ISN'T IT?
YES, I LIKE EVERYONE HERE!
HAHAHA
THAT... THAT IDIOT... I CAN'T BELIEVE HE COULD BE THAT STUPID.
HE'S A FORMIDABLE FOE.
SIGH. WHAT WAS THE POINT OF THAT?
...
BADUMP BADUMP
WAS JUST A BIT TAKEN ABACK
END OF BOOK 4

Love Hina

VOL. 5

IN THE NEXT INSTALLMENT OF LOVE HINA ...

Even with all the Hinata House habitants pitching in to help at a beach cafe run by Keitaro's Aunt Haruka, the girls find time for crazy beach antics, keeping themselves entertained as Keitaro and Naru trudge through the awkwardness between them. But the meddling roommates never fail to ease the tension among friends — that is, until an unexpected guest pops up at a summer beach festival. With any luck, Keitaro will come away from the summer beach stay with more than just unpleasant memories.

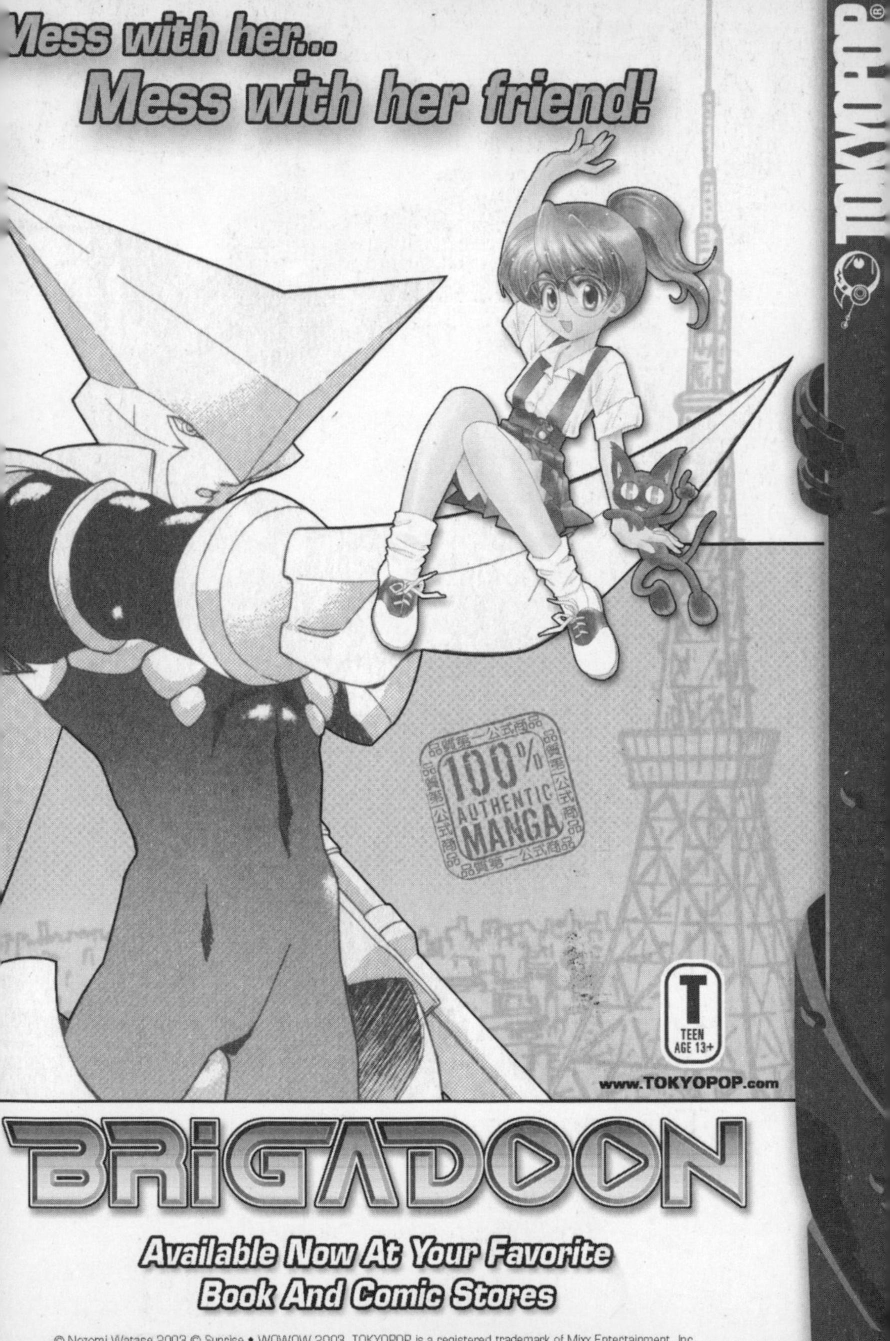
Mess with her...
Mess with her friend!
TOKYOPOP®
100% AUTHENTIC MANGA
品質第一公式商品
T
TEEN
AGE 13+
www.TOKYOPOP.com
BRiGADOON
Available Now At Your Favorite
Book And Comic Stores

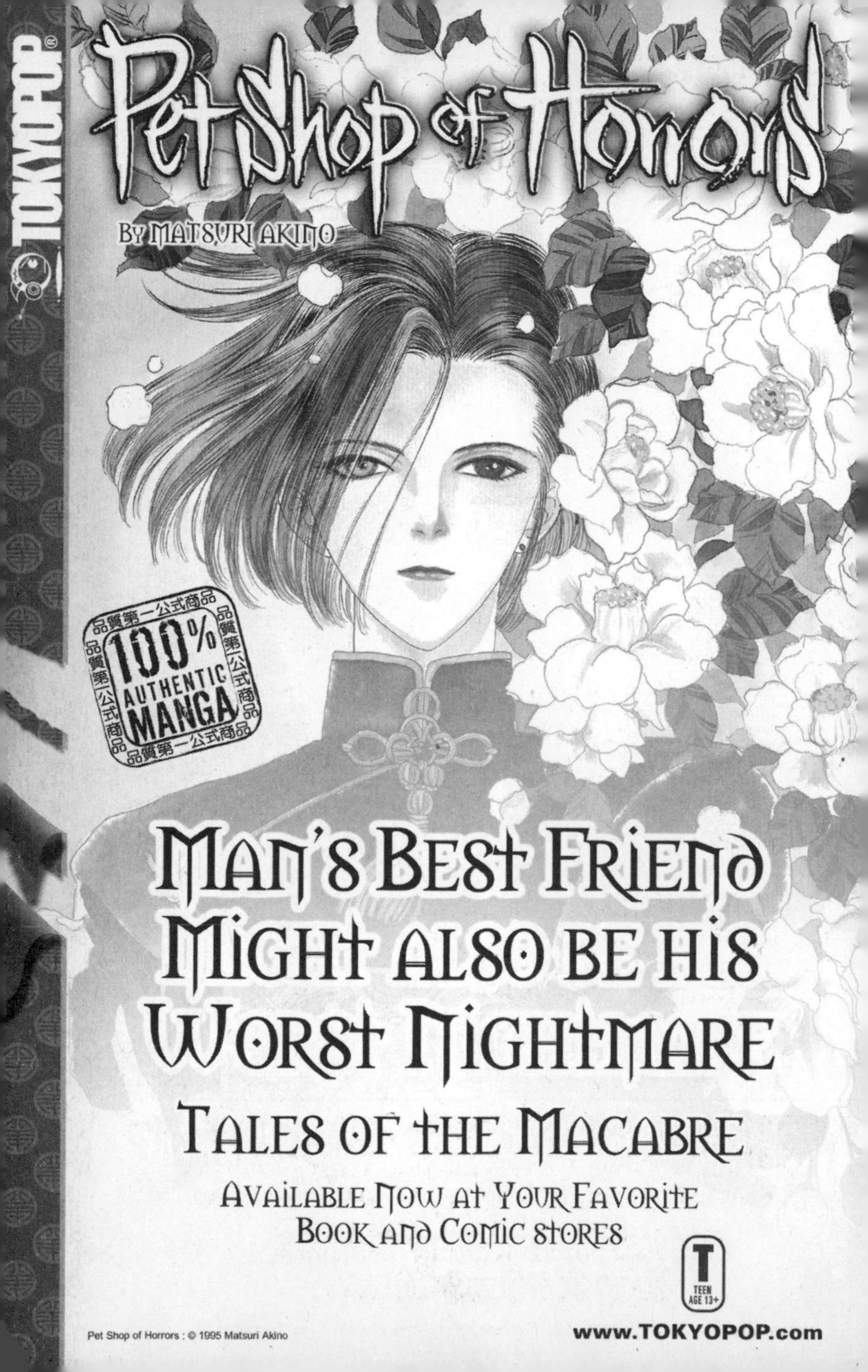
TOKYOPOP
Pet Shop of Horrors
BY MATSURI AKINO
品質第一公式商品
100% AUTHENTIC MANGA
MAN'S BEST FRIEND MIGHT ALSO BE HIS WORST NIGHTMARE
TALES OF THE MACABRE
AVAILABLE NOW AT YOUR FAVORITE BOOK AND COMIC STORES
T TEEN AGE 13+
Pet Shop of Horrors : © 1995 Matsuri Akino
www.TOKYOPOP.com

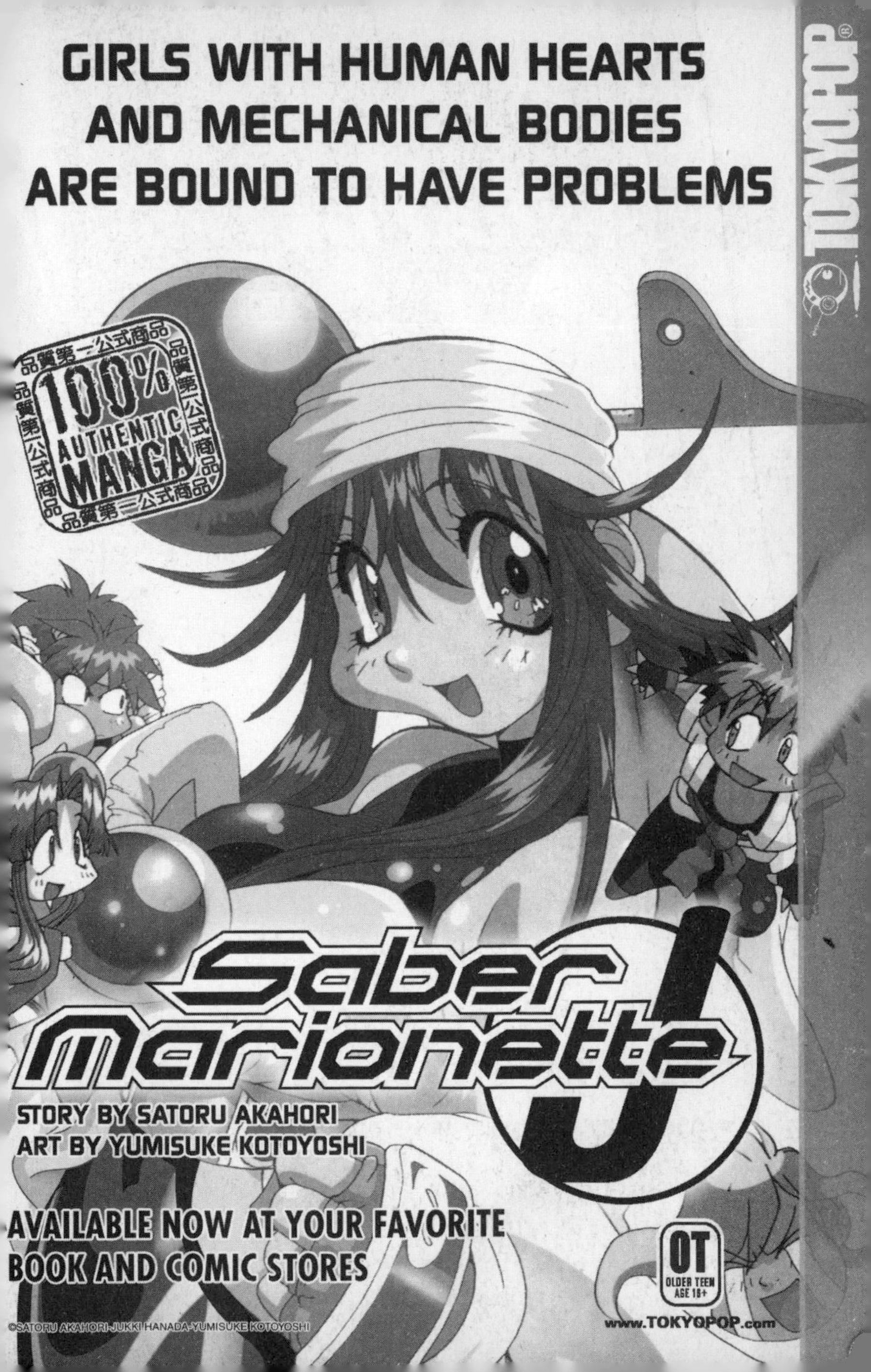
GIRLS WITH HUMAN HEARTS
AND MECHANICAL BODIES
ARE BOUND TO HAVE PROBLEMS
TOKYOPOP®
品質第一公式商品
100% AUTHENTIC MANGA
Saber Marionette J
STORY BY SATORU AKAHORI
ART BY YUMISUKE KOTOYOSHI
AVAILABLE NOW AT YOUR FAVORITE
BOOK AND COMIC STORES
OT
OLDER TEEN AGE 16+
©SATORU AKAHORI·JUKKI HANADA·YUMISUKE KOTOYOSHI
www.TOKYOPOP.com

STOP!

This is the back of the book.
You wouldn't want to spoil a great ending!

This book is printed "manga-style," in the authentic Japanese right-to-left format. Since none of the artwork has been flipped or altered, readers get to experience the story just as the creator intended. You've been asking for it, so TOKYOPOP® delivered: authentic, hot-off-the-press, and far more fun!

DIRECTIONS

If this is your first time reading manga-style, here's a quick guide to help you understand how it works.

It's easy... just start in the top right panel and follow the numbers. Have fun, and look for more 100% authentic manga from TOKYOPOP®!